MARINE CARGO OPERATIONS

MARINE CARGO OPERATIONS

A Guide to Stowage

FOURTH EDITION

CAPTAIN ROBERT J. MEURN, USNR
Master Mariner

CORNELL MARITIME PRESS
A Division of Schiffer Publishing, Ltd.
4880 Lower Valley Road, Atglen, PA 19310

Other Schiffer Books by the Author:

Survival Guide for the Mariner, 2nd Edition, 978-0-87033-573-0, $35.00

Other Schiffer Books on Related Subjects:

Dictionary of Maritime and Transportation Terms, 978-0-87033-569-3, $19.95

Tanker Operations: A Handbook for the Person-in-Charge, 978-0-87033-620-1, $50.00

Schiffer Books are available at special discounts for bulk purchases for sales promotions or premiums. Special editions, including personalized covers, corporate imprints, and excerpts can be created in large quantities for special needs. For more information contact the publisher:

Schiffer Publishing Ltd.
4880 Lower Valley Road
Atglen, PA 19310
Phone: (610) 593-1777; Fax: (610) 593-2002
E-mail: Info@schifferbooks.com

For the largest selection of fine reference books on this and related subjects, please visit our web site at:
www.schifferbooks.com
We are always looking for people to write books on new and related subjects. If you have an idea for a book please contact us at the above address.

This book may be purchased from the publisher. Include $5.00 for shipping. Please try your bookstore first. You may write for a free catalog.

In Europe, Schiffer books are distributed by
Bushwood Books
6 Marksbury Ave.
Kew Gardens
Surrey TW9 4JF England
Phone: 44 (0) 20 8392 8585; Fax: 44 (0) 20 8392 9876
E-mail: info@bushwoodbooks.co.uk
Website: www.bushwoodbooks.co.uk

Designed by Stephanie Daugherty
Type set in Trajan Pro/Times New Roman
ISBN: 978-0-87033-623-2
Printed in China

DEDICATED TO CAPTAIN CHARLES L. SAUERBIER,
who authored the first edition and co-authored the
second and third editions.

Contents

CHAPTER 4
PLANNING THE STOWAGE AND PREPARATION OF THE CARGO SPACES

CHAPTER 5
STOWAGE OF GENERAL CARGO

CHAPTER 6
STOWAGE OF HAZARDOUS CARGO

CHAPTER 7
PROPER CARE FOR THE CARGO: VENTILATION OF CARGO HOLDS

CHAPTER 8
MARINE MATERIALS HANDLING EQUIPMENT

APPENDIX 1
STOWAGE FACTORS OF COMMONLY CARRIED
BREAKBULK COMMODITIES

APPENDIX 2
PROBLEMS PERTAINING TO
MARINE CARGO OPERATIONS

APPENDIX 3
STOWAGE OF BULK GRAIN

INDEX

ABOUT THE AUTHOR

ABOUT THE BOOK

PREFACE

T HE SAFE AND ECONOMICAL CARRIAGE of goods continues as an ongoing mission of the shipping industry. This fourth edition has a twofold purpose. It aims to help the shipping industry fulfill its mission by presenting formally and systematically the basic principles and techniques of cargo operations, and it seeks to acquaint merchant officers present and future with the principles of stowage and their implications as they apply to the responsibilities of a carrier.

The method of presentation grew out of experience within the classroom, which is believed to be an excellent testing ground for the methodology used in the presentation of any idea or group of ideas. The discussions are slanted toward the individuals who make up the shipping "team" and whose work is one of the most important factors in accomplishing the shipping industry's mission. The "team" includes the operations manager, the terminal superintendent, the marine superintendent, the stevedore, the ship's master, and their staffs.

Attempts have been made to set forth and discuss as many of the tasks, concepts, and facts affecting cargo operations as could be encompassed within a book of reasonable size. The discussion is directed toward the ship's master and his deck officers, but the substance of the discussion is no less valuable to other members of the team. These members of the team are often underrated, even though they are in an ideal position to observe and evaluate operating methods. They can do much to improve any given system. A lack of information among these men may prove very costly. Compliance with the three "C's" (Communication, Cooperation, and Coordination) is vital for members of the team. One need only study the litigation resulting from cargo claims for only a short time to be convinced that in many cases damage to cargo and the resulting legal action were needless.

Communication and cooperation should insure coordination in the movement of cargo. Much of the success of a shipping venture depends on intelligent coordination of movement among all individuals and groups participating in the business of overseas commerce. This coordination should be present from the domestic shipper's terminal in the hinterland, through the marine terminal, to the foreign consignee, and then, with other commodities, back to the shores of the mother country. We hope that this book will contribute to this coordination of movement by giving a better understanding of the full shipping cycle to many who are involved in it only partially.

Much of the text is based on scientific fact, but there are a number of recommendations regarding methods, procedures, and even philosophies that are based purely on opinion. Such opinion is based on much study and half a century's experience in the marine shipping industry. There is undoubtedly room for argument on some of these points, and there may be some omissions that will come to the mind of the careful reader.

Much of the research alluded to in the first three editions have indeed led to astonishing innovations in cargo operations over the last five decades. These innovations are described in this edition.

The greatest impact on the waterfront over this time has been made by the innovation of *containerization*. When the first edition was published in 1956, the viability of containerization was just being tested by Mr. Malcolm P. McLean. He was interested in knowing if carrying truck vans by water from Houston to New York would be feasible and economical. He had two, T-2 tankers covered with a platform that formed a raised deck upon which the truck vans could be secured for the voyage. The "test" proved that the idea was sound. The next year, 1957, the Pan Atlantic Steamship Company (later known as Sealand, S.S. Co.) converted the *S.S. Gateway City* from a breakbulk carrier to the world's first cellular containership. She was able to carry 230, 35 foot containers. Obviously, the impact of the "Box" has been great.

It is not possible to acknowledge all intellectual debts within the space allotted to this preface. However, there is need to mention a few people who made major contributions. Mr. Harold Kingsley rewrote Chapter 2, "Cargo Responsibility." As an admiralty lawyer practicing in New York, he provided insight and advice that will be extremely informative and valuable to the ship's officer. Captain Jim McNamara, president of the National Cargo Bureau, provided Appendix 3, "Stowage of a Grain Bulk Cargo." The contributions of Marilyn Hetsel, Simulation Services Manager at the U.S. Merchant Marine Academy, were instrumental in the production process. Her knowledge of computer technology was vital and ensured that all deadlines were met. Joseph Liotta Art & Design contributed a number of figures for the third and this edition. My wife Christine, whose counsel and advice were invaluable in the preparation of this, as well as my previous four books. Last but not least in acknowledgement is the author of the first edition. Captain Charles Sauerbier assisted this author in the second and third edition. Captain Sauerbier's first edition was published in 1956 by John Wiley & Sons and because of his original concepts, *Marine Cargo Operations* is acknowledged to be the most read, referred to, and quoted book in the shipping industry.

Robert J. Meurn

Kings Point, New York
August, 2010

MARINE CARGO OPERATIONS

CHAPTER 1

INNOVATIONS TO THE CARRIAGE OF GOODS AT SEA

INTRODUCTION

THE BUSINESS OF SHIPPING IS governed by the spirit and the political makeup of the period. With the growth of independent states as a result of the Renaissance, there arose conflicting nationalisms. By the 18th century every kind of restriction on and inconvenience for trade was in force. There was no way for commerce to break its fetters except through violence. Navigation Acts and monopolies resulted in illegal trading, smuggling, and privateering, and these frictions caused wars. The 19th century was slow to resolve these tangles. It became clear that agreements on such issues as shipowners' liabilities, common forms of chartering, and marine insurance were mutually desirable. The International Maritime Committee did much valuable work toward the end of the century in clarifying and simplifying the mass of confused regulations hampering the shipping business. The responsibilities and liabilities of the shipowner with respect to the handling, loading, and stowage of cargo are defined primarily in the Carriage of Goods by Sea Act of 1936 and the Harter Act of 1893. One of the principal purposes of the Harter Act was to prevent shipowners from evading their obligation to properly load, stow, care for, and deliver cargoes carried on their vessels.

With a view toward making uniform the rules governing the responsibilities and immunities of shipowners under a bill of lading, a code of rules known as the "Hague Rules" was drawn up in 1921 by the Maritime Law Committee of the International Law Association. These Hague Rules form the basis of the Carriage of Goods by Sea Acts of Great Britain and the United States. There can be little doubt that responsibility for proper stowage rests primarily on the shipowner, and on the master as his/her representative.

Because domestic markets are limited, nations must turn to world markets for commerce. Nations can draw upon gold reserves for only so long, and soon learn they must trade or fade. The sea-power historian, Alfred Thayer Mahan, taught that national sea power is a politico-military force composed of naval and commercial fleets capable of transiting the oceans of the world at will. Served by overseas bases strategically located throughout the world, such sea powers exploit worldwide markets and sources of raw materials to the fullest possible extent.

Trade, of course, requires movement of goods. The only practical method of transporting large volumes of goods across the oceans of the world is in merchant ships. A ton of cargo may be moved in a ship for only a fraction of the cost of air transport. If a nation is going to trade with the rest of the world, it must utilize merchant ships. A nation's vessels plying the shipping routes of the world have a stabilizing effect on freight rates charged to that nation's businesses. Economically, the need for a strong, healthy merchant marine is tremendous.

Innovations in the Carriage of Goods at Sea

The most astonishing and whole-hearted acceptance of any principle of materials handling in the past half century has been that of unitization. It has been proven that materials handling becomes more efficient as the size of the unit increases.

Over the past decades, billions of dollars have been invested by the shipping industry in the production of marine containers, the construction and modification of ships to carry those containers, the development of marine terminals to handle efficiently both the ships and the containers, and, lastly, the manufacture of other equipment and systems to support the maritime intermodal triangle of container, ship, and marine terminal. This does not even take into account the expenditures of other transportation interests generally considered only land oriented: railroads, truckers, equipment-leasing companies, and so forth. After this very busy and costly era of development, it would seem that a plateau of attainment and rest might be in order. Such is certainly not the case!

Intermodal containerization has grown from approximately 30,000 twenty-foot-equivalent units (TEU) to current worldwide inventory estimates of 16 million TEU. Growth estimates dwarf even this incredible increase. As regards ships to carry these TEU, not only will the number and size be increased, but there is also a supersized containership with a 10,000 TEU capacity.

This would seem to imply that the era of the breakbulk ship has ended. Although the number of breakbulk vessels has dwindled, the need for their flexibility of service still exists. Therein lies the advantage of such vessels. Even though a containership may be far more productive and cost effective, it is so *only* in the carriage of containers. A breakbulk vessel can carry breakbulk cargo; dry and liquid bulk cargo; outsized cargo such as lumber, rails, and piping; refrigerated cargo; heavy lift cargo; and yes, even containers.

The concept of lower costs is more likely to change carrier attitudes toward breakbulk handling than is that of new equipment. Carriers tend to think in terms of unit costs and to disregard improvements in traditional handling methods without bothering to assess their net benefits. Effective breakbulk handling can require more intensive management than does containerization, but is rarely accorded it due to a tradition of fragmented responsibility. With adequate thought and simple technology, breakbulk handling rates can almost match those of containerization, and for much lower investment and operating costs. Optimum results depend on proper handling at the source, which principally involves efficient slinging. Carrier resistance arises from expenditure on nonreusable slings, but this can be recouped by only a small productivity increase. Reduction of worker resistance to the use of slings depends on proper consultation and on convincing dock labor that it involves no increase in effort, or reduction in safety.

The type of vessel required depends upon the trade route. Containerization cannot be the answer for a less developed country; the economic viability of this technique depends on the nation's ability to stuff into containers a major portion of its trade goods, to create a series of inland depots to receive the goods, to stuff and de-stuff containers, to redesign its railroad system and its road system, to abandon intermediate ports, and to redesign its major ports. This may take several generations. It is obvious that the trade route will determine the mode of transportation. In view of this, the intent of this first chapter is to discuss the major innovation in the carriage of goods at sea in the past 50 years, namely, containerization.

CONTAINERIZATION

The concept of containerization was not a new one when Malcolm P. McLean initiated the container revolution in April 1956 with the sailing of a converted T-2 tanker, the *Ideal X*. Malcolm McLean brought about containerization in much the same way that the forklift truck brought about palletization in 1935. The *Ideal X* was converted to allow for cargo movement by both truck and ship, thereby forming an integrated transportation system. In examining this innovation the remainder of this chapter will discuss the container, the ship, the terminal, and the lashing of containers aboard ship.

The Container

Containerization is considered the most successful solution to the problem of moving cargo in international trade. Containerization has achieved its primary purpose of minimizing the handling of cargo. It ensures the efficient, reliable, and rapid delivery of the undamaged goods with through-transportation that can utilize all modes of transport. The end result is intermodalism. Intermodalism can best be depicted by the example of a "house to house" or "door to door" container. A shipper will stow (a term preferable to "stuff") a container, and the consignee will unload ("strip") the container. The cargo is only handled twice, which fulfills the objective of containerization.

To allow this intermodalism, several aspects of transportation had to be studied and some had to be altered. Trailer manufacturers had to develop a chassis that the container could easily and swiftly be lifted from or placed on and locked into position for road transport. Larger road networks had to be developed in various countries, including areas throughout Europe. Interfacing with the railroads became important. Transportation of containers by rail necessitated altering various bridge and tunnel clearances. Lift requirements for piggyback containers had to be adapted for the Association of American Railroads. Through the efforts of the American National Standards Institute (ANSI) and, on a world scale, the International Organization for Standardization (ISO), containers have reached a certain degree of standardization. The term "ISO container" is a well-recognized one in the transportation industry.

The use of a container vessel fleet for a trade route with appropriate marine-materials-handling equipment can provide substantial cost savings.

a. The container, being standard, can easily be interchanged among the various transport modes. This allows intermodalism.

b. A decrease in transit time has a tendency to decrease inventory costs because a shorter lead time is required at reorder points.

c. A closed and sealed container provides protection against pilferage because what goods are in the container is not common knowledge.

d. The handling of goods themselves is dramatically reduced. This is especially true of the "house to house" container, with which the goods are handled once by the shipper and once by the consignee. (The container may be handled several times, but the goods are handled only twice.)

e. The container can serve as protection against the elements, thereby reducing the need for increased packaging.

Container operation is not without its indigenous problems, however. These include the following:

a. Equipment balance necessitates having the required number and types of containers located conveniently for the shipper's access. The container must be structurally sound, clean, and seaworthy. If it is not, the possibility of cargo damage increases.

b. The container must be correctly loaded. If it is not, the cargo, the container, and the handling equipment may be damaged. When "house to house" containers are used, responsibility for proper stowage shifts from the carrier to the shipper, who may have less expertise in cargo stowage.

c. Certain types of cargo may not be transportable by container simply because of the restrictive size or carrying capacity of the container.

d. Certain containerships are limited in their ports of call, due to poor capabilities for the loading or unloading of containers at some terminals.

CONTAINER MATERIALS

The construction materials used in assembling containers are steel, plywood/fiberglass, and aluminum. *Steel* containers are strong but heavy and susceptible to corrosion. Steel keeps damage from puncturing and collisions with equipment to a minimum. *Plywood/fiberglass* containers generally have steel frames and smooth walls of ¾–inch plywood reinforced by fiberglass that do not reduce internal space. These walls are easy to maintain, and when maintained properly will not corrode. Such containers are not comparable in strength to aluminum or steel types. *Aluminum* containers are made of wide, lightweight aluminum sheets and have one-piece roofs and sides. Their light weight is a considerable advantage in over-the-road transport. The interiors are generally lined with plywood for protection and insulation. Aluminum is more resistant to corrosion than steel.

BASIC CONTAINER ELEMENTS

Since the container is the package that is handled by the steamship, an understanding of the terms commonly used to talk about containers is a necessity (see Fig. 1-1). *Side rails* provide the strength to resist bending (compression and tension) when the container is lifted at the corners. The *bottom structure* bears the weight of the cargo resting on the floorboards (wood planks on plywood) and distributes this weight to the cross members' (I or Z beam) understructure. In addition, the I or Z beams distribute weight to the bottom side and end rails. *Corner castings* are steel fittings that allow the insertion of lifting devices. They also provide a means for handling, stacking, and securing. *Corner posts* are the steel vertical strength members that make stacking possible. The stress is transmitted through the corner castings. The *sides* and *front* are the flat sidings attached to the side and front posts, which are bolted to the top and bottom rails. These aluminum posts may be inside or outside the siding on aluminum containers. Steel-container siding is made of corrugated steel sheets, which eliminates the need for posts. Plywood/fiberglass containers do not use posts for their fiberglass-reinforced plywood panels. The *roof* is usually made of the same material as that of the side panel. It is desirable to have one-sheet construction to resist water entry. The *security seal* (see Fig. 1-2) is used in conjunction with the locking door handle. Once the door is closed and the seal is in place, the door cannot be opened without the seal breaking. Such seals are number coded. The *door gasket* is attached to the door edges to help provide a waterproof seal.

THE CONTAINER CHOICE

There are several different types and sizes of containers to meet the varying needs of shippers. A thorough knowledge of these container types allows the shipper to plan shipments effectively. Selection of the most suitable container can be

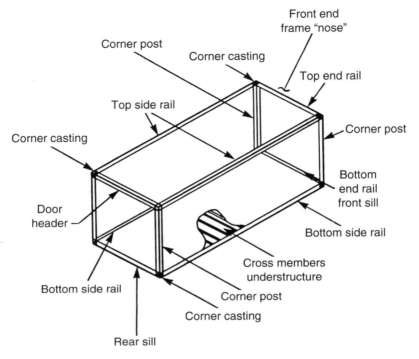

Figure 1-1. Container elements.

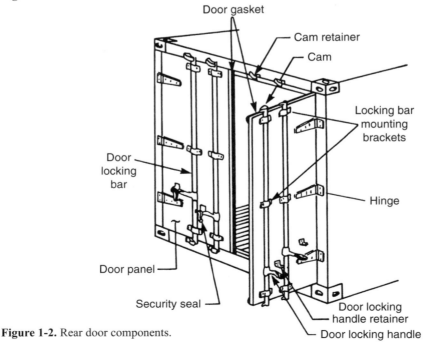

Figure 1-2. Rear door components.

done by conferring with a container-leasing company, the carrier, or referring to *The Official Intermodal Equipment Register.* The *Register* contains, among other things, the dimensions and capacities of the various containers currently in use. Typical information for some of the more commonly used containers is found in Table 1-1.

TABLE 1-1
Commonly Used Containers

Exterior Door	Approximate Interior Dimensions	Interior Approximate Dimensions	Approximate Weight	Door Openings
W × H × L	W × H × L	(Cubic Feet)	Capacity (lbs)*	W × H
8' × 8' × 20'	92" × 87" × 230"	1,065	40,000	89" × 84"
8' × 8'6" × 20'	92" × 93" × 230"	1,138	40,000	89" × 89"
8' × 8'6" × 24'	92" × 94" × 282"	1,411	45,900	90" × 89"
8' × 8'6" × 35'	92" × 93" × 415"	2,054	50,000	90" × 90⅞"
8' × 8' × 40'	92" × 88" × 473"	2,216	50,000	89" × 84"
8' × 8'6" × 40'	92" × 93" × 473"	2,342	55,000	90" × 89"
8' × 8'6" × 40'	92" × 105" × 473"	2,644	55,000	90" × 102"
8' × 9'6½" × 45'	92" × 106½" × 534"	3,035	64,300	92" × 102½"

* It should be realized that there are weight and size limits on containers for state and interstate over-the-road transportation. This in formation may also be found in *The Official Intermodal Equipment Register.*

CONTAINER TYPES

The following are some of the different types of containers, along with possible commodity applications:

Flatracks (Fig. 1-3) are used for cargo that does not conform to the normal dry cargo container. The cargo may be awkward or too large; the flatrack allows such cargo to be carried on containerships. The ends are collapsible and can be interlocked for cost-saving in handling and storage. Examples of cargo not susceptible to water damage that may be carried in this container are boilers, generators, machinery (agricultural, construction), and transport vehicles (boats, buses, tanks, and trucks).

Ventilated containers provide ventilation and protection against water damage. They are similar to the basic dry cargo container and therefore may be used as such on the return leg of the voyage. Cargo carried in these containers includes fruits and vegetables, green coffee (bagged), and spices (bagged).

Half-height containers (Fig. 1-4) are normally only 4 feet high and are designed for cargoes of high density (i.e., those that are heavy and take up little space). They act as a space saver, because two can fit into the space occupied by one standard container. Cargo carried in these containers includes steel products such as pipes, rolls, and beams; drums; and ores.

Tank containers (Fig. 1-5) have many different configurations. Their function is to carry bulk liquids in small lot shipments. Shipping in tanks is an alternative to drum shipping and may save labor. Examples of cargo carried in this container include chemicals (hazardous and nonhazardous), potable liquids, liquid foods, gas, and helium.

The *open or canvas-top* container (Fig. 1-6) allows loading both through the top with an overhead crane and through the rear doors by conventional means. It is advisable that cargoes susceptible to water damage be kept in a weatherproof pack inside the container. Overheight cargoes may be carried in this container. Examples of cargo carried in such containers include machinery, lumber, and pumps.

The *high cube* containers (Fig. 1-7) are large-volume containers (9 ft 6 in. high) specifically for low-density (light, large) cargo. Such containers may present problems in foreign countries with low rail and bridge clearances. Examples of cargo carried in this container include household goods, stoves, refrigerators, washers, furniture, carpets, tobacco, and cargoes with high stowage factors.

Bulk containers (Fig. 1-8) answer the need for reducing the expense of bagging dry bulk commodities that flow freely. Certain bulk products require

Figure 1-3. Flatrack container.

Figure 1-4. Half-height container.

Figure 1-5. Tank container.

Figure 1-6.
Open or canvas-top container.

Figure 1-7. High cube container.

Figure 1-8.
Bulk container.

Figure 1-9.
Refrigerated container.

additional protection such as polyethylene liners. Examples of cargo carried in these containers include grains, cereals, flour, malts, sugar, fertilizers, and coal.

Reefer (refrigerated) containers (Fig. 1-9) have precise temperature control capabilities for situations in which refrigeration or freezing is necessary. They run on diesel, electrical, or liquid gas power, and can be used for ocean transport, storage, or over-the-road transport.

Other specialized containers include livestock, produce, insulated, tilt, side door, and automobile containers.

STOWING (STUFFING) THE CONTAINER

For the sake of clarity, we shall use the term "stowing" to denote placement of the container aboard the ship. The term "stuffing" shall mean the placing or packaging of the goods within the container. This term (stuffing) is a misnomer because it suggests packing a container in a careless manner, which is not how stuffing should be done.

Prior to the advent of containerization, the shipper had to rely on the expertise of the stevedore to stow the cargo aboard ship properly so as to withstand the hazardous rigors of an ocean voyage. But with modern house-to-house containerization, the shipper "stuffs" the container. Therefore, the responsibility of proper packaging has shifted from the carrier to the shipper. Because of this shift in responsibility, the shipper should be aware of all forces that the container (and the cargo contained within) will encounter from the start of its journey to the final destination. These forces are due to the motions of the road, railroad, and the ship. *Road motions* include acceleration and deceleration (braking); impact (coupling of the chassis with the truck and backing up against loading docks); and vibration, sway, and road shocks from poorly paved roads. *Railroad motions* include acceleration and deceleration, impact from coupling, vibration, and sway. *Ship motions* (see Figs. 1-10 and 1-11) include rolling, yawing, pitching, surging, sway, and heaving. In addition, there are wave-impact stresses such as panting and pounding. *Panting* is a stress due to unequal water pressures on the bow as it passes through successive waves. *Pounding* results from the bow lifting out of the water and then slamming down onto the crest of the next wave.

It is apparent that the ocean voyage presents the most hazardous situation for the container. To stuff for the worst conditions is to stuff for the oceanic leg of the integrated transportation system.

The principles of stowing a breakbulk ship are applicable to the stuffing of containers. Containers must be loaded so as to prevent movement within them. The distribution of weight should be even throughout the length and breadth of the container, with heavy cargo on the bottom and light cargo on top. The permissible floor load capacity must be adhered to, and cargo within the container must be compatible; for example, wet hides should not be packed in

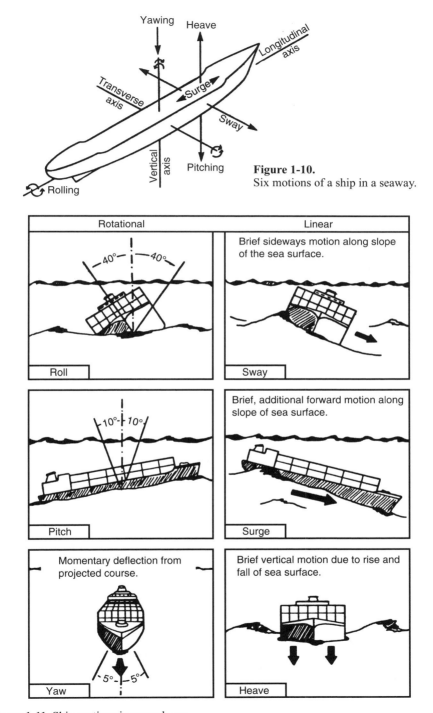

Figure 1-10.
Six motions of a ship in a seaway.

Figure 1-11. Ship motions in a rough sea.

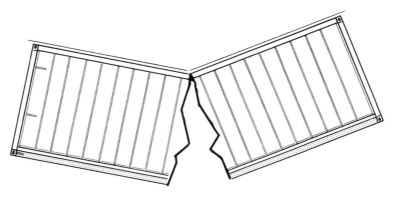

Figure 1-12. Container too heavy in the middle.

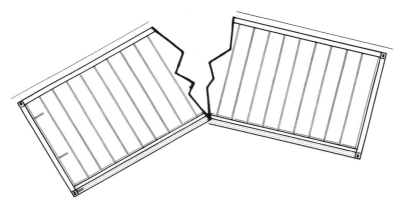

Figure 1-13. Container too heavy at both ends.

Figure 1-14. Improper loading; container heavy at front end.

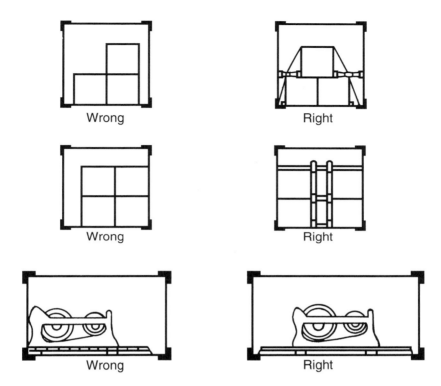

Wrong   Right

Wrong   Right

Wrong   Right

Figure 1-15. Right and wrong weight distribution in a container.

a container with food stuffs; the hides will taint the foodstuffs. Also, wet cargo should never be stowed on top of dry cargo. Finally, all void spaces should be filled to prevent shifting of the cargo. Not adhering to these principles will cause the types of damage depicted in Figures 1-12 to 1-15.

In addition to the motions (forces) already mentioned, the container experiences *transfer forces* (forces experienced between modes) such as lifting, stacking, racking, and restraint. *Lifting* emanates from rapid acceleration and deceleration. *Stacking* results from forces applied at the corner castings (in the marshaling yard and aboard ship). *Racking* forces are side forces that tend to make the top and bottom of the container no longer square with its sides. *Restraint* results from forces applied by the various lashing systems used aboard ship.

As was stated above, the principles of stowing a breakbulk ship are similar to those of stuffing a container. The techniques involved in securing cargo in a breakbulk ship are also similar to those used for securing cargo in a container. The use of dunnage, whether lumber, plywood, steel strapping, or fiberboard, for bracing and shoring is discussed in detail in Chapter 5. Adherence to these techniques will help to minimize damage to the cargo and the container.

The Ship

Container stowage aboard conventional breakbulk ships is difficult and time consuming. One limiting factor is the hatch opening, which usually does not extend for the full breadth of the vessel. Stowing in the wing spaces below deck requires additional horizontal motion. To alleviate this problem a ship of cellular construction was developed. The containership, with hatch openings extending for almost the full breadth of the vessel, incorporates vertical cell guides that allow confined positioning below deck and vertical stacking (see Figs. 1-16 and 1-17).

Figure 1-16.
Cell guides for vertical stacking.

Figure 1-17. Profile view of vertical stacking below and on deck. The hatch covers are designed for heavier deck load capacity because of the weights incurred when containers are stacked on deck.

THE OPERATION

The overriding consideration in performing cargo operations on containerships is keeping port time to a minimum. To achieve this end, a cargo stowage plan and the sequence of container loading is arranged by shoreside personnel prior to the ship's arrival in port. The chief mate has only a brief period to look at the stowage plan, since cargo operations usually commence immediately on the docking of the ship.

Once the containership has docked, the lashings are removed from the on-deck containers and the shoreside gantry crane commences discharging.

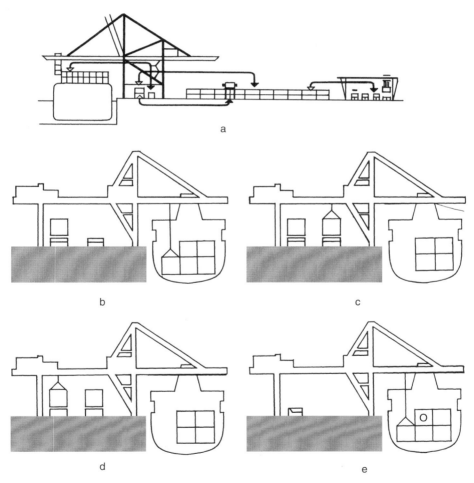

Figure 1-18. (a) Crane sequence of operations in discharging an import container and loading an export container. (b) Crane engages container. (c) Import container lifted onto trailer waiting ashore. (d) Crane engages export container on trailer. (e) Export container loaded into ship's hold. Spreader then off-loads container marked "O."

Figure 1-19. Container spreader that locks into the tops of containers for lifting aboard ship. **(a)** Locks on to container aboard vessel. **(b)** Lifts container off vessel. **(c)** Releases container onto hustler.

The hatch cover is then removed. The crane will then begin discharging cargo below deck, removing containers from one vertical cell only (usually six or seven containers) until that column or cell is empty. This allows loading to begin and to run in conjunction with unloading. Time is saved because every time the crane with its spreader moves it is carrying a container (see Figs. 1-18 and 1-19). The actual loading and unloading operation is quite simple, but planning where each container is to be located aboard ship can become quite complex. Because of the vast number of containers aboard ship, it is necessary to have a location identification system. A numerical system has evolved that utilizes the three dimensions involved in cargo stowage. This system calls for numbering containers longitudinally from forward to aft by hatch and bay number, transversely beginning at the centerline and moving outboard (the port side being designated by successive even numbers, the starboard side by successive odd numbers), and vertically beginning at the tank top and moving upward to the uppermost tier on deck (see Figs. 1-20 and 1-21). The bay concept arose to accommodate the fact that it is possible to stow two, 20 foot containers in the same cell as one, 40 foot container and thus it is necessary to differentiate between the two sizes on the cargo plan.

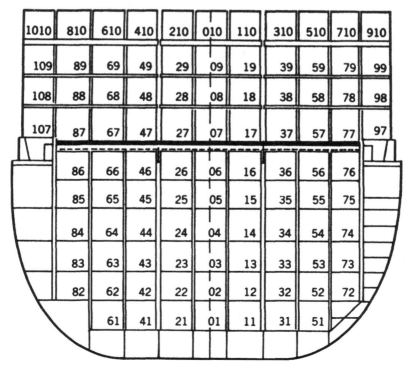

Figure 1-20. Transverse and vertical numbering system for containers aboard a containership.

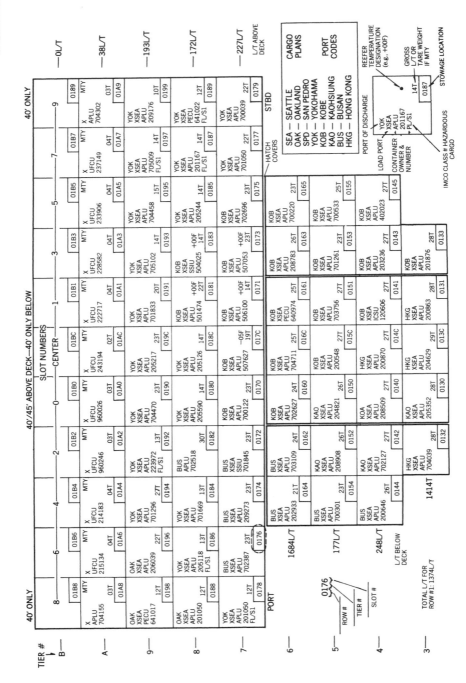

Figure 1-21. Computer plan layout illustrating bay concept.

STOWAGE CONSIDERATIONS

Stowage considerations that pertain to containerships include stability, trim and list, vessel stresses, stack height and weight limitations, port of discharge, and hazardous cargo regulations.

Considerations of *stability, trim,* and *list* dictate that it is necessary to stow the heaviest containers below deck, with the bottom tiers heavier than the ones on top; to build up the stacks of containers on deck that are closest to the ship's centerline (again with the heavier containers on the bottom); and to distribute weight evenly between the port and starboard sides to limit ballasting and to prevent a list. It should be noted that under certain listing conditions a containership cannot work cargo owing to the inability of the container to be inserted into the cell guides. Finally, the weight must be distributed longitudinally so as to give the desired trim.

Vessel stresses (shear stresses and bending moments) should not exceed the design limits of the vessel. To this end no more than two consecutive hatches, depending on design limits, should be empty at the same time, nor should they carry only empty containers.

Stack height is a concern when stowing a high cube (9 ft 6 in.) container under deck, since this type of container will occupy the space of two, 8 foot 6 inch containers. This results in lost volume. Stowing of high cube containers on deck is also a problem, due to lashing system constraints.

Stack weight limitations must be considered in that the total weight of the stack should not exceed the deck load capacity of the tank top for under-deck stowage or the deck load capacity of the hatch cover for on deck stowage. In addition, the strength of the bottom container must also be considered, since stacks may be as high as 11 containers under deck and as high as 5 containers on deck.

The use of more than one crane at the *port of discharge* will probably dictate a need for bay separation when stowing the cargo. Because of their size, container cranes cannot load or discharge adjacent bays (see Fig. 1-22[a-c]).

Hazardous cargo regulations dictate certain stowage restrictions that are set by the Department of Transportation in the United States and the International Maritime Organization (IMO) for international shipping.

In addition to these considerations, there may be *special cargo stowage restrictions.* For example, refrigerated containers are generally loaded on the first tier on deck for accessibility to a power source. These containers should be stacked only one high to allow servicing at sea. First-tier on-deck stowage of containers containing wet animal hides or other odorous cargoes must also be considered. Aluminum containers must be stowed in a protected location away from possible damage by heavy seas. They should not be stowed on deck forward or in the out board *slots.* During *cold* weather it is necessary to stow "Keep from Freezing"

(KFF) cargo under deck. Open or canvas-top containers must be stowed under deck or at least under another container on deck. High cube containers should be stowed on deck, taking into consideration any lashing constraints. Flatracks and value cargo containers should be stowed below deck to limit access.

Some of the considerations and restrictions noted above could be included on a port detail sheet to assist proper stowage planning. Table 1-2 is a fictitious port detail sheet that includes some of this information.

TABLE 1-2
Port Detail Sheet

Port of Call:					
Berthing	Depth of Channel/ Berth	Berth Use	Docking Side	Shift Starting/ Finishing Times	Holidays
	Channel—40' Berth—38' Channel width—900'	Multiuse No first come, first serve	Star board side-to	0730–1530 1530–2330 2330–0730	
Cranes	Number & Type of Cranes	Crane Moves/Hour	Types of Spreader	Crane Reach Height/Across	Bay Separation Necessary for Crane
	4-Paceco	18.0	Telescoping	5 high all bays / 13 across all bays	2 bays for all cranes
Stowage	Stowage Preference	Reefer Capacity	KFF Facility	Heavy-Lift Capacity	Hazardous Cargo Restrictions
		Terminal plug-in	Keep from freezing, limited	Mobile crane 150 tons	
Pier Facilities	Fuel Available	Freshwater Available	Customs	Terminal Equipment	
	Yes, by barge	Yes, at berth	At terminal	Straddle Carriers Forklifts	
Cost	Cost/box				
	Normal move $ Restow $ Bay shift				

The Containerized Terminal

At the breakbulk terminal, the equipment, starting at the ship, consists of the following: First, there is the married fall rig or the ship's crane, with a capacity of about 3 tons unless it is doubled up for heavier lifts. Most loads handled by a breakbulk ship do not exceed 1 ton. When the load reaches the pier apron it is either picked up by a forklift truck or landed on a dock trailer and hauled away by a small warehouse tractor as part of a three-trailer train. In the transit shed, protected from the elements, the load is stacked with a forklift truck. Some types of cargoes can be handled better with the Ross Carrier, which is a type of straddle truck much smaller than those seen today in use at containerized terminals. For heavy lifts and special cargo types, floating cranes or special heavy-lift cranes

Figure 1-22 (a) and (b). Adjacent container cranes. *Bottom photo courtesy Frederick Kurst.*

Figure 1-22 (c). Adjacent container cranes. *Courtesy Frederick Kurst.*

mounted on the ship are used. The equipment list is short and almost universal: ship's gear, forklift truck, tractor-trailer trains, and straddle truck. Whether the terminal is of high or low volume, the same basic set of equipment and methods is used. For high volumes the ship is simply worked longer hours and more hatches are worked. In the past, some breakbulk ships with double gear at four hatches and single gear at two hatches (six-hatch vessel), side ports in the upper and lower 'tweendecks, and overhead chutes and conveyors in operation would require as many as 23 gangs working the vessel. The entire operation required an army of men (as many as 400) and many machines.

    Containerization has changed things. The circumstances and controls are not the same when working with the "box." Gone are the 1- to 3-ton lifts. The lift may be as much as 40 tons if the container is a 40 footer loaded with dense cargo. However, if so, the container must be lightened before being hauled over the road due to limits on total weight of cargo and equipment. Some of the containers will be empty because of the need to keep the supply of containers somewhat equal throughout the system. On the average, about 75% of the containers handled will be loaded, and the average load will be about 14 tons. As a result, the married fall rig cannot be used, and the ship's own heavy-lift gear, formerly used for a few lifts, is just too slow to work a large number of containers and at any rate cannot reach over them. The dockside equipment has changed, too; we will look now at the equipment found at container handling terminals.

GANTRY CRANE WITH TROLLEY

One of the most common types of cranes used to move containers to or from the ship is the gantry crane with a trolley controlling the hook. The trolley is positioned vertically over the container by running it out on the gantry tracks; the operator then carefully lowers a spreader with fittings that mesh with four corner slots on the container. One control locks the spreader onto the container, which can then be hoisted clear of the hold. On fully containerized vessels the containers are stacked one on top of another in vertical cells constructed with heavy metal guides at the four corners.

Several manufacturers make these gantry cranes, some of which are installed on the ship to make the ship self-sufficient. When Sea-Land Service, Inc. pioneered this system, the ships needed to carry the container handling cranes on board, as the terminals they visited were not equipped to handle the containers. The ability to handle the containers with ship's gear is still important on vessels that act as feeders from smaller, less well equipped ports to the larger major container-oriented ports. Large mobile cranes with slewing booms are also used to lift the containers on and off the ship, but these cranes cannot match the cycle times of the gantry-and-trolley type cranes.

Two types of gantry-and-trolley cranes have been developed. In one, known as the A-frame design, the boom that extends out from the dock over the ship is topped up when not in use and lowered to the horizontal position when a ship is positioned alongside the dock. The other type has a lower profile; its boom is always in the horizontal position but slides inboard and outboard. The uprights supporting the latter type of crane are spaced quite far apart, usually enabling the containers to be handled over a greater distance, sometimes as long as that from areas inland to the pier apron. Both types provide a boom that is long enough that the trolley can be positioned over any point on the vessel in line with the gantry tracks as the trolley travels athwartships.

The crane is mounted on rails on the dock and can be moved forward or aft by the operator. Thus, the hook can be positioned vertically over any point on the ship. The cycle time of the hook on these cranes is 2 to 4 minutes, depending on the design of the crane and the weight of the load being handled. Cranes with sliding or telescopic booms with wide spans between their uprights provide more space for landing containers on the pier apron. The cranes at Elizabeth, New Jersey, facility can land as many as seven containers abreast of one another. This capability reduces the dependence on the tractor's chassis meeting the hook cycle exactly. The short cycle time and average load of about 14 tons obviously enables high tonnages to be handled per ship hour. (A 2-minute cycle time for the hook of a breakbulk married fall system is good, but the hook only carries a 1-ton rather than a 14-ton load.)

EQUIPMENT ON THE TERMINAL SIDE

Once the gantry or slewing crane has landed the container on the dock, various types of equipment are used to place the container in a marshaling area and from there onto a road chassis for the haul to the consignee. Three systems have evolved for this purpose over the brief history of containerization. These systems may be designated by the equipment that they use. The three common systems are (1) the Chassis System, (2) the Straddle Carrier System, and (3) the Straddle Gantry Crane System. Additional equipment other than that which we will discuss under these three names is also found in use at containerized terminals. These additional pieces of equipment will be described separately.

The Chassis System

The chassis system (see Fig. 1-23) was the system first developed and used by Sea-Land when that company pioneered containerization in 1956. The container from the ship is landed directly onto a road-haul chassis waiting on the pier apron. Either a tractor that can operate over the road or, more commonly, a yard tractor then pulls the chassis with its container load to a slot in a large marshaling area. Once the yard tractor takes the chassis from the pier apron to the designated slot in the marshaling area and drops it off with its container load, the yard tractor then picks up an empty chassis and returns to the pier apron to receive another container from the ship. The number of yard tractors working in the system will depend on the hook cycle of the ship. With a crane discharging a container every 2 minutes,

Figure 1-23. A 40-foot chassis.

about four tractor-chassis trains would be needed. The distance between the slots in the marshaling area and the pier apron is also a factor. The most important consideration is that enough tractors must be working in the cyclical system to make sure the hook on the ship does not have to wait.

One immediately evident advantage of this system is that no other handling of the container is necessary. The customer (consignee) can take the chassis with the container directly from the terminal to his/her facility. The consignee has a certain amount of time to unload the container and bring the chassis and container back to the terminal.

The chassis system requires a lot of land and a large inventory of chassis. For example, the terminal facility in Elizabeth, New Jersey, covers 232 acres and provides space for more than 6,600 chassis. Besides the marshaling space for the chassis with containers, there are supporting facilities such as a gateway control area with 20 lanes for trucks: 7 for entry, 7 for exit, and 6 that may be for either entry or exit, depending on the need. A freight consolidation station servicing trucks and railroad cars with less than container load (LCL) shipments is under a 306,000 ft² (over 7 acres) building. Another, 100,000 ft² complex is provided for repair and maintenance work on the many types of equipment that must be kept in good condition. There are also administration buildings. The pier is 4,520 feet long and can accommodate six large container vessels. It is equipped with six gantry cranes of the low-profile extension boom type.

The Straddle Carrier System

The straddle carrier (see Fig. 1-24) picks up one container from under the hook spot on the dock and transports it to a predesignated slot in the marshaling area. Some straddle carriers can stack the containers three high. However, there is a need to be able to get at any one of the stowed containers for customer servicing. This involves placing the container on a consignee's road-haul chassis with tractor. Because of this need, the stacking limit is one and a half high for 20 foot containers and one high for 40 foot containers. This means that for four slots, assuming 20 foot containers and a 45° parking pattern, as in Fig. 1-25, two would be one high and two would be two high. With this pattern the straddle truck can shuffle the upper containers to get at any of the bottom containers. The 45° pattern makes it unnecessary for the straddle truck to maneuver down long lines of containers, which may damage containers and is slower.

The rate at which a straddle carrier can handle containers determines the number needed to support any given operation. One straddle carrier can handle about 12 containers/hour if receiving them from the ship's hook and taking them to a marshaling area. The containers are landed on the pier apron and a carrier with a spreader sling moves over the container and drops the spreader down on top of the container so that special fittings mesh with the container's corner fittings. The operator then locks the spreader onto the container, picks it up, and carries it away to the marshaling area.

Figure 1-24. The straddle carrier.

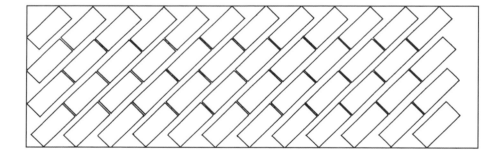

Figure 1-25. *Top:* The 45° parking pattern that may be used for containers in the marshaling area handled by straddle carriers. In the 200 by 65 ft area, sixty-six, 20 ft containers can be placed so that all are readily available. With allowances for aisles between blocks, the number of containers stored per acre will be slightly less than if they were stored in parallel rows. *Bottom:* Diagram illustrating why stacking containers one-and-a-half high is necessary for easy availability. Of the six, 20 ft containers in the row, numbers 1, 5, 6, and 4 are easily available. To obtain container number 2 or 3, the operator must place number 5 or 6 on top of 1 or 4; then number 2 or 3 can be picked up and passed over the remaining containers to place the desired container on a chassis or under the ship's hook. If the containers were stacked two-high throughout, the bottom containers would still be accessible, but not without considerable time being taken to shuffle and move other containers.

Figure 1-26. The straddle gantry crane system.

Picking up a container and placing it on a chassis bed is a slower process, because the operator must carefully maneuver over the chassis bed and lower the container so it meshes with special fittings that will secure it to the chassis. The rate of loading onto chassis is about 8 containers/hour.

Once a loaded inbound container is at the terminal, it does not remain there very long. The ship operator will have contacted all consignees and notified them as to when their shipment would be ready for delivery. The consignee then has a limited time within which he/she must come and remove the container, take it to his/her own facility, unload it, and bring it back. About 48 hours is allowed for the consignee to come and pick up his/her shipment, and he/she has about the same time to unload it and bring it back to the terminal. If he/she keeps it beyond the specified time he/she is charged a daily rental fee. The outbound containers are delivered to the terminal so as to coincide with the ship's schedule. It is the responsibility of the freight department to coordinate these movements.

The Straddle Gantry Crane System (SGCS)

The straddle gantry crane (SGC) (Fig. 1-26) is not used to transport the container from or to the pier apron. A tractor and chassis train is used for that purpose in this system. One lane under the SGC is reserved for the tractor and chassis. The SGC is used to pick up the container from the chassis and place it in a predesignated slot in the marshaling area.

If the container is being loaded onto a ship or an outgoing road-haul chassis, then the SGC picks up the container and places it on the chassis. Thus, the transport between the marshaling area and the ship is by the yard chassis; the SGC does the handling. As we have already seen, straddle carriers perform both the transport and the handling.

It may appear that the straddle carrier would be the more economical of the two systems, because of its flexibility. Under some operating conditions, it may be. However, when the number of containers that must be handled is high, there may be some economy in switching to the use of the SGC and chassis trains to service the ship's hook or to load trucks. The SGC system utilizes the customer's equipment and driver to move containers between the yard entrance gate and the stack in the marshaling area. The savings resulting from its use are thus due to a reduction in the cost of needed equipment, especially when the terminal workload is such that there is a need for a high truck-loading rate. For example, the SGC can handle 15 truck-loading operations and 30 ship-loading operations per hour, whereas the productivity level for the straddle carrier is such that when the need for multiple units develops in order to keep up with delivery and receiving rates of containers passing through the terminal, then the SGC system, at some point, becomes more economical.

Other Types of Container Handling Equipment

Certain equipment at the container terminal has been designed for special tasks. Three examples are the *front-end loader* (Fig. 1-27), the *side loader* (Fig. 1-28), and the *shifter* (Fig. 1-29).

Some ships have their own container handling equipment as shown in figure 1-31. This equipment allows greater flexibility, but does take up space that can be utilized for the carriage of additional containers.

FIXED AND VARIABLE COSTS OF TERMINAL OPERATIONS

The primary objective of the container terminal is to provide good and complete service to its customers, the consignees and shippers. This service is the receipt and delivery of the containers with as little delay and difficulty as possible. The terminal is the interface between the ship and the land transport systems. Its efficiency can be measured by the *cost per container handled.* If we know the total cost of an operation and the total number of containers handled per year we can determine the cost per container.

The total *cost* is composed of fixed and variable costs. The fixed costs for the terminal consist of the money invested in the land and in the equipment. Once the land and equipment have been procured, the annual costs remain fixed regardless of how many containers are handled. The variable costs are those

Figure 1-27. Front-end loader.

Figure 1-28. Side loader.

Figure 1-29. The shifter.

that depend on the number of containers handled and the size of the installation being set up. These costs include labor, repair and maintenance, development costs (paving, buildings, etc.), and administration costs.

Estimating Equipment Needs and Costs

Let us assume that we must load 76 containers on chassis per hour to meet an over-the-road delivery schedule, and that we also need to operate the ship's hook at the rate of 30 containers/hour. What equipment would be needed for each operation? Table 1-3 gives the required information.

TABLE 1-3
Equipment Comparison

Factor	Straddle Carrier	SGC
Ship handling rate	12	30
No. units needed to handle 30 containers/hour	2.5	1
Truck-chassis loading rate	8	15
No. units needed to handle 76 containers/hour	9.5	5
Yard-chassis trains needed	0	4
Standby units needed	1	0

According to this analysis, the straddle carrier system would need 13 units, and the SGC system would need 6 units plus four yard-chassis trains. If we obtained the cost of the various needed components, we could determine the annual cost of the capital investment for equipment.

Estimating Land Needs and Costs

The area needed for marshaling is less with the SGC than with the straddle carrier system. This is for two reasons: (1) the ability of the SGC to stack containers higher and (2) the space between containers can be less with the SGC. With the straddle carrier, the space between rows of containers must be 4 feet to control damage to containers as the straddle carrier runs down the rows. With the SGC, the space between rows can be reduced to 1 ft, and the lanes between blocks can be narrower.

The height of stacking with the straddle carrier is limited to two containers high, or for good customer service, which is important, to one and a half containers high. Three high is possible but not practical except for the storage of a few containers when selectivity is not important. The carrier can pass over a stack two high while carrying a container, but cannot pass over a stack three high. The SGC can stack three or four high and retain the ability to pick out of the stack any of the containers for delivery.

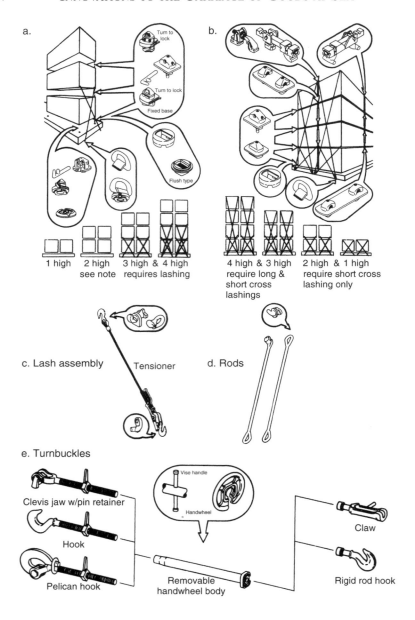

Figure 1-30. Lashing components. **(a)** Lock-Lash System. **(b)** Stack-Lash System. **(c)** The lash assembly shown is used on the Lock-Lash or Stack-Lash Systems. The strength of the lash is determined by the loads involved. End fittings should be selected to suit lashing arrangement and deck fittings. **(d)** Rod strengths should be determined by dynamic analysis using the ship's characteristics. End fittings and best arrangement can be selected to suit individual operating requirements. **(e)** Turnbuckles. *Courtesy Peck and Hale, Inc.*

To estimate the fixed cost of the needed land, we must know the level of productivity that must be met. For example, let us assume that the terminal must be capable of holding 2,000 containers. The land needed for the straddle carrier system would be 2,000/167 or about 12 acres. For the SGC system the land needed would be 2,000/403, or about 5 acres. With these data, plus the cost per acre of land, we could determine the annual fixed cost of the land.

The Lashing of Containers Aboard Ship

Great strides have been made in lashing systems since the inception of containerization. New equipment is continually being introduced and today there are several systems available. Information on which system might be best for an individual ship can be obtained from the manufacturers of the various

Figure 1-31. Lashings with tensioners and turnbuckles. Note twist locks at the bottom.
Courtesy Peck and Hale, Inc.

Figure 1-32. Use of rigid rods and turnbuckles. *Courtesy Peck and Hale, Inc.*

Figure 1-33.
The buttress system.
(a) Buttress system in place.
(b) Buttress towers aboard
   the *Sea-land Freedom*.

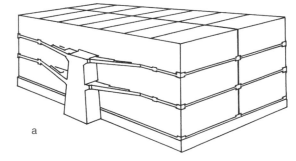

Figure 1-34. Removable stacking frames. **(a)** In place aboard ship. **(b)** On the pier.

container securing systems. It is commonplace for the manufacturer, such as Peck & Hale, to run a computerized dynamic analysis of container accelerations, which determine the required lashings and allowable weights.

Three common systems in use today are the locking, lashing, and buttress systems. The *locking system* can be utilized with relatively lightly loaded containers stacked no more than two high. Locking is achieved by the use of stacking fittings such as twist-lock stackers and stacking cones (see Fig. 1-30a). The *lashing system* (Fig. 1-30b) uses wire rope (Fig. 1-30c), rigid rods (Fig. 1-30d), chains, or combinations thereof with various tensioning devices such as turnbuckles (Fig. 1-30e). Stacking fittings are used in conjunction with the lashing equipment for alignment of the container and additional restraint. Diagonal lashings are usually preferable to vertical lashings because they provide antiracking strength (see Figs. 1-31 and 1-32). The *buttress system* uses buttress towers that are permanently fixed to the deck at the fore and aft ends of each hatch. Removable stacking frames that allow several containers to be blocked and locked as one integrated unit fit into each of the buttresses. After a tier of containers has been loaded, the stacking frame is placed on top and the next tier is loaded on top of the stacking frame. The frame thus provides a rigid means of restraint. This system reduces container securing time but cannot accommodate containers of different heights except on the uppermost tier (see Figs. 1-33 and 1-34).

DOCUMENTATION

The carriage of goods at sea by its most predominant mode (the containership) must be concerned with the documentation utilized. What follows is an outline of the export and import documents along with a flow chart of their place (see Fig. 1-35) in the transportation process.

CONCLUSION

Following similar patterns of other commercial transportation industries, the global fleet of containerships, measured by container slots, is dominated by a handful of super carriers. In fact, the top 20 companies control about 82% of cellular ships, and it would appear that this trend will continue.

The supply of vessels is a function of carriers' ability to look into their crystal balls to determine how many ships they can build, operate, manage, and scrap given the cycle patterns of global economies and customer demand for their services. With global trade expected to grow at an annual rate of between 3.5 and 5% over the next few years, despite the fact that national economies have been growing at about half of that rate, carriers are desperately trying to maintain a perfect balance between supply and demand.

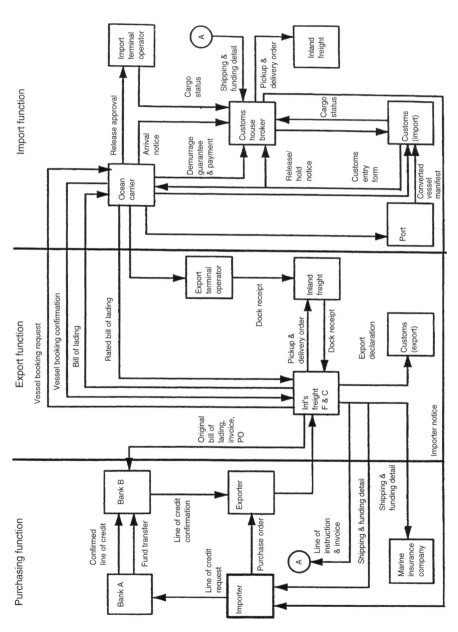

Figure 1-35. Documentation outline and flow chart.

CHAPTER 2

CARGO RESPONSIBILITY

INTRODUCTION

A COMPETENT SHIP'S OFFICER SHOULD HAVE a basic familiarity with the laws governing carriage of goods by sea. By understanding where the responsibility for cargo lies throughout its carriage, a ship's officer will be better prepared to avoid cargo loss or damage. In an effort to explain the necessity of and reasons behind some of the routine duties required of the ship's officers and crew members, we will provide here an overview of the laws governing cargo handling. In addition, we will give suggestions on ways to meet the requirements of the various laws governing cargo handling and thereby reduce shipping costs and strengthen the carrier's position in case of litigation over cargo damage.

THE HARTER ACT OF 1893

Under the general maritime law, the common carrier had historically been regarded as the insurer of all cargo carried. Prior to the passage of the Harter Act of 1893, the shipowner was held responsible for cargo damage unless he/she could prove that such damage was due to one of the following causes:

1. An act of God.

2. An act of public enemies.

3. Inherent vice.

4. Fire.

Because the English allowed shipping companies to protect themselves by disclaimers contained in the bills of lading, the American shipping companies were at a disadvantage. Thus, in 1893, Congress passed the Harter Act, which gave some protection to our shipping companies.

With the passage of the Harter Act, shipowners obtained six additional exceptions under which they would be not liable for cargo loss or damage:

1. Errors in navigation or mismanagement of the ship.

2. Perils of the sea.

3. Insufficiency of the packaging.

4. Seizure under legal process.

5. Act or omission of shipper.

6. Saving or attempting to save life or property at sea.

Thus, the shipowner enjoyed 10 immunities, counting the four previously enjoyed. Congress also demanded that the shipowner fulfill three definite responsibilities in order to enjoy the 10 immunities:

1. He/she must properly stow and care for the cargo.

2. He/she must exercise due diligence to properly equip, man, and provision the ship.

3. He/she must exercise due diligence to make the vessel seaworthy in all respects.

The Harter Act has no provision relieving the carrier of responsibility for damage or loss caused by fire; however, shipowners are covered by the Fire Statute of 1851. This statute protects shipowners by excluding liability of the shipowner and vessel for fire unless the fire occurred as a result of the shipowner's or its agents' neglect. Employees such as the master and crew members are not agents of the shipowner under this statute; the term "agents" in the statute refers to shoreside management. The problem with the Fire Statute of 1851 is that it applies only to bareboat charterers, shipowners, and the vessel. Time and voyage charterers are left exposed and liable for damages and losses caused by fire.

The Harter Act applies only to vessels operating in the domestic trade. For the shipowner to enjoy the benefits of the six additional exceptions to liability, the Harter Act must be incorporated as governing the relations between the parties in order to apply. The Harter Act does not apply to tug-tow relations. The shipowner is responsible for the cargo from yard to yard. Thus, it behooves the ship's officers to insure that the cargo is properly cared for while on the dock prior to loading and after discharge from the vessel.

Besides directing the shipowner to issue a bill of lading, the Harter Act also prohibits the shipowner from avoiding the responsibilities specified above. However, the carrier can accept more responsibilities by so contracting with the shipper. The carrier has the burden of proving freedom from negligence if he/she is to enjoy the benefits of the Harter Act. If the cargo is damaged by two causes (attributable to the shipowner and/or the cargo owner) and the parties to an action are unable to establish who caused what, the ship owner must pay for all the losses or damages suffered by the cargo interests.

With respect to tug-tow relationships, the barge is not considered cargo of the tug. However, if there is cargo on the barge and the bill of lading states that the Harter Act applies with respect to the cargo, then the barge owner is responsible for the cargo on the barge so carried.

Even if the cargo is carried aboard a foreign vessel, if it is being shipped in the domestic trade of the United States, the Harter Act applies. Thus, in *Knott v. Botany Worsted Mills,* a foreign vessel engaged in domestic U.S. trade was held responsible for water damage to wool. The water came from drainage off an adjacently stowed cargo of sugar. The shipowner was held to be negligent in its care and custody of the cargo. The failure to trim the vessel properly was construed as negligence in care and custody.

Section 3 of the Act, referring to errors in navigation and management of the vessel, was interpreted interestingly by the courts in *May v. Hamburg.* The vessel was stranded in a German river, and the court ruled that the shipowner used due diligence in making the vessel seaworthy and that the stranding was caused by an error in navigation; therefore, no liability for loss or damage could be assigned to this stranding. However, the shipowner sent a managing agent to examine the ship for necessary repairs. While en route to the repair yard, the vessel was involved in a second accident in which it was again stranded. When the court examined the case, they decided that when the shipowner sent its agent to Germany, it was as if a new voyage had commenced. Thus, the shipowner had to prove that it exercised due diligence to make the vessel seaworthy in all respects for *that* voyage. Since it was unable to prove that due diligence was exercised after the first stranding, the shipowner was liable because the damage was not from an error in navigation. The most significant element of the *Hamburg* ruling is that the damage did not necessarily have to be causally related to unseaworthiness. If the shipowner cannot prove that it exercised due diligence to make the vessel seaworthy in all respects, it loses the six exceptions to liability granted by the Harter Act.

The importance of determining the cause of damage to cargo is illustrated by numerous water damage cases. Whenever sea water gets into the hold, in order to enjoy the benefits of the exceptions of the Harter Act, the shipowner must prove that it was not negligent and that the cause comes under one of the exceptions of Harter. In the case of the *Folmina,* a classic case on the common occurrence of salt water damage to cargo, the court was unable to determine how this sea water got into the hold. The shipowner claimed salt water damage to the cargo was a peril of the sea and disclaimed liability. However, the court ruled that the doubt as to the cause of the entrance of the sea water must be resolved against the carrier.

Even when there is evidence that the cargo damage was caused partially by the carrier's negligence, the carrier has the burden of proving what portion was caused by the excepted peril. In *Schnell v. The Vallescura,* the cargo of onions, which, required ventilation, was damaged by decay. The vessel encountered heavy weather en route and was therefore unable to ventilate the cargo properly for part of the voyage. However, the court also noted that the vessel neglected to ventilate the cargo at night during fair weather. Because the vessel was unable to prove what portion of the damages were attributable to the excepted peril of the heavy weather, the Supreme Court ruled that the vessel must bear the total cost of damage to the cargo.

As is obvious from these cases, it is important that the ship's officers obtain and log all facts surrounding any damage to cargo.

THE CARRIAGE OF GOODS BY SEA ACT OF 1936

In an effort to provide more protection to merchant shipowners and more certainty in establishing the relationship of the ship to its cargo, Congress passed the Carriage of Goods By Sea Act (COGSA) in 1936. COGSA differs from the Harter Act in that it has its own fire clause protecting time and voyage charterers. It is not necessary to insert clauses in the bill of lading to obtain the benefits of COGSA, and the shipper must establish a causal connection between damage to cargo and unseaworthiness of the vessel to recover for such damage. COGSA applies to vessels carrying goods between an American port and a foreign port. However, it may apply to vessels in the domestic trade if the bill of lading so states. In such a situation, COGSA supersedes the Harter Act.

Under COGSA, the carrier is responsible for the cargo from tackle to tackle. Thus, as soon as the cargo is loaded aboard the ship, the carrier's responsibility commences, and as soon as the cargo is discharged from the vessel, the carrier's responsibility ends. Recent court decisions, however, have tended to extend the responsibility to arise as soon as the carrier loses or obtains custody of the cargo (i.e., when it enters or exits the yard).

COGSA may be incorporated into a charter party by specific reference. The charterer would thus be able to benefit from the provisions of the act. By inserting a so-called Himalaya clause[1] into the bill of lading, the carrier can extend the protection of COGSA to stevedores employed to handle the cargo. As long as the stevedores are assisting in the loading and discharge of the cargo and the language of the Himalaya clause is clear and unambiguous, the courts have permitted COGSA to be extended to protect the stevedores.

COGSA also sets up some statutes of limitation. If cargo is damaged, the claimants have 1 year from the date of delivery to proceed against the carrier; if the cargo is not delivered on the date specified in the bill of lading, the time period is 1 year from the time the cargo should have been delivered. In addition, a claimant has 3 days from the time of delivery within which to make a complaint of latent defects in cargo—failure to complain in three days does not affect a time limit, but shifts the burden of proof to the claimant to show the damage occurred in the carrier's custody.

The additional immunities granted to the carrier under COGSA are:

1. Act of war.

2. Quarantine restrictions.

3. Strikes or lockouts.

4. Riots and civil commotion.

5. Insufficiency or inadequacy of marks.

6. Latent defects not discoverable by due diligence.

7. Any other cause arising without the actual fault and privity of the carrier.

The additional responsibility set upon the carrier by COGSA is the necessity to make all cargo spaces fit and safe for stowing the cargo.

[1]*Himalaya* is a vessel; the name of the clause stems from a case involving that vessel. The clause extends all limitations and exonerations of liability of a carrier to independent contractors. These independent contractors include stevedores and longshoremen doing work normally done by the carrier.

Summary of Immunities

To sum up all of the immunities of the carrier under COGSA, neither the carrier nor the ship shall be responsible for loss or damage to cargo arising from any of the following:

1. Error in navigation or mismanagement of the ship.

2. Fire or loss caused by the fault or privity of the carrier.

3. Perils of the sea.

4. Act of God.

5. Act of war.

6. Act of public enemies.

7. Arrest or seizure under legal process.

8. Quarantine restrictions.

9. Act or omission of the shipper.

10. Strikes or lockouts.

11. Riots or civil commotion.

12. Saving or attempting to save life or property at sea.

13. Inherent defect, quality, or vice of the goods.

14. Insufficiency of packaging.

15. Insufficiency or inadequacy of marks.

16. Latent defects not discoverable by due diligence.

17. Any other cause arising without the actual fault and privity of the carrier.

The Carriers' Responsibility

Just as in the Harter Act, the carrier, to enjoy the immunities of COGSA, must fulfill the following conditions:

1. He/she must exercise due diligence to make the ship seaworthy.

2. He/she must exercise due diligence to man, provision, and equip the ship properly.

3. He/she must properly care for and stow the cargo.

4. He/she must make all cargo spaces fit and safe for stowing the cargo.

Sample Cases

In an effort to clarify the real meaning of the exemptions and responsibilities delineated by COGSA, we shall summarize below cases wherein the courts have interpreted their meanings. Through understanding how the courts have interpreted the provisions of COGSA, a ship's officer should be better able to grapple with the various problems encountered in cargo handling.

IMPROPER STOWAGE VERSUS INSUFFICIENCY OF PACKAGING

In the case of *Martin v. S.S. Ensley City,* a ship at Basra, Iraq, loaded 732 cases and 319 bags of licorice extract from open lighters. The licorice had been shipped by rail from Turkey and had been on the dock waiting for the ship for about 1 month. The cases were marked with the words: "Stow away from the boilers."

When loading commenced, the temperature of the atmosphere was about 115°F. The master of the ship noted that some of the cases were broken and in some instances the licorice was oozing out. He had all the damaged containers re-coopered and he endorsed the bill of lading to the effect that the cases were badly damaged and re-coopered but that the ship could not be responsible for the loss of contents or a short delivery.

The entire cargo of licorice was stowed in the forward part of the number 4 'tweendecks, directly aft of the engine room. The cargo extended from the deck of the compartment to within 12 inches of the overhead. The cases were stowed about eight high, with the bags on top. The ship proceeded to an East African port and loaded chrome ore. Some of this chrome ore was placed just aft of the licorice, with a temporary wooden bulkhead erected between the two cargoes. During the voyage, no temperatures were taken of the hold spaces, nor were any inspections made. In Baltimore, where the licorice was to be discharged, it was found that the extract had broken out of most of the cases and bags in a glutinous state and therefore had become a hard mass. Many of the cases and bags were stuck together. Wood, nails, and other foreign material were imbedded in the licorice. This made it impossible to remove the cargo from the ship case by case or bag by bag. It had to be broken apart with picks before it could be removed from the hold. Recovery was sought for the expense of removing it, melting it down to remove the foreign material, and making it marketable.

In court, the shipper argued that the damage was due to improper stowage. He claimed that the licorice should have been stowed in one of the lower holds, preferably in the number 1 lower hold, where the temperature was less than in the number 4 'tweendecks, and also that dunnage should have been used between tiers to allow better air circulation.

The carrier claimed that the licorice extract was not in good condition when loaded and that its stowage was entirely proper. It also claimed that any change in the condition of the licorice during the voyage was due to inherent vice and to the insufficiency of the packaging.

It was brought out in court that the recognized place for stowing such cargo was below the waterline of the ship, where temperatures are lower than in the upper deck. The carrier introduced as evidence the temperatures of another ship that had carried licorice extract successfully in this upper deck, but the court rejected these records because it was purely a matter of speculation whether the temperatures on the first ship were the same as those on the second. In fact, there were two things that made it seem likely that the temperature on the second ship was probably higher. First, chrome ore in bulk will heat up when damp. Such cargo was stowed adjacent to the licorice, and although there was no evidence that it did or did not heat up, the court could not accept the submitted temperatures with so much conjecture about them. Secondly, the ventilators in the after part of the 'tweendecks where the licorice was stowed led into a special locker, which prevented full circulation of the air in that space. This was not the case on the other ship.

It may have been true that the temperatures on the two ships were the same, but the ship's officers failed to take any temperature measurements and log them; therefore, the carrier had no proof of proper temperatures.

The court held in favor of the shipper, saying that he had proved, as he must, that the cargo was in a marketable condition when delivered to the ship, but that on arrival in Baltimore it was not marketable. The court also concluded that the proximate cause of the change was not insufficiency of packaging or inherent defect, but improper stowage.

UNSEAWORTHINESS AS A CAUSE OF LOSS UNDER COGSA

In *Riverstone Meat Company v. Lancashire Shipping Company (The Muncaster Castle)*, cargo was damaged by sea water due to an improperly replaced valve inspection cover. The shipowner argued that he exercised due diligence to make the vessel seaworthy in that he delegated the tasks to a reputable shipyard. The court disagreed, stating that the warranty of seaworthiness and duty of due diligence are nondelegable. Thus, the shipowner was held liable for all cargo damage caused by the sea water.

ERRORS IN NAVIGATION AND MANAGEMENT UNDER COGSA

In *Mississippi Shipping Company v. Zander and Company (The DelSud)*, the court created the concept of voyage by stages. *The DelSud*, while in Santos, Brazil, struck the concrete pier, resulting in a hole in the side of the vessel. This occurred while the ship was being turned around for the purpose of leaving. The court ruled that the voyage had already commenced. The vessel then sailed to Rio de Janeiro without anyone noticing the hole, and from there to Curacao and New Orleans. In New Orleans, extensive salt water damage to the cargo was discovered. The cargo claimants from the port of Santos and ports of loading prior to Santos argued that the vessel should have been made seaworthy on departure from Rio. The court ruled that the failure to make repairs at an intermediate port, such as Rio or Curacao, was an error of management for which the vessel and carrier were not liable. As long as the vessel owner exercised due diligence to make the vessel seaworthy prior to departure from the loading port for the respective cargo, any subsequent unseaworthiness would be seen as an error in management or navigation. Thus, for cargo loaded at Santos, the voyage commenced with respect to that cargo at Santos, and the shipowner had a duty to exercise due diligence to make the vessel seaworthy for that cargo prior to departure from that port.

It is important to note that if a shipowner or his/her representative comes aboard the vessel to take full command of a situation involving repairs, the courts look at this situation as destroying the continuity of the voyage. The shore staff is then required to exercise due diligence in inspecting the vessel and making it seaworthy lest the shipowner forfeit his/her immunity. Applying the ruling of the court, the shipper of cargo loaded in Curacao, if that cargo was damaged by the leakage caused in Santos, would be able to recover from the shipowner for his/her failure to exercise due diligence to make the vessel seaworthy at the port of loading.

Although the concept of voyage by stages is somewhat beneficial to the shipowners, it would be prudent for the ship's officers to inspect the vessel thoroughly whenever there is a suspicion of damage to vessel or cargo.

THE FIRE EXCEPTION OF COGSA

COGSA specifically excepts liability for damage caused by fire unless the fire was caused by the actual fault or privity of the carrier. The Act also obviates the need for repeal of the Fire Statute. The Fire Statute holds that the owner was not liable to the shipper for losses caused by fire on board "unless such fire is caused by the design or neglect of such owner." As previously noted, the COGSA exception covers any carrier, whereas the Fire Statute does not cover time and voyage charterers. The courts have interpreted actual fault or privity to have the same meaning as design or neglect. As it stands, it seems a nearly impossible burden for the cargo owner to prove that the fire was caused through the actual fault, privity, design, or neglect of the shipowner or shoreside personnel. However, in *Complaint of Tai Chi (S. S.Eurypylus* (1984 A.M.C.985, 574 F. Supp. 418), the carrier was held liable for fire damage where the Court held the cargo interests had carried their burden by proving the fire was caused by habitual storage of oxygen and acetylene cylinders just outside the engine room, and the engine room door was always left open. All within the knowledge of the shipowner.

Cargo damage claimants have been successful in contending that unseaworthiness of firefighting equipment should make the vessel owner liable for damage, notwithstanding the fire exemption. Despite the Supreme Court's ruling that due diligence to provide a seaworthy ship is not a prerequisite to enjoying the benefits of the Fire Statute or COGSA's fire exemption, two appellate courts have ruled otherwise. These courts have been harshly criticized by the majority of the appellate courts, which claim that the design and neglect test is the exclusive one to be applied in a fire damage situation.

"Neglect," as thus used, means negligence, not the breach of a nondelegable duty. For the shipper to recover, he/she must prove that the carrier caused the damage, by proving either that a negligent act of the carrier caused the fire or that such an act prevented the fire's extinguishment. Thus, it is incumbent upon the ship's crew to maintain the firefighting equipment in top condition. Not only must firefighting equipment be adequately maintained, but the crew must be properly trained in firefighting. Thus in *Hasboro v. St. Constantine* (1980 AMC 1425), the Court held the vessel owner liable for fire loss where the crew was unable to extinguish the blaze because of inadequate training in firefighting techniques. The Court concluded that the shipowner had notice of the lack of training, as the vessel owners' shoreside superintendent engineer was the person designated by management with the duty and obligation of controlling and overseeing the firefighting training which was to be given the officers and crew.

Jurisdictional Clauses in Bills of Lading Under COGSA

Often bills of lading contain forum selection clauses indicating where disputes concerning the contract of carriage are to be resolved, for instance, that all disputes shall be submitted to the Federal Courts in New York. These clauses are valid under COGSA, including foreign forum selection clauses as long as the carrier's liability under COGSA is not lessened. The seminal case is *Vimar Segurosy Reaseguros, S.A. v. MIV Sky Reefer,* which involved damage to a shipload of oranges and lemons being carried from Morocco to Massachusetts. The bill of lading for the fruit contained a "Governing Law and Arbitration" clause requiring that all disputes be referred to Tokyo arbitration and the application of Japanese law. The cargo interests, nonetheless, filed suit for the cargo damage in Federal Court in Massachusetts. The carrier asked the Court to stay the Massachusetts action and compel arbitration in Tokyo in accordance with the bill of lading. The United States Supreme Court held for the carrier, finding that the bill of lading foreign forum selection clause was enforceable because it was not shown that the carrier's liability in this forum and under Japanese law would be less than that under COGSA.

Damages Under COGSA

If the value of the cargo has not been declared somewhere on the bill of lading, the carrier and ship are not liable for any loss or damage to the cargo exceeding $500 per package or, in the case of goods not shipped in packages, per customary freight unit. It is important for the parties involved in any dispute over cargo damage or loss to define clearly what the customary freight unit or package is. Although a ship's officer should exercise special care for all of the cargo, if he/she sees a bill of lading listing a large number of packages, he/she should take extra precautions to make sure that the cargo is properly cared for. This, of course, is because the $500 package limitation is multiplied by the numerous packages listed in the bill of lading, which could result in excessive liability for the vessel in the unfortunate event of damage or loss.

The growing trend is for the courts to consider the bill of lading as manifesting the intent of the parties. Thus, if under the heading "number of packages" the bill of lading lists one container, some courts are likely to rule that the intermodal container is the package. Although this has been disputed among the various courts, if the container is supplied, stuffed, and delivered by the shipper to the carrier in a sealed condition, most courts are likely to rule that the container is the package for the purposes of COGSA. These courts reason that the carrier has no knowledge of the contents of the container unless they are delineated in the bill of lading. Thus, if the bill of lading reads as previously stated, the carrier's lack of knowledge of the contents of the container will not disqualify him from claiming the $500 per package limitation. Even if elsewhere on the bill of lading there is a description of, for instance, the number of containers on a pallet, if under the heading "number of packages" the pallet is listed as the package, the court will not rule the former description to be binding on the carrier. In brief, the courts generally treat the number of packages delineated in the "number of packages" section of the bill of lading as binding upon the parties for the purposes of the package limitation. Thus, pallets, containers, and pails, as well as loose cases and drums, can all be ruled to be COGSA packages, depending on their positions on the bill of lading.

ADVANTAGES OF UNIFORM ALLOCATION OF CARGO RESPONSIBILITY

With the trend toward greater uniformity in laws applying to cargo, assignment of liability is becoming more predictable. Unification of law makes it easier for local parties involved in international transportation to be certain of foreign law so that adequate planning and protection may be assured. To the extent that cargo interests and carriers are able to predict which law will govern a potential dispute, they are able to avoid disputes and arrive at settlements without resorting to litigation.

Except where national laws apply, existing modal transportation conventions provide a significant amount of uniformity of laws for modal carriage. For example, the Warsaw Convention unifies the laws of international air transport, the Hague Rules provide a uniform regime for maritime carriage, and the CIM and CMR Conventions (European Train and Road Transportation Conventions) provide uniformity on a regional basis for rail and truck transport, respectively. For domestic rail and truck carriage, the Interstate Commerce Act mandates substantial uniformity among the 50 states. In fact, this national law goes one step further; it regulates multimodal transportation among surface modes.

Although a significant amount of legal uniformity has been attained, there are several gaps among the various governing laws and treaties that cause problems to shippers and carriers alike. One example of lack of uniformity confronting multimodal cargo interests and carriers is provided by a comparison of the limits on liability in the various conventions and national laws. Whereas the national laws tend to provide compensation up to the full value of the goods, the liability limits under the international conventions range between $13.63/lb under the CIM Convention and $500/package under the U.S. (COGSA). Under the Hague Visby Rules as amended by the Brussels Protocol of 1979, which is applicable in most major shipping nations other than the U.S., the package limitation is set forth as 666.67 SDRs (Special Drawing Rights—an average of several currencies) per package, or a weight limitation of 2 SDRs per kilogram, whichever is greater. As of March 2010, an SDR was worth $1.53. Where heavy, dense cargoes, such as basic steel commodities are involved, the weight limitation frequently equates to no limitation at all. Also, the Hamburg Rules, adopted by many third world nations, provides a package limitation of 835 SDRs per package, or 2-1/2 SDRs per kilogram, whichever is higher. And the latest U.N. proposed regime, the Rotterdam Rules, would provide 875 SDRs per package, or 3 SDRs per kilogram, whichever is higher. U. S. law does not forbid the adoption by contract of foreign law, as long as it increases the carrier's liability, so that even where COGSA applies by law, the carrier may have voluntarily increased its limitation by a bill of lading or charter party clause.

Under U.S. law, the package limitation protection can be lost where the carrier commits an unreasonable deviation from the bill of lading contract, by either geographically deviating from the contemplated voyage or by unauthorized on deck stowage.

The variety of liability limits makes it difficult for banks, insurers, carriers, and cargo interests to identify the risk involved in carriage affected by more than one convention. The only time liability is uniform is when the carriage of cargo is governed by one convention. In addition, there is a substantial lack of uniformity regarding the defenses against liability in the various conventions and national laws. A variety of defenses exists among the various regimes, ranging from the 17 defenses under the Hague Rules (COGSA) to the strict liability regime of the U.S. Interstate Commerce Act. Furthermore, a great disparity exists among the laws that apply to international multimodal carriage, because there is no single international law that governs the interfacing among the various modal conventions. It is sometimes impossible to ascertain or predict the applicable law. Thus, if the carriage mode in which loss or damage occurred is not clearly established, the interested parties must fend for themselves. Concealed damage to cargo that is shipped by several modes of transport under various conventions leaves the interested parties stranded in the gaps. If they cannot prove that a particular convention applies, a legal stalemate results. Thus, the claimants must pay higher insurance premiums to cover the risks incurred in these "gaps." While uniformity may be coming soon, the keeping of accurate records of cargo condition on ships will insure that the point of damage is determined.

CARGO CLAIMS AND MINIMIZING LOSSES

We will now summarize the possible causes of damage that may bring the carrier under the exception clauses of the Harter Act and COGSA, thereby exempting him from liability. Causes beyond the vessel's or cargo's control are typically excepted. Such causes include:

1. Fire.

2. Act of God.

3. Perils of the sea.

4. Quarantine restrictions.

5. Government restraints.

6. Strikes or civil commotions.

Several claims attributable to the ship permit the vessel to escape liability. These claims are:

1. Errors in navigation or mismanagement of the ship by the crew.

2. Unseaworthiness despite due diligence in caring for and stowing the cargo.

3. Latent defects; that is, those not apparent to usual inspection (e.g., metal fatigue).

4. Assisting vessels in distress.

5. Deviation for the purpose of saving life and property.

Claims arising due to problems originating within the cargo itself are excepted:

1. Inherent vice or poor condition prior to loading.

2. Fault or omission of the shipper or cargo owner (in shipping instructions, etc.).

3. Insufficiency of marking.

4. Insufficiency of packaging.

Any claims arising outside the normal course of seagoing transportation or scope of the contract of transport are also excepted claims permitting the carrier to escape liability:

1. Flood or fire at port warehouse.

2. Negligence of third party for whom the carrier is not responsible (e.g., shipper's freight forwarder).

Finally, time limitations on claims may free the carrier from liability.

Good Practices for Loss Prevention

When handling outward-bound cargo, it is important that the shipboard personnel check all markings. They should make sure that the marks on the bill of lading and the manifest are in concord. Any errors may cause fines to be imposed by customs authorities. The officers, prior to sailing, should survey the pier for cargo accidentally left behind. In addition, the tightness of all lashings should be checked; if the ship is carrying containers, all interbox connectors should be locked; all watertight doors and holds should be sealed; and, lastly, accurate bilge soundings should be obtained. It is prudent when multifarious cargo is being carried for the chief mate to ascertain that all of the containers or parcels aboard are listed in the vessel's stowage plan and are stowed in the exact locations indicated in the plan.

Special procedures should be used when loading incomplete or damaged cargo. The mate on watch should either reject the cargo or make sure that the bill of lading is amended accordingly. When cargo is insufficiently packaged, the mate should, if possible, give the shipper time to correct the defect or, if not, correct it at loading. The chief mate should mark the bill of lading "insufficient packaging." It is important that this statement be placed on the bill of lading, as it will assist shoreside personnel in repudiating any claims. If anyone tries to issue a letter of indemnity against a clean bill of lading, and the shipboard personnel consent, they may be liable for fraud. In addition, if caught in this act, the carrier would be deprived of all defenses and limitations contained in the bill of lading under the various conventions.

Regarding stowage, ship's officers should make sure that for the cargo stowed on deck there have been no "underdeck" bills of lading issued. It is important that the ship's deck department be aware of the various Federal regulations governing the proper stowage and separation of various cargoes. A daily inspection of the cargo areas over the course of the voyage will help prevent false claims against the vessel. If the mate makes entries in a log as to the condition of the cargo and the cargo spaces, and observes how the cargo is riding as the vessel proceeds in a seaway, possible losses and damages may be avoided, as well as spurious claims.

During discharge of general cargo, a check should be made for heavily damaged cargo; if found, it should be safely stored and re-coopered. If the cargo is badly damaged or wet, it may be wise to call in a surveyor. Consolidating cargo that is consigned to one recipient on the pier will facilitate rapid, efficient delivery. High-value cargo should be tallied from the vessel. This will help to minimize theft. Local stevedores should be instructed to check the containers and parcels that are damaged or missing their seals. This should be done as soon as such items are discharged. In addition, shipboard reports should be attached to the stevedore reports to ascertain where the damage or loss occurred.

It is important that the vessel have the proper documentation for the cargo and that no cargo be released without receipt of the original bill of lading. Carriers should require that the person issuing the bill of lading sign it and write his/her title on the front. This will assist the claims personnel in tracing the facts surrounding the shipment, including the details on the bill of lading. If the consignee or claimed consignee offers a letter of indemnity with a bank guarantee in order to effectuate release of the cargo, the carrier personnel or company staff in the respective port should obtain clearance from the home office prior to releasing the cargo without receiving the original bill of lading.

When the cargo is lost or damaged, it is incumbent upon the ship's officers to write a report describing the facts surrounding the loss or damage as soon as possible. The sooner the report is written, the more accurate it will be. The information is more accessible if the report is completed quickly; thus, good relations are enhanced with both the shipper and the home office. Last, prompt reporting saves both the shipper and the company money.

It is important that the ship's officers give accurate and detailed descriptions of all surrounding circumstances, no matter how seemingly insignificant. If possible, photographs should be obtained and log entries made regarding the chronology of the events surrounding the loss or damage to the cargo.

In addition to the log entries on cargo damages, times of starting and finishing unloading, and so forth, the officers should make entries on cargo gear inspections, malfunctioning of any cargo gear or hydraulic equipment, and, of course, bilge levels.

Because the ship's officer makes a countless number of log book entries during his/her career, there is always the danger that he/she will become careless about the manner in which they are made. The distribution of responsibility for the cargo should make it evident that the log book entries can affect the shipowner's position materially.

When a hold is inspected to determine its fitness for receiving cargo, the determination and some details concerning it should be noted carefully in the log. The timing of fueling and of bilge soundings reflect due diligence, or the lack of it, so definitively that the prosaic task of sounding bilges must never be overlooked, nor, what is just as important, should the entries in the log. Monthly inspections of all cargo gear should be entered in the log book simultaneously with entries in the chief officer's cargo gear register. All efforts to ventilate a hold properly or to determine or control conditions in a hold before or during the voyage should be indicated clearly in the log. If this is not done, the officer is jeopardizing his/her employer's position in the eyes of the court in case of litigation, as well as his/her own position in the eyes of his/her employer. All efforts to prevent the elements from entering the hold during loading operations or from reaching cargo in lighters alongside the ship should be logged. Every time a lashing is checked or set up or added to deck cargo, this fact should be entered in the log.

Whenever there is any doubt as to whether an action to protect cargo is warranted, the decision should be in favor of doing it. But it is just as important to log the fact that the action was taken. All such special entries should be signed and the time of the action indicated. Entries should never be erased, and it is a poor policy to add entries long after the action has, or should have, taken place in an effort to deceive a surveyor or counsel. Postscripts to the log can be uncovered easily, leaving the responsible officer in an embarrassing position. When honest mistakes are made in writing an entry, officers should delete them by drawing a single neat line through the error, leaving it clearly discernible.

A DECK OFFICER'S RESPONSIBILITY
IN THE STOWAGE OF CONTAINERS

Although containers are stuffed at the factory or at the terminal, the deck officer must look beyond just the box. The deck officer's responsibility for safe carriage of cargo has been discussed elsewhere. This section looks at the phenomena of containerization and how the deck officer must not forget all those principles applied to break, bulk, refrigerated, or special cargos. Containerized cargo operations can only be successful and profitable if all deck officers understand the complete operation: preplanning, loading, transporting, and discharging. The responsibility belongs to the deck officer, not just the cargo supervisor or an agent overseas.

The container plan (Fig. 2-1) must be understood and utilized in the stowage of a containerized vessel. The deck officer must know their vessels configuration and the plan that refers to that configuration (Fig. 2-2).

To find or stow a container by position, we need to be talking the same language. To describe a container's position, some standard terms are used and may vary by specific companies or vessels (refer to Fig. 2-3). When identifying a container's position fore and aft on a vessel, the term "bay," "row," or "hatch" are used. To identify the container's position athwartships, the term "cell" is most commonly used and is numbered outward from the center, even to port and odd to starboard. To identify a container's position by height above the keel, the term "tier" is most commonly used. Take another look at Figure 2-3. The container indicated is in position 7F35, which is bay 7 forward, cell 3, tier 5. Containers may be identified fore or aft if the container is 20 feet in length. There may also be separate "rows" for 20-foot containers.

Now that we know how to identify a container's position, let's take a look at another example for some very important information that the deck officer needs to know about a container (see Fig. 2-4). The position here is occupied by container number SCXU4706936 it was loaded at Charleston and is to be discharged at Alexandria. It is a 40-foot flat rack (special container) and has a gross weight of 18 tons. It is over high and over wide. As in Figure 2-5, you may also identify a container's hazardous materials class—"3.3" in this case (see chapter 6). This information is extremely important for the deck officer so as to prevent over-stowage, or over or under carriage. The plan helps to protect against improper hazardous material stowage.

It is the responsibility of the deck officer to be able to glean from the plan all the necessary information to compute the vessel's stability and bending moments, trim, and list. The deck officer should always check weight totals of the plan—vertical (tier) totals for stability, bay or row totals for trim and bending moments, and cell totals for list and ballast requirements. Many modern container vessels utilize wing tanks for automatic list control, however, without

Figure 2-1. Container plan.

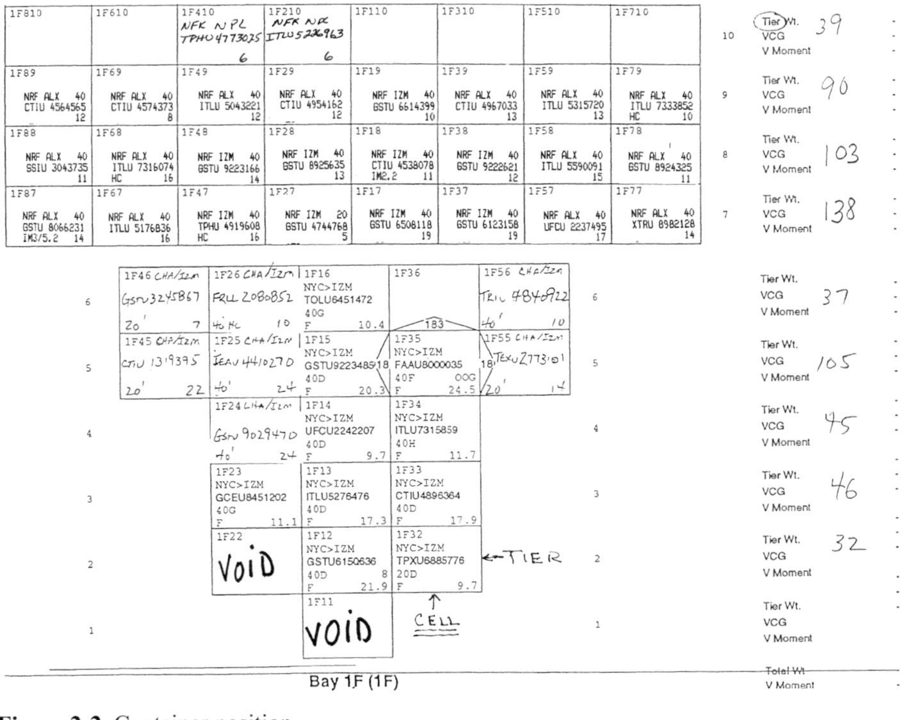

Figure 2-2. Container position.

Bay 1F (1F)

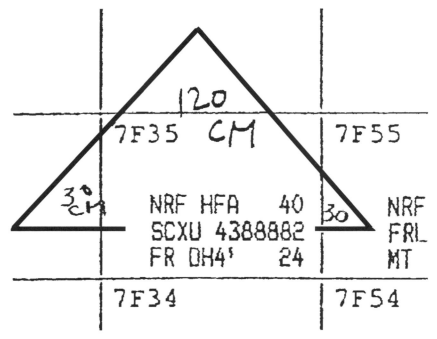

Figure 2-3. Container location.

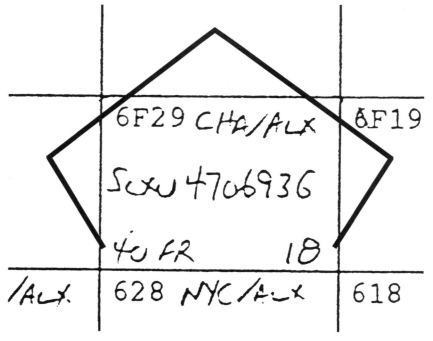

Figure 2-4. Container identification.

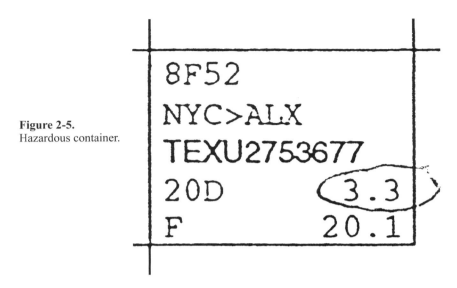

Figure 2-5.
Hazardous container.

proper prior planning this could lead to list conditions that could stop or slow down a container operation (see Fig. 2-6).

To have a successful container operation, the deck officer needs to understand the vessel's ports and cargo restraints. An example would be gantry widths, heights, and reach. Rules on handling special cargo, such as yachts or break bulk cargo should be accessible. There is usually a port information book on your vessel and if not, use a questionnaire to make one up.

Once the plan is clearly understood, it becomes the tool for planning cargo operations. Today, this is usually done by cargo supervisors either from the company, the ship's agent, or the stevedores. The preplan allows you to check your vessel's calculations as in Figure 2-7 and 2-8. This must also be combined with all the vessel's other variables such as fuel, water, and ballast (Fig. 2-9)

The preplan allows the deck officer to verify and check the hazardous cargo manifest (Fig. 2-10), the reefer manifest (Fig. 2-11), and the stowage of any cargos requiring special care, (i.e., heavy lifts, tank containers, or cargo requiring extra lashing). The expense of not making these checks can be very costly. These losses can result in fines for improper stowage of hazardous cargo; reefer temperatures being misread; and cargo stowed on flat racks not being checked and causing either ship, cargo, or container damage (Fig. 2-12).

The deck officer needs to be familiar with the job of shore side cargo planners, an awareness of how a preplan works (Fig. 2-12 and 2-13), how to eliminate or reduce shifting (the movement of containers already onboard for the purpose of stowing new cargo). The cost of these moves can substantially reduce the profit of any container operation. The deck officer should be aware of the difference between a shift through shore and a shift onboard. The profit and, sometimes, loss of a container vessel operation can be directly related to

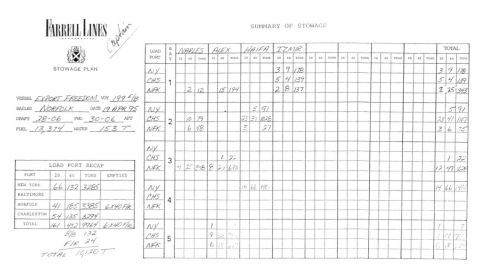

Figure 2-6a. Summary of stowage.

	BREAKBULK	
NFK - ALX	3 DOZERS	119T
NFK - HFA	1 COMBINE	13T
	B/B	132T

TIER WEIGHTS

BAY/TIER	1	2	3	4	5	6	7	8	TOTAL	9
10	12	53	16	72	16	24	23	74	290	
9	90	73	68	86	122	77	57	69	642	56
8	103	135	111	119	82	102	83	849		71
7	138	155	153	189	166	184	170	118	1273	125
6	44	157	-	127	-	71	61	118	578	59
5	142	143	216	135	157	126	105	163	1187	86
4	46	121	153	155	154	147	158	180	1114	107
3	46	128	160	164	165	151	159	219	1192	X
2	39	179	175	172	162	149	160	207	1243	
1	X	129	133	270	179	238	158	141	1248	
TOTAL	660	1273	1185	1494	1240	1249	1153	1372	TOTAL	10120

REMARKS

SUMMARY OF STOWAGE

LOAD PORT	BAY	NAPLES			ALEX			HAIFA			IZMIR											TOTAL		
		20	40	TONS	20	40	TONS	20	40	TONS	20	40	TONS	20	40	TONS	20	40	TONS	20	40	TONS		
NY	6				4	38	692													4	38	692		
CHS					4	22	533													4	22	533		
NFK								1		24										1		24		
NY	7																							
CHS																								
NFK		2	14		5	39	6	51	1079											6	58	1132		
NY	8	32	7	513	12	7	320													44	14	833		
CHS		13	29	535				1		4										14	29	539		
NFK																								
NY	9																							
CHS																								
NFK		1	12	93				4	11	227	7	5	184							12	28	504		
TOTAL		50	93	1642	43	168	3720	51	165	3964	17	26	638							161	452	9964		

DISCH MOVES - 143 - 211 - 216 - 43

Figure 2-6b. Summary of stowage.

"moves" (how many times a container is moved). The best scenario is loading and discharging a container just one time.

The deck officer should be keenly aware of the preplan for dealing with list problems, and how much ballast is onboard. Remember, in a container operation, time is money. If a ship or cargo operation is delayed due to a list or trim problem, it can be very costly. Plan and stay ahead (see Fig. 2-13).

FARRELL LINES -- CONTAINERSHIP BENDING MOMENT NUMERAL

ITEM		WT. COLUMN LONG TONS/100	FACTOR	WEIGHT NUMERAL	ITEM	WT. COLUMN LONG TONS/100	FACTOR	WEIGHT NUMERAL	BUOYANCY NUMBER TABLE Δ(L. TONS/100)	BUOYANCY NUMERAL
Light Ship(Inc.Fixed Bal)		104.65	><	263.0	Flume Tk No. 1 Upper	0.60	0.33	0.20	280	537
Crew & Effects		0.20	3.51	0.70	Flume Tk No. 1 Lower	0.60	0.33	0.20	270	515
Stores		0.29	3.26	0.95	Flume Tk No. 2 Upper	0.60	1.28	0.77	260	493
Fore Peak Tk	¢	---	4.95	---	Flume Tk No. 2 Lower	0.60	1.28	0.77	250	471
Deep Tk No. 1	P	2.85	4.25	12.12	Container Bay No. 1	---	3.13	---	240	450
Deep Tk No. 1	S	2.85	4.25	12.12	Container Bay No. 2	---	2.36	---	230	428
Deep Tk No. 2	P	---	3.72	---	Container Bay No. 3	---	1.52	---	220	408
Deep Tk No. 2	S	---	3.72	---	Container Bay No. 4	---	0.75	---	210	387
Double Bottom No. 1 P		---	2.44	---	Container Bay No. 5	---	0.08	---	200	366
Double Bottom No. 1 S		---	2.44	---	Container Bay No. 6	---	0.87	---	190	347
Double Bottom No. 2 P		2.29	1.03	2.36	Container Bay No. 7	---	1.17	---	180	327
Double Bottom No. 2 S		2.29	1.03	2.36	Container Bay No. 8	---	2.48	---	170	307
Double Bottom No. 2 ¢		---	1.09	---	Container Bay No. 9	---	4.38	---	160	288
Double Bottom No. 3 P		2.57	0.51	1.31					150	268
Double Bottom No. 3 S		2.57	0.51	1.31	Summary	132.42	><	330.27	140	251
Double Bottom No. 3 ¢		---	0.52	---					130	231
Double Bottom No. 4 P		1.64	1.98	3.26	Corresponding Buoyancy				120	212
Double Bottom No. 4 S		1.64	1.98	3.26	Num.			235.84	110	189
Double Bottom No. 4 ¢		---	2.13	---	Resulting Bending Mom.				100	164
Settling Tank	P	1.99	4.28	8.55	Numeral (Must be < 100)			94.43	90	157
Settling Tank	S	1.99	4.28	8.55						
Aft Peak	P	---	4.77	---						
Aft Peak	S	---	4.77	---						
Reserve F.W. Tk	P	0.38	3.15	1.20						
Reserve F.W. Tk	S	0.37	3.15	1.18				CONDITION:		
Potable Water Tk	P	---	3.08	---				BALLAST - ARRIVAL		
Potable Water Tk	¢	0.10	3.08	0.30						
Distilled Water Tk	S	0.45	3.08	1.41						
Oily Bilge Water Hldg Tk ¢		0.90	3.99	3.59						

Figure 2-7. Summary of stowage preplan.

When refrigerated containers are being loaded, the deck officer should know who plugs them in and where they can be found, who the cargo supervisor is and where they can be located, and who the hatch boss is and that you are both on the same plan. A few containers stowed in the wrong position and not found on the terminal could lead to excessive shifts and a change in the pre-stow stability.

All of today's modern container vessels calculate their stability by computer. There are many software programs in use today and many are vessel specific. With that in mind, today's container ship deck officers must become familiar with their ship's particular program, however, a review of the long-form stability found in each vessel's stability booklet allows the deck officer not to become complacent and assume the figures found in the computerized printout infallible. The following figures give you a review of what the deck officer should be familiar with on their container vessel: Stability form (Fig. 2-15), hydrostatic properties (Fig. 2-16 and 2-17), required GM curve (Fig. 2-18), trim table (Fig. 2-19). Calculations utilizing these forms are further discussed in Chapter 3 and should be reviewed again in discussion of container vessels.

One of the most important responsibilities of a deck officer on container vessels is the knowledge and understanding of the vessel's particular lashing systems. The movement of vessels has been discussed in Chapter 1 and the theory of lashing containers is no different than that for break bulk cargo: "Prevent movement." This is accomplished by using many different systems with the same philosophy of trying to keep all the containers together as one unit. To this end, the containers are landed on pins that do not allow athwartship movement. Sometimes, these stacking cones or pins lock in place, others do not. The

```
PORT:       NORFOLK    BARRELS FUEL OIL ABOARD  14227
VOYAGE:     199        TONS OF CARGO N BOARD      10121  STOW  5 HIGH
COMPARTMENSTS  TONS  VCG   MOMENTS
LIGHT      SHIP  10440  25.8  269352     KM 32.77  →  LIST   0.3
STORES/EQUIP      100  53.1    5310      KG 30.22  NORFOLK
CREW EFFECTS       20  47.0     940      GM  2.55  4 HIGH
CARGO ABOARD    10121  42.5  429892      FS  0.44
                                         GM  2.11
   FUEL    FSMOM                    →     GM  1.62  REQUIRED    ←
#2 DT P/S   760   662  18.8   12438 →     GM  0.49  EXCESS GM  ←
#1 DB P/S   900   336   2.6     875  ------------------------------------------
#2 DB  C    750   307   2.5     768 →    1430  BALLAST  TONS  ←
#3 DB  C    750   307   2.5     768 →   10121  CARGO    TONS  ←
#4 DB  C   3520   294   2.5     734 →    2175  FUEL     TONS  ←
SETTLERS   2620   269  29.4    7912 →   57.10  BEND PERCENT    ←
LUBE OIL           10  50.8     508 →   24452  DISPLACEMENT   ←

   BALLAST                          →      53  CARGO OFF CENTER
FORE PEAK    30    30  20.9     627 →       0  BALST OFF CENTER
#1 DT P/S   300   100  19.1    1910 →      53  NET OFF CENTER
#2 DB P/S     0   456   2.6    1186  ------------------------------------------
#3 DB P/S     0   516   2.6    1342 →    0.27  DEGREES OF LIST
#4 DB P/S     0   328   2.6     853  ------------------------------------------
AFT PK P/S    0     0  29.9       0       BALLAST OFF CENTER
UPPER FLUM    0     0  29.6       0   DTP    50    DTS    50
LOWER FLUM    0     0  19.9       0   2P    228    2S    228
                                      3P    258    3S    258
   WATER                              4P    164    4S    164
PORTABLE P  234    58  39.1    2268   APP     0    APS     0
DISTILLED    95    28  39.1    1095   PORT  700    STB   700
RES. FEED   330    60   2.6     156  ------------------------------------------
SLOP        383    10   4.6      46   1273      PORT MOMENTS
TOTAL     10672 24452         738980  1273      STBD MOMENTS
                                         0      NET OFF CENTER
              CARGO                   THIS IS      BALLAST ONLY
BAYS (1-8) TIER TONS VCG  MOMENTS  ----------------------------------------
             11      0  96.9       0            FUEL
             10    250  88.4   22100   TANK          STATUS
              9    641  79.9   51216   #2D/T  4327   BBLS
              8    847  71.4   60476   #1P/S  2200   BBLS
              7   1273  62.9   80072   #2C/L  2010   BBLS
              6    611  51.5   31467   #3C/L  2010   BBLS
              5   1171  43.0   50353   #4C/L  1920   BBLS
              4   1115  34.5   38468   SETTS  1760   BBLS
              3   1202  26.0   31252   TOTAL BARRELS ABOARD
              2   1250  17.5   21875
              1   1248   9.0   11232   FUEL   14227  BBLS

BAY (9)      10      0  94.9       0
              9     63  86.4    5443
              8     66  77.9    5141
              7     32  69.4    9161
              6     59  56.3    3322
              5     86  47.8    4111
              4     07  39.3    4205
```

Figure 2-8. Vessel moments.

BE PREPARED. FOR EMERGENCY

FARRELL LINES

DANGEROUS CARGO MANIFEST (Always Look up each Cargo)

LOADING PORT	NORFOLK	VESSEL	RESOLUTE		VOY.	42	OFFICIAL NUMBER	612715	NATION	U.S.A.

DISCHARGE PORT	PROPER SHIPPING NAME	CLASS	U.N. NO.	IMDG PAGE	EMERG. RESPONSE TELEPHONE NO.	EMS NO.	MFAG NO.	B/L NO.	TYPE & NO. OF PKGS.	GROSS WEIGHT	CONTAINER NUMBER	STOW POSITION
NAPLES	COATING SOLUTION	FLAMMABLE LIQUID 3.2	1139	3200	18004249300	—	—	2M4720	2 CT	454 #	MLCU 4484904	6-77
" "	COATING SOLUTION	FLAMMABLE LIQUID 3.2	1139	3321	"	—	—	"	1 CT	1,110 #	MLCU 4484904	✓
" "	FLAMMABLE LIQUID, NOS (CONTAINS ETHYL ALCOHOL)	FLAMMABLE LIQUID 3.2	1993	3230	"	—	—	"	1 CT	829 #	MLCU 4484904	✓
" "	FLAMMABLE LIQUID, NOS (ETHANOL/DIETHYL TRILAMIDE)	FLAMMABLE LIQUID 3.3	1993	3345	"	—	—	"	1 CT	41 #	MLCU 4484904	✓
" "	METHYL ETHYL KETONE	FLAMMABLE LIQUID 3.2	1193	3226	"	—	—	"	1 CT	960 #	MLCU 4484904	✓
" "	ADHESIVES, containing a flammable liquid	FLAMMABLE LIQUID 3.3	1133	3302	"	—	—	"	1 CT	16 #	MLCU 4484904	✓
" "	FLAMMABLE LIQUID, NOS (CONTAINS ETHYL ALCOHOL)	FLAMMABLE LIQUID 3.2	1993	3230	"	—	—	"	1 CT	80 #	MLCU 4484904	✓
" "	ACETONE SOLUTIONS	FLAMMABLE LIQUIDS 3.2	1090	3172	"	—	—	"	1 CT	609 #	MLCU 4484904	✓
" "	BATTERIES, WET, FILLED WITH ACID electric, storage	CORROSIVE 8.0	2794	8120	"	"	—	2M4720	4 CT	5,193 #	FRLL 2050185	4-67
" "	CORROSIVE LIQUIDS, NOS (STANNIC CHLORIDE)	CORROSIVE 8.0	1760	8147	"	.	.	"	1 CT	2 #	FRLL 2050185	✓
" "	CORROSIVE LIQUIDS, NOS (METHYLENE CHLORIDE/ PHENOL/CARBOLIC ACID)	CORROSIVE 8.0	1760	8147	"	"	—	"	1 CT	30 #	FRLL 2050185	✓
" "	BATTERIES, WET, NON-SPILLABLE electric, storage	CORROSIVE 8.0	2880	8121	"	"	—	"	1 CT	65 #	FRLL 2050185	✓

PREPARED BY	Eva L. Rufnozuk	DATE	1 May 94	MASTER	John Hazel

Figure 2-9. Vessel summary.

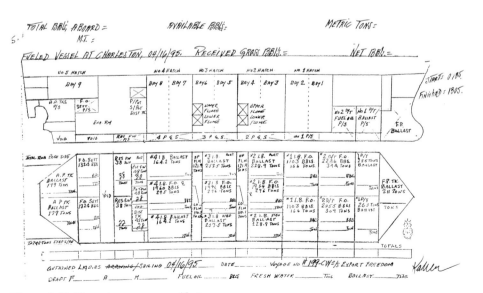

Figure 2-10. Hazardous cargo manifest.

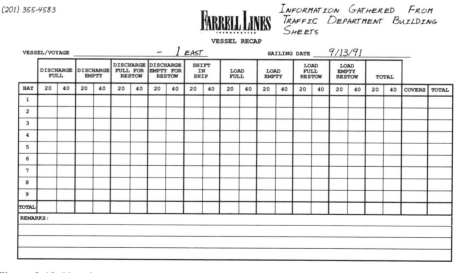

MASTER

SS ___RESOLUTE___ Voy # _42EB_

Dear Sir:

REFRIGERATED CARGO-ON DECK

FARRELL LINES

The following refrigerated containers are aboard your vessel.

LOAD PORT	DISCHARGE PORT	STOWAGE	CONTAINER NUMBER	COMMODITY	REQUIRED TEMP.(F)
NORFOLK	CADIZ	9F27	FAAA 560449-5	MILITARY PROVISIONS	0°
NORFOLK	NAPLES	9-17	FRLU 500057-9	MILITARY PROVISIONS	0°

CC: Chief Engineer
    Chief Mate
    1st ASST.

Terminal Manager

Figure 2-11. Reefer manifest.

(201) 355-4583

FARRELL LINES

INFORMATION GATHERED FROM TRAFFIC DEPARTMENT BUILDING SHEETS

VESSEL RECAP

VESSEL/VOYAGE ___ − 1 EAST   SAILING DATE ___9/13/91___

BAY	DISCHARGE FULL 20	40	DISCHARGE EMPTY 20	40	DISCHARGE FULL FOR RESTOW 20	40	DISCHARGE EMPTY FOR RESTOW 20	40	SHIFT IN SHIP 20	40	LOAD FULL 20	40	LOAD EMPTY 20	40	LOAD FULL RESTOW 20	40	LOAD EMPTY RESTOW 20	40	TOTAL 20	40	COVERS	TOTAL
1																						
2																						
3																						
4																						
5																						
6																						
7																						
8																						
9																						
TOTAL																						
REMARKS:																						

Figure 2-12. Vessel recap.

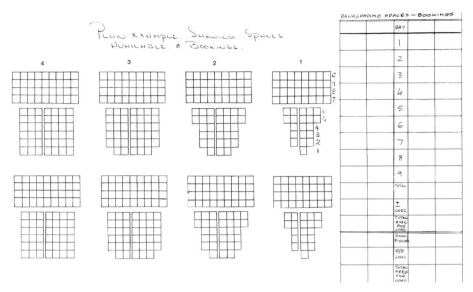

Figure 2-13. Vessel plan.

EXPORT FREEDOM			VOY. NO. 199			DATE: 5/8/98			SAIL / ARR. PORT: Haifa Israel			
CARGO: BAYS 1-8			**COMPARTMENT**	**CAP. TONS**	**MOMENTS FULL COMP.**	**ACTUAL TONS**	**V.C.G.**	**ACTUAL MOMENTS**	**MAX. F.S.MOM.**	**F.S.MOM. 98% FULL**	**ACTUAL F.S.MOM.**	
TIER	TONS	VCG	MOMENTS									
				LIGHT SHIP			10,440	25.8	269,352				
10	0	88.5	0	STORES & EQUIP.			100	53.12	5,312				
9	58	79.9	4634.2	CREW & EFFECTS			20	47.0	940				
8	227	72.4	16207.8	CARGO: (FROM LEFT COL.)			3,980		1,45573.4				
7	379	62.9	23839.1	FUEL:									K.M. 33.09
6	299	51.5	15398.5	#2 D.T. P	344	6,539	344	19.0	6,536	380	365	365	K.G. 25.60
5	462	43.0	19866	" " S	310	5,726	187	18.5	3,459.5	380	365	380	G.M. 7.49
4	475	34.5	16397.5	#1 D.B. P&S	332	854	336	2.5	840	1,720	900	900	F.S.CORR. 30
3	517	26.0	13442	#2 D.B. ¢	297	730	61	2.5	152.5	3,520	750	3,520	
2	616	17.1	10533.6	#3 D.B. ¢	297	730	307	2.5	767.5	3,520	750	750	CORR. G.M. 6.64
1	592	9.0	5328	#4 D.B. ¢	295	729	69	2.5	172.5	3,520	750	3,520	REQ. G.M. 2.5
CARGO	**BAY 9 ONLY**			SETTLERS P&S	399	11,722	277	29.4	8,143.8	2,620	1,560	8,620	DIFF. 4.19
9	0	-86.4	0	LUBE OIL	10	508	10	50.8	508				
8		77.9	3,661.3	BALLAST:									
7	90	69.4	6,246	F.PEAK	211	4,403	30	20.9	627	30		30	DRAFT.
6	51	56.3	2,871.3	#1 D.T. P&S	570	10,885	120	19.1	2292	310		310	F.
5	70	47.8	3,346	#2 D.B. P&S	458	1,181	373	2.6	969.8	2,620		1310	A.
4	97	39.3	3,812.1	#3 D.B. P&S	515	1,318	515	2.6	1339	4,080		0	M. 22-04
TOTAL	3980		145573.4	#4 D.B. P&S	328	867	328	2.6	852.8	1,490		0	* From G.M. Curve
				A.PEAK, P&S	359	10,733	0	29.9	0	2,100		0	
				UPPER FLUMES	242	7,146	0	29.6	0	6,428		0	
				LOWER FLUMES	220	4,171	0	19.0	0	6,428		0	
				FRESH WATER:									
				POTABLE, P&C	98	3,822	70	39.1	2737	234		234	
				DISTILLED, C	45	1,785	54	39.1	2111.4	95		0	
STABILITY				RES.FEED P&S	75	195	70	2.6	182	330		0	
				TOTAL			1,7691		452,868.2			14,269	
							(T.DISPL.)		(T.MOM.)			(T.F.S.M.)	

Figure 2-14. Stability form.

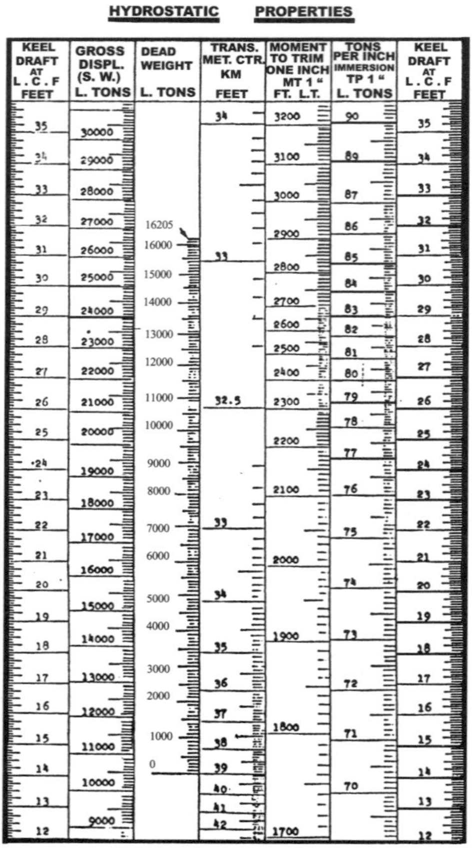

HYDROSTATIC   PROPERTIES

KEEL DRAFT AT L.C.F FEET	GROSS DISPL. (S.W.) L. TONS	DEAD WEIGHT L. TONS	TRANS. MET. CTR. KM FEET	MOMENT TO TRIM ONE INCH MT 1" FT. L.T.	TONS PER INCH IMMERSION TP 1" L. TONS	KEEL DRAFT AT L.C.F FEET

Figure 2-15. Hydrostatic properties.

2 TIERS REQUIRED GM FEET	KEEL DRAFT AT L.C.F FEET	LONG'L CENTER OF FLOTATION AFT or Lp/2 In FEET	LONG'L CENTER OF BOUYANCY AFT or Lp/2 In FEET	KEEL DRAFT AT L.C.F FEET	3 TIERS REQUIRED GM FEET

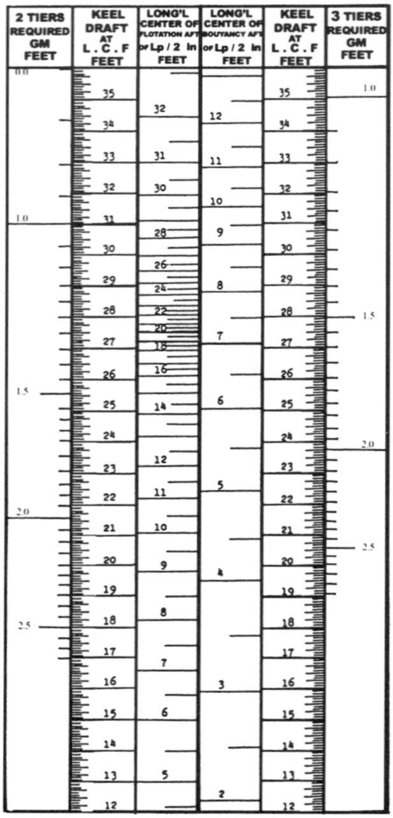

Figure 2-16. Hydrostatic properties.

deck officer must know their ship's system. Twist locks can be right-handed, left-handed, or automatic. Right and left-handed should never be mixed on the same vessel. With the container stacks all pinned, lashings—either wire or stiff rod—are put in place to pull the containers tightly down by use of turnbuckles or tension levers. The lashings are crossed to prevent stacks from falling over as a vessel rolls. None of these lashings are any good unless the deck officer has checked for tension and that twist locks are indeed locked. The following pages give some examples of container lashing equipment (Fig. 2-19 through 2-23).

Containerization leads us to think of these boxes, flat racks, tanks, open top gondolas, and pontoons as the cargo. When looking at today's modern day cargo ship carrying 6,000 or 7,000 TEU, we say, "Look at all those boxes." However, as a container vessel deck officer, we cannot lose sight of the cargo that is inside those boxes. The U. S. Coast Guard requires a daily log entry

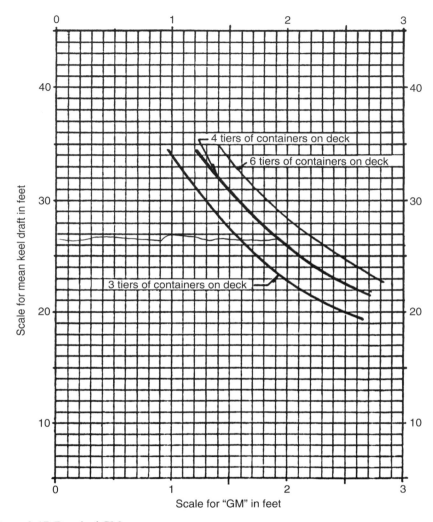

Figure 2-17. Required GM curve.

that all dangerous cargos have been checked and found secure. We check the container lashings and log the entry.

Following is a list of container stowage do's and don'ts. The deck officer must be aware that the vessel's cargo is not just the boxes, but many types of cargo with many characteristics. The theories contained in this text on ventilation, tainting, and securing requires vigilance and care. When noise is heard within a container such as a reel of wire rolling, an odor is detected coming from a hazardous container, or liquid is seen leaking from a container, the deck officer must not ignore these signs of potential damage to the real cargo inside the box.

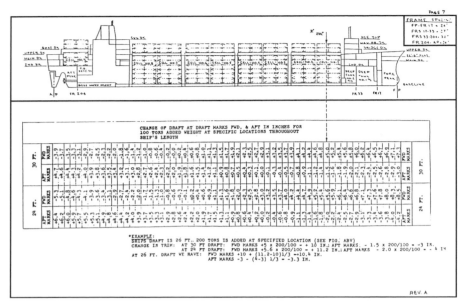

Figure 2-18. Trim table.

Figure 2-19. Twist locks in a locked and unlocked position on a chassis.

Figure 2-20. Rigid rod lashing: two-tier configuration using turnbuckles as tensioners.

Figure 2-21. Double stacker.

Figure 2-22. Automatic twist locks.

Figure 2-23. Twist locks used to connect containers to hatch cover through deck shoes.

Container Stowage DOs and DON'Ts

Do

Choose the most suit able container to accommodate the cargo.

When the container arrives at the loading facility, thoroughly inspect the equipment for soundness.

Keep within the load limits of the container; never over load.

Distribute the weight of the cargo evenly over the floor of the container. Never stow heavy, dense items in one section and light, voluminous items in an other.

Stow all cargo tightly.

Observe all the handling instructions on the cargo, such as "Do Not Drop" or "This Side Up."

Stow goods with sharp corners and projections separate from other types of merchandise. Use dividers and separating material.

Place any packages containing liquid on a double tier of dunnage. This will reduce the chance of damage if the packages leak. This should also be done for the entire load when general cargo is mixed with liquid cargo.

Use cargo liners for obnoxious cargo, e.g., green hides, car bon black.

Use all tie-down systems already incorporated in the unit to secure cargo.

Observe all the rules concerning hazardous cargo. Use appropriate labels and placards to identify containers loaded with dangerous goods.

Stow hazardous-type cargo at the rear of the container (by the door).

Include all necessary documentation.

Record the seal number and the container number on all shipping documents.

Secure and stow for the worst conditions.

DON'T

Do not use tools, grips, or other loading devices unless the goods can withstand such handling.

Never stow heavy goods on top of light goods. Place heavy items on the bottom, light ones on top.

Never smoke while loading and unloading containers.

Do not load goods in a container with damaged packaging.

Avoid stowing wet or damp goods together with dry goods.

Do not use dunnage which is incompatible with the cargo.

Do not stow without placing plastic or water-repellent shrouds over the top and sides of the load to protect against damage from water and condensation.

Do not ship until all container doors are closed and sealed properly.

Do not accept equipment which is not in good order and poses a threat to safe arrival of cargo.

Never stow goods with marked odors close to goods that can be contaminated by odors.

CHAPTER 3

MATERIALS HANDLING PRINCIPLES AND THE PRINCIPLES OF STOWAGE

MATERIALS HANDLING PRINCIPLES

THERE ARE SEVERAL EXCELLENT BOOKS on the subject of materials handling. They discuss guiding principles for the materials handling engineer in great detail and give numerous examples of their application. The reader desiring a more detailed coverage of the field of materials handling is advised to read one of these books, for example, *Materials Handling*, by John Immer. In the following pages, we will survey the most important basic principles and discuss some of their applications with reference to machines and techniques used in the maritime field.

Professor Immer has classified the various principles under four categories: *planning, operating, equipment,* and *costing* principles.[1] They are listed here in what is considered the order of their relative importance. After the first few, it becomes difficult to judge their relative importance; in fact, the last eight or nine discussed may be considered equal in importance.

After reading the comments under each principle listed, the reader may reflect that the ideas set forth seem quite obvious and fundamental. This is true. But it is also true that adherence to the principles is the only effective way to produce an efficient materials handling operation. For example, the first principle is simplicity itself, yet compliance with the idea is one of the most promising ways of obtaining effective cargo operations.

The Operating Principle of Unitization

Materials handling becomes more efficient as the size of the unit handled increases.

Some of the most radical changes in ship operation are based on this principle. The SEABEE operation had carried this idea further than any other segment of the shipping industry. The *unit* here is a barge. Compliance with the unitization principle has produced a profitable operation despite the fact that other principles of ship stowage and materials handling may have been disregarded. An optimum application of this principle was the SPLASH (Self Propelled Lighter Aboard Ship) Vessel, wherein cargo can float aboard as one unit.

The pallet load, the container, lighters, barges, and integrated tug barges are developments that are slowly being exploited more and more by foresighted operators the world over. They are all based on the principle of unitization.

Rigged as they are for handling the loads of yesteryear, there is a limit on the size of the units that can be handled economically on present-day general cargo ships. The unitization principle may produce radical changes in the future ship as the cost of labor and specialized routes make themselves more evident. Use of a containership with all containers loaded and waiting when the ship docks should and does lower the materials handling costs tremendously. If the overall operation was coordinated to such a degree that these containers were packed by the shipper and delivered to the terminal ready for loading, the efficiency will be even greater.

At any rate, the small single carton or single bag is being eliminated and combined into larger units. Those operators who become conscious of this fact and bend their efforts toward this end first will be the first to realize the great potential savings.

The Equipment Principle of Terminal Time

The shorter the terminal time, the greater the efficiency of the materials handling equipment.

The only time that a piece of materials handling equipment is making money for its owner is when it is actually moving cargo. This principle can be used by the operating manager as a guide to deciding on the merits of one type of materials handling equipment as compared with another. Other factors being somewhat equal, the system that reduces the terminal time to the smallest value is obviously the best. This idea applies to all materials handling equipment, large or small.

It appears that there will be large increase in profits awaiting the first group that finds a successful means of reducing the terminal time of the general cargo carrier. The ideal arrangement would be to have a single container that is loaded and waiting for the ship when it arrives in port, as with a SPLASH vessel. Then, by pumping out ballast, a powered unit with a buoyant body could rise up and engage the cargo container. Once sufficiently strong connections had been made between the cargo containers and the powered buoyant part, the load could be taken to sea.

The Operating Principle of Gravity Utilization

Move materials by the use of gravity where possible.

At the marine terminals of the world, this principle has long been exploited when the cargo can be carried on the ship in bulk form. The best example of the use of gravity for loading ships is the ore carrier of the Great Lakes. Grain docks and some oil docks utilize gravity to a large degree also. Here we have a force provided by nature that will move cargo with a minimum cost if a suitable pipe or chute to direct the flow is provided. In some operations gravity has been used successfully to load bagged and cased products also.

At a Great Lakes terminal, iron ore is often stored in large bins and then released in runs of 60 to 80 tons. When released, the ore simply pours into the ship's hold. In one test at one of these terminals, 12,500 tons of iron ore was loaded in 16 minutes. On the average, these terminals load the ore at the rate of 5,000 tons/hour. The number of men required for the operation is less than that in a single gang of longshoremen handling general cargo.

The Planning Principle of Improved Flow or The Straight Line

Efficiency in materials handling is increased by the elimination of switch-backs and vertical movement.

This principle recognizes the simple fact that the shortest distance between two points is a straight line, and inasmuch as *motion is money,* the most economical flow for materials is in a straight line. This principle is badly violated on almost every terminal in the world. The cargo may flow almost in a straight line up to the ship's side on the pier apron due to a well-organized and carefully planned receiving operation, but what happens at the pier apron? The cargo's ultimate position in the ship is only a few feet away in a horizontal or almost horizontal direction, but as ships load today, the cargo travels in a circle to get there. To eliminate some of this inefficiency, it seems that a greater utilization of side ports should be made. There is no arguing the physical fact that it requires only a comparatively small amount of energy to move a ton of material along a smooth horizontal surface, whereas it takes a tremendous amount of energy to raise that ton only a few feet.

It is unlikely that perfect satisfaction of this principle will ever be approached with existing docks and ships, but all future development should be directed toward that end. RO/RO vessels and vessels utilizing side ports to load bananas come as close as possible to compliance with this principle (see Fig. 3-1).

The Planning Principle of Air Rights

Dock area is increased by utilizing the third dimension

This principle may be considered too high on the list, but with the limited dock space on many existing terminals it is quite obvious and fortunate that the idea is being exploited fairly well on today's piers. Satisfaction of this principle is now possible with the use of high-stacking forklift trucks and pallets, whereas it was impossible before such equipment was available. Even with the cargo stacked as shown in Figure 3-2a, some piers are heavily congested. Imagine the effect

Figure 3-1. Loading bananas through a side port.

of having to spread all the cargo out; all inefficiencies would be compounded and many present operations might even be rendered completely uneconomical. Hence, although it is almost taken for granted on today's terminals, the principle's importance, as well as its simplicity, cannot be denied.

The Costing Principle of Determining Handling Costs

For an intelligent analysis of any handling system, the costs of the handling operation must be known.

This is a difficult problem, but management should make every effort to determine the costs of every step in the terminal's operation. How else can one system be compared with another to determine which is truly the best from an economic standpoint? One system may be more productive than another, yet be more costly. This cost analysis must be done by experts in industrial engineering and cost accounting. The facts obtained may reveal astonishing weaknesses in any given system and allow better planning in the future, or perhaps point the way to immediate desirable changes.

The Operating Principle of Safety

High productivity with economy is impossible without safety.

Everybody agrees that safety is a necessity, but too many people fail to remain safety conscious when planning and executing plans, including materials

Figure 3-2a. Utilization of air rights with a high-stacking forklift.

Figure 3-2b. Utilization of air rights increases effective dock area.
Courtesy Frederick Kurst.

handling plans. Cargo operations on the marine terminal, and especially on the ship, have a high potential for developing unsafe conditions. Management and labor must be constantly reminded to enforce safety regulations.

One of the worst violations of a common safety rule at the marine terminal is the lack of proper lighting, especially in the hold of a ship. A well-designed system would be one that provides light in all parts of the hold interior even when cargo is stowed in various bays. The light provided should be *bright,* not a yellow glimmer. This is not all; the well-designed lighting system must be reliable and rugged so that it cannot be made inoperative by working cargo into and out of the spaces. Finally, it must be accessible to the ship's officer and inaccessible to unauthorized persons. The use of a number of cluster lights (Fig. 3-3) in a hatch is inefficient; also, they are vulnerable to sudden breakage and constitute a fire hazard. Besides all these defects, their use normally results in leaving some spots that are not being actually worked in darkness, and these, of course, make ideal places for the sneak thief to go to work on the cargo. Can it be that with all the modern materials and design talent in the lighting engineering industry, ships must continue to go their way shrouded in darkness? Any additional cost for a ship with a well-designed lighting system is warranted.

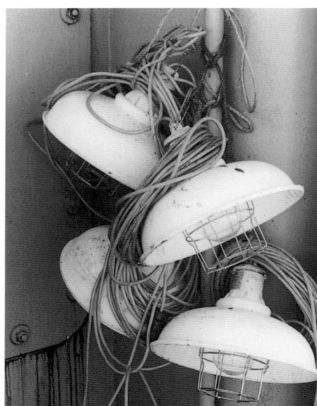

Figure 3-3.
Portable cargo lights.
Notice protective wire
guards around bulbs.

The Costing Principle of Equipment Amortization

Purchasing new handling equipment is warranted if the expense of the new equipment is exceeded by savings sufficient to amortize the cost in a reasonable time.

The economies realized as a result of abandoning old methods and equipment have in certain cases paid off the costs of new equipment in 3 months. This, of course, is an extreme case but it serves to point out how costly the old methods must have been. Just what the amortization period should be when making a decision regarding new equipment is something that must be decided after considering many things, including such items as legal allowances for depreciation rates and period of expected use. Some managements have adopted the policy of approving the equipment that gives the lowest handling costs, regardless of the time required to pay for itself; this policy guarantees that long-term savings will not be overlooked. The life expectancy of most equipment is about 10 years, although for some it may be as high as 20 years. It seems sensible to set the amortization period somewhere near but below the life expectancy. Approximately 5 to 6 years is an average, reasonable time. Note, however, that it is difficult, if not impossible, to determine the potential savings to be gained by changing methods of operation unless the handling costs are known. This places emphasis on the importance of the principle of determining handling costs. A lack of knowledge of handling costs is probably one reason why mechanization was slow to come to the marine terminal and why, in general, new methods and equipment are not readily adopted.

The Equipment Principle of Flexibility

Materials handling equipment becomes more useful, and therefore more economical, as its flexibility increases.

This particular principle cannot be followed blindly, but should be used with caution in the face of all other facts about a given operation. Obviously, the forklift truck and pallet system is far more flexible than the elevating platform and skid. Forklifts may be used to handle skids as well as pallets if necessary, but elevating platform trucks can handle skids only. Besides this, the forklift truck can be fitted with attachments that make it possible to handle bars, pipe, rolls of paper, drums, bales, and many other items without pallets or skids. Thus, it is quite clear which is the better handling equipment.

The general cargo carrier that can handle truly *general* cargo of all types and sizes without delay for refitting is the best such carrier. For instance, for flexibility she should be able to carry general packaged merchandise; a limited quantity of bulk liquid cargoes; 50,000 to 100,000 ft^3 of refrigerated cargo; heavy lifts up to 50 or 75 tons; and bulk grain with a minimum of expense for fittings, long lengths, and dangerous cargoes and containers. Trailer ships represent the antithesis of flexibility; they can call at only one type of specially built dock and can carry only one type of cargo. In spite of their merits, they would be condemned if judged solely by the principle of flexibility.

The Operating Principle of Mechanical Equipment

Heavy units are moved most economically through the use of mechanized equipment when gravity cannot be used.

Practically all units on the marine terminal may be classed as heavy; therefore, mechanization should have great advantages. Mechanical equipment reduces worker fatigue, which is a safety consideration and also may affect productivity. Mechanization speeds the handling process and, if union regulations allow, reduces the number of workers. The reduction in the number of men has a twofold advantage: Both the possibility of injury and the cost of labor are reduced. It is important to point out that the men remaining on the job will not be required to do as much heavy labor, and that mechanization will produce jobs in the service area. Without mechanized equipment, it becomes impossible to utilize overhead clearances economically by stacking cargoes high on the dock. One of the biggest obstacles to more and better mechanization of materials handling methods on the terminals and on the ships, especially on the ships, is the attitude of labor. This problem may be solved by education and training over a long period, but it will not be easy. What labor seems unable to accept is that more mechanization and better use of present mechanization makes industry more stable, gives it a healthy financial foundation, and eventually will use more men. At the same time, the men will be relieved of back-breaking manual labor. With labor and management cooperating fully on a completely mechanized, costwise operation, this branch of water transportation would probably be able to flourish once again.

Equipment Principle of Standardization

After thorough experimentation, it is economical to standardize the equipment and methods of materials handling.

The advantages of following this principle are a reduction in the number and makes of parts for making repairs and an increase in the efficiency of the personnel making the repairs. It is even desirable to standardize such simple pieces of materials handling equipment as pallets; the objective here would be to economize not on the cost of the pallets, but on the maintenance, handling, and storage costs.

It should be obvious that the maintenance and repair of a heterogeneous mixture of handling equipment is not as economical as that of standard equipment. The important thing is to make certain that the standard equipment chosen is the best, based on all the other principles mentioned in this section.

Operating Principle of Maintenance and Repair

It is economical to avoid breakdown through correct maintenance and to anticipate repairs and replacements.

It should be obvious that it is not good business to run equipment until it breaks down and then perform corrective maintenance. It should be equally clear that some regular inspection and check-off system, as with a preventive maintenance program for lubrication and replacement, is necessary to prevent unexpected breakdowns. Even the simple pallet needs attention. If one has a standardized set of pallets, a supply of boards cut to fit the pallets can be maintained. When an end board or any other part of the pallet is found to be cracked or damaged, this part should be replaced immediately. In this way, the total number of actively used pallets is kept high and greater damage is prevented.

Planning Principle of Coordination of Handling and Movement

Greatest economy is realized when the handling and movement of materials is coordinated.

This is merely another way of stating the fact that the greatest materials handling economies will be obtained through the complete overall planning so that all functions dovetail together in a smooth flowing organization. Here the importance of cooperation, communication, and coordination cannot be overemphasized. What the receiving clerk does with the cargo when it is delivered to the pier should not be done without consideration of the stevedore's activities when he/she picks it up for loading on board the ship. Full coordination is impossible without a well-prepared tentative cargo plan and without maximal scheduling of delivery to the pier. Companies that neglect to organize the flow of cargo to their dock and work without, or with, an incomplete tentative plan are violating this basic principle, and their activities are certain to be inefficient.

Planning Principle of Making the Organization Handling Conscious

For full cooperation, create full understanding of the philosophy that motion is money, extra handlings are evil, and reduced handlings are good.

This principle suggests the establishment of an educational program including management, as well as labor. It may take the form of voluntary participation in a time and motion study, attendance at the showing of a materials handling film with discussions, suggestions relative to materials handling, or a series of lectures on the need for increased productivity through mechanization. To summarize: in the process of handling materials it may be beneficial for all concerned to remember that they must COPE (Costing, Operating, Planning, Equipment) with these principles. Knowledge of the principles helps to explain why one way of doing a job is better than another and why one piece of equipment is better for a given job than another.

PRINCIPLES OF STOWAGE

The fundamental objectives when cargo is stowed in a ship are (1) to protect the ship, (2) to protect the cargo, (3) to obtain the maximum use of the available cubic of the ship, (4) to provide for rapid and systematic discharging and loading, and (5) to provide for the safety of the crew and longshoremen at all times. These objectives may be referred to as the five principles of stowage.

STOWAGE PRINCIPLE 1: PROTECTING THE SHIP

The problem involved in meeting this first objective is the correct distribution of the cargo weight. The distribution must be correct vertically, longitudinally, and transversely. The weights must not be concentrated on any deck in such a fashion that the structure's supporting strength is exceeded.

Vertical Distribution of Weight

Vertical distribution affects the stability of the ship. If too much weight is in the upper decks of the ship, the ship will have a small amount of stability and be in a condition known as *tender.* If too much weight is concentrated in the lower holds, the ship will have an excess of stability and be in a condition known as *stiff.* The tender ship has a long, slow, easy roll. The stiff ship has a fast, whiplike roll that makes her especially uncomfortable in a heavy sea and is often the cause of cargo shifting transversely.

If a ship is excessively stiff, she will roll with such violent motion that damage to the ship can be caused by heavy wracking stresses on the hull. Some of the defects caused by these heavy wracking stresses will be apparent immediately after they occur, such as cracked porthole or window glass in the superstructure, standard compasses being whipped from their pedestals, and topmasts or antennas being shaken loose. Some defects having their basic cause in these wracking stresses will never be attributed to the improper vertical distribution of the cargo. These defects, which may not be discovered until the ship undergoes a thorough inspection in a dry dock, include cracked seams, hull weaps, and leaking tanks.

Longitudinal Distribution of Weight

Longitudinal distribution affects the trim of the ship and the hogging and sagging bending stresses that the ship's hull must withstand. The trim is the difference between the drafts of the ship fore and aft. The ship should be loaded so that she has an even trim or a trim slightly by the stern, 6 inches to 1 foot. A trim by the head, if only a few inches, does not affect the speed of the ship. Trimming

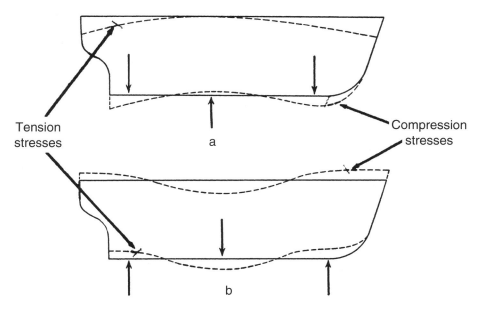

Tension
stresses

a

Compression
stresses

b

Figure 3-4. (a) Hogging—too much weight in ends. **(b)** Sagging—too much weight amidships.

by the head is usually avoided, however, because if the ship is deeply loaded and in a heavy seaway, there is more possibility that damaging green seas will be shipped on the foredeck. Hogging occurs when the ship has too much of the total weight concentrated in the ends and the hull bends as shown in Figure 3-4a. Hogging results in compression stresses being imposed on the keel and tension stresses on the sheer strake and main deck. Sagging occurs when too much weight is concentrated amidships and the hull bends as shown in Figure 3-4b. Sagging results in tension stresses being imposed on the keel and compression stresses on the sheer strake and main deck. If a ship is hogged or sagged when lying in still water, these excessive stresses will be accentuated when the ship is in a seaway, and the result may be a cracked deck or hull plate. Excessive hogging or sagging as a result of improper longitudinal distribution of cargo or ballast has been the cause of many ships breaking in two. But for every ship that has cracked into two pieces, there are hundreds of cases in which the shipowner has had to pay for the repair of cracks, large and small, in hull and deck plating. Many of the resulting expenses and delays could have been avoided by more intelligent longitudinal distribution of the cargo, voyage after voyage.

Transverse Distribution of Weight

Transverse distribution offers no problem. When stowing the cargo, the only necessity is to make sure that the weight is equal on both sides of the ship's centerline. This is accomplished by starting all loading on the centerline and stowing outboard, loading equal amounts in the wings, or, in the case of heavy lifts, putting them on the centerline if possible. If heavy lifts cannot be put on the centerline, then by careful planning, an equal weight must be placed on the side opposite the heavy lift.

Although it is rarely of practical use, it is interesting to know that the period of the ship's roll can be affected by the concentration of the weight transversely. If the mass is concentrated inboard along the centerline of the ship, the roll will be very rapid and the period of the roll will be decreased. Conversely, if the weights are concentrated outboard in the wings, the roll will be slowed down and the period of the roll will be increased. Theoretically, then, this is a device that could be used to give a stiff ship a more comfortable roll. If a ship is unavoidably loaded stiff, the roll can be slowed down by concentrating weights outboard. Such refinements are seldom practicable, although they are possible.

Importance of Weight Distribution

Improper weight distribution due to improperly loaded cargoes has cost many shipowners much time and money in the past and in all probability is still costing time and money. Ships have been lost at sea due to the shifting of cargoes or ballast, caused primarily by violent rolling in a heavy seaway. For every ship lost, there are probably thousands of cases of minor but nevertheless costly damages. Improper longitudinal distribution of weights does contribute to structural failure of ships. These failures are of such a nature that in many cases the shipowner's organization may not be aware of the cost in time and money that improper distribution is causing. This is because minor failures might be attributed wholly to heavy seas or the age of the ship, whereas these factors only contribute to the failure and the principal blame should go to the improper longitudinal distribution of cargo and ballast. The longitudinal distribution of weight should be calculated, recorded, and attested to by the master of every ship that sails. Furthermore, some tabular or mechanical means for calculation of the bending moments of the hull should be employed. This should be in addition to an onboard computer to monitor stress points.

To facilitate a complete discussion of the first fundamental objective of cargo stowage, the basic principles of stability, trim, and longitudinal stresses will be covered in this chapter.

THE SHIP'S STABILITY

Stability is the tendency of a ship to return to an upright position when inclined from the vertical by an outside force. This discussion shall be concerned only with *initial stability,* which can be defined as the tendency of a ship to right itself when inclined less than 15°. Stability at large angles and damage stability are topics that every well-informed ship's officer should understand, but the discussion of them would be too lengthy for our coverage here and would not aid the discussion of the first objective of good stowage.

THREE IMPORTANT POINTS

For a study of initial stability we constantly refer to a diagram of a ship's midship section (see Fig. 3-5) and the relationship between three points on it. These points are known as (1) the center of buoyancy *(B)*, (2) the center of gravity (*G*), and (3) the metacenter *(M)*.

Archimedes' principle of buoyancy is the basis of any explanation regarding the stability of a floating body. This principle states that a body submerged wholly or partially in a fluid is buoyed up by a force equal to the weight of the fluid displaced. On a ship, the total of the upward forces of buoyancy is considered to be concentrated at point *B*. Actually, there are hydrostatic forces acting over the entire submerged surface of the ship's hull, but the total upward force is the force of buoyancy and acts through point *B*. This force of buoyancy acting through *B* is opposed by an equal force acting downward through point *G*. When a body is floating, the forces through *B* and *G* are equal. The force through *B* will never exceed the force through *G*. The force through *G* may exceed the force through *B,* in which case the body will sink. When the forces through *G* and *B* are equal, the body will float. If the floating body is at rest, that is, not revolving transversely or longitudinally (rolling or pitching), then the forces through *B* and *G* are exactly opposed: They are acting along the same vertical line. The force acting through *G* is the sum of the weights of all elements making up the ship's structure. For convenience, we consider them as acting through this single point *G*.

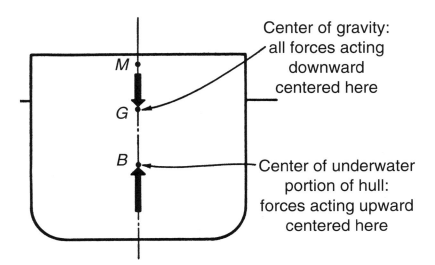

Center of gravity: all forces acting downward centered here

Center of underwater portion of hull: forces acting upward centered here

Figure 3-5. Ship's midships section.

Point *B* will always be at the exact center of the underwater portion of the ship's hull. Point *G* will always be at the exact center of the entire mass of which the ship is composed. This mass includes every part that lies above or below the waterline, everything in the ship or on the ship. The addition of a weight, the removal of a weight, or the shifting of a weight will change the position of *G*. The only thing that will change the position of *B* is a change in the shape of the underwater portion of the hull. The underwater portion of the hull changes shape, of course, whenever the ship rolls or pitches; thus *B* moves about as the ship works in a seaway.

The Vertical Position of *G*

The first step is to examine the problem of determining the *position of the center of gravity of a system of weights*. We use a physical law that may be explained mathematically as follows: *If a number of weights are part of a system of weights and each weight is multiplied by its distance from a reference line or surface, then the sum of all these products will equal the sum of all the weights times the distance of the center of gravity of the system from the reference line or surface.* This is a very important concept and the reader should not proceed until he/she is certain that he/she understands it. The rule as stated above applies to masses, but it can be made applicable to volumes as well. It can be used to find the position of a center of gravity in three dimensions; however, our problem in stability is somewhat simplified by the fact that our *G* will always be considered to lie on the ship's centerline, and we will be concerned only with the height of *G* above the keel of the ship.

Before proceeding further, it must be pointed out that the product of a weight and a distance *(W × D)* in each case is a *moment*. A moment is defined as the product of a force acting through a distance. The units used on ships are long tons for *W* and feet for *D*; hence the units of moments are foot-tons. Knowing this, we can restate the important law given above as follows: *The sum of all the individual moments in a weight system is equal to the moment caused by the total weight of the system being concentrated at the distance of G from the reference line.* The law holds for finding the position of *G* upward in a vertical direction with reference to a horizontal line. This latter method is the way we consider the problem when working to locate *G* on a ship. A numerical example pertaining to the vertical position of *G* follows. In this example, we will shift also to the terms used on board ship.

Numerical Example

In Figure 3-6 the reference line is the keel of the ship. The lower hold has 3,000 tons in it, with the center of this weight 8 feet above the keel; the lower 'tweendecks has 2,000 tons centered 22 feet above the keel; the upper 'tweendecks has 1,000 tons 30 feet above the keel; the deck load of cargo amounts to 500 tons 38 feet above the keel. There are 2,500 tons of fuel, water,

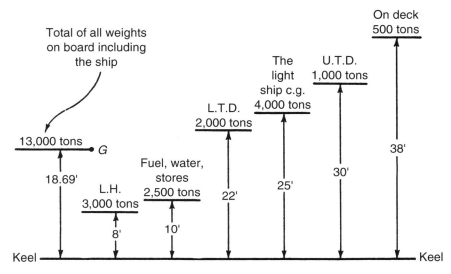

Figure 3-6. Keel reference line.

and stores on board, with the center of this weight 10 feet above the keel. The light ship structure has a weight of 4,000 tons and the vertical height of its center of gravity is 25 feet above the keel. The question we want to answer with all these data is: How far does the center of gravity of all these weights (G) lie above the keel? Referring to the general statement of the problem, we proceed to multiply each weight in the system, which is in this case the displacement of the ship. To obtain the answer we seek, we divide the sum of all the moments by the ship's displacement.

25	×	4,000	=	100,000 ft-tons	Light Ship Moment
38	×	500	=	19,000 ft-tons	On-Deck Moment
8	×	3,000	=	24,000 ft-tons	L/H Moment
22	×	2,000	=	44,000 ft-tons	LTD Moment
30	×	1,000	=	30,000 ft-tons	UTD Moment
10	×	2,500	=	25,000 ft-tons	Fuel, Water, Stores

x	×	13,000	=	242,000 ft-tons

Distance of G above keel   Total weight   Sum of all moments

Dividing 242,000 by 13,000, we obtain the value of x.

$$x = 18.69 \text{ ft}$$

Thus we see that G lies 18.69 feet above the keel of the ship.

The 13,000 tons is the weight of the ship and all she contains under the conditions given in the problem. This figure is the *displacement* of the ship, indicated in formulas by the Greek letter delta (Δ). The weight of the cargo and the fuel, water, and stores, 9,000 tons, is known as the *dead weight lifting capacity* of the ship if this weight puts the ship down to her maximum legal draft. The *cargo deadweight* is the 6,500 tons of cargo. The weight of the ship with nothing on board, 4,000 tons, is known as the *light ship displacement.*

The solution of a practical problem requires all of the data given above. The weight of the cargo in the various compartments is obtained from the stowage plan. The distances of these weights above the keel are obtained partially from data concerning each compartment given on a ship's *capacity plan* (see page 4-6) and partially from estimates made by the officer. If the compartment is filled with a homogeneous cargo, the weight can be considered to be centered vertically. If it is loaded with heavy goods on the bottom and lighter goods on top, assume the center of the weight to be about one-third of the height of the compartment above the deck of the compartment. To find the center of all the fuel, water, and stores weights is a smaller problem solved in the same manner as the general problem. The weights of the fuel and water and the tanks in which they are contained must be obtained from the ship's chief engineer. The weights of stores and their positions with reference to the keel must be estimated as closely as possible. The weight of the light ship and the position of its center of gravity must be obtained from the ship's capacity plan or from stability data supplied for the ship by the builders. These data are determined by means of the inclining experiment.

SHIFTS IN POSITION OF *G*

The position of *G* is affected by addition, subtraction, or shifts of weights in the system. It is important that the reader be capable of calculating these shifts in the location of *G*. When considering stowage problems, it is often necessary to estimate the shift in *G* owing to a change in the stowage plan or to the consumption of large masses on the ship, such as the burning of fuel oil from the double bottom tanks.

The first problem that we will examine is a shift in *G* owing to an addition or subtraction of weight in the system. Later, we will examine the shift in *G* caused by movement of a mass within the system. We refer to the basic law and consider a system comprised of the original total weight and the single added new weight. The reference line will be a horizontal line passing through the known position of *G*. The distance between our reference line and our biggest weight in our two-weight system is zero, and hence the moment is also zero. This is important. One other moment remains. This is the product of the additional weight and its distance from the old position of *G* (see Fig. 3-7). The sum of these products is equal to the value of the last product. We divide the sum of the moments by the old displacement plus the newly added weight. The quotient will be equal to the shift of G. The new position is referred to as G' ("G prime") and the distance of the shift is indicated by GG'. The shift is always toward the position of the added weight. Do not forget the formula for GG'.

$$GG' = \frac{D_1 W_1}{\Delta + W_1} \tag{1}$$

where

W_1 = added weight.

D_1 = distance of added weight from old center of gravity.

Δ = displacement of ship before adding W_1.

When subtracting a weight, the same reasoning applies. The shift of G is away from the weight removed and the value of the weight system is the displacement less W_1. Equation for GG' becomes:

$$GG' = \frac{W_1 D_1}{\Delta - W_1} \tag{2}$$

The shift of G (GG') caused by a shift of a part of the weight system, such as moving 100 tons up or down on the ship, is found using equation 3.

$$GG' = \frac{W_1 D_1}{\Delta} \tag{3}$$

where

GG' = shift of G (always in the direction that the weight is shifted).

W_1 = the weight that is shifted.

D_1 = distance that W_1 is shifted.

Δ = the ship's displacement.

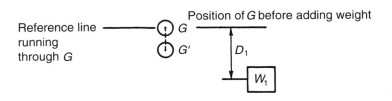

Figure 3-7. Product of additional weight and distance.

NUMERICAL EXAMPLE

Given: A ship displacing 15,000 tons with a *KG* of 30 feet; 2,000 tons of fuel oil is burned from the double bottoms; this mass had a *KG* of 2 feet. *(Note: The distance of G above the keel is generally referred to as KG. This notation will be used hereafter.)*

Required: The ship's new *KG*.

Solution: This is a case of removing a weight from the weight system; hence we use equation 2: W_1 equals 2,000 tons. D_1 equals 28 feet. Hence, the GG′ equation becomes:

$$GG' = \frac{W_1 D_1}{\Delta - W_1} = \frac{2,000 \times 28}{13,000} = 4.3 \text{ ft}$$

Since *G* has moved up 4.3 feet, the new *KG* is 34.3 ft.

Another method of solution uses the moments involved, as follows:

W		KG		Moment
15,000	×	30	=	450,000
- 2,000	×	2	=	- 4,000
13,000				446,000

$$\text{New } KG = \frac{446,000}{13,000} = 34.3 \text{ ft}$$

One more type of problem remains to be clarified with respect to the position of *G* and its shift due to the movement of weight on the ship. We have considered the solution for the shift in *G* due to the addition or removal of a single weight. There may be need to calculate the final position of *G* after loading several weights and discharging several weights. In this problem, it is necessary to consider each addition and removal separately and to separate all the movements into those that will move *G* up and those that will move *G* down. A net moment is obtained by adding these two sums. The net moment is divided by the *final* displacement to obtain the shift in *G*.

NUMERICAL EXAMPLE

Given: A ship with a *KG* of 20 feet. The displacement is 10,000 tons.

Two weights, W_1 and W_2 are loaded. W_1 = 500 tons and is placed 23 feet above the keel. W_2 = 500 tons and is placed 5 feet above the keel.

Two weights are discharged. $W_3 = 1,000$ tons removed from 12 feet above the keel. $W_4 = 1,000$ tons removed from 40 feet above the keel.

Required: The problem is to determine the ship's *KG* after the above operation. We actually would have four problems here if we solved each separately by equations 2 and 3. It is easier to combine the data to form one problem. The procedure is to make two columns: In one column, list all the moments resulting in an increase of *KG;* in the other, list all those resulting in a decrease.

Solution: Before adding and removing the weights, the ship had a *KG* of 20 feet. Carefully check the effect of each weight on the *KG*. W_1 is added 3 feet above the initial *G*, which we are going to use as a datum level; hence, the movement of $3 \times W_1$ will increase our ship's *KG*. W_2 is added 15 feet below our datum level, and the moment will decrease the *KG*. W_3 is removed from 8 feet below *G*, and *G* will move away from a removed weight; thus, this moment will increase *KG*. W_4 is removed from 20 feet above *G*; thus, the moment will decrease *KG*. Next we calculate each of these moments, giving a plus sign to those that increase the *KG* and a minus sign to those that decrease the *KG*. Add the moments. Next divide by the final displacement of the ship. The quotient is the distance in feet that *G* has moved up or down. If the net moment has a minus sign, the movement is down and *KG* has been decreased. If the sign is plus, the movement of *G* is up and *KG* has been increased. The solution of the above problem is as follows:

Increase of KG (+)			Decrease of KG (-)		
500	× 3 =	1,500 ft-tons	500	× 15 =	7,500 ft-tons
1,000	× 8 =	8,000 ft-tons	1,000	× 20 =	20,000 ft-tons
		+ 9,500 ft tons			- 27,500 ft-tons

+ 9,500
- 27 ,500

- 18,000 ft-tons (net change in moments)

A total of 2,000 tons was discharged and 1,000 tons were loaded; hence, the final displacement is 1,000 tons less than the initial 10,000 tons, that is, 9,000 tons.

Final step to solve for *GG′*:

$$GG' = \frac{-18,000}{9,000} = -2 \text{ ft}$$

Therefore, the new *KG* is $20 - 2 = 18$ feet.

Determining the Position of B

The position of B can be calculated in a manner similar to that used to calculate G, except that volumes are used instead of weights. The calculations are complicated by the fact that these volumes are bounded by curved surfaces, but they are not exceptionally difficult. The reader should refer to a standard reference if he/she wishes to learn exactly how these calculations are made. For the practical determination of stability, there is no need to make the calculations involving the location of B. The reader needs only to be aware of the fact that B moves about as the vessel is inclined and why it moves.

Movement of B

The definition of B must be recalled before we attempt an explanation of how and why B moves about when the ship is inclined. Point B is the geometrical center of the *underwater* portion of the hull. Looking at Figure 3-8, we note that B is on the centerline of the ship. If the ship is upright and floating, G is either directly above or below B on a line perpendicular to the waterline. G is illustrated as above B on the diagram in Figure 3-5. If the ship is inclined as shown in Figure 3-8, a wedge of volume is removed from the underwater portion of the hull on the side away from the inclination and transferred to the side toward which the ship is inclined. What will happen to B? Obviously, B will move in the direction of the submerged side. This can be appreciated intuitively, for the center of the underwater portion now lies toward this side. The amount of the shift of B is not too important in our explanation of factors involved in stability, but a brief exposition of the method for calculating it is presented below.

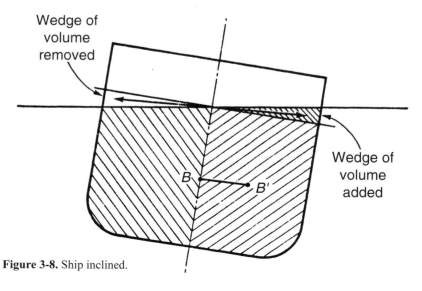

Figure 3-8. Ship inclined.

CALCULATING THE SHIFT OF *B*

The technique for calculating a shift in *B* involves the same principles used with respect to finding the center of a system of weights. The only difference is that in place of weight values, volume values are used. Hence, the equations used to calculate GG' can be used to calculate BB'. In the case of the movement of *B* because of a shift of the volume wedge from one side to the other, equation 3 can be used, with the units changed as necessary:

$$BB' = \frac{v \times d}{V}$$

where

    BB' = the distance that *B* shifts.

    v = volume of the wedge.

    d = distance that the center of the volume wedge moved.

    V = volume of the entire underwater portion of the ship.

The focus of the point *B* as the ship is inclined to larger and larger angles is an ellipse. This fact is of significance when studying stability at large angles of inclination.

THE METACENTER (M)

The third and last point to be examined is the metacenter, *M*. To locate the metacenter, the naval architect takes the curvature of a circle that has the same curvature as a very small segment of the elliptical path of *B* and draws radii of this circle. They intersect at the center of the circle; this point is *M*. *M* moves about as the ship is inclined. This fact can be appreciated because the curvature of an ellipse is at a minimum at the extremities of the minor axis and at a maximum at the extremities of the major axis. Therefore, the radii will be changing continually, and the point *M* will follow. For small angles of inclination, *M* will fall on the centerline of the ship. As the angle of inclination approaches 10°, *M* moves upward and away from the side toward which the ship is inclined. When considering *initial* stability, it is assumed that *M* is always directly on the centerline. The distance from *B* to *M* is notated as *BM* and known as the metacentric radius. The force of buoyancy acting upward through *B* always passes through *M*, which will always be directly over *B* in a vertical direction normal to the waterline.

DISTANCE FROM KEEL TO *B* AND *M*

The distance from the keel to point *B* is known as *KB* and is calculated by the naval architect. *BM* is also calculated. The sum of *KB* and *BM* gives *KM*, a value of great importance in the calculation of initial stability. The value of KM varies with the ship's draft. For the ship's officer to know his/her ship's KM, he/she must refer to a set of hydrostatic curves or have a table giving the KM of the ship for the various drafts. The draft referred to is the mean draft, of course. This means that KM varies with the displacement. For the ship's stability to be calculated, the KM must be known. All ships should have a deadweight scale with the KM given on it or a table of KMs by draft or deadweight. Hydrostatic curves may be used if available, but they are more difficult to read and cumbersome to use.

Determination of Stability

The three points that must be understood clearly for an appreciation of ship stability have now been examined. The reader may already realize that a ship increases her stability with a lowering of G. The distance between G and M is referred to as the ship's GM. When a ship is inclined, initially B moves away from the centerline, G remains stationary, and for small angles we will assume that M remains stationary. Thus, our points would be located as seen in Figure 3-9a if G was initially below M. The angle of inclination has been exaggerated in this diagram so that the elements of the figure can be seen more easily. Note that the forces through B and through G are no longer opposed to each other. They are forces acting through a distance; thus, they create a moment. The distance through which these forces act is the line GZ. GZ is perpendicular to the line BM, the metacentric radius. The moment tends to revolve the ship in a direction opposite to the inclination. In other words, it tends to push the ship back into an upright position. This moment is called the righting moment.

Stable, Neutral, and Unstable Equilibrium

When G is below M, the ship possesses *stable equilibrium* and tends to return to an upright position if inclined by an outside force. The tendency to right herself depends on the ship's displacement and the value of GZ, because the righting moment is the product of displacement and GZ.

If points G, B, and M are located as shown in Figure 3-9b, the point G has moved up until the distance GZ has become zero and there is no righting moment. In this position, GM is also zero. GM and GZ vary directly. The ship is in a condition of *neutral equilibrium* when GM and GZ both equal zero. When a ship possesses neutral equilibrium, she will remain in whatever position she is placed, within certain limitations. If G is moved up beyond M, the points and forces involved will act as shown in Figure 3-9c. In this condition, the ship possesses *unstable equilibrium.* The ship will not remain in an upright position, but will assume a list either to the port or to the starboard. The angle of the list will depend on the distance of G above M. The greater the distance, the greater the angle of list.

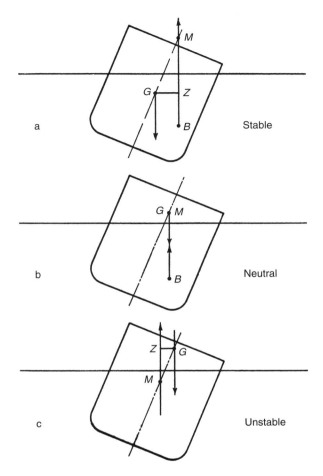

Figure 3-9. Stable, neutral, and unstable equilibrium.

LISTING DUE TO NEGATIVE *GM*

'

The ship will not capsize just because she has unstable equilibrium, unless *G* is too far above *M*. When *G* is above but close to *M* the ship will assume a small list. This list may be increased to a dangerous magnitude if *G* is moved up as a result of burning fuel oil from the ship's double bottom tanks. The reason why the ship assumes a small list and does not continue over is explained by the fact that the metacenter, *M*, moves up as the angle of inclination varies between 0 and 20°. Thus, *M* moves above *G* if *G* is sufficiently close to *M*, for *G* is stationary. When *M* is above *G*, the ship attains stable equilibrium, but she will have a permanent list to the port or starboard. The list will change from one side to the other when a force, such as centrifugal force during a radical course change or from strong winds or seas, is applied to the hull.

The ship's officer should be able to recognize a ship with negative *GM* by her behavior in a seaway. A ship with negative *GM* will have a list, but the list may change from port to starboard and back again with such forces on the hull as wind and sea or centrifugal force when applying heavy rudder. The ship will always have a long, slow, sluggish roll.

CORRECTING A LIST DUE TO A NEGATIVE *GM*

A common, and often serious, mistake made in the field of stability is that of not recognizing a list caused by negative *GM* or unstable equilibrium and therefore taking corrective measures that are improper.

If a ship has a list of 5 or 6° caused by off-center weights, that is, by *G* being to port or starboard of the centerline, the obvious correction is to move weights toward the high side. However, if a list is caused by negative *GM,* the movement of weights to the high side would cause the vessel to right itself partially and then suddenly take a much greater list to the opposite side. The sudden rush toward the opposite side would take place after about one-half of the previous angle of list had been removed. The list to the opposite side would be greater because it would be the result of two poor conditions: (1) negative *GM* and (2) off-center weights.

The only way to correct a list due to negative *GM* is to add, remove, or shift weights so that *G will be moved down.*

Lumber carriers are frequently victims of negative *GM* conditions. To prevent or correct a list due to this condition, the double bottom tanks should be kept as full as possible. After a long voyage, the double bottom tanks may be so empty that the ship will have an excessive list on arrival in port. In such a case, the lumber deck load should be carefully removed in layers. It would be a serious blunder to attempt to right the ship by discharging from the low side first. The list can be removed by pumping salt water into the empty double bottom fuel oil tanks, but this is generally avoided if possible. Once salt water gets into the fuel oil system of the ship, the engineers may have endless trouble with it.

GM AS A MEASURE OF STABILITY

In the triangle *GZM* of Figure 3-10b, the angle at vector *Z* is a right angle.

From elementary trigonometry we have:

$$\sin \theta \;=\; \frac{GZ}{GM} \tag{5}$$

from which we get:

$$GM \;=\; \frac{GZ}{\sin \theta} \;=\; GZ \times \csc \theta \tag{6}$$

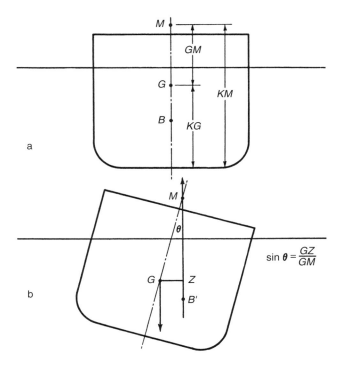

$$\sin \theta = \frac{GZ}{GM}$$

Figure 3-10. Calculating *GM*. **(a)** Stable equilibrium. **(b)** Ship inclined, thereby creating triangle *GZM*, where *GM* and *GZ* vary directly.

From equation 6, we see that *GM* varies directly as *GZ*. It has already been pointed out that *GZ* is one of two factors that determine the tendency of the ship to right herself. Because *GM* and *GZ* vary directly, *GM* is a measure of stability also.

CALCULATING *GM*

All of the points that we have examined are illustrated in Figure 3-10a. They are arranged to indicate a positive *GM*. To calculate *GM*, data to calculate *KG* are required. In addition, a table of *KMs* for all the drafts from light to loaded is required. Then, $KM - KG = GM$. Once we know the *GM* of the ship, we have some knowledge of her stability and we know how she will react to a heavy seaway. With experience, such information gives the ship's officer a basis for making correct and prompt decisions concerning stability.

NUMERICAL EXAMPLE

Given: A ship with a light ship displacement of 4,500 tons. Light ship *KG* = 25 feet. The following weights are on board: fuel, water, stores = 2,000 tons with *KG* of 20 feet; lower hold cargo = 2,000 tons with *KG* of 10 feet; and 'tweendeck cargo = 1,000 tons with *KG* of 30 feet. *KM* for a displacement of 9,500 tons = 24.5 feet.

Required: The ship's *GM.*

Solution: We know the *KM,* so we only have to calculate *KG; KM* will be obtained from a table based on displacements or drafts. To calculate *KG,* we find the vertical moments of all the weights (including light ship), add these moments, and divide by the displacement. The result is the *KG.* Then *KM − KG = GM.*

$$
\begin{array}{rcl}
4{,}500 \times 25 & = & 112{,}500 \text{ ft-tons} \\
2{,}000 \times 20 & = & 40{,}000 \text{ ft-tons} \\
2{,}000 \times 10 & = & 20{,}000 \text{ ft-tons} \\
1{,}000 \times 30 & = & 30{,}000 \text{ ft-tons} \\
\hline
9{,}500 & & 202{,}500 \text{ ft-tons}
\end{array}
$$

$$202{,}500 \div 9{,}500 = 21.3 \text{ ft} = KG$$

$$24.5 - 21.3 = 3.2 \text{ ft} = GM$$

LIGHT AND LOADED DISPLACEMENT *GM*s

Stability is the tendency of a vessel to right herself. This tendency is measured in the units of the righting moment, which are foot-tons. Considering a constant *GZ,* it can be seen that when a vessel is light, say displacing 6,000 tons, the righting moment will be considerably less than when the vessel is loaded, say displacing 14,000 tons. The righting moment should be kept at a nearly constant value; hence, the *GM* that produces a comfortable and safe ship in the light condition will produce a very stiff ship in the loaded condition. The average *loaded* merchant ship is safe and comfortable with a *GM* between 2 and 3 feet. The *GM* of the ship with only 1,000 or 1,500 tons of cargo or ballast on board should be 4 to 5 feet. The important point here for the ship's officer to remember is that when the ship is only partially loaded, the *GM* must be larger than when the ship is fully loaded.

A light ship may have a *GM* of 8 to 12 feet. With some fuel, water, and stores on board, this will generally be reduced 2 or 3 feet. The resulting *GM* will generally be too large for a ship even in the partially loaded or ballasted condition. At light drafts, the *KM* is reduced rapidly as the displacement increases; thus, adding weight so that the position of *G* remains fixed will reduce *GM* by dropping the metacenter down closer to the center of gravity.

DISTRIBUTION OF PARTIAL LOADS

It is neither feasible nor necessary to specify the precise distribution that should be given partial loads. The important thing is to be aware that if only 500 to 1,000 tons are being carried, the load should be carried in the 'tweendeck areas. If the cargo amounts to 2,000 to 3,000 tons, the metacenter may drop so rapidly that some cargo will be required in the lower holds for a safe and comfortable *GM*. Each ship and her partial load will present a particular problem that should be solved on the basis of the facts available. The above is a discussion of the general case, and is not intended to lay down any precise rules or imply what should be done in a particular case. However, it can be stated safely that if a ship capable of lifting 7,500 to 10,000 tons cargo deadweight is lifting only about 1,000 tons, none of that weight should be in the lower holds.

ESTIMATING VERTICAL DISTRIBUTION

It is often stated with reference to the stowage of cargo that, as a general guide for proper vertical distribution of cargo when carrying full loads, about one-third of the weight should be in the 'tweendecks and about two thirds should be in the lower holds. **This rule should not be used.** Such distribution will often give a ship an excessive *GM*. The rule also leaves much doubt as to what should be done when the ship has three decks or four decks. The only safe procedure is to calculate the correct vertical distribution by the methods outlined above. However, if for any reason it is necessary to estimate the desired vertical distribution of a full load and data for calculating the amounts are not available, the safest procedure is to place in each compartment a proportion of the total weight equal to the ratio of the individual compartment's bale cubic to that of the ship's total bale cubic. This can be expressed by the following formula:

$$\frac{v}{V} \times T = t \qquad\qquad (7)$$

where

V = total bale capacity of the ship.

v = bale capacity of the compartment or series of compartments at equal distances from the keel.

T = total tonnage to be loaded.

t = number of tons of the total load that should be placed in the compartment or compartments in question.

This method cannot be used when taking on partial loads or under ballasted conditions, as is evident from the above discussion.

NUMERICAL EXAMPLE

Given: On a vessel, the bale cubics are as follows:

U. T .D.	=	145,865 ft³
L. T .D.	=	134,025 ft³
L.H.	=	164,550 ft³
Total	=	444,440 ft³

The cargo deadweight is 8,000 tons. No other information is available.

Required: The vertical distribution of the 8,000 tons.

Solution: Simply multiply 8,000 by the ratio of each compartment's cubic to the cubic of the entire ship.

$$\frac{145,865}{444,440} \times 8,000 = 2,640 = \text{tons in U. T .D. area}$$

$$\frac{134,025}{444,440} \times 8,000 = 2,440 = \text{tons in L. T .D. area}$$

$$\frac{164,550}{444,440} \times 8,000 = 2,920 = \text{tons in the L.H. area}$$

Note that the weight is divided up to equal about one-third for each level in this particular case. The resulting *GM* would depend on the tankage of the ship, which can cause the *GM* to vary widely. Tankage is the distribution of the weights in the numerous tanks on the ship. Free surface effect would also have to be given consideration, as in any practical calculation of *GM*.

Trim Calculations

DEFINITION OF TRIM

Trim is defined as the difference in drafts forward and aft on the ship. The trim of a ship is a function of the moments developed by weights acting forward of the ship's tipping center as opposed to those acting aft of the tipping center. With a ship on an even keel, the points mentioned in the explanation of stability would be arranged as shown in Figure 3-11a. These are the same points except that they are analyzed on the profile of the ship instead of the midship section. The center of gravity and the center of buoyancy are in the same place vertically as before. *M* is much higher and is identified as the longitudinal metacenter. The *GM* is a few hundred feet in length and is designated the longitudinal *GM*. It is important that the reader review the explanations of how *G, B,* and *M* are located and why *G* and *B* move.

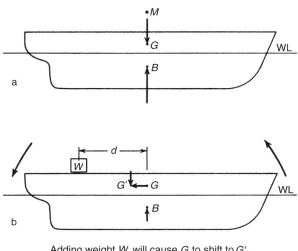

Adding weight *W* will cause *G* to shift to *G'*.

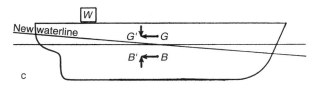

Figure 3-11. Change of trim.

When a ship is on an even keel and at rest, the points G and B are vertically one over the other. If they are not, the ship will revolve slightly, causing B to move until it comes under G. Hence, if we take the ship on an even keel and place a weight aft of point B or G, point G will be moved aft. The situation then would be as illustrated in Figure 3-11b. This condition cannot exist, because the forces acting upward through B and downward through G are now acting through a distance, and this produces a moment. This moment will tend to revolve the ship counterclockwise as viewed in this diagram. As the ship trims by the stern, a wedge of volume is shifted from the forward part of the vessel to the after part. This causes B to shift aft and eventually come directly under G again, as shown in Figure 3-11c. When this occurs, the ship will come to rest with a change of drafts forward and aft. The ship will have changed trim.

MOMENTS PRODUCING A CHANGE OF TRIM

The change of trim can be expressed as a function of two completely different moments. The reader should be able to see that GG' multiplied by the displacement is one moment that causes the ship to revolve. The displacement used in this calculation is the displacement in the final condition. Another moment, which would be equal to the first one mentioned, is the product of W times D, where W is the individual weight being considered at a distance D from the tipping center of the ship. Either of these two moments may be used to calculate the change in trim, but the methods used in each solution differ slightly. As the vessel revolves in changing trim, it does so about the center of flotation, which is the geometrical center of the water plane at which the ship is floating. This point is also known as the tipping center and is notated as T. C. The tipping center changes its position as the displacement increases, generally moving aft.

CHANGE OF TRIM VALUES

When given a set of drafts for two different conditions, the change of trim between the two conditions is calculated by first noting the trim in each case. Next, if the trim is in the same direction in both cases, the change in trim is found by subtracting the smaller from the larger.

NUMERICAL EXAMPLE

Given: A ship with the following initial and final drafts:

	Fwd., ft and in.	Mean, ft and in.	Aft, ft and in.	Trim, in.
Initial:	20 06	20 08 ½	20 11	5 aft
Final:	26 00	27 00	28 00	24 aft

Required: The change in trim.

Solution: By inspection it can be seen that 24 less 5 inches gives a *change of trim* of 1 foot 7 inches by the stern.

If two trims are in opposite directions, the change of trim is found by adding the two trims.

NUMERICAL EXAMPLE

Given: A ship with the following initial and final drafts.

	Fwd., ft and in.	Mean, ft and in.	Aft, ft and in.	Trim, in.
Initial:	20 00	19 06	19 00	12 fwd.
Final:	20 00	20 04	20 08	8 aft

Required: The change in trim.

Solution: Inasmuch as the trim is by the head in the initial condition and by the stern in the final condition, the change in trim is found by adding the trim. Thus, the *change in trim* is 1 foot 8 inches by the stern.

MOMENT TO CHANGE TRIM 1 INCH *(MT1)*

As stated above, the change of trim can be expressed as a function of either of two moments. When calculating the effect of loading, discharging, or shifting partial loads, that is, when the change of displacement is small, the moment obtained by multiplying the weight involved *by* the distance through which it acts is most commonly used.

When loading or discharging a weight, the moment is obtained by determining the distance between the center of flotation and the position of the weight and multiplying by the value of the weight. The change in trim is determined by dividing the above moment by a value known as the *moment to trim the ship 1 inch.* This value is notated as *MT*1 and is found on the hydrostatic curves of the ship and on the deadweight scale. This value increases with displacement. If the exact position of the center of flotation is not known, the moment may be calculated about the midship section of the ship. If this is done, however, an error will be introduced. The center of flotation will generally be well forward of the midship section at light drafts. At loaded drafts, it may be slightly aft or slightly forward. The equation for the change of trim is:

$$\frac{W \times D}{MT1} = \text{Change in Trim} \tag{8}$$

When shifting a weight, the moment is obtained by multiplying the weight by the distance that the weight is moved.

A typical trim problem is solved by first entering on the deadweight scale the ship's existing mean draft and finding the corresponding *MT*1. One then determines the trimming moment and divides by the *MT*1. The result will be the change in trim in inches. If the ship's tipping center is exactly at the midpoint longitudinally, the *change in draft* readings forward and aft are obtained by dividing the total *change in trim* by 2 and applying it to the old draft readings. If the ship's tipping center is not precisely at the midpoint, the change of *draft* (not trim) forward can be found by multiplying the change in *trim* by the ratio of the distance of the tipping center from the forward perpendicular to the total length on the waterline. In the same manner, the change in draft aft can be found. The sum of the changes in draft should equal the total change in trim. In practice, the error produced by assuming that the tipping center is at the midship section, whether it is or not, is less than the inaccuracies that enter into the actual reading of the drafts. Hence, the extreme precision obtained by multiplying by the ratio mentioned above is unnecessary.

A trim problem involving a shift of weight.

Given: A ship with an *MT*1 of 1,200 pumps 200 tons of fuel oil from a forward tank to an after tank, a distance of 60 feet. The drafts before the shift were: forward, 23 feet 8 inches; aft, 23 feet 4 inches; mean, 23 feet 6 inches.

Required: The total change in trim and the final drafts.

Solution:

$$\frac{200 \times 60}{1,200} = 10 \text{ in. total change in trim by the stern}$$

Assuming the tipping center is amidships, the draft aft is increased 5 inches and the draft forward is decreased 5 inches. Therefore, the new drafts would be: forward, 23 feet 3 inches; aft, 23 feet 9 inches; mean, 23 feet 6 inches.

In the above problem, if the ship was 480 feet on the waterline and the tipping center was 10 feet forward of the midship section, the exact change in drafts would be:

$$\frac{\text{Distance of tipping center from fwd.}}{\text{Length on the waterline}} \times \text{Change in trim} = \text{Change in draft fwd.}$$

$$(230/480) \times 10 = 4.79 \text{ in.}$$

$$\frac{\text{Distance of tipping center from aft}}{\text{Length on the waterline}} \times \text{Change in trim} = \text{Change in draft aft}$$

$$(250/480) \times 10 = 5.21 \text{ in.}$$

From this problem, it is seen that the error produced by assuming the T.C. to be amidships, when it was actually 10 feet forward, amounts to less than a quarter of an inch.

A trim problem involving the addition of weight.

Given: A ship with an *MT*1 of 1,000. 150 tons are loaded 100 feet aft of the tipping center. The drafts before loading were: forward, 19 feet 2 inches; aft, 19 feet 4 inches; mean, 19 feet 3 inches. Tons per inch immersion (T.P.I.) is 50.

Required: The total change in trim and the final drafts.

Solution: The *MT*1 and the T.P.I. are found on the deadweight scale. T.P.I. is defined as the number of tons required to increase the mean draft 1 inch. It is obvious that to determine the final drafts, this figure would have to be known unless the deadweight scale was on hand to refer to. In practice the deadweight scale would be available, but when working problems the T.P.I. is usually stated.

The initial step in calculating the final drafts is to increase all the given drafts by an amount equal to the *mean sinkage*. The mean sinkage is obtained by dividing the number of tons loaded by the T.P.I. In this problem it amounts to 3 inches. The reasoning used in the solution is that the weight is loaded directly over the tipping center first then shifted to the actual position. Thus, the mean sinkage is added to all the given drafts first; then with these new drafts the change of trim is applied exactly as in the simple shift of weight problem already solved. Therefore, applying the mean sinkage to the given drafts we obtain: forward, 19 feet 5 inches; aft, 19 feet 7 inches; mean, 19 feet 6 inches.

Calculating the change of trim:

$$\frac{150 \times 100}{1,000} = 15 \text{ in.}$$

The change forward is -7½ inches, and aft it is + 7½ inches. The final drafts would be: forward, 18 feet 9½ inches; aft, 20 feet 2½ inches; mean, 19 feet 6 inches.

The T.P.I. is found by taking the area of the water plane for the draft in question and dividing by 420. That is:

$$\frac{\text{Area of water plane}}{420} = \text{T.P.I.}$$

The derivation is simple. The number of tons required to sink a ship 1 foot is equal to the weight of sea water displaced by the volume of a 1-foot layer of the hull. Thirty-five cubic feet of sea water weighs 1 ton. Therefore, to find the tons required to immerse a ship 1 foot, we simply divide the volume of a 1-foot slice by 35. The volume of a 1-foot slice is equal to the area of the water plane multiplied by 1 foot. This is expressed by the equation:

$$\frac{\text{Area of the water plane} \times 1}{35} = \text{Tons per foot of Immersion}$$

But we want to know the tons per inch, and an inch is exactly one-twelfth of a foot. Letting A.W.P. stand for area of the water plane, we have:

$$\frac{\text{A.W. P.}}{12 \times 35} = \text{T.P.I.}$$

which is the same as:

$$\frac{\text{A.W. P.}}{420} = \text{T.P.I.}$$

Calculating MT1

When asked to calculate the *MT1*, the problem is to find the value of $W \times D$ (the trimming moment) that will produce a change of *trim* of 1 inch or, what amounts to the same thing, a change of *draft* at either end of ½ inch. One-half inch can be expressed also as ¹⁄₂₄ foot. We will say then that our problem is to find an equation for $W \times D$ that will produce a change of *trim* of ¹⁄₁₂ foot or a change of draft forward and aft of ¹⁄₂₄ foot. When we do this, we will designate such a $W \times D$ as *MT1*. Referring to Figure 3-12, if the weight, *W*, is moved aft some distance *D*, then *G* will move aft to some point *G*. A moment will be set up causing the ship to revolve counter clockwise as viewed in the diagram. This will cause *B* to move aft until it is again under the center of gravity; that is, *B* will move to point *G'* or directly below this point and become *B'*.

Starting with the ship on an even keel, the right triangle *MGG'* has been formed. Also, right triangle *OAC* has been formed. *AC* equals ¹⁄₂₄ foot. *OA* equals one-half the length of the ship, which we notate as *L/2*. The angles *GMG'* and *COA* are both equal to theta *(θ)*.

From trigonometry:

$$\tan \theta = \frac{GG'}{GM} \tag{9}$$

$$GG' = \tan \theta \times GM \tag{10}$$

Also:

$$\tan \theta = \frac{1/24}{L/2} \tag{11}$$

From equation 3:

$$GG' = \frac{W \times D}{\Delta} \tag{12}$$

Solving for $W \times D$ (our trimming moment):

$$W \times D = GG' \times \Delta \tag{13}$$

Setting the right-hand sides of equations 9 and 11 equal to each other and solving for GG':

$$GG' = \frac{GM}{12L} \tag{14}$$

Substituting the right-hand member of equation 14 in 13, we have:

$$W \times D = \frac{GM \times \Delta}{12L}$$

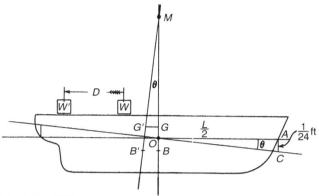

Figure 3-12. Calculating *MT*1.

Because $W \times D$ produced a change of trim of 1 inch and by definition *MT*1 is the notation used for this particular moment, we substitute *MT*1 for $W \times D$ and obtain:

$$MT1 = \frac{GM \times \Delta}{12L} \tag{15}$$

CHANGING DRAFT AT ONE END OF VESSEL ONLY

The application of the principles of trim calculation to determine where a given weight should be loaded on a ship so that no change in draft will occur at one end of the ship may prove useful to the ship's officer. If the weight, *W*, is known and the T.P.I. is known, the mean sinkage is obtained by dividing *W* by T.P.I. Let us suppose that we wish to load *W* so that no change will occur in the present draft aft. It is immediately clear that we must load the weight at some point forward of the tipping center. It must be loaded so that the change of *draft* aft is equal to the mean sinkage due to loading the weight. The change of draft is considered equal to ½ the change of trim; therefore, the change of trim obtained as a result of loading this weight must be equal to twice the mean sinkage. Now we have two formulas that we combine and then solve for the distance, *D*, that the weight must be from the tipping center.

$$\frac{W}{T.\,P.\,I.} = \text{Mean sinkage}$$

However, we have said that mean sinkage must be removed from the draft aft in order not to have any change aft. In other words, the change of trim must be equal to twice the mean sinkage or 2W/T.P.I. From equation 8 we have:

$$\frac{W \times D}{MT1} = \text{Change of Trim}$$

Knowing that our change of trim must be equal to 2W/T.P.I., we substitute in the above equation:

$$\frac{W \times D}{MT\,1} = \frac{2W}{\text{T.P. I.}}$$

Solving for D:

$$D = \frac{2 \times MT1}{\text{T.P.I.}} \tag{16}$$

NUMERICAL EXAMPLE

Given: A ship with the following drafts must load 200 tons: Drafts forward, 19 feet 0 inches; aft, 19 feet 6 inches; mean, 19 feet 3 inches. $MT1$ is 1,400. T.P.I. is 50.

Required: Where shall the weight be loaded so that there will be no change aft?

Solution: Using equation 16:

$$D = \frac{2 \times 1,400}{50}$$

$$D = 56 \text{ ft forward of the tipping center}$$

If this problem is stated without mentioning the weight involved, the solution is the same with the exception that the weight may be found by knowing the mean sinkage required and the T.P.I. For example, supposing the problem had asked for the position and the amount of the weight needed to give the ship an even trim with a mean draft equal to the present maximum draft. The present mean draft is 19 feet 3 inches, and the problem states that it must be 19 feet 6 inches when the weight is loaded. Therefore, the mean sinkage must be 3 inches. Now, from our equation for mean sinkage:

$$\frac{W}{\text{T.P.I.}} = \text{Mean sinkage}$$

we have:

$$W = \text{T.P.I.} \times \text{Mean sinkage}$$

$$W = 50 \times 3$$

$$W = 150 \text{ tons}$$

Thus, we know the weight required; the solution for the remaining part of the required data is the same as in the first problem. The final draft in the second problem would be: forward, 19 feet 6 inches; aft, 19 feet 6 inches; mean, 19 feet 6 inches.

Calculating Trim with Large Changes of Displacement

When a ship is laid out during the planning stage of the cargo operation, the weights should be so distributed longitudinally that the final trim will be within an acceptable range. The methods of calculating trim and changes of trim discussed above have assumed that comparatively small parts of the ship's total cargo capacity were being used; therefore, small changes in displacement were envisioned. When loading a complete or even a half or quarter shipload, there will be a large change in displacement. A large change in displacement makes it very important that the correct *MT*1 and tipping center be used. T.P.I. will not be used for finding mean sinkage. Mean sinkage is determined accurately only by finding on a deadweight scale the correct drafts for the different dead weights involved.

First Method: Moments about the Tipping Center

Two methods may be used to calculate the trim when large changes of displacement are involved. The first method is based on the concepts already discussed. Care must be used to choose the *MT*1 for the final condition and the average position of the tipping center between the initial and final condition. In this first method, the trimming moments are taken about the tipping center.

Table 3-1 is a form that may be used to record the data when loading a large number of weights throughout the ship so that the net effect of all the trimming moments can be calculated. The first question that arises in the use of this form when determining the moments about the tipping center involves the position of the tipping center. The tipping center is constantly changing its position. The best that can be done is to pick the tipping center for the average position. It must be pointed out that the geometrical centers of all compartments and tanks must be known relative to the mid ship section. The centers of such compartments and tanks must then be computed relative to the tipping center that has been calculated.

The T.P.I. is not used to determine the final mean draft. Using a mean T.P.I. would introduce a large error into the calculations. The mean sinkage is determined by referring to the deadweight scale, as mentioned above.

The final *MT*1 value must be used. This is obvious because it has already been pointed out that we assume all the weight to be loaded over the position of the mean tipping center first. After calculating the effect on mean sinkage, we imagine the weight is shifted so as to produce the trim. The reader should study the elements of the solution of the problem represented by Figure 3-13a.

TABLE 3-1
Form for Calculation of Change in Trim about Tipping Center (T.C.)*

Compartment	Weight, tons	Distance from Amidships, ft	Distance Fwd. of T.C., ft	Distance Aft of T.C., ft	Trimming Moments	
					Fwd., ft-tons	Aft, ft-tons
		(This fact is needed because T.C. position is given from the midship section of the ship as a reference line.)				

Total weight ———   Total trimming moments: Fwd. ——— Aft.———

$$\frac{\text{Net trimming moments either fwd. or aft}}{Final\ MT1} = \text{Change of trim}$$

Final $MT1$ = ———
Mean position of $T.C.$ = ———

* With large changes of displacement, use dead weight scale to obtain *final* mean draft. Apply this to original condition and then apply change of trim to obtain *final conditions.*

Second Method: Moments about Longitudinal B.

A more accurate and more commonly used method of calculating trim involving large changes of displacement will be explained next. Before attempting this explanation, however, the reader is reminded that all of the previous methods involving trim considered moments about the tipping center, or longitudinal center of flotation, of the ship. However, it was stated at the beginning of the discussion on trim that trimming moments may be considered also to act about the center of buoyancy. In the first method, we considered the total weight involved as acting through a distance from the tipping center. In this second method, we consider the weight as causing a shift of G. This shift of G creates the trimming lever GG' as illustrated in Figure 3-13b. The weight acting through the distance GG' is the *displacement* of the ship, and, thus, the *trimming moment* is formed. Figure 3-13 shows two diagrams. Diagram a points out the trimming moment of the first method. Diagram b points out the trimming moment of the second method. The reader should not proceed without a clear understanding of these points.

The second method requires that the final longitudinal position of G be calculated along the same lines as the vertical position of G was calculated in the study of transverse stability. From hydrostatic curves or suitable tables, the longitudinal position of B is obtained for the condition of even keel. The distance of G from B is the trimming lever, and the weight involved in the trimming moment is the displacement. Once we have the trimming moment, we simply divide by the $MT1$, as before, to obtain the change of trim.

Inasmuch as the longitudinal position of G must be calculated, it is obvious that the location of the geometrical center of every cargo compartment and tank must be known with reference to some longitudinal point. The midship section can be used as the reference point, but if this is done, it is necessary to bring plus and minus quantities into the calculations that unnecessarily complicate the solution. It is recommended that either the forward or after perpendicular be chosen as the reference point.

Change of Trim with Second Method and Partial Loads

The second method of calculating trim may be used for calculating change in trim for partial loads as well as the first method. Suppose a ship capable of lifting 10,000 tons deadweight has all but 3,000 of those tons on board, and the problem is to plan the loading of the last 3,000 tons so that a suitable trim is obtained. The procedure is the same as that for starting with a light ship except that the longitudinal positions of B and G must be determined in a different manner. If the ship is on an even keel, the location of B can be determined by looking it up on suitable tables or from the hydrostatic curves for the ship. However, if the ship has a trim by the head or stern, the location of B (and therefore of G also) is obtained by using the equation for determining the change of trim by the second method. We have:

$$\frac{GG' \times \Delta}{MT\,1} = \text{Change of trim}$$

Solving for GG':

$$GG' = \frac{MT1 \times \text{Change of trim}}{\Delta}$$

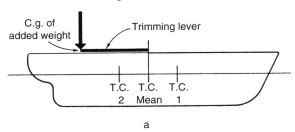

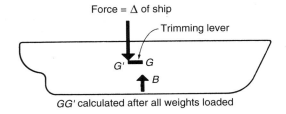

GG' calculated after all weights loaded

Figure 3-13. Calculating trim.

All of the factors in the right-hand term are known. The value of GG' is applied to the position of B as if the ship had been on an even keel at the mean draft. B must be either forward of or aft of the latter position, depending on whether the ship has a trim by the head or stern, respectively. The distance that it is forward or aft will be equal to GG'.

A record of the distances forward and aft of G' at which the 3,000 tons are disposed is kept, and the final position of G' (call it G'') is calculated. Thus $G'G''$ becomes the trimming lever, and the weight involved is the final displacement. The change of trim and final draft are determined as outlined previously.

The Use of Trimming Tables

Trimming tables are generally found below the profile view of the ship on the capacity plan. The tables are constructed to show the change in *draft* forward and aft when a weight of 100 tons is placed on the vessel. The effects on the drafts forward and aft can be determined by looking in the box directly below the point on the ship where the weight is placed. If the weight being considered is more than or less than 100 tons, the effect is increased or decreased proportionately. For example, if a 300-ton weight is loaded, the figures in the boxes are multiplied by 3.

In each box there is a plus or minus sign. These signs indicated how the values in the boxes are to be applied to the initial draft figures. These signs are for a loading process. Therefore, if the weight is discharged, the signs must be reversed. The changes in draft in the boxes take into consideration the change in mean draft due to mean sinkage.

Because the $MT1$ changes with draft, a set of numbers for each draft in increments of 1 foot would be better than for just the two drafts illustrated. It will be noted that the two drafts are 10 feet apart. This makes it possible to interpolate in calculating the change in drafts for a mean draft lying in between or slightly beyond the two drafts listed. Choosing the table for the nearest draft generally yields sufficient accuracy for most operating conditions.

LONGITUDINAL STRESSES

The following discussion is not intended to be a thorough presentation of the involved subject of strength calculations as applied to the hull of a ship. A summation of the elements of the problem and their relationship to the responsibilities of the ship's officer is our prime objective. It is hoped that the discussion will also clarify the approach to the problem that the ship's officer should take.

THE STRENGTH EQUATION

Let us say that we have the problem of determining the stress in pounds per square inch on a ship's deck or bottom under a given set of conditions, wherein the type of sea that is running and the distribution of weight in the ship are specified.

Without deriving the equation here, we will accept the following mathematical statement as truth, for we need to use it in our solution of the above problem.

$$M = \frac{I}{y} \times p$$

where

M = the bending moment of the hull girder.

I = the moment of inertia of the hull girder.

y = the distance from the neutral axis of the hull girder to the most remote member of the hull girder.

p = a measure of the resistance offered by the material of which the hull girder is made; hence, it is given in units of stress, pounds per square inch.

The section modulus. The ratio of *I* to *y* is also known as the section modulus of the hull girder. It depends on the form and distribution of material in the construction of the hull girder. *I/y* may be notated as *S*. The section modulus of the ship is calculated by the naval architect, and if we are to have the necessary data to calculate the answer to the problem stated above, we must know *S* for the hull of the ship.

Bending Moment and Stress of Material

Two other factors remain in our equation: *M*, the bending moment of the hull under our specified conditions of sea and load, and *p*, the stress of the material. The latter is what we must find ultimately; hence, our discussion will not revolve around the problem of determining *M* in our equation.

Finding the Bending Moment

The first step is to determine the weight of the ship per linear foot starting from one end of the vessel. This is the weight in tons of each foot of length and includes the weight of the ship's structure and all the deadweight items aboard her, such as cargo, fuel, water, and stores. This is a difficult task.

The next step is to calculate the buoyancy of the ship per linear foot of length. This is a relatively easy task. All that must be done to obtain the buoyancy of a linear foot is to calculate the volume of the underwater portion of the hull for a 1-foot slice longitudinally and divide by 35. At this point, let us note that *total* weight must always equal the *total* buoyancy; however, the weight at any one point may exceed or be less than the force of buoyancy acting on that point of the hull.

Let us consider a single slice of the hull as illustrated in Figure 3-14. If the force of buoyancy on this particular slice exceeds the weight or vice versa, the edges of the slice will experience a shearing stress. If the next and each

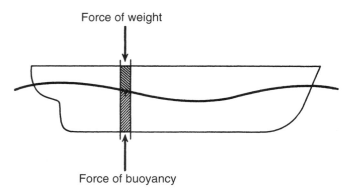

Figure 3-14. If a particular slice of the ship's hull is considered, as indicated, it becomes obvious that unless the weight and buoyancy forces are equal, this slice is resisting a shearing stress tending to push it upward or downward. The ship profile is depicted as floating in a trochoidal curve with a height $\frac{1}{20}$ of the ship's length; the naval architect defines this as a *standard sea.*

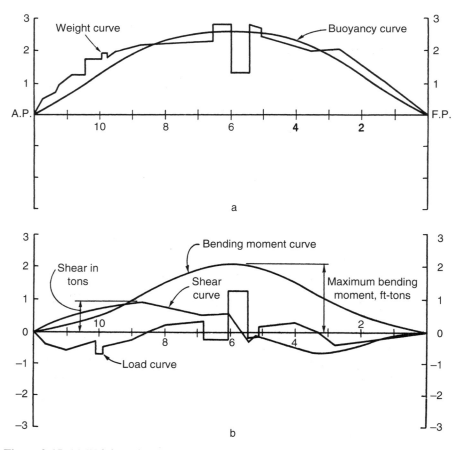

Figure 3-15. (a) Weight and buoyancy curve. **(b)** Load and shear curve.

succeeding slice experience this shearing stress, a force acting through a distance exerts itself on the hull of the ship. A force acting through a distance is termed a moment, and in this case it is called a *bending moment* because as the hull girder resists the force, it bends. If the shearing stress is large or acts over a considerable distance, the bending moment will be large.

THE STRENGTH CURVES

The buoyancy and weight in tons per linear foot are plotted as curves as shown in Figure 3-15a. Next, the difference between the weight and buoyancy values at every point is plotted. An excess of weight is assigned a negative value and plotted below the base line; an excess of buoyancy is assigned a positive value and plotted above the base line. The curve resulting from this plot is known as the load curve, and is shown in Figure 3-15b. The total area under it (counting area below the base line as negative area) should be equal to zero.

Next, the integral of the load curve, called the shear curve, is plotted (see Fig. 3-15b). Finally, the integral of the shear curve, called the *bending moment curve,* is plotted (see Fig. 3-15b).

All of the curves shown in Figure 3-15 are simply for purposes of illustration. The conditions depicted parallel those of a ship in still water. The strength curves for a ship in a standard wave with crest amidships would have more buoyancy amidships and less at the ends. Conversely, if the ship were in a wave with the trough amidships, the buoyancy would be reduced amidships and be increased at the ends. The weight curve would, of course, remain the same, unless the load conditions on the ship were changed.

The abscissas on all five curves are in units of length. The ordinates on the weight and buoyancy curves are in units of tons per linear foot. The ordinates on the shear and load curves are in tons, and the ordinate of the bending moment curve is in units of foot-tons.

Going through this process, the maximum bending moment as well as the bending moment at any given point may be obtained. With this value, the stress, tension, and compression on the hull bottom and deck plating can be calculated, providing we know the section modulus, because:

$$P = \frac{M}{S}$$

where

M = the bending moment, which we have calculated.

S = the section modulus for the hull, which we must obtain from the design naval architect.

The naval architect specifies structural members for all decks and other parts of the hull to withstand the tension and compression stresses that are found to exist in them when the ship is placed in a standard sea under a standard load condition. This is done for both a hogging and a sagging condition.

Standard Sea and Standard Load

The standard sea is one in which the height is $1/20^{th}$ the length of the ship and in the form of a trochoidal curve. For a hogging condition, the crest of the sea is assumed to be amidships. The buoyancy amidships would then be at a maximum. For a sagging condition, the trough of the sea is assumed to be amidships. The buoyancy would then be at a minimum amidships.

The standard load for a ship with machinery spaces amidships assumes the midship tanks to be empty, the end tanks full, and all cargo compartments full. This is a poor loading pattern for such a ship, for it results in an initial hogging tendency.

The standard load for a ship with machinery spaces aft assumes the cargo spaces to be full and the end tanks empty. This will create an initial sagging tendency in such a vessel.

Obviously, the load and the sea can be exaggerated so as to produce excessive stresses; however, the naval architect does not design the ship to withstand the worst possible conditions, but rather what might be termed "reasonably bad" conditions. Then a suitable safety factor is worked into the calculations for determining the final scantlings used to construct the ship.

It should be apparent that if the ship is loaded with an extreme concentration of weight in the center hatches or in the end hatches and subsequently the ship meets with extremely heavy seas, the stresses on the hull girder will become dangerously high.

The Beam Theory

We have been referring to the hull of the ship as a beam or girder. The ship is really a complicated built-up shape, and much of the theory of stresses on the hull is based on the assumption that hull stresses are quite similar to beam stresses. The experience of naval architects has proved that this assumption is a reasonable one. Figure 3-16a illustrates a beam heavily loaded on its midlength. This parallels a ship in the sagging condition. Note that the steel of the upper decks is under a compression stress, and the bottom is under tension. Figure 3-16b illustrates a beam supported at its midlength and loaded on its ends. This parallels a ship's hull in the hogging condition. Note that the steel of the upper decks is under tension stresses, and the bottom is under compression. If these tension or compression stresses become greater than the ship is designed to withstand, the plating will fail. Under tension, the plating will crack or tear apart. Under compression, the plating will buckle.

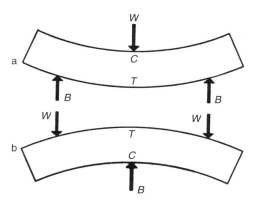

Figure 3-16. The beam theory: W = excess of weight; B = excess of buoyancy; C = steel in this area under compression; T = steel in this area under tension.

PRACTICAL APPROACH TO THE PROBLEM

The ship's officer must make certain that his/her ship is never loaded in such a fashion that extreme hogging or sagging will occur. In actual practice, however, it is difficult for the ship's officer to obtain data to make calculations concerning the bending moments of the vessel as she sails each voyage. What, then, should be the practice to remove this "blank spot" in the average ship's officer in his/her knowledge of his/her ship? Three solutions are set forth below:

1. The shipowner should see that every ship is supplied with necessary data, such as strength curves, section modulus, geometrical locations of all spaces, and other information, to facilitate the calculations of bending moments and possibly the stresses. Then, instructions in how to use the data should be provided where necessary. All ship's officers should then prepare tabular methods of calculating the hogging and sagging moments under conditions of loading for each voyage. With the proper data and background, any ship's officer can make up a similar set of tables and diagrams to work out the hogging and sagging tendencies for his/her particular ship. If a tabular method has been devised for the ship upon which he/she is sailing, the ship's officer should work with it until he/she is thoroughly acquainted with it. Then he/she should use it consistently. The hogging and sagging tendencies of his/her ship in waves of standard proportions should become as familiar to the ship's officer as the sailing drafts of his/her ship.

2. If his/her ship is equipped with a mechanical device for the calculation of hogging and sagging bending moments, the ship's officer should be thoroughly familiar with its use and the significance of the data it provides him.

3. If his/her ship is equipped with an onboard computer that monitors enough stress points, the ship's officer should be very familiar with the instructions for

operation and should correlate the findings with those of tabular and mechanical devices, if available. In addition, a correlation can be made in port before sailing by observing the drafts fore, aft, and mean. All vessels should be inscribed with midships draft marks to facilitate verification of these measurements.

Approximating the Longitudinal Distribution

If the time, the data, or the materials to take advantage of any of the previously mentioned suggestions are lacking, an estimation of correct longitudinal distribution for ships with their engine room spaces amidships can be made. The method is based on the same premise as is the method for roughly estimating the vertical distribution. The amount of weight that should be placed in each longitudinal compartment is equal to the ratio of the cubic of that compartment to the cubic of all the cargo compartments. This may be expressed by the following equation:

$$\frac{v}{V} \times T = t$$

where

   v = the volume of the compartment in question.

   V = the volume of all cargo compartments.

   T = the total weight to be loaded.

   t = the weight to be loaded in the compartment in question.

Caution must be exercised when using such a method. If used for ships with the engine room spaces aft, it would lead to excessive sagging moments.

Onboard Computers

Onboard computers such as the LOADMAX 200 (see Fig. 3-17) compute all stability and trim calculations. In addition, stress points are monitored on the vessel and indicators show where limits are exceeded. There is also a graphic display of shear force/bending moment. Data is entered via a keyboard, and most onboard computers have a printer so that a permanent record may be obtained. Thus, a history of various loadings plus figures for the most optimal load may be maintained.

Checking on the Hull Deflection

Simply noting where the actual waterline amidships is as compared to the true mean draft affords a check on the amount that the hull is deflected. Draft marks amidships are found on many bulk carriers; therefore a check on the waterline's

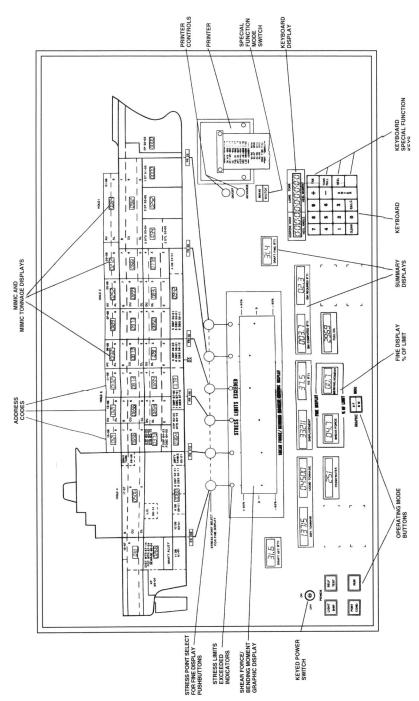

Figure 3-17. Typical onboard computer. *Courtesy Raytheon.*

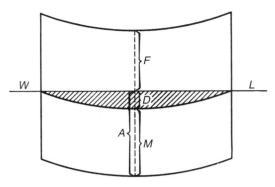

Figure 3-18. Sagging condition.

position can be made by inspection from the dock. A practical check on hull deflection for all ships may be made by subtracting the mean draft amidships from the hull's depth to obtain the freeboard. Next, a plumb line is prepared to equal the freeboard in length. With the upper end of the plumb bob at the statutory deck line, the position of the lower end is noted. If the lower end of the plumb line is in the water, the ship is sagged. The amount of the deflection is equal to the difference between the actual freeboard and the calculated freeboard. It can be determined by noting the number of inches the line must be shortened to make the plumb bob level with the waterline. This should be done on both sides of the ship, using the mean of the data received. The ship is hogged, in the above test, if the end of the plumb line is out of the water.

Figure 3-18 is a diagram of a barge in a sagging condition. Observe that the vessel is floating on an even keel with waterline WL. If we read the drafts forward and aft and divide by 2, we obtain a mean draft equal to M. The draft amidships is equal to A because of the sagging condition. In the method outlined above for checking on hull deflection, our plumb bob would be immersed in the water to the depth of D. If the plumb bob were this distance above the waterline, the hull deflection would be due to hogging.

NUMERICAL EXAMPLE

Given: A tanker has the following drafts: forward, 13 feet 0 inches; aft, 18 feet 0 inches. The depth of the ship is 40 feet. After measuring the freeboard on both sides of the ship and taking the average, the mate arrives at a figure of 24 feet 0 inches.

Required: Is the ship hogged or sagged? If so, how much?

Solution: The mean draft *amidships* is equal to 15 feet 6 inches; therefore, the freeboard amidships should be 24 feet 6 inches, providing no hull deflection exists. But, the actual freeboard is 6 inches less than it should be, so we conclude that the ship is sagging 6 inches.

Correction for Density

When a ship is floating in water that is brackish, another correction to the displacement as read from the deadweight scale must be made. This is called the *correction for density* and is necessary because the deadweight scale is prepared assuming the ship is floating in salt water. The correction amounts to the displacement as read from the deadweight scale multiplied by the difference between the specific gravity of the water in which the ship is floating at the time of reading the drafts and the specific gravity of sea water, which is taken as 1.026. This can be expressed in the following equation:

$$c = \Delta \times (\text{S.G.}_1 - \text{S.G.}_2)$$

where

c = the correction in tons.

S.G._1 = specific gravity of sea water (1.026).

S.G._2 = specific gravity of the water in which the ship is floating.

Δ = displacement as read from the deadweight scale using the true mean draft.

The density correction is always subtractive.

Obviously, the ship must be equipped with a suitable hydrometer for measuring the density of the water in which the ship is floating.

Draft correction for density. Because of the difference in density between pure sea water and fresh or brackish water, the ship's mean draft will change when going from one to the other. This change in draft or correction may be found by a number of equations.

To obtain the fresh water draft if the salt water draft is known, multiply the latter by the ratio 36/35. If the fresh water draft is known, the salt water draft can be found by multiplying the fresh water draft by 35/36. The results will be approximate, but accurate enough for most practical purposes; 35 ft³ of salt water weighs 1 long ton and 36 ft³ of freshwater weighs 1 long ton (approximately); hence the source of this useful ratio.

A general equation based on the specific gravity differences and the T.P.I. concept is as follows:

$$c = \frac{\Delta \times \text{Difference in specific gravity}}{\text{T.P.I.}}$$

From this equation, assuming a specific gravity of 1.026 for salt water and 1.00 for freshwater, an equation for the difference in draft between fresh and salt water is:

$$c = \frac{\Delta}{40 \text{ T.P.I.}}$$

where

Δ = displacement in tons.

c = difference in draft in inches.

T.P.I. = tons per inch immersion.

Concentration of Weights

The weights may be distributed transversely, vertically, and longitudinally so that no damage can be caused to the ship, yet there remains one aspect of the problem of handling weight distribution on the ship that has not been discussed. This is the problem of loading weights so that the total weight on any deck, or part of any deck, is not so great that damage will be done to the ship structure.

Deck Load Capacities

The deck load capacities of all decks of the ship must be known if a decision is to be made concerning this problem. The deck load capacities are given on most capacity plans. If they are not recorded there, the ship's officer should make every effort to find these values and place them on the plan. The data are given in pounds per square foot and may be defined as the average load that the deck can support. This does not mean that if the deck load capacity is exceeded on any single square foot, the deck will fail to support it. It is a figure that can be used to determine the design load of the deck of a given compartment or part of a compartment. For example, the deck load capacity of the weather deck of the average merchant ship is on the order of 350 lb/ft². This means that if a heavy lift is being loaded on deck that has a base 100 ft² in area, the left could weigh as much as 35,000 pounds without endangering the structure. In other words, divide the area over which the load will be spread into the number of pounds in the load; if the result is equal to or less than the deck load capacity, there is no reason for shoring up. If the result is greater than the deck load capacity, shoring up under the deck may be necessary.

Although the foregoing indicates that only the area over which the load is actually resting should be used in determining the deck load, this allows for a considerable margin of safety. The load is distributed over an unknown area extending out beyond the precise limits of the container. Some engineering data suggest that it is safe to assume that the supporting area extends out from the container one-half its length and breadth all around. Thus the area that contributes to the support of the land is four times the area of the base of the container. Obviously, this assumption will lead to trouble when carrying loads that extend over very large areas of the deck, such as over the entire beam of the ship. The assumption may be used with caution, however, when considering single small containers.

NUMERICAL EXAMPLE

Given: A vessel has a number 4 lower hold deck capacity of 528 lb/ft².

Required: Could you load 100 tons of boiler plate that covers an area of 8 feet by 40 feet?

Solution:

$$\text{lb/ft}^2 = \frac{\text{tons} \times 2{,}240 \text{ lb/ton}}{W \times L \text{ (area)}} = \frac{100 \times 2{,}240}{8 \times 40} = 700 \text{ lb/ft}^2$$

Therefore, the answer is no, unless dunnage is used to distribute the weight over a larger area.

HEIGHT LIMITATION

When loading small dense units of cargo, such as steel billets, lead ingots, or tin plate, the height of the stowed cargo block must be limited. If such cargo is loaded too high, the deck load capacity will be exceeded and the ship structure will be damaged.

Two things must be known to calculate the height in feet up to which it is safe to load any given cargo. First, the deck load capacity must be known. Second, the stowage factor of the cargo must be known. The stowage factor is defined as the number of cubic feet required to stow one long ton of the cargo without any broken stowage. Knowing these values, the following equation may be used:

$$h = \frac{c \pm f}{2{,}240}$$

where

h = the maximum height to load the cargo.

c = deck load capacity.

f = the cargo's stowage factor.

2,240 = the number of pounds in 1 long ton.

NUMERICAL EXAMPLE

Given: A stowage factor of 14 and a number 4 lower hold deck capacity of 528 lb/ft².

Required: How high can railroad steel be loaded?

Solution:

$$h = \frac{c \times f}{2,240} = \frac{528 \times 14}{2,240} = 3.3 \text{ ft}$$

Utilizing Free Space over Dense Cargo

Obviously, if the cargo is very dense it cannot be stowed very high. Cargo with a stowage factor in the order of 10 can be stowed only 2 or 3 feet high in 'tweendeck areas, whereas in the lower hold the height will be limited to about 7 feet. This leaves several feet of free space over such cargoes that cannot be used if the dense cargo is stowed to the limit of the deck load capacity. We therefore violate our third principle of stowage in that we do not obtain maximum utilization of all available cubic.

When two cargoes are available, one with a very low stowage factor and the other with a high stowage factor, it may be desirable to limit the height of the heavy cargo below the full limit of the deck so that the free space on top can be filled with the lighter cargo. If general cargo is to be stowed over such heavy concentrated cargo, an average stowage factor may be estimated and the height of the dense cargo limited accordingly.

CALCULATING THE HEIGHT LIMIT OF DENSE CARGO

WHEN OVERSTOWING WITH LIGHT CARGO

We consider a column 1 foot square and equal in height to the cargo compartment. This column must be filled with a mixture of light and heavy cargo such that its total weight equals the deck load capacity of the compartment. Note that the cubic capacity of this column is equal to the height of the compartment. Hence, we have a problem somewhat similar to the full and down loading problem.

In this problem, we may work with densities or stowage factors. In the general solution that follows and the numerical example, densities are used because the values are considered easier to work with. Our problem is to determine the number of cubic feet that each cargo type must occupy out of the total cubic in the 1 ft² column. This number of cubic feet is also the height of each cargo type needed to fill the space and use up all the deck load capacity.

Deriving a general solution

Let

a = density of light cargo.

b = density of heavy cargo.

h = number of cubic feet in a 1 ft² column in the compartment.

c = deck load capacity in lbs/ft².

x = cubic feet of light cargo in the column h.

y = cubic feet of heavy cargo in the column h.

Then

$$x + y = h \qquad (17)$$

and

$$ax + by = c \qquad (18)$$

$$a \times (x + y = h) = (-) \, ax + ay = ah \qquad (19)$$

$$by - ay = c - ah$$

$$y = \frac{c - ah}{b - a} .$$

$$x = h - y$$

But since column h is 1 foot square, x and y may also be read as units of height alone.

NUMERICAL EXAMPLE

Given: Steel billets with a stowage factor of 12 are to be stowed in a compartment 12 feet high with a deck load capacity of 400 lb/ft². General cargo with an average stowage factor estimated at 160 is to be stowed over the steel.

Required: How high should the steel be tiered to allow the free space over the steel to be filled with the general cargo and not exceed the deck load capacity?

Solution: First solve for the density of the steel billets and the general cargo.

2,240/12 = 186 lb/ft³ = density of the steel

2,240/160 = 14 lb/ft³ = density of the general cargo

Let x = cubic feet of general cargo and y = cubic feet of steel. Then:

$$x + y = 12$$

$$14x + 186y = 400$$
$$\underline{(-)14x\,(-)\,14y = (-)168}$$
$$172y = 232$$

$y = 1.35$ ft³ steel

$x = 10.65$ ft³ general cargo

Therefore, the steel should be tiered 1.35 feet high and the general cargo 10.65 feet high.

Stowage Principle 2: Protecting The Cargo

The first objective and principle of good stowage have been thoroughly discussed and it should be apparent that to meet these, a ship's officer must *know his/her ship*. The second objective and principle objective of good stowage can be met fully only by officers who *know their cargo*. Knowing your ship is an easier task than knowing your cargo. In the first body of knowledge there are certain fundamental, unchanging, and consistent principles of mathematics and physics to be mastered. This takes a little time and effort, but once understood there is an end to the required effort for practical operating purposes. In the second body of knowledge, many of the factors involved change from shipping route to shipping route and even from ship to ship. The problems may vary from time to time on the same ship. The ship's officer, to know his/her cargo, must always be alert to the changing commodities received on board. Changing commodities bring new problems, and it is an absolute necessity continually to seek empirical information to know what is permissible.

To know what is the *best* thing to do under a given set of conditions is not always possible; in some cases the true answer to a question may not be known by anyone. There is no organized program of research to determine the exact answers to many of the problems met within practical cargo operations. Each ship is a laboratory of a sorts, but the facts that emerge from company investigations of poor out-turns of cargoes are not publicized through any medium; indeed, in some cases the facts are guarded with great care. The most skillful cargo officers are those with years of worthy experience and gifted with good judgment. But the best experience and the best judgment will pay higher dividends if backed with a good foundation of facts gained from the experience and the judgment of those who have passed the same way before.

SEGREGATION OF CARGO

One of the fundamental requirements in the protection of the cargo is the proper segregation of the various types. This also is one of the most difficult requisites to meet when carrying full loads of general cargoes. (It offers almost no problems on ships carrying only one or two items,)

Segregation refers to the stowage of cargoes in separate parts of the ship so that one cannot damage the other because of its inherent characteristics. Wet cargoes must be kept away from dry cargoes. Generally, certain areas of the ship will be specified for the stowage of wet items when the ship is laid out during the planning stage of the cargo operation. In the same way, other areas will be specified for dry, dirty or clean cargoes. Although segregation is called for in the case of odorous and delicate cargoes, special sections are not specified for their stowage. Each time the ship is laid out, care must be taken not to make a gross error in this respect. Segregation of light and heavy cargoes is necessary with respect to their vertical positions. Heavy items must always be given bottom stowage in any compartment. Refrigerated cargoes must be given stowage in spaces especially equipped to handle them, and segregation among items under this single category must also be given attention. Finally, the stowage of any dangerous cargoes must be in strict accordance with the segregation required by the provisions of the regulations issued by the U.S. Coast Guard, the Department of Transportation, and the International Maritime Organization (IMO).

Wet cargo, as used in this discussion, refers to items that are liquid but in containers. With such cargo comes the possibility of leakage, and the stowage should be such that in case of any leakage the liquid will find its way to the drainage system without damaging any other cargo. Wet cargo does not refer to bulk liquid commodities; the latter requires obvious special stowage in deep tanks. Examples of wet cargoes are canned milk, beer, fruit juices, paints, lubricating oil, and so on.

Dry cargo refers to the general class of items that cannot possibly leak and furthermore can be damaged by leakage from the wet cargo. This category includes flour, feed, rice, paper products, and many more items.

Dirty cargoes are those commodities that are exceptionally dusty and always tend to leave a residue behind them. The residue, of course, will contaminate other cargoes. Examples are cement, antimony ore, charcoal, and lamp black.

Clean cargoes are those that leave no residue, are not likely to leak, and generally will not cause any damage to any other cargo, but are themselves highly vulnerable to contamination.

Odorous cargoes are those commodities that give off fumes that are likely to *taint* certain susceptible cargoes if they are stowed in the same or even in adjacent compartments. Examples are kerosene, turpentine, ammonia, greasy wool, crude rubber, lumber, and casein. Some odorous cargoes may taint more delicate cargoes and yet are susceptible to tainting themselves.

Delicate cargoes are those that are highly susceptible to damage by tainting from the odorous types. Examples are rice, flour, tea, and cereals.

Fragile cargoes are those commodities that are susceptible to breakage. Examples are glass, porcelain, and marble.

Hygroscopic cargoes are cargoes that have the ability to absorb or release water vapor. Examples are all grains, wood products, cotton, wool, sisal, jute, paper, and other products of an animal or vegetable origin.

To discuss segregation thoroughly, a discussion of commodities is necessary. A worthwhile coverage of the subject of commodities cannot be undertaken in this book. The intention here has been to point out the necessity of giving segregation the serious consideration it warrants when planning the stowage. The ability to adjudge correctly whether cargoes need segregation comes only with experience. It is also necessary to consider the fact that cargoes may possess several inherent characteristics and may, for example, be classified as not only dry but also delicate and clean.

DUNNAGING

A second requirement in the stowage of cargo so as to protect it is the correct use of dunnage. The word dunnage as it is used in relation to modem cargo stowage refers to the wood that is used to protect the cargo. The common dunnage board is a 1- by 6-inch piece with a length of 10 to 12 feet. The lumber used for dunnage is classed technically as number 4 or 5 stock in the board or rough merchandise grades. For special uses such as when stowing heavy lifts or steel products, heavier lumber is used, such as 2- by 10-inch deals, 6- by 8-inch timbers, or split pieces of cord wood. Refrigerated cargoes require strips of common building lath as dunnage, which measure ⅜ by 1½ by 48 inches. In all cases, the dunnage should be dry and clean. Dunnage that has been contaminated by previous cargo or is wet from any cause should not be used. If it is badly contaminated, it should be discarded. Once wetted by salt water, its use may cause more damage than can be justified by any savings made by attempting to salvage it. Green wood is a very poor risk for use as dunnage.

TYPE OF WOOD

For some uses, it makes little difference what type of wood is used. For example, any wood can be used if the dunnage is to be used in stowing steel rails or providing drainage under bags of antimony ore. However, for dunnaging sugar, hides, marble, and certain other commodities, only well-seasoned dry, clean pine, spruce, or fir should be used. If oak, redwood, or mahogany is used with the latter group of commodities, staining will result. Generally, it is poor practice to accept anything but dry clean pine, spruce, or fir, because the dunnage is used for various cargoes and the operation cannot depend on what type of dunnage is in the hold. As the cost of lumber increases, more use is being made of plywood. Regardless of the type or quality, the wood, especially cheaper grades, must be inspected to insure it is dry and unstained.

AMOUNT OF DUNNAGE ON THE SHIP

The average general cargo carrier requires approximately 100,000 board feet of dunnage, which will weigh about 150 tons. Depending entirely on the type of cargo being stowed, the amount specified above may be increased or decreased by 25%. In some cases, the amount of dunnage may be much less than 75,000 board feet, but it will rarely be over 125,000. The average general carrier requires replenishment of her dunnage to the amount of about 25,000 board feet after each voyage because of the need for condemnation of part of the supply during the voyage. Dunnage control should be regulated by the operations department and not left entirely up to each ship. Ship's officers should give dunnage (see Fig. 3-19) the same care as the cargo, for two reasons: First, the dunnage is stowed with the cargo, so that unless the dunnage is clean and dry the cargo will be damaged by it; second, the cost of dunnage wood has increased.

THE USE OF DUNNAGE

Dunnage is used to protect cargo by preventing:

1. Contact with free moisture.

2. Condensation.

3. Crushing.

4. Chafage.

5. Spontaneous heating.

6. Pilferage.

Dunnage is also used to facilitate rapid and systematic discharge. The following discussion will include an explanation of how each of the above six results are obtained through the use of dunnage.

Preventing Contact with Free Moisture

The term *free moisture* has been used in this category to eliminate confusion with damage caused in some instances by the transfer of hygroscopic moisture. No amount of dunnaging will prevent the latter type of trouble; the only effective means of preventing such damage in general cargo is by proper segregation.

Figure 3-19a. Bag stowage on a floor of dunnage three tiers high. One dunnage board has broken at a knot, seen in the lower right-hand corner. Before bags are stowed over this floor, this break in the floor should be made solid. Another interesting point in this view is the bag-on-bag stowage, which clearly shows the spaces left between the bags for ventilation purposes. Finally, the bags have "dog ears," which enable easy handling without the use of hooks.

Figure 3-19b. This dunnage is used to strike a level platform that will reduce crushing from uneven pressures.

Free moisture refers to water in the liquid form that might be present in a cargo hold as a result of a leak in the hull plating, an adjacent tank, deck, or openings into the hold or of heavy condensation. Also included in this category, insofar as dunnaging is concerned, is liquid from any wet cargo.

The first dunnage used in the stowing of most cargoes is used for this purpose. This is the dunnage laid on the deck upon which the first tier of cargo is stowed. To provide for drainage under the cargo, the first dunnage should be laid with the length toward the drainage system and spaced about 6 inches apart. There should be at least two tiers of dunnage, the bottom tier laid to provide the drainage and the top tier to support the cargo. Thus, on a modern ship with drain wells aft and running transversely, the first tier of dunnage would be laid fore and aft. The second tier should always be perpendicular to the first and may be spaced 2 or 3 inches apart. On ships with side bilge systems, the first dunnage laid in the lower holds should run diagonally, slanting aft from the centerline.

If bags are being stowed on top of such a floor, the dunnage should be spaced not more than 1 inch apart. Wide spacing of dunnage floors upon which bags are to be stowed results in the bottom bags being split and a heavy loss of contents through leakage. If the commodity in the bag requires ventilation, spacing the dunnage a little is advantageous. If the commodity does not require ventilation, the floor will be better if made solid.

Necessity for multiple layers of dunnage: When laying the bottom tier of dunnage where there is a high probability of drainage from some source, the number of tiers of dunnage running toward the drainage system should be increased. Five tiers may be laid with a sixth tier on top as a floor with some cargoes that need maximum circulation of air, as well as drainage. The ship's officer should not be timid about requiring that dunnage be laid correctly. *It is a basic requisite of proper care and custody,* and can prevent costly damage. Longshoremen the world over are very apt to lay dunnage floors in a slipshod and highly inadequate manner. Common deficiencies are laying it so that the best drainage is not provided, laying an insufficient number of tiers, and improper spacing. The ship's officer must be in the hold of the ship to prevent gross negligence in this initial step in stowing cargo.

Vertical dunnage: To prevent contact with steel members of the ship and thereby preclude the possibility of wetting with condensation, vertical dunnage is installed between the cargo and all steel members. The members referred to are the stanchions, frames, ladders, transverse bulkheads, partial longitudinal bulkheads, and ventilator shafts running through the space. This dunnage may be put into position by standing it up against the vertical member, and temporarily held in place by one container of cargo being stowed against the bottom. Another way is to stand the dunnage up in place and tie with rope yarn, then wrap heavy paper around the dunnage and member together and tie with more rope yarn. The rope yarn serves the purpose of holding the dunnage in place until the cargo is safely stowed.

The dunnage drainage floor and the vertical dunnage to separate the cargo and the steel members complete the dunnage used to prevent contact with free moisture.

Dunnage to Prevent Condensation

The dunnage that prevents condensation is the dunnage that is placed in the cargo to facilitate the circulation of air currents. It is by thorough ventilation that high-dew point air is removed from hold interiors, and this is necessary to prevent condensation. When laying the floor upon which to stow certain cargoes, such as fish meal in bags, deep tiering is utilized to help circulation under the cargo and thus remove moisture-laden air. Such floors may be five tiers deep with a sixth layer on top upon which to stow the cargo. Blocks of cargo may be separated vertically by laying crisscross dunnage separation at convenient intervals, normally about 5 feet. Venetian ventilators, which are made from dunnage wood, may be worked into some cargoes for ventilation purposes. The venetian vent is made with two pieces of dunnage measuring 1 by 6 inches and about 10 feet long. These two boards are separated by slanting pieces of lumber measuring about 1 by 2 inches and nailed to the side to form a support and separation for the two solid pieces and to form openings along the vent's entire length. Figure 3-20 is an illustration of a venetian ventilator. This type of fitting is used so frequently with rice cargoes that occasionally it is referred to as *a rice ventilator.*

Use of the Venetian vent or rice ventilator: The Venetian vent is inserted within bagged cargoes. At 5-foot intervals, the vents are laid longitudinally and transversely to form continuous air channels in both directions. Generally two longitudinal lines are laid running in the same vertical plane as the hatch carlings (fore and aft hatch coamings), and two transverse lines are laid in the same vertical plane as the hatch end beams. These four lines intersect at the four corners of the hatch, and at these points a vertical vent is fitted. This arrangement continues for the full depth of the cargo. When the cargo is stowed, such a system provides continuous internal movement of air and is an effective aid in the prevention of heavy condensation.

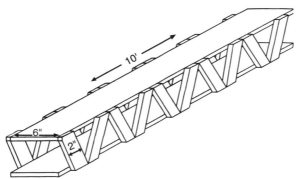

Figure 3-20.
A Venetian vent or rice
ventilator made out of dunnage.

If the ship is operating on a route where the outside temperatures may fluctuate between two extremes, or if the hatch is extremely long, the vents may be inserted at more frequent longitudinal and transverse intervals.

Sweat battens: The permanent dunnage attached to the frames of the ship is also an aid in ventilation. This dunnage is known as cargo battens or sweat battens and may be secured either vertically or horizontally. It is generally made of 2- by 6-inch lumber held in place by clips that are bolted to the inboard flange of the frame. The sweat battens prevent the cargo from filling up the frame spaces and hence these spaces are reserved to act as vertical air ducts.

Deep dunnage floors, crisscross dunnage floors, Venetian ventilators, and the sweat battens complete the dunnage used to prevent condensation.

Dunnage to Prevent Crushing

Dunnage that is used to prevent crushing of cargo is that which is placed in the hold to prevent the cargo from shifting, to spread weights evenly so that pressure is equalized on lower tiers in deep holds, and to maintain levels.

Eliminating voids: Cargo seldom fits exactly into a hold. When stowing athwartships, a void nearly always appears at either side or along the centerline of the ship into which no cargo will fit. It is a standard rule never to leave a void in a stowed cargo block; such voids must be filled with something. The best thing to place in such voids is cargo that is small and durable, known as *filler cargo.* However, if filler cargo is not available, dunnage must be used. The dunnage may be used to build up bracing between the two sides to prevent movement of the cargo, or dunnage may be piled directly into the void. The need for dunnage to fill in such voids often occurs in the wings of compartments where there is much curvature, such as the end lower holds. This dunnage is used for two reasons: first, for filling in the void; and second, for maintaining a level tier. Figure 3-21 illustrates such a use of dunnage. Filling voids is a precaution against shifting, which results in crushed cargo.

Toms, shores, and braces: Large pieces of cargo that stand alone and blocks of cargo that are not supported on one of their sides require shoring or bracing to prevent shifting and possible crushing.

Shoring is the process of using 6- by 8-inch timbers or similar pieces known as shores to secure cargo. The shore runs from a low supporting level *up* to the cargo at an angle.

Bracing is the process of using timbers to secure cargo by running the brace horizontally from a support to the cargo. The timbers used for this purpose are known as braces or, more correctly, as *distance pieces.*

Figure 3-21. Dunnage to fill wing voids. The triangular void filledwith dunnage helps to form a level surface upon which the next tier of drums will be stowed. This is a well-laid dunnage floor and well-stowed cargo. *Courtesy of Joe Liotta Art & Design.*

Tomming is the process of using timbers to secure cargo by running the timber from an upper support *down* to the cargo either vertically or at an angle. The timbers used for this purpose are known as *toms.* Tomming is used to secure top tiers of cargo that are not secured by other cargo being stowed over them. Cargoes that need tomming, especially in the 'tweendeck areas, are steel products, such as rails or billets pipes; bombs; and similar items. In the lower holds, tomming may be employed, but the overhead clearance may be so great that it is better to use lashings.

Shoring and bracing are usually all that can be done when securing deck cargo. Tomming can be used on deck only when the cargo is below the level of a mast house or other deck structure and a tom can be fitted into position. Tomming should be used whenever possible, even if shoring is also used.

Below decks, bracing or tomming is preferable to shoring. Shoring transmits a lifting effect to the cargo that is undesirable. Shoring may loosen in heavy weather unless carefully wedged and supported. Tomming presses downward against the cargo, and when the ship is heaving in a heavy seaway, the rising of the cargo only presses the tom more tightly against the overhead support. The shore, however, works with the sea and the cargo may be lifted upward. When it settles, the shore may fit loosely and eventually its supporting effect may be completely lost.

Examples of shoring, tomming, and bracing are illustrated in Figures 3-22 to 3-25.

Peck & Hale shoring net: The shoring or tomming of cargo shown in Figures 3-22 to 3-25 clearly shows interference with free space, which might be more convenient to leave clear. It is also quite obvious that a good deal of lumber is consumed along with the labor of constructing the shoring. It may also happen that cargo may be stowed next to a block of cargo in the wings for part of a voyage but that during another part the adjacent cargo will be removed. In such a case, shoring must be erected at an intermediate port or the cargo must be broken down by shifting some of it into the hatch square. This requires labor and materials, and in some parts of the world the materials for erecting the shoring may not be available.

The Peck & Hale shoring net, as illustrated in Figures 3-26 and 3-27, is an answer to these problems. It provides a means of support for the cargo bulkheads without the use of shoring or tomming.

Dunnage floors: Dunnage floors, solid or spaced, are laid between tiers of cargo in cardboard containers in deep lower holds. This is very important if the cargo is known to be fragile or prone to leakage. A floor is not needed between every tier. It is recommended that the first floor be laid after three tiers, the second floor after another three tiers, the third floor after six additional tiers, and a fourth floor after still another six tiers. No more than four floors will be needed. The first two floors are the most necessary. The purpose of all these floors is to prevent the spread of damage in case one of the inside containers fails. For example, if a bottle or can of beer began to leak in a carton stowed in the third tier up from the bottom of a hold in which cartons were stowed from the deck all the way up, what would happen if no dunnage floor were used?

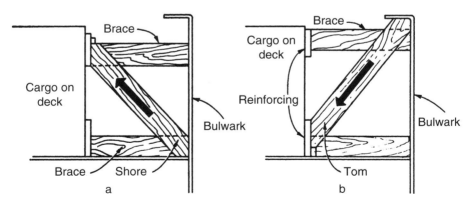

Figure 3-22. A sketch of deck cargo being secured with shores (**a**) and toms (**b**). Bracing or distance pieces are used in both cases. Note that when a force, as from a sea striking the opposite side, pushes the cargo against the shore, the shore tends to lift the cargo up. If the cargo is lifted upward, the shoring itself, including the braces and lashings, may be loosened and eventually cause the cargo to shift. The tom, on the other hand, forces the cargo downward toward the deck. Tomming is better than shoring, but a combination of both should be used. Lashings should always be used also. Wherever a brace, shore, or tom exerts pressure against the cargo, reinforcing should always be used.

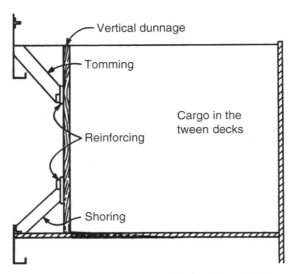

Figure 3-23. Tomming and shoring of cargo stowed in the wings of the 'tweendeck space. It is important to place reinforcing wherever pressure will be exerted by the toms or shores; it is also important to cut the vertical dunnage so it fits snugly between the deck and overhead or to use wedges to take up slack. If the cargo being shored is not in lengths, such as cartons or cases, the reinforcing shown here should run longitudinally to exert pressure all along the face of the cargo block; the vertical dunnage pieces should be more numerous, although each vertical piece may not need to be secured with a shore and tom.

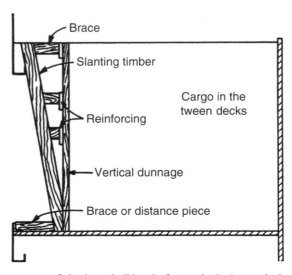

Figure 3-24. An easy way of shoring a bulkhead of cargo in the 'tweendecks, providing timbers of about 4 by 6 inches are available. The slanting timber should be cut to just fit with the greatest dimension running athwartships. The braces are not likely to be displaced, because they will work downward with the working of the cargo and tend to tighten themselves.

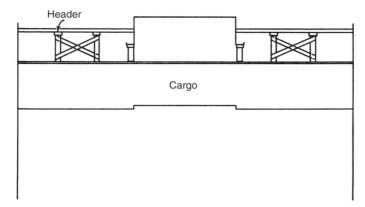

Figure 3-25. Tomming over the type of cargo that might be displaced by heavy working of the ship in a seaway. Examples of such cargo include cylinders, bombs, pipes, or steel billets. It is important to tie the toms together with dunnage wood as shown and to use cleats on either side of the upper end of the tom nailed to the header. Wedges should be driven under the lower ends of the toms to make them fit tightly. This view is looking forward or aft. The headers run longitudinally, with the toms spaced at intervals of approximately 6 feet.

The beer would wet the carton and reduce its strength and in all probability the adjacent inside containers would be called upon to support the entire weight of all the cases between them and the surface of the stowage. Without the support of the outside carton and with one inside carton gone, the adjacent bottle would break and the one adjacent to that would break in turn. This procedure would be accelerated in heavy weather. Eventually, a large amount of damage would be caused in the area of the first broken bottle or collapsed can. The stowed block would sag in toward the damaged area, and damaged cargo would be found throughout the bottom layers. The inside cartons would not stop failing until the damage reached the upper layers, where the superimposed weight would be lessened.

Now, if dunnage had been laid between the third and fourth tiers, the weight on the bottles adjacent to the broken bottle would have been partially taken up by the bridge of dunnage over the third tier. In fact, an entire carton could be left out of the third tier without causing any damage. The floor of dunnage over the third tier would simply bridge the gap, and there would be a negligible increase in pressure on other containers in the tier. Thus, it is seen that floors of this type prevent crushing.

Preventing Chafage

Chafage of cargo is a source of damage when cargo rests against the edges of structural members or other dunnage. Vertical dunnage placed against the permanent sweat battens is used to prevent small cargo from becoming hung up on the upper edges of the battens. If this should happen as the ship works in a seaway, the sides of the cardboard cartons may be sheared off or bagged cargo

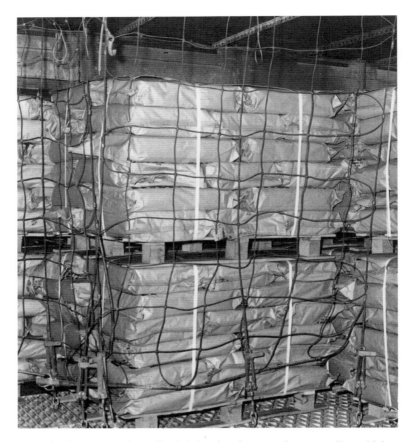

Figure 3-26. Shoring nets used to split triple hatches for general cargo and/or vehicles. *Courtesy Peck and Hale, Inc.*

may be torn. In general, the dunnage placed in the cargo to prevent chafage is not extensive. The use of dunnage for the other purposes set forth herein precludes chafage. There are exceptions, however, as mentioned above, and the ship's officer should be on the alert for situations that call for additional dunnage to prevent chafage.

Preventing Spontaneous Heating

Some cargoes require dunnage to provide air channels through the stowed cargo block in order to carry away heat generated by the cargo. If such heat is not carried away, the temperature will gradually rise and serious damage may result. Refrigerated cargoes of ripening fruit are the best example. Ripening fruit creates a large amount of heat, and cool air currents must pass through such cargoes or areas will become comparatively warm and the ripening process will be accelerated, with resulting damage in the form of

Figure 3-27. Peck and Hale net shoring system used to secure palletized stowage in wing of hatch. *Courtesy Peck and Hale, Inc.*

overripe product at the discharge port. Dunnage placed between every tier *of* the cargo in the form of strips of building lath provides the necessary air channels. It is important that the lengths of the strips lie in the direction of the air currents.

Other examples of cargoes requiring such dunnaging are onions, fish meal, and charcoal. These latter cargoes do not use building lath. They may use 1- by 6-inch dunnage, crisscross floors, or even the Venetian ventilator. As can be seen, the dunnaging used to prevent spontaneous heating is the same as that used for the prevention of condensation. In most cases, dunnage used to aid circulation of air fulfills both objectives.

Pilferage: Dunnage for the protection of cargo from pilferage is mentioned for the sake of completeness. This dunnage takes the form of a rough fence or barrier around cargo that is subject to pilferage but for some reason cannot be stowed in a special locker.

Additional dunnage uses: Dunnage is also used to separate cargoes. In this form it aids the discharge process rather than protecting the cargo as in all of the above examples. When used as separation, strips of dunnage or solid floors are laid between layers of the cargo. Separation is necessary when the same type of cargo is destined for separate ports or for different consignees at the same port. Clear and definite separation makes the cargo easier to discharge in consignee blocks. In the same way, the separation lessens the probability of overcarrying the cargo.

<h2 align="center">Lashings</h2>

Cargo becomes damaged when it is not secured in its stowed position. Dunnage may be used for this purpose, as outlined in the preceding section. Another means of securing cargo, and one that is especially useful for securing on-deck cargo, is the use of lashings. Lashings should be of steel chain, wire rope, or steel strapping. Lashings of fiber rope should never be used when attempting to secure cargo on the deck of a ship for a long voyage. Fiber rope stretches under stress and chafes easily. In emergencies, or other circumstances, it may have to be used. If used, it should be checked often, and when slackness appears, additional line should be used to frap the original lashings tighter. Never remove the original lashings with the idea of replacing them.

Regardless of the material used, the first requisite for the use of lashings is the installation of pad eyes at points along the deck that will afford the best leads for securing cargo. This is a requirement that the ship's officer should take care of as soon as he/she knows where the cargo is to be stowed. This applies whether the cargo is being stowed below deck or on deck, so long as it is going to be necessary to lash it down.

Chain lashing is secured by using a shackle at the lower or deck end of the chain, passing the chain over or around the cargo in whatever manner seems to be most appropriate for the job on hand, and securing the other end by the use of a pear link, pelican hook, and turnbuckle. The pear link provides a movable link to which the turnbuckle can be attached without having to use the opposite end of the chain. The chain will not always be the exact length needed and it is too expensive to cut it to fit each time it is used; hence, it is necessary to have this adjustable method of securing one end. After securing the pelican hook and the pear link, the turnbuckle may be set up by inserting a piece of wood in the barrel and twisting. Once the lashing is tight, the wood should be left in the barrel and lashed to something to prevent the turnbuckle from backing off and becoming slack. For the same purpose, a short stick should be inserted through the pear link on one side of the turnbuckle.

Chain is used when securing extremely heavy objects on deck, and for lumber deck loads. The most common size is ¾-inch diameter with a 36-inch turnbuckle and shackles of 1 or 1½ inches.

Wire rope is secured by using clips to form eyes where needed; the eyes are secured to the pad eyes with shackles. The wire rope is passed between the deck and the cargo or over the cargo and finally attached to a turnbuckle with a pelican hook. Wire rope is more workable than chain and can be pulled tight by hand very easily, after which the clips can be applied. When the clips are on, the rope is seized, then cut. The turnbuckle is set up to tighten the lashing; the same precaution against backing off that was mentioned in the case of chain lashings must be taken.

The most common type of wire rope used for this purpose is ⅝-inch, 6 × 19 plow steel wire. Old cargo falls should be saved for use as lashings of this type. Three-quarter-inch wire rope is used whenever the object being secured is heavy enough to warrant it.

STOWAGE PRINCIPLE 3: MAXIMUM USE OF AVAILABLE CUBIC

Controlling Broken Stowage

The stowage of cargo so that the greatest possible amount of the cubic capacity of the ship contains cargo is primarily a matter of controlling the *broken stowage*. Broken stowage has been defined as that space within a loaded ship that is not occupied by cargo. Therefore, the space that contributes to the broken stowage is space between containers of irregular shape containers with curvature, space filled with dunnage, and the space over the last tier into which no cargo can be fitted for one reason or another. Broken stowage is expressed as a percentage of the total available cubic. Broken stowage on uniformly packaged commodities will average about 10%; that on general cargo will average about 25%. Both of these values may be affected by several variables. Some of these variables, as shall be seen, are within the control of the shipowner's organization; some are not. The control of broken stowage starts with the laying out of the ship and continues throughout the actual stowage process.

Use of Filler Cargo

Filler cargo is defined as small durable packages or pieces of cargo that may be stowed in the interstices or voids between larger pieces. As has already been pointed out, it is a violation of basic principles to leave a void anywhere within a stowed cargo block. Hence, if a void occurs, it either must be filled with dunnage, braced or shored with dunnage, or filled with filler cargo. Unless filler cargo is used, the broken stowage is increased. The *smallness* of these pieces of durable cargo is in comparison with the cargo in which the voids appear. For example, when stowing large frames of structural steel, wooden boxes of foodstuffs may fit in and around the pieces of steel in such a way as to qualify as filler cargo. On the other hand, when one is stowing cases of foodstuffs in the wings of a lower hold and a row has to be shut out because of the curvature, smaller pieces of boxed merchandise or bundles of pipe may be used as filler cargo. Thus, whatever an officer judges to be suitable for stowage in void spaces becomes filler cargo.

The efficient use of filler cargo is dependent on the terminal manager's administrative policies with respect to it. The first step is to have all personnel alerted to the need for spotting shipments that are suitable for such use. Next a system must be set up whereby such cargo is assembled to be ready for use when needed during the loading process. This must be organized or the use of filler cargo will be haphazard.

Choosing Cargo to fit the Hold

When laying out the ship, decisions are made as to what cargoes go where. During this stage of the cargo operations, a ship may be "blown up" (given an excessively high broken stowage percentage). This can be caused by the decision to stow large crates and cases in the end lower holds, where small curved items should go. Planning to stow drums for the first port of call in a 'tweendeck where only nine-tenths of a drum can be stowed in the space remaining over the last tier will result in much broken stowage. The latter mistake could be rectified during the actual loading process (as many such mistakes are), providing a readjustment is possible or additional cargo can be obtained for stowage over the drums. Generally this cause of broken stowage is pretty well controlled: in practice, however, the principle of choosing cargo to fit the hold should always be kept in mind.

Skill of the Longshoremen

The final factor in the control of broken stowage is probably the most variable. The skill, industry, and interest of the longshoremen art: definitely important factors in whether a ship is stowed compactly. The use of excessive amounts of dunnage in lieu of filler cargo and the failure to stow some items in neat and uniform rows and tiers are two ways that longshoremen can do the greatest amount of harm insofar as the control of broken stowage is concerned.

When stowing drums or crates and cases of odd sizes, the extra effort needed to two-block adjacent containers may prevent many longshoremen from doing the job right. A large number of loosely stowed cargo not only will increase the broken stowage but may set the stage for disastrous shifting during heavy weather. When stowing bagged goods that are flowing into the ship through chutes, longshoremen may step aside and allow a large number of the bags to fall at random; after a time, and before the chute becomes jammed, a few of the uppermost bags can be set straight. There may be no indication of the improper stowage except as reflected in the rise in broken stowage percentage for the compartment. The poor stowage will come to light, of course, when the cargo is discharged.

The judicious use of dunnage and filler cargo and the manner in which placed in stowage are all ways of controlling broken stowage. Still another is the measuring of the holds before stowage of bales or any items that may be stowed in such a way that more than one vertical dimension can be obtained from the container. If the hold measurements are taken and compared with the cargo's measurements, a decision can be made quickly regarding how the cargo should be placed in the hold so that the last tier will come as close as possible to the top of the hold. Inasmuch as the space over the last tier contributes to broken stowage, it can be seen that this results in better control of the value.

In summary, the best use of available cubic is obtained by paying attention to three factors: (1) the use of filler cargo, (2) the choice of cargo to fit the hold, and (3) the skill of the longshoremen.

STOWAGE PRINCIPLE 4:

RAPID AND SYSTEMATIC LOADING AND DISCHARGING

Prevent the Long Hatch

The rules for providing for rapid and systematic loading and discharging are few. One of the first rules is to prevent the stowage of a disproportionate amount of cargo for any one port in any one hatch. A hatch that is so stowed is known as *a long hatch.* The ship's time in port is controlled by the maximum number of gang hours in any one hatch; therefore the work should be divided evenly among all hatches. For example, if a five-hatch ship has 3,000 tons for a given port and hatches 1, 3, 4, and 5 have 400 tons apiece whereas hatch number 2 has 1,400 tons, the ship will be in port just as long as if all hatches had 1,400 tons. In other words, it would take as long to discharge the 3,000 tons as it would 7,000 tons, provided the 3,000 was stowed as stated above and the 7,000 was divided evenly in all five hatches.

Prevent Overstowage

Another obvious rule is to prevent cargo from being overstowed. *Overstowage* does not mean that the cargo necessarily has cargo stowed directly over it, but simply that cargo is blocking the discharge in one way or another. Overstowage is prevented by thorough planning before the loading operation commences.

If cargo is overstowed, it necessitates the shifting of the blocking cargo before any discharge can take place. It may require that some cargo be completely discharged and then reloaded. All of this activity is costly in time and money and should be avoided.

Prevent Overcarriage

The third rule for obtaining rapid and systematic discharge encompasses three factors, all of which may be described as means of preventing *overcarried* cargo.

Overcarried cargo is cargo that is inadvertently left in the ship and taken beyond the port of discharge on the ship's itinerary. Thus, it is obvious that overcarried cargo represents the antithesis of rapid and systematic discharge operations. It will be seen that the three devices that reduce the possibility of overcarried cargo are also natural aids to rapid discharge.

Port Marks

The first device is the use of *port marks*. Port marks are geometrical designs placed on cargo in various colors so that the destination can be noted at a glance without reading carefully all the printing upon the case. These port marks are in the form of green circles, blue diamonds, red crosses, or other such markings. When blocks of cargo are so marked in the hatch, the ship's officer at the port of discharge can more easily, and with more certainty, check on the completeness of the discharge. This check is necessary every time a port is discharged. The longshoremen should never be allowed to cover up a hatch until a ship's officer has personally inspected the hold to make certain all cargo for the port is out. This check must be made sometimes under adverse conditions, such as during foul weather in the middle of the night. The ship's officer in charge of the deck should be aware, of course, of the approximate time that the discharging is to be completed, and should be on hand to check the hatch at the time of completion. If the cargo is well marked with port marks, the check will be more definite.

In most cases, the port marks are placed on the cargo by a member of the dock force. During the stowage, these marks may be stowed so that they are not visible in the hold; this makes them useless for the above purpose. The remedy is to place additional marks on the cargo after stowage, or to put the marks on the cargo in such a fashion that they will always be visible.

Block Stowage

The second device is to provide for block stowage insofar as possible, that is, to eliminate small segments of cargo in several locations in any one hatch and to make some attempt to assemble large blocks at one level in one compartment. This may not be possible because of the need for segregation, but an effort should be made to attain such stowage. Block stowage is accomplished through planning.

Related to this problem is the need for keeping consignee marks in blocks within any one port block. This is mainly useful to the dock force in segregating the cargo as it is being discharged. When discharging, the necessity of spotting the cargo on the dock by consignee for organized delivery may prove to be a difficult and time-consuming problem, especially if the cargoes with several consignee marks are discharged simultaneously. The segregation is a simple task if one mark comes out at a time until all cargoes bearing that mark are discharged. The planning and stowing of the cargo should provide for consignee marks being kept together and marked off in the hatch by some separation system.

Proper Separation

The last device to be mentioned with regard to the prevention of overcarriage is the proper separation of cargoes. *Separation* refers to the material used to separate blocks of cargo by port and/or consignee. If blocks are separated, the longshoremen are directed, more or less, through the cargo. If the separation is omitted or incomplete, confusion is the result, and some cargo may be inadvertently left in the ship.

Some cargoes need no separation because they are different in nature and mistaking one container for another is impossible. For example, when a ship is discharging bags of rice for one port and the adjacent cargo for the next port is barrels of flour, there is no possibility of mixing the rice and the flour. This may be termed "natural" separation.

Separation between cargoes of the same type with different consignee marks and in bags is obtained by the use of strips of burlap. Heavy paper may also be used. Dunnage boards widely separated are used, but dunnage worked into the stowage of bags may lead to chafing and tearing of the bags, with a consequent loss of contents.

When separating general cargoes, heavy paper with appropriate marks on the exterior is used. This refers to the separation of miscellaneous cargoes, such as small cartons and cases containing general merchandise bound for different ports but stowed adjacent to each other. Such stowage is most likely to result in the overcarriage of a few items if port marks and separation are not given proper attention.

Lumber needs careful separation of consignee marks. This cargo may be separated by laying strips of rope yarn athwartship spaced about 6 feet longitudinally over the stowed mark. Painting stripes across the stowed block is also used, but should not be used when working with milled or surfaced lumber in the finishing grades. Wire and staples are used, but this method of marking off is not desirable because the staples left in the lumber obviously are liable to cause trouble when the lumber is being worked. Wire and staples are not as easy to handle as rope yarn or paint, and the efficiency of marking off is no greater.

Wire may be used when separating structural steel, steel pipe, or steel rails. Paint and dunnage strips may also be used for separating steel products.

In summary, provision for rapid and systematic loading and discharging depends on three factors: (1) preventing long hatches, (2) preventing overstowed cargo, and (3) preventing overcarried cargo.

STOWAGE PRINCIPLE 5:
SAFETY OF CREW AND LONGSHOREMEN

Cargo should be stowed so that during the discharging process it is unlikely that unsafe areas will develop for the men working the cargo or the men working about the ship. An example of a situation in which discharging cargo may result in the formation of unsafe areas is when workers discharge a block of cargo before moving to another block even though high and perhaps unstable bulkheads are formed all around the square where the longshoremen are laboring. Instances have occurred also in which the manner of discharging either aggravated the situation or actually created it needlessly.

The objective of providing for the safety of crew and longshoremen is so obvious that it is often ignored. There should be no unstable bulkheads of cargo, any unsafe areas should be roped off, warning signs should be used and enforced, and proper lighting must be provided. The ship's officer must always keep in mind that he/she is responsible for the safety of crew and longshoremen aboard.

CHAPTER 4

PLANNING THE STOWAGE AND PREPARATION OF THE CARGO SPACES

PLANNING COMPLICATIONS

W HEN FACED WITH THE PROBLEM of planning for the stowage there are a number of factors that directly or indirectly complicate this task.

Diversity of the Cargo

The diversity of the cargo, in its inherent characteristics, as well as its shape and weight, is first and foremost on the list. If all cargoes could be stowed together in any compartment or in any order vertically and longitudinally, the problem of planning would be reduced in difficulty by over 50%. The fact that cargoes must be separated in definite ways complicates their segregation. When there is only one cargo, or even when there are several that can be stowed together, planning for good stowage is greatly simplified.

The Number and Sequence of Ports

If all the cargo is going to one port, it is obvious that the planning problems are greatly reduced. Under such conditions, it is impossible to overstow or to overcarry cargo or to make long hatches.

It is interesting to note, however, that a situation making it difficult, if not impossible, to satisfy all the objectives of good stowage can be created by an itinerary of just two ports with just two cargoes. The reader might consider, for example, a ship booked to carry a full and down load of steel rails for port A and cartons of packaged cereals for port B, with the ship to call at port A first. How would such a cargo be stowed? Remember the necessity of correct weight distribution, segregation of light and heavy cargoes vertically, control of broken stowage, and rapid and systematic discharge. The booking of such a cargo would be a gross error, of course, on the part of the freight traffic department unless the sequence of ports could be reversed.

The Shape of the Hold

This factor must be considered in regard to the question of control of broken stowage. All factors of stowage may be well satisfied, but if the plan calls for large cases to be stowed in the lower holds of the end hatches, the broken stowage percentage will be high. If possible, bagged cargoes or smaller curved items should be stowed in such areas. This is an example of the give and take that must go on when planning the stowage of any cargo.

Obstructions in the Hold

Obstructions in a hold should be kept to a minimum by the designers. If obstructions exist in the hold, otherwise-perfect stowage may have to be changed because the cargo will not go in around the obstructions or, if it will, the broken stowage may rise an unwarranted amount. These facts reduce the commercial value of any ship.

Heated Bulkheads

Bulkheads that are heated may make it necessary to stow cargo such as lard, wattle bark extracts, and similar items in other spaces when all other factors are best satisfied by placing them in the heated compartment. This fact, of course, requires a change in the plan and results in a complication.

Optional Cargo Shipments

Optional cargo is cargo that is loaded for discharge at any one of several ports at the option of the shipper. Such shipments are sometimes difficult to keep from being overstowed. They must be ready for discharge at all of several ports instead of only at one. Only a limited amount of optional cargo can be stowed without the necessity of shifting cargo for its discharge.

Unavailability of Cargo

Cargo may be booked and planned for stowage, but the shipper may fail to deliver it to the dock when it is time to load. Such a situation makes it necessary to change the entire plan. The degree of the change depends on the amount of cargo involved and other conditions.

THE TENTATIVE CARGO PLAN

Importance of the Tentative Cargo Plan

With only two cargoes and two ports creating difficult problems, as illustrated in the above hypothetical case, the reader can appreciate more readily the problems that may arise when stowing a hundred commodities for several ports. General cargo carriers operate under the latter conditions consistently. The operation may be further complicated by the need to load as well as discharge cargoes at intermediate ports on the itinerary.

The correct way to prevent costly mistakes from occurring during the loading process is to lay out the ship as far in advance as possible. The preliminary laying out of the ship is the plan for stowing the vessel made up from the engagement sheet or recapitulated data from such a source. This first plan is called the *tentative plan* to eliminate confusion with the other plan known as the *final stowage plan*. There are terminals in operation where large vessels are loaded without the benefit of a formal tentative plan. However, to do so is contrary to the best operating principles. It is true, of course, that when the sample type of ship is loaded in regular and frequent intervals over runs that are almost identical year in and year out, the importance of the tentative plan will be less than when a ship is being loaded for the first time on a new run. With years of experience with the same ship, the same cargo in general, and the same run, the loading methods will be very similar; however, they will never be identical. The differences will always warrant a rough tentative plan at the least. With respect to weight distribution, the same mistake might be made for years and quite unnecessarily cause gradually increasing costs for repair and maintenance. The latter mistake would be rectified only if the final stowage plans were analyzed. Lacking this check and continuing to load the ships by intuition, the shipowner may operate his/her fleet with less-than-optimal efficiency.

Preparation of the Tentative Cargo Plan

Data for preparing the plan are obtained from copies of the engagement sheet kept by the booking clerk. The booking may not be complete when he/she starts to make up the plan. This will complicate the task to some extent and necessitate a number of changes during the actual loading process. The object is to have some basis for making initial decisions when starting the loading operation and to have an instrument with which to brief all supervisory personnel about the operation.

As mentioned above, when the same ship receives similar shipments voyage after voyage to be loaded for the same consignees in approximately the same amounts, the tentative and final stowage plans, if analyzed constantly, should reflect the best answer for stowing the cargo on board in accordance with the five objectives of good stowage. The development of new products and changes in demand for the old will cause a gradual change in the types and amounts of cargoes found on old and established runs. The change will be so gradual that there will be little difference in the tentative plan between one voyage and the next, but there will be change. The need for analyzing the stowage from time to time will always be present on the general cargo carrier.

Provisions of the Tentative Plan

The tentative plan provides for loading cargo bound for the last port of call first, that is, on the bottom tiers. (The layers of cargo are referred to as *tiers*. The athwartship for fore-and-aft lines of stowage are referred to as *rows*.) The plan will show limitations on the stowage as to height and bulkheads fore, aft, and athwartship. The approximate amounts in tons and numbers of units expected to be placed in the indicated spaces will also be shown. All of these data may be changed during the actual stowage in order to expedite the total operation.

Heavy cargoes must be loaded on the bottom tiers. A complication arises immediately when a heavy item must be loaded so that it can be discharged at one of the early ports on the itinerary. There are several ways to meet this problem. One of the most common is to split the hold transversely, leaving at least one section of the hatch available to the hook, and, if necessary, to subdivide the two parts further longitudinally. A second solution is to save a part of or the entire hatch square for the first port. A third device is to use the upper decks for the heavier pieces bound for the early ports. A fourth is to resort to on-deck stowage if it is allowable by the terms of the bill of lading. A fifth solution, and the least desirable, is to stow the heavy item under cargo bound for a later port. This may be the only possible answer under some conditions, but it requires the shifting of cargo to get the load discharged and means added time and expense for the cargo operation. It should never be used without having exhausted every other possibility.

The tentative plan will provide for the correct distribution of weight vertically and longitudinally. The tentative plan will also reflect the correct segregation of the cargo. The problem of segregation is that of stowing the cargoes so that one cannot cause damage to another, and this may be the most difficult problem to solve. Compromises will have to be made in this regard at times.

Finally, the tentative plan will provide for an amount of cargo in each hold such that no one hold will require a disproportionate number of gang hours of work to discharge the cargo.

Using the Tentative Plan

Once it is prepared, the plan can be used to judge whether the finished ship will be in accordance with the best principles of stowage. If for any reason a change is required, the old plan is a beginning point. A very important use of the plan is to tell how many gangs are needed from day to day and what gear is required. Many daily decisions will be made more quickly and accurately if based on a good tentative plan.

The ship superintendent or walking boss needs the plan to see how the ship is to be stowed. If changes must be made, he/she can always consult with the pier superintendent. Having the tentative plan, however, makes the entire operation run much more smoothly and guarantees better results.

Whereas the use of the tentative plan as outlined for the above officers within the shipowner's organization is fairly uniform from company to company, the use of the plan by the master of the ship and his/her officers varies from full use to a complete lack of use.

The Ship's Officers and the Tentative Plan

Cargo operations represent a high operational cost for a general cargo carrier. Every effort should be expended to make the procedures as efficient as possible under practical operating conditions. One of the things that can be done in this respect, but is neglected in many cases, is the briefing of the ship's officers regarding all the plans for loading the ship.

To begin with, a copy of the tentative plan should be presented to the master of the ship, so that this officer can make a preliminary analysis of it. The approximate draft, metacentric height, bending stresses, and segregation should be clearly noted on the plan. These are the bases for judging whether a given layout is good or bad. The master of a ship should know whether the ship he/she is to take to sea is going to be loaded as he/she would load her. It is the responsibility of the operations department to see that every ship master has the data needed to ascertain this fact. In some instances, the master of the ship has little if any influence on the way his/her ship is to be loaded; regardless of the reason, this is not right. Such cases may stem from the method of operation of the company or from the laissez faire attitude adopted by the master him/herself.

In every case, the master of the ship should make some analysis of the tentative plan for the stowing of his/her ship. He/she should either approve or disapprove of the stowage. If there are things of which he/she disapproves, there should be a clarification of the issue with the pier superintendent. In the final analysis, the master of the ship is the officer responsible for the way the ship is stowed. This fact must not be forgotten by anybody.

The master should brief all of the ship's officers in regard to the loading operation. This briefing should be in the form of a conference on the ship with the pier superintendent and walking boss present if possible. The chief officer should have a copy of the tentative plan, and after the loading conference the other deck officers should carefully note those items that will require checking during the actual operation.

Under this system, the ship's officers will be able to stop serious mistakes in loading before they occur. The ship owner will be able to utilize the years of experience of the officers with the cargoes they carry. Too frequently, the officers are completely uninformed about the operation taking place on their ship. All information about the proceedings is often held by the pier superintendent and walking boss, and not systematically passed on to the officers. Direct questions may be answered readily, but not enough information is given to enable the officers of the ship to assist fully in the cargo operation. Lacking full and complete data, the officers feel unfamiliar with problems that in many cases could be handled better if they were properly briefed.

The practice of briefing subordinates concerning any operation in which they are going to take part is a fundamental principle of leadership. Conducting a briefing makes all hands feel more as if they have a personal stake in the outcome and gives them a feeling of participation that is very important for the attainment of efficiency. Under a cooperative relationship between the master and his/her officers, any ship will function in a more efficient manner than under an impersonal and uninformed relationship. Compliance with the three C's of *Communication, Cooperation,* and *Coordination* cannot be overstressed.

THE CAPACITY PLAN

When laying out the ship, certain information concerning the ship must be readily available. The data needed are incorporated on a plan of the ship known as the *capacity plan*. A full and complete capacity plan answers the questions of whether a given cargo shipment can be stowed in any given compartment or part of a compartment and what the effect on the ship will be.

The information that a capacity plan should have upon it is as follows:

Compartmentation: An inboard profile view of the ship showing all of the compartments of the ship including the holds, tanks, store rooms, quarters, and working spaces.

Volumes: The volumes of all the above spaces are not specified. The volumes of the tanks and the cargo holds are given. The *bale* capacity and the *grain* capacity of each cargo compartment capable of receiving dry cargo are given. The bale capacity is the cubic capacity measured vertically from below the beam flanges down to the upper side of the tank top plating or the spar ceiling if any exists. Transversely, the measurements are from inside the sweat battens, and longitudinally from inside any stiffeners or insulation on the bulkheads. The grain capacity is the cubic capacity measured from inside the plating of all six sides less the volume taken up by the structural members extending into the hold. In other words, the bale capacity is the volume of the hold that can be utilized when stowing bales and the grain capacity is the volume that can be utilized when stowing the grain. The bales cannot go in between all the frame and beam spaces, but the grain will flow around such members.

The volumes of the complete hold may be recapitulated in a table on the plan, but the profile plan of the ship should be broken up into such units of space as are often used in actual stowage of cargo. Figure 4-1 is an illustration of how the profile plan of the ship may be subdivided to make this part of the capacity plan more useful.

Below the profile plan of the ship, plan views of the various decks appear. On these plan views, the cubics of the compartments should be broken up into smaller units. On a hatch that has three sections, the plan view of the decks should have the space divided up into fifteen separate parts. Such a division is shown in Figure 4-2. When speaking of or making written notations about these spaces, the terms applied to areas 1 and 3 are *forward winged out*, or simply *forward wings*. If the position refers to only one wing, it should be designated by name, such as *forward port wing*. Area 2 is *forward amidships*. Areas 13, 14, and 15 are referred to in the same manner except that they are aft. The entire area on each side of the hatch in the wings is referred to as *wings abreast*. More explicit designation may be given by reference to the section of the hatch. For example, wings abreast would mean the cargo was stowed in areas 6, 7, 12, 4, 9, and 10. If cargo was stowed only in the approximate limits of area 10, this may be designated *starboard wing abreast aft*. Areas 5, 8, and 11 are designated the *hatch square*. It should be emphasized that there is no universally accepted terminology for designating all of these areas. These areas may simply be given numbers or referred to as bays, a term used on many piers to designate certain stowage areas. The terms used need only be descriptive of the position to be acceptable.

Safety area: When cargo for one port is stowed in a 'tweendeck space and will remain there while it is necessary to work the hatches below, this cargo should not be stowed too close to the edge of the hatch opening. Cargo should be kept 3 feet back from the edge of the hatchway. It is a good practice to paint a white or red line this distance from the edge as a guideline for longshoremen

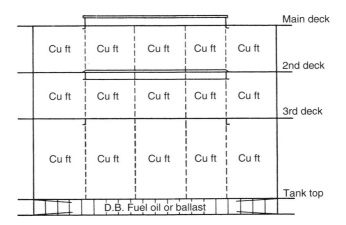

Figure 4-1. Subdivision of the profile view.

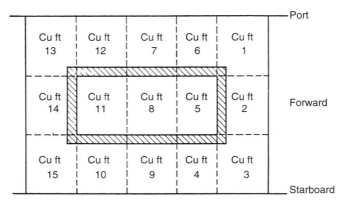

Figure 4-2. Subdivision of the plan view. The shaded area is a 3-foot safety area in which cargo should not be stowed if the compartment below will be open.

(see Figs. 4-2 and 4-3). The space between this line and the edge of the coaming may be called the *safety area* or, in some cases, it is appropriately named *no-man's land*. The cubic of this space may sometimes be included in the hatch square cubic figure and sometimes in that of the appropriate areas surrounding the hatch. Just how it is handled is not too important, but the area in which it is included should be known.

This safety area serves to prevent longshoremen from falling into the open hatch when working around the space when opening or closing hatches, and also provides room for the ship's personnel to pass safely. Also, when cargo is being loaded or discharged, it lessens the probability that the cargo stowed in the 'tweendeck area will be struck in such a fashion that a cargo is damaged or knocked below so that a longshoreman is injured.

Clearances: The distance between the bottom of the hatch coaming and the deck, as well as the lengths, widths, and heights of all the compartments, should be notated on the capacity plan. The distance from the forward edge or after edge of a hatch coaming to the opposite lower end of the compartment below should be included, because this measurement will tell the planning officer at a glance whether a given length of pipe or timber will go into the compartment in question. It should be kept in mind that if a given length will just squeeze by the obstruction when being stowed in the beginning, then only one tier will be possible. As the cargo builds up, the drift, as this measurement is called, will be reduced. The length of clear deck run on the weather deck is also an important clearance and should be indicated on the plan. This measurement controls the size of single items that can be stowed on deck.

Deck load capacities: To enable the planning officer to know whether a given cargo can be stowed on a given deck insofar as the structural strength of the deck is concerned, all decks of the ship should have their capacities in pounds per square foot notated upon them. If the deck capacities are not given

Figure 4-3. Number 4 hold of SS *Mallory Lykes* with a 3-foot safety line shown.

one may have to resort to the National Cargo Bureau rule of thumb of 45 times the height of the compartment in feet. Of course, this rule of thumb can be utilized only for the 'tweendecks and lower holds.

Geometrical centers: To make the capacity plan useful for calculation of trim and stability problems, the distances of the geometrical centers of all cargo compartments and tanks above the keel and from one of the perpendiculars should be given. The center of gravity of the contents of a compartment above the keel will not coincide with the figure given on the plan unless the compartment is filled with a homogeneous mass. When the compartment is not filled with a homogeneous mass or is only partially filled, an estimate must be made of the location of the center of gravity. For example, if the compartment is filled with a general cargo with the heavier items on the lower layers, the center can be assumed to be about one-third of the height of the compartment above the deck of the compartment. If half of the compartment's capacity is filled with one cargo, the center of the mass will be one-fourth of the height of the compartment above the deck of the compartment, and so on. Refer to Figure 4-4 for a numerical example. For an explanation of the need for such data see chapter 3.

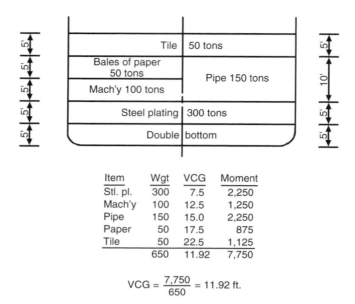

Item	Wgt	VCG	Moment
Stl. pl.	300	7.5	2,250
Mach'y	100	12.5	1,250
Pipe	150	15.0	2,250
Paper	50	17.5	875
Tile	50	22.5	1,125
	650	11.92	7,750

$$VCG = \frac{7,750}{650} = 11.92 \text{ ft.}$$

Figure 4-4. Vertical center of gravity (VCG) of hold.

Trimming table: Below the profile view of the ship, a trimming table will be found. This table enables the quick determination of the effect of a small change in longitudinal weight distribution on the trim of the ship. When calculating the final trim after loading a large amount of cargo, it is just as simple and more accurate to use the methods outlined in chapter 3. The use of the trimming table is explained on page 3-40. It is important to keep in mind that most of these tables are based on a units of 100 tons.

Deadweight scale: The deadweight scale is found on all capacity plans; however, the data given with the scale are often incomplete for all the needs of the planning officer. This scale is simply a diagram of the draft of the ship marked off in increments of 1 inch. The displacement of the ship and deadweight carrying capacity corresponding to the draft are always given. To make the deadweight scale more complete, the T.P.I., *MT*1, and *KM* of the ship should also be given. All of these data vary with the draft. The *deadweight carrying capacity* for any given draft is the *displacement* of the ship for the given draft less the *weight of the light ship*. The cargo deadweight carrying capacity cannot be recorded upon this scale, because this value varies with the amount of fuel, water, and stores on board. Under any given set of conditions, the cargo deadweight carrying capacity may be calculated if the number of tons of fuel, water, and stores on board is known. The latter value is subtracted from the deadweight carrying capacity taken from the deadweight scale to obtain the *cargo deadweight capacity*.

Also reflected on the deadweight scale is the freeboard of the ship. As explained in chapter 3, the freeboard of the ship, as derived by taking the mean of the forward and after drafts, will coincide with that reflected on the deadweight scale only if the ship is neither hogged nor sagged. If the ship is hogged, the actual freeboard will be greater than that taken from the scale. If the ship is sagged, the actual freeboard will be less. This fact can be used as a check on whether a ship is hogged or sagged.

Capacities and arrangement of cargo gear: The capacity of each boom or crane should be notated on the capacity plan so that the planning officer will have these important data at hand. Often a question regarding whether a given piece of gear can take a given load rigged in one way or another must be answered. For similar reasons, the length of each boom or crane and rigging itself should be depicted upon the plan.

Miscellaneous data: Besides providing the data mentioned above, which are needed to plan quickly and thoroughly for the stowage of cargo, the capacity plan is also a source of such information as the principal dimensions of the ship, pitch of the propeller, boiler, and engine data.

With all these data, the original plan can be made up and the resulting *GM*, trim, and layout of the ship can be obtained. Furthermore, in case of a need for changing the stowage, the effects on the *GM*, trim, and bending stresses can be readily obtained.

It should be pointed out that the *KM* is omitted on almost all deadweight scales by naval architects. However, the *KM*s for each draft can be obtained from other sources. If a capacity plan with these data already recorded on it is available from the builders, it should be requisitioned. The officer doing this will know his/her ship much better and be able to function in a far more efficient and competent manner.

THE FINAL STOWAGE PLAN

The tentative stowage plan is a guide to loading the ship. When the ship is completely loaded, the stowage of the cargo will resemble the tentative plan but will never be precisely in accordance with it. The numerous changes, large and small, cannot be kept on the tentative plan so that it will serve as a final plan. It is necessary to construct a final stowage plan as the ship is loaded compartment by compartment. This plan must show in great detail the actual stowage of the ship. It must depict all ports and as many of the individual port marks as is practicable.

Use of the Final Plan

The final plan is used by the stevedore of the discharging port to plan the discharging operation. It is used by the ship's officers to know the stowage of their ship so that in case of an emergency they can estimate the seriousness of the situation and more intelligently plan for action to cope with it. Also, it is analyzed by the master to determine the metacentric height, the appropriate bending moments, what might have been done to better the trim if it is extreme in any way, and judge the quality of the stowage generally. Later, if he/she deems it warranted, the master may recommend to the operations department a change in past methods or offer constructive suggestions. He/she can do none of these things unless he/she has a good final stowage plan and analyzes it thoroughly.

Without an accurate, complete, and clear final stowage plan, there can be no efficiency in the discharging operation and the safety of the ship and crew is impaired greatly.

Construction of the Final Plan

The constructions of the tentative and final stowage plans are almost identical except that the tentative plan will not be so detailed. This section will describe the construction of a final plan and explain some of the notations. It must be pointed out that the notations are not standardized throughout the merchant marine. The variations are minor, and once the reader has a general idea of the way these plans are laid out, he/she can read all plans after a few minutes of study.

The stowage plan is generally constructed on a profile plan of the ship with the bow depicted to the reader's right. The stowage of all 'tweendeck areas is presented as a plan view; that of the lower holds, as an elevation. Now inasmuch as a profile view of the ship is used to draw the plan, a plan of the 'tweendeck hatchways must be drawn on the plan to be used as a reference in locating the cargo stowed therein. Figure 4-5 shows the blank form for one hold, assuming the ship has two decks and three sections to the hatchway. Obviously, nothing is proportional or to scale on the blank form. As the limitations of the stowage are drawn on the plan, some approximation of proportion should be attempted. For example, if a cargo runs one half the distance from the forward bulkhead aft to the hatch edge, the plan should show that cargo as running half the distance. This may not be possible to do when a number of cargoes or ports are stowed in the same area. It becomes impossible because the space between cargoes, when the division is small, is not large enough for legible printing on the actual plan.

Two types of plans are found in use. One of these may be described as the *commodity plan* and the other as the *block plan*.

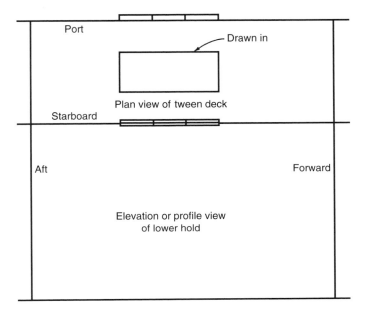

Figure 4-5. Cargo hold blank form.

COMMODITY TYPE PLAN

The commodity plan shows as much of the detail of the stowage as possible on the profile of the ship; that is, the limitation of all cargo is outlined on the plan. In the spaces prepared, the names of the commodities, the marks, the tons, and the number of packages are recorded. This is usually all the data that will be needed to plan for the discharge of the cargo or for action when fighting fire or in case of an emergency. This type of plan presents a *picture* of the stowage that can be readily interpreted. The officer sees the segregation immediately on viewing the plan.

BLOCK TYPE PLAN

The block plan shows the limitation of the cargo, but in the spaces on the profile of the ship, numbers are placed. Each number refers the reader of the plan to a line on a table or list placed on the plan below the profile of the ship or on a separate sheet of paper. On this line, the cargo represented by the number is fully described. The block plan makes it possible to give more detail concerning the stowed cargo if it is desired. The only room needed on the face of the plan is that necessary to print a number, which is small indeed. Then almost as much detail concerning the cargo as appears on the manifest may be written on the line corresponding to the reference number. There is generally some system to the numbering of the cargo blocks: All the numbers in the number 1 hold will be in the 100s, all those in the number 2 hold in the 200s, and so on. To make the identification of items more easy and less susceptible to mistakes, the initials or first syllable of the port of destination may follow the number. Furthermore, the number may be underlined in a distinctive color representing the port of discharge. Both types of plans should be color coded to make reading them easier and more foolproof.

Example of a Commodity Stowage Plan

To understand some of the methods of showing the stowage on a plan, the reader is referred to Figure 4-6. The reader should follow step by step the stowage and recording of the stowage on the plan. The lower hold has a depth of 25 feet and the 'tweendecks a depth of 11 feet.

Stowage 1: Port Allen, 20,000 cartons of canned soup in the forward part of the lower hold.

Comments: Stowed 11½ feet deep from the forward bulkhead aft to take in one section of the hatch and all the way across the ship. The mark is *S.P.* in a diamond.

Stowage 2: Honolulu, 32,000 cartons of canned beer in the after part of the lower hold.

Comments: Stowed 12½ feet deep up to the edge of the hatch; then drops down about 4 feet at the square of the hatch and continues forward taking up two sections of the hatch. In the wings, it continues at a level of 12½ feet. The mark is *N.M.*

Stowage 3: Honolulu, 200 cartons of shoes stowed in the square of the hatch over the beer 4 feet deep.

Comments: This view is an elevation; hence the wing stowage is separated from the hatch square stowage on the plan by the use of a slanting line through the common athwartship area. The cargo in the square of the hatch should come out first and it is shown above the slanting line to indicate this fact. The mark is *N.W.T.*

Stowage 4: Hilo, 800 bags of soy beans.

Comments: These soy beans are in the two wing bays and must come out after the Kona rice; hence the stowage is shown below the slanting line. The mark is *W.A.L.*

Stowage 5: Kona, 400 bags of rice.

Comments: Stowed in the way of the hatch square for a depth of 4½ feet. Same depth as the soy beans except that it is amidships. It comes out first; hence it is on top of the slanting line. One section of the hatch is used. The mark is *Z.T.9.*

Stowage 6: Honolulu, 12,000 cartons of chewing gum.

Comments: Stowed 6 feet deep all the way across and including two sections of the hatch. The mark is *F.W.W.*

Stowage 7: Honolulu, 5,000 cartons of shredded wheat.

Comments: Stowed 6½ feet deep all the way across including two sections of the hatch. The mark is <J.P.>.

Stowage 8: Honolulu, 3,200 cartons of shoes.

Comments: Stowed 9 feet deep all the way across to include one section of the hatch. The mark is *N.W.T.* The stowage of block number 8 completes the lower hold.

The following stowage is in the 'tweendeck:

Stowage 9: Port Allen, 8,000 pigs of lead.

Comments: These lead pigs would have to be stowed not more than 20 inches high; this would leave considerable space above them for lightweight cargo. But the 'tweendeck stowage is shown on the plan view. This corresponds to the problem of showing the stowage of a lower hold on an elevation when the cargo is not the same all the way athwartships. The slanting line is used; forward of the line, we place the cargo that is to come out last. Thus the Port Allen cargo is overstowed by the Hololulu. In 'tweendeck storage this is not done very often. Generally the cargo blocks run from the deck to the overhead. The mark is *G.I.D.*

Stowage 10: Honolulu, 100 tons of general merchandise.

Comments: Stowed forward of the hatch over the Port Allen lead. No marks have been listed because they are so numerous that the space doesn't permit it. The hatch list or manifest would have to be consulted to know exactly what the cargo comprises. The term *general merchandise* denotes less than carload lots of drugs, hardware, furniture, appliances, canned goods, dry goods, shoes, clothing, and tools. Note that with the general merchandise, the cargo stowed forward of the hatch in the 'tweendecks weighs 500 tons. Unless the area of the deck multiplied by the deck load capacity equaled 500 tons or more, this stowage would quite likely cause damage to the ship.

Stowage 11: Port Allen, 3,000 lead pigs.

Comments: Stowed over a large area about 20 inches high like those forward. Total weight amounts to 150 tons. Since the Port Allen lead is aft of the slanting line and the stowage is aft of the hatch, it is overstowed by the Hilo feed. The mark is *G.I.D.*

Stowage 12: Hilo, 1,800 bags of feed.

Comments: These bags of feed come out before the Port Allen lead. They are stowed over the lead in the same way that the Honolulu general merchandise is forward. The mark is *F. & G.*

Stowage 13: Honolulu, 3,000 bags of feed.

Comments: Stowed from the edge of hatch aft to the Port Allen lead and Hilo feed and from the deck to the overhead and all the way across the ship. The mark is *W.F.L.*

Stowage 14: Port Allen, 30 tons of general merchandise.

Comments: Stowed in the port and starboard wing bays of the third section of the hatch. Space limits even an abbreviated description on both sides, so the two sides are used for a short notation of the cargo. The arrow on the port side refers the reader to the other side for more information.

Stowage 15: Kona, 30 tons of general merchandise.

Comments: Same stowage as given the Port Allen general.

Stowage 16: Honolulu, 1,600 cases of computers.

Comments: These are stowed in the wing bays of the forward section and in the square of the hatch of the forward section from the deck to the overhead. The mark is <S.S.>.

Stowage 17: Honolulu, 3,000 bags of U.S. mail.

Comments: One or two sections of the 'tweendeck square may be saved for mail received during the last hours of loading. Mail may be placed over other cargo in the square. It makes good beam filler cargo when space is at a premium.

Stowage 18: Honolulu, one millstone.

Comments: This is an 8-ton lift, and as such it requires special rigging for handling and must be conspicuously entered on the plan. It is only one item and the space on the plan is far out of proportion to what it occupies, but it is necessary to draw such items to the attention of all who use the plan so that rapid discharge is assured.

Stowage 19: Honolulu, one bulldozer.

Comments: On-deck cargo is shown in whatever way is most convenient with full notation. Heavy lifts must always be well marked. If ship's gear cannot handle the lift, some statement should inform the reader of this fact.

Stowage 20: Hilo, 6 drums of nitric acid.

Comments: The stowage of explosives and other dangerous articles must be illustrated clearly and accurately on the final cargo plan. Besides the ordinary data for other cargo, such cargo must have its classification and the required label clearly printed on the plan and underlined. Thus, nitric acid, which is classified as a corrosive liquid and carries a white label, is recorded as shown on Figure 4-6. All hazardous cargoes must also be listed on the Dangerous Cargo Manifest.

The plan in Figure 4-6 is of the commodity type. A hatch list is made up that gives more complete data about every shipment stowed in each compartment. Thus, with the commodity type plan and the hatch list, the stevedore discharging the ship knows all that is necessary.

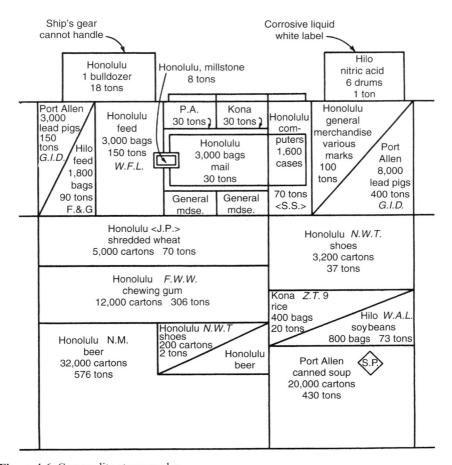

Figure 4-6. Commodity stowage plan.

The corresponding block plan would be as illustrated in Figure 4-7. Below the profile drawing of the ship and stowage, a table such as Table 4-1 would be placed. By cross reference between the plan and the table, the same information would be obtained as from the other type of plan. The numbers all being in the 200s means that the hold we have been discussing is the number 2 hold. A combination of the two types of plans is also frequently seen, depending on the preference of the plans clerk.

TABLE 4-1
Cargo Description for Figure 4-7

Number	Description
201	Port Allen, 20,000 cases of canned soup, 430 tons, for *S.P.*
202	Honolulu, 32,000 cartons canned beer, 576 tons, for *N.M.*
203	Honolulu, 200 cartons shoes, 2 tons, for *N.W.T.*
204	Hilo, 800 bags of soybeans, 73 tons, for *W.A.L.*
205	Kona, 400 bags rice, 20 tons, for *Z.T.9*
206	Honolulu, 12,000 cartons chewing gum, 306 tons, for *F.W.W.*
207	Honolulu, 5,000 cartons shredded wheat, 70 tons, for <J.P.>
208	Honolulu, 3,200 cartons shoes, 37 tons, for *N.W.T.*
209	Port Allen, 8,000 pigs lead, 400 tons, for *G.I.D.*
210	Honolulu, general merchandise consisting of: 20 cases drugs, for F.G.; 12 bags pipe fittings and 5 bundles pipe, for J.S.; 400 cartons shoes, for Y.P.; 8 cases household effects, for C.L.S.; 1,000 cartons dry groceries, for K.K.; five refrigerators, for H.A.; 17 cartons radios, for H.P.; and miscellaneous Sears and Roebuck packages. Total: 100 tons.
211	Port Allen, 3,000 pigs lead, 150 tons, for *G.I.D.*
212	Hilo, 1,800 bags feed, 90 tons, for *F. & G.*
213	Honolulu, 3,000 bags feed, 150 tons, for *W.F.L.*
214	Port Allen, general merchandise: 32 cases dry goods, for Z.T.; 64 cases hardware, for P.A.H.; 160 cases computer components, for G.I.S.; 400 cartons dry groceries, for D.S.L.; 16 cases drugs, for R.X.; and miscellaneous Sears and Roebuck packages. Total: 30 tons.
215	Kona, 2,000 bags feed, for G.G.; 200 cases computer components, for K.S.; 1,500 cases drugs, for K.G.H. Total: 30 tons.
216	Honolulu, 1,600 cases computer components, 70 tons, for <S.S.>
217	Honolulu, 3,000 bags mail, 30 tons.
218	Honolulu, 1 large millstone with sling attached, 8 tons. Readily accessible in square of hatch aft.
219	Honolulu, 1 bulldozer, 18 tons. Ship's gear can not handle.
220	Hilo, 6 drums nitric acid, 1 ton. Corrosive liquid, white label.

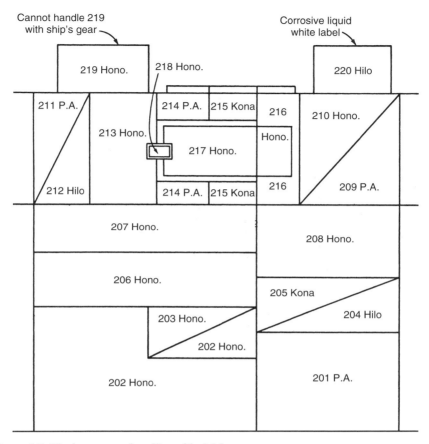

Figure 4-7. Block stowage plan. (See table 4-1.)

Preparation of the Final Plan

The final stowage plan is prepared by a member of the receiving clerk's staff known as the *plans clerk* or by the ship's officers. The procedure varies from company to company. In some companies, the ship's officers keep no records and accept the plan made up by the dock force. In others, one plan is made up by the ship's officers and another by the plans clerk. In certain cases the officers may keep only a rough copy of the stowage and use it to check the plan from the dock. In a third method of operating, only one plan is maintained, and this by the officers. Whenever a plan is kept by the officers, the second or third officer will have a direct responsibility of entering the data on a master plan. The chief officer will confer with the officer keeping the plan from time to time. In this way he/she can keep abreast of the operation while taking care of other duties. In case of a change in the tentative plan or a development of any kind that is not in accordance with the best principles of stowage, the chief officer would be notified; then he/she would attempt corrective measures. If the chief officer is not satisfied with the corrective measures, he/she may make an appropriate log book entry, notify the master, and/or write a formal report concerning the incident.

Of the three means of keeping the final stowage plan, the second system is superior. The least desirable, of course, is the first, which places complete reliance on a plan kept by a member of the dock force. In spite of their experience and sincerity, plans clerks will from time to time make mistakes in the construction of the plan. Some of these mistakes may be serious.

One reason for the plans clerk making mistakes is that to a large extent, he/she does not witness the actual stowage. As a result, the precise limitations of the stowage are not accurately depicted on the final plan.

The best way for a final stowage plan to be made for the use of the ship is to have the officers prepare it from actual observation of the stowage in the holds and data received from the receiving clerk's office. Thus the officer noting the stowage of cargo block number 201 in Figure 4-7 would make a rough notation on a blank plan showing the limitations of the stowage. If the plan was of the commodity type, he/she would enter the type of cargo and probably the marks. Obviously, he/she would not know the exact number of cartons or the total weight; these data he/she would have to be obtained from the receiving clerk's office.

Keeping a plan as outlined above guarantees that the officer will know the stowage well. It is not a difficult task, although it may seem difficult to anyone who has not actually performed it. But difficult or easy, the advantages are great. The ship's officers will have a clearer knowledge of the stowage, and in gaining it they will have circulated from hold to hold keeping a watchful eye on the entire operation. The actual procedure in keeping the plan requires that the officer start in the number 1 hold and, after observing the stowage activities there, proceed to the number 2 hold and finally all the way aft to the last hold. He/she should carry with him/her a small book with a cargo compartment drawn on each page. The book should be small enough to fit into a pocket. In this book, he/she should make notations of what he/she observes. When the ship has been completely observed, the officer transfers these data to a master rough plan. The blank that forms this plan may be kept in one of the officer's cabins or in the chart room. All officers should observe the progress of the plan's construction and check back in the holds from time to time to ascertain its accuracy.

One officer should be responsible for making hourly trips through the holds as described above and entering the information on the rough master plan. On some of the rounds through the ship, there may be no change from the last observation. But when a change does occur, the officer should be on hand to see where the old mark left off and the new mark started. If a tentative plan is available, all officers will know approximately when changes are to be made, and they can plan their work more intelligently. They can be on hand to check on the security of the cargo that is going to be stowed under and on the laying of dunnage or separation, and in general to see how the stowage of the last cargo is finished and the next cargo commenced.

If a plans clerk is also keeping a plan, it may be used to check the plan kept by the ship's officers. This, the second system mentioned above, is the best because it provides for a check on the accuracy of each.

Disposition of Final Plan

When the ship has been completely loaded, a smooth plan is made up from the rough original, duplicated, and the copies distributed. Copies should be sent ahead of the ship to all the discharging ports, and copies should also be distributed to the operations department and to all deck officers of the ship.

PREPARATION OF THE CARGO SPACES

Cargo is stowed in the holds and tanks of the ship. In the hold areas, special compartments may be built, such as cargo lockers for valuable or easily pilfered items, magazines for the stowage of explosives, and insulated compartments for refrigerated cargoes. Prior to the loading of any cargo in any compartment, be it a container, tank, magazine, reefer space, special locker, or plain hold, the compartment must meet minimum standards of cleanliness. In some instances, the cleanliness of the hold is not of major importance, for example, when loading bagged cement. In most cases, however, an improperly prepared hold may result in heavy damage claims due to tainting or contamination. If the shipper can prove that the attention paid to the preparation of a hold area was less than that warranted by good seamanship and thereby create grounds for claiming improper care and custody, he/she has a good chance of collecting damages. It is the duty of the chief officer to have all cargo compartments prepared for the receipt of cargo and to make log book entries concerning the efforts expended along these lines.

Standard Procedure for Cleaning Holds

Holds may be cleaned by the ship's crew or by ship service company gangs hired on a contract basis. The choice of the type of labor to be used is most commonly made by a member of the operations department on an economic basis. When ships are in places where cheap labor is available, then such labor should be used. However, when the choice is between the ship's crew members and a shoreside contractor in a port of the United States, the differential in cost may favor using the ship's crew. Another factor in favor of using the ship's crew may be good labor relations on board the ship; the decision should be given careful consideration.

The actual process of cleaning a general carrier's holds is simple and routine, providing that no special problem of cleaning is created by the carriage of extremely odorous or dirty cargoes. The equipment needed for each hatch is as follows: one dirt sling, two endless rope slings, enough brooms for all hands in the cleaning gang, rope yarns, and some cluster lights. The cleaning starts in the upper 'tweendeck. The first task is to clear a small space of all debris and start piling all the clean dunnage in a neat stack over two, 2- by 4-inch battens spaced about 6 feet apart. If 2- by 4-inch battens are not available, a double height of 1- by 6-inch boards will suffice. After the usable dunnage has been salvaged, the condemned dunnage should be slung up in the rope slings. If two rope slings are not enough, use more. All the paper and other debris should be rolled up and placed in the dirt sling, which consists of an ordinary rope net sling with a lining of canvas to prevent the dirt from falling through. Every ship should have at least one dirt sling for every hatch, and perhaps one or two extra.

If the ship is in port, the debris, including the condemned dunnage, must be dumped on the weather deck of the ship. This should be done in such a way that the safety of crew members walking fore and aft is not impaired. If the pile of debris on deck gets too large, the loads should merely be slung up and left in the hold ready to be hooked up and dumped over the side when the opportunity presents itself. If the working circumstances are such that the decks and holds must be cleared, the mate must make arrangements for trucks or railroad cars to come alongside and receive the debris to be discharged from the hold being cleaned

When the good dunnage has been stacked up in one wing where it will be available as needed for the next cargo, the condemned dunnage slung up ready for discharge, and the paper, debris, and dirt swept up and placed in a dirt sling ready for discharge, the cleaning process is complete.

Washing the Interiors of Dry Cargo Holds

Occasionally, it may be necessary to wash the interior of a dry cargo hold. Washing is always done *after* the hold has been cleaned according to the system described above as the standard procedure for cleaning holds. After carrying cargoes that leave behind heavy dust or glutinous residue, the simple sweeping outlined above would be insufficient to clean the hold if the next cargo were a delicate or clean type of commodity.

The washing procedure is simply that of using a wash deck hose below decks to direct a solid stream of water over all the surfaces of the hold and toward the drainage well. If possible, the washing should be done alongside a dock where fresh water can be used directly from a dock outlet. If the washing is done at sea, the preliminary wash may be with salt water, followed by a thorough rinse with fresh water. If the washing is done with salt water without a rinse of fresh water, the salt residue left after drying will pick up moisture from the air and may damage cargo coming in contact with it. Probably the worst feature of allowing the salt water to dry on the hold interior is the increase in the corrosion rate that will result.

A period of 2 or 3 days should be allowed before attempting to load another cargo in a freshly washed hold. This time is needed for drying. If the outside atmosphere is relatively dry and windy and a good stream of air is directed into the hold with the hatches removed for a maximum exhaust circulation, the drying process should not take more than 36 hours. However, in the case of high outside humidity or heavy rain, the drying period may extend to several days. If the ship is equipped with a dehumidifying system, the hatches can be closed and the system placed on recirculation with dry air, which will result in one hatch being well dried out in 3 hours. If an exceptional condition arose in which every hatch of the ship had to be washed, the drying of all hatches could be accomplished in one day.

Deodorization Methods

If drain wells or parts of a given hold become contaminated by odorous cargo residue, they may have to be treated with a simple deodorizing wash. A solution consisting of ½ pound of chloride of lime mixed with 2½ gallons of fresh water is quite effective. If the area is only slightly affected, it may simply be swabbed down with this solution. If it is very dirty, it should be washed with a solid stream of fresh water from a wash deck hose and then swabbed down with the chlorated lime solution. If the odor persists, sprinkle some of the powder over the area. High test hypochlorate (HTH) is a more powerful deodorizing agent that also comes in powder form. Compared with chlorated lime, smaller amounts of HTH are used when making up solutions for deodorizing holds. A tablespoonful of HTH added to a bucket of fresh water makes a fairly strong solution; no more than this should be used. This powder should not be left in the area, where it might contact cargo directly. If the solution is too strong, it may eradicate the odors of the past cargo but the odor from the HTH may cause damage itself.

Preparation for Bulk Commodities

The preparation of a dry cargo hold for the loading of bulk commodities generally involves more than the simple cleaning described above. One thing that always must be done is to prepare the drainage system to pass water but to retain the bulk commodity. In the case of the drain well plates in the lower hold, this involves either covering with burlap and inserting the edges underneath the plates or, more preferably, covering the opening with two layers of burlap and cementing the edge down. The cement that is applied to the edge should be flattened and not built up. If the cement is rounded off or built up in any way, there is more danger of its getting knocked loose and allowing the bulk commodity to fill up the drain wells. If this occurs, there is no way of pumping water out of the compartment in case of a leak from any source. Ignoring such a detail could mean the loss of the ship.

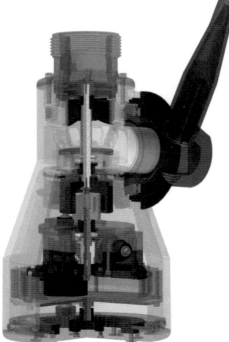

Figure 4-8.
Butterworth tank washing machine. The hose is connected to the threaded upper end. The water turbine is connected to a shaft, which in turn rotates an eccentric crank. The eccentric crank operates a pawl that rotates a worm. This rotating worm meshes with a worm gear and by this means the nozzles are rotated in a vertical plane. At the same time, a stationary gear rotates the entire assembly in a horizontal plane. *Bottom illustration courtesy Troy R. Humphries and Dan G. Elko, Butterworth Group.*

Additional protection for the burlap covering is afforded by placing a small wooden box about 6 inches high with the bottom removed over the drain well opening. This covering is referred to as a *high hat* in some trades. It is not absolutely necessary, but the added protection may be well worth the trouble.

When stowing bulk copra, the interior of the hold is entirely covered with fiber mats. Bulk coal requires no interior covering, but pipes must be inserted in the hold *before* the coal is loaded so that temperatures can be taken in the interior of the stowed cargo. In the case of bulk grain, a longitudinal bulkhead may be built along the centerline of the ship in the lower holds if more than a specified amount is loaded. If the grain is loaded so that it completely fills the hold, special feeders may be built in the 'tweendeck spaces.

The above examples are presented to show the type of special preparations that may have to be taken before loading certain cargoes.

Standard Procedure for Cleaning Tanks

On tankers, machines are used almost exclusively for the washing of the tanks. Hand washing methods are used for washing tanks on most dry cargo ships, but machines are used in some instances. A brief description of washing by machine will be given below.

When washing by hand, the temperature of the water cannot be as high as when using a machine. Consequently, the tanks are heated by steaming. Washing by machine eliminates the need for this prolonged steaming. The fact that steaming is not necessary is one of the principal advantages of washing by machine. Steaming a tank causes expansion and later contraction of the hull, which may result in hull damage, especially after being repeated many times. Steaming also accelerates corrosion of the tank interior. If a machine is used, the ship must be capable of delivering at least 180 gallons of salt water per minute to the machine at a temperature of 185°F under a pressure of about 180 pounds per square inch. This will supply one machine. If two machines are to be run simultaneously, the ship must have a heat exchanger and pump capable of doubling the above supply. Two types of machines are used. One is the Butterworth machine, pictured in Figure 4-8, and the other is the Pyrate machine. They operate on the same principle. The water is discharged under high pressure and high temperature, and as it strikes the surface of the tank it cleans the surface of all oil, wax, and dirt. The machine rotates in two planes and the stream from each nozzle covers every inch of the tank that can be reached by a straight line from the machine's position in the tank during its operation. From this last statement, it can be seen that surfaces behind beam knees, bilge brackets, and web frames will not be struck by the solid stream of hot water. Therefore, these surfaces must be reached by repositioning the machine so that they are struck by the solid stream or by hand hosing and cleaning after the machine has been removed.

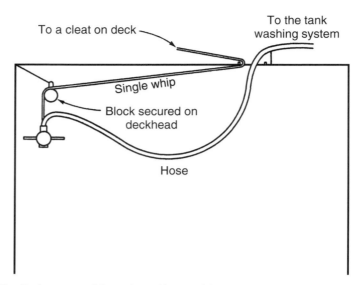

Figure 4-9. The displacement of the tank washing machine make an improved wash.

The machine may be lowered into a tank through a special hole cut through the deck for this purpose or through a manhole from one side. If lowered through a manhole, a block with a bull line or single whip to hold the machine in the center of the tank must be rigged. If the special hole is used, it should be cut through the center of the tank. Regardless of the method used to suspend the machine in the tank, the cleaning routine is the same. A recommended method is to lower the machine to within 5 feet of the bottom of the tank and run it for about 30 minutes, draw the machine up to within 5 feet of the top of the tank and run it for about 15 minutes, and then lower it 5 feet and run it for another 15 minutes. Continue lowering and washing at 5-foot increments until within 5 feet of the bottom again. Run the machine at this lower level for 30 minutes to complete the process.

All the time that the machine is running, the pumps should be slowly pumping out the wash water. This keeps a steady stream of water running toward the suction foot and carries away some of the sludge and dirt that would otherwise be floating on the surface of the water in the tank. This sludge would adhere to the sides of the tank at the lower levels and make the cleaning job much more difficult. The reason for operating the machine at the lower position first is to warm up the tank and knock down the worst of the scale and dirt at the beginning of the operation.

The length of time and number of drops may be increased or decreased depending on the condition of the tank and the degree of cleanliness desired. Figure 4-9 shows the method of rigging up a machine to wash from different positions by the use of blocks and single whips. The machine is assumed to be entering the tank through a manhole, but the same thing can be done if it is lowered through a tank washing hole.

After washing as outlined above, the tank is opened and ventilated with a mechanical blower. The rigging of wind sails is not always practicable.

After ventilation, workers must be sent into the tank to muck it out. *Mucking out* may be defined as the process of scraping up scale and sediment left in the tank and placing it in a bucket that is then hauled out of the tank and dumped either over the side or on deck to be shoveled over the side when the ship is at sea. This process is done entirely by hand and is a slow job. It should be done thoroughly. The mucking out process is followed by wiping down the interior, spot cleaning the dirtier areas with a hand hose or by wiping with a solvent and rags.

Washing by Hand Hose

The majority of dry cargo vessels still are not equipped with the machines, pumps, and heat exchangers for cleaning tanks mechanically; therefore, the tanks must be washed by hand. Washing by hand starts with the steaming of the tank by turning on the steam smothering line. The steaming period may run for 4 to 8 hours depending on the condition of the tank before the process starts. If the tank has been carrying black fuel oil and is to be prepared for a product that is easily contaminated, the tank will require at least 6 hours of steaming.

After the steaming period, the tank must be allowed to cool for 1 to 2 hours. The cooling time will depend on the outside temperature, and no definite time limit can be specified.

As soon as possible, a worker should be sent into the tank with a wash deck hose and washing by hand should commence. This person should have a line around their shoulders and under their arms and be tended by another worker from the deck. A vapor-proof light should be lowered into the tank so that the worker in the tank can see where the stream of water is being directed from the hose. This worker must work from the top of the ladder leading into the tank, which is an awkward and dangerous position from which to handle a hose. To prevent an accident, the worker should be lashed to the ladder before the hose is passed down to him/her. At the first stage of the washing process, this worker's head should be no father down into the tank than a foot or so, just enough to enable him/her to see the interior. The blower should be rigged and a supply of fresh air should be supplied to the worker continuously. The worker will start washing the overhead and continue down the bulkheads and sides of the tank. At the beginning, the heat will be intense and the worker should be relieved after not more than 10 minutes of washing. Gradually, the time for each worker in the tank can be increased as the tank cools down. It is important to start the hand washing before the tank cools excessively, because as the tank cools the waxy elements in the oil tend to coagulate and become difficult to wash away. The steaming period should melt most of the wax and grease and make it easier to wash the tank. The hand hose cannot be handled at the high pressures and temperatures used with a machine. The temperature of the water when washing by hand should be 125°F and the pressure 125 pounds per square inch. This is about as much pressure and as high a temperature as a worker clinging to a slippery ladder can handle. If started while the tank is still warm, this washing procedure will be effective. While the washing process is being carried out, the tanks should be slowly stripped by operating the pumps steadily. This is for the same reason as mentioned in the case of machine washing, to have a steady stream of water running toward the suction foot and to prevent a rise in the dirty water level in the tank.

As the washing continues, the tank will be cooling down and the worker handling the hose in the tank will have to go farther and farther down. After he/she has done all the washing possible with the hose, the tanks should be well ventilated with a mechanical blower. Following the ventilation process, ll hands should be sent into the tank for wiping down and mucking out. When the tank has been wiped down and mucked out, it should be clean, dry, and ready for the next cargo.

Whether washing a tank by hand or by machine, if the tank is not cleaned sufficiently well after the regular washing process there is no alternative except to repeat the process. However, if only certain spots are found to be dirty, the interior may be cleaned in those areas only.

If a tank has been used for dry cargo for some time and the principal defect in the tank's condition is heavy rust and dirt accumulation, the interior may have to be scraped and chipped before washing. This depends on the type of cargo that is to be loaded into the tank (see Fig. 4-10).

Figure 4-10. Forward deep tank awaiting discharge of jeeps while after deep tank has dunnage removed in preparation for cleaning.

Before any tank is loaded, the interior is inspected by a representative of the shipper, the shipowner, and one of the ship's officers. The shipowner will, for his/her own protection, generally have a surveyor certify the tank as being clean, the surveyor being a qualified representative of the cargo underwriters, probably from an organization such as the National Cargo Bureau, Inc.

CHECKING THE CONDITION OF THE CARGO HOLD

To the casual observer glancing down into a ship's hold, it does not appear that there are many things that could go wrong with the space below. It has the appearance of a big steel container with spaced wooden lining against the frames and little else. Yet before an officer can make an entry in the ship's log relative to the condition of the cargo spaces, he/she must have checked in one way or another a long list of items. Some of these things must be checked each time the ship empties her holds; others, such as the striking plate under the bilge sounding pipe, need to be checked very infrequently. These items are listed and commented upon briefly in the following sections.

Permanent Dunnage

The term *permanent dunnage* refers to the sweat battens secured to the frames, the spar ceiling laid over the tank tops, the wooden sheathing sometimes secured to the transverse bulkheads separating boiler rooms or engine rooms from adjoining cargo holds, and any wooden casings around pipes or conduits going through the cargo spaces. These items can be inspected as the ship is being discharged. That is to say, there is no need to make a special inspection trip through the ship to keep informed about their condition. The policy should be set by the chief officer for all officers to take note of the condition of these items as they travel from hatch to hatch during their normal day's work of observing the cargo operations. If something is noted to be missing or broken, the chief officer should be given the information as soon as possible. In the case of sweat battens, the chief officer should replace the missing sweat batten during the lunch hour or whenever there will be no longshoremen in the hold. In this manner, the ship's sweat battens will always be in first-class condition. If casings or the spar ceiling is noted to be damaged, it may be repaired by the ship's force, but more than likely a requisition to the company's repair department will have to be made. The sweat battens can usually be taken care of by the ship's force in the manner described above, and the work and trouble are negligible. If the batten is missing about a height that can be easily reached from the tank tops, the cargo provides a convenient platform upon which to work.

Limber System

The term *limber system* refers to the drain pipes and drain holes that constitute the means for carrying off all liquids to the drain well in a hold. In other words, limber is a synonym for drainage. The limber system or drainage system must be checked each time a ship has been discharged. If a ship is on a run where cargo is always coming in and going out, the check must be made whenever practicable.

In the 'tweendecks, the principal thing to be checked is the drain pipe leading down to the ship's drain well in the after end of the hold. This drain pipe can be checked by pouring water from a bucket down the pipe and observing whether the water flows through or not. Obviously, two people are needed to see if the flow is obstructed or not.

If the flow is obstructed, the pipe should be cleared with an ordinary wire snake or by using a rubber plunger. If the pipe cannot be cleared by these methods, it must be removed and either renewed or cleaned out. Cargo should not be stowed in a 'tweendeck space where the scupper drains are plugged up. One reason for this is because of the tremendous effect on stability that the free surface in the upper levels of a ship has. The free surface effect itself is the same whether high or low in the ship, but the added weight of the liquid trapped in the upper levels adds to a poor situation. If it becomes necessary to use a fire hose in the 'tweendeck where there are no drains, the water will create a condition that endangers the ship. One of the contributing causes to the capsizing of the *Normandy* in 1941 at a dock during the fighting of a fire in her in New York City was the fact that the water from the fire hoses collected in the upper decks and *remained* there. If the water could be drained to the lower levels through freely running pipes, the ship might have been saved.

These drains from the upper decks to the drain well are located in the after end of the hatch. This fact must be kept in mind when stowing certain cargoes. Cargoes that are known to drain heavily should normally be loaded near these drains. There are exceptions; for example, if the cargo is of such a nature that it would obstruct drainage from other cargoes, then it should be stowed away from the drains. In the latter case, however, it would be highly important to make sure that the dunnage was laid to form an efficient drainage system under the cargo stowed near the drain pipes. Lack of attention to such details on the part of stevedores or ship's officers may be the cause of costly damage to cargo.

DRAIN WELLS

In most modern ships, the tank top plating continues outboard in a horizontal plane and connects with the hull plating. A drain well is provided for draining off any water or other liquids that might find their way into the ship's hold. The drain well is located between the last two frames and floors of the hold. It drops down below the level of the tank tops to within about 18 inches of the outer bottom, runs athwartship for several feet, and stops about 18 inches inboard from the turn of the bilge. Fig. 4-10 illustrates the construction.

When the ship has side bilge construction, it is important to check all of the limber (drainage) holes through the bilge bracket where the hull and tank top intersect. These holes should be clear. This bilge system is not open to the hold. It is usually covered with boards 2 inches by 12 inches. These boards are known as the *limber boards* and their purpose is to keep dirt and cargo residue from entering the limber system. They are removable for inspection purposes. It is necessary, therefore, to open up the bilges by removing these boards each time one inspects them.

In holds equipped with the drain well system, there is a perforated plate that covers the drain well and must be kept clean. If the holes become plugged, no water or liquid cargo can drain into the well; hence, if the hull plating is pierced or water finds its way into the compartment in any way, there will be no way for it to be removed. It will back up into the hold and cause free surface, which will impair stability, or rise vertically and damage the cargo.

The liquid that finds its way into either the drain well or the after part of the side bilge is removed from the compartment through a bilge suction pipe that is connected to a bilge pump manifold in the engine room. The pipe used to pump out the well or bilge is 3 inches in diameter. It terminates about 1½ inches above the lowest point in the well or bilge. When checking the limber system, the ship's officer should always check the wire cage or perforated box covering the suction foot in the well or bilge. The wire cage or perforated box acts as a strainer of the liquid picked up by the suction, and it must be clean and clear. This strainer is known as the *rose box*. The rose box keeps rags, bits of wood, and other debris from being sucked into the bilge suction pipe. If the rose box is neglected, it will eventually become clogged; this will make it impossible to pump out the hold in case of leakage.

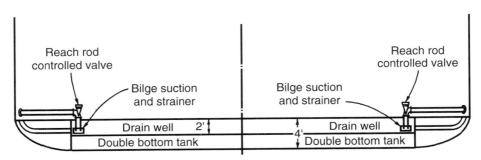

Figure 4-11. Drain well. The drain well may run almost all the way across the ship as shown here or it may be only 4 feet transversely. Its depth is about 2 feet, and it is located just forward of the after bulkhead of the compartment. The opening into the drain well is 2 to 4 feet long in a transverse direction. This opening must be made dust tight but not watertight when stowing bulk commodities.

STOP-LIFT-CHECK VALVES

The bilge suction pipes have valves inserted in them just above the level of the suction foot. These valves are known as stop-lift-check valves. The action of this valve is as follows: if the valve stem is turned clockwise as far as it will go, the valve is closed. If the valve is opened one and a half turns, its action is the same as any lift-check valve. If the valve stem is turned counterclockwise for several turns, the valve is raised off its seat and acts as an open valve.

Ordinarily, this valve should be set to operate as a lift-check valve. That is, it should be backed off about one and a half turns. In this position, if suction is lost when pumping the bilges, the contents of the pipe will not be vomited back into the well. This fact makes it easier to regain suction and to retain suction when pumping liquids at low levels, which is almost always the case when pumping out the bilges and drain wells of cargo ships.

The valve should be closed when there is danger of flooding an adjacent compartment through the bilge system, as in the case of a collision. This may not be necessary unless the pipe is broken by the impact, but it should be done as a safety precaution. Part of every ship's collision drill should include the closing of these valves by crew members instructed in the procedure.

The valve will have to be opened wide if it becomes necessary to pump water into the hold through the bilge system. This may be the only way to extinguish some types of fires.

This valve should be checked to see that it turns freely each time that it becomes accessible after discharging cargo. It is important to reset it, however, as required by the chief engineer. It may be opened wide in some cases so that the lift-check feature is not utilized.

REACH RODS

Obviously, stop-lift-check valves cannot be reached when the hold is filled with cargo. To operate them from the deck, they are fitted with *reach rods*. These are simply extensions of the valve stem running up through the main deck through watertight glands and fitted with a wheel for turning. They must be checked to see that they are not broken and that they turn freely. If they are rusted and frozen, the ship may be placed in a dangerous condition in case of an emergency. It is recommended that the reach rods and bilge suction valves be checked at the same time. This can be accomplished by one person turning the reach rod from the weather deck level while another person observes the action in the hold.

The 'tweendeck drains, drain wells, rose boxes, bilge suction valves, and reach rods make up an important group of items all related to keeping the drainage system of the ship functioning in the best manner. These items should be checked each voyage and if any one is not working correctly it should be repaired before cargo is loaded.

BILGE SOUNDING PIPE

To determine whether a given compartment is taking water, each one is equipped with a pipe running from an accessible upper deck down to the drain well or bilge called the *sounding pipe*. At regular periods, an iron or brass rod is lowered down this pipe until it strikes the bottom of the well or bilge. The rod is coated with chalk, and if any water or other liquid is in the bilge its presence and depth will be indicated on the rod. This chore is performed by a designated seaman and is called *sounding the bilge*. It should be done at least twice a day under ordinary circumstances, every half hour when taking on fuel oil or other liquids in the ship's tanks, and immediately after a period of heavy weather. There may be times when the bilges cannot be sounded because of heavy seas placing water on deck continually; during such times, orders should be given to the watch engineering officer to pump all the bilges at least once a watch. Such orders would generally be given by the master of the ship through the chief engineer.

THE STRIKING PLATE

After several years of daily sounding, the steel directly below the bilge sounding pipe will wear away. If a pinhole develops in this spot from wear and corrosion, oil or water from the tank below can enter the hold. The amount of oil that can enter the hold might be sufficient to cause damage to cargo in the lower tiers, especially if the tank were pressed up and the ship had a large trim by the stern. Another bad feature of such a hole is the possibility of contamination of any drinking water carried in the tank below.

To guard against the possibility of the steel directly below the bilge sounding pipe wearing out, this area is covered with a small doubling plate called the *striking plate*. This plate does not wear out quickly and hence need not be inspected every time the drainage system is checked. However, every officer joining a ship should satisfy himself that this plate is not worn through on both sides of every compartment. This can only be done by opening up the drain well and sighting the plate or running a finger over it to feel the amount of wear. If it is badly worn, it should be renewed at the first opportunity. It is not necessary to renew the entire plate; the worn spot can be filled with a bead of weld metal.

Electrical Conduits and Outlets

Conduits and outlets can also be checked as the cargo is being worked. Whenever a defect is noted, a repair requisition should be sent in immediately or the defect should be taken care of by the ship's force.

Ladders

As a safety measure, a broken rung in a ladder should be repaired as rapidly as possible. If a ladder is damaged during the cargo operation and cannot be repaired immediately, the longshoremen must be provided with a Jacobs ladder or other means of climbing into and out of the hold. Rungs can be replaced very easily by the ship's force. The uprights of the ladder can be bored with a ⅝-inch hole and a ½-inch steel bar, threaded at both ends, can be secured in place with nuts. This may be used as a temporary repair measure, providing the uprights are not bent out of line. Ladders are frequent casualties in ship's holds and their repair goes on continually.

Plating and Pipes

The hull plating, tank top plating, deck plating, and the plating of the transverse bulkheads forming one side of a tank should be surveyed constantly by the ship's officers as they make their frequent visits to the holds. Prior to loading cargo, a special inspection should be made for evidence of leaks. Leaks may be spotted by the presence of rust streaks or oil traces. Such measures also apply to pipes running through the compartment, especially the flanges of such pipes.

Manholes and Side Ports

These openings into the hold should be checked more frequently than any of the other items mentioned. Obviously, they should be checked when they are closed and made ready for sea. If any of the dogs are difficult to turn, they should be made free at the first opportunity, which may not be at the time of closing. The gaskets should be kept clean and intact. If gaskets are made of flax or woven fiber material of any kind, they should be kept oiled and free of paint. If they are made of rubber, they should be kept clean and free of oil, grease, and paint. The knife edges against which the gasket presses when the door of the opening is closed should be clean and free of broken or jagged places.

While at sea, side ports should be checked twice daily. This is not of great importance when the ship is light and the weather is fair, but if the ship is loaded and the seas are running up the hull and placing hydrostatic pressure over the side port as the ship works in the seaway, it is extremely important. If possible, some means of gaining access to the side port without having to open a manhole on the weather deck should be made. This can be accomplished by building crawl holes in the cargo in the shelter deck spaces leading from entrances other than the manhole openings on the weather deck, if such openings exist.

If a side port is found to be leaking while at sea, it should be caulked with oakum. Directly in the way of most side ports, a drain will lead to the drainage system of the hold. This drain should be kept clear so that in case of leakage the entering sea water can be drained off quickly. In such a case, it would be common sense to have the bilges serving the compartment pumped frequently by the engineer officer on watch. In very bad weather it may be impossible to have the bilges sounded periodically because of water on deck and generally unsafe conditions in the exposed area of the bilge sounding pipe opening on the weather deck.

Firefighting Equipment

The carbon dioxide outlets should be checked to see that they are not broken and are clear. The inlets to the smoke detecting system should be checked also to see that they are clear and in good working order.

Hatch Covering Equipment

It may not be necessary to place this item on the checkoff list; however, it is important to have all such equipment in good order. If tarpaulins are used, there should be at least three and they should be without holes or weak seams.

Ventilation Ducts

The most important thing that needs checking with respect to the ventilation ducts leading into the holds is that the system of closing them off from the outside atmosphere is in good working order. In the case of fire, it is imperative that all openings to the atmosphere be closed and kept closed. In some instances, it may be necessary to close these openings because of heavy seas coming on board. It should be seen to, of course, that these same openings into the hold are clear so that the hold can be ventilated correctly during the voyage.

CHAPTER 5

STOWAGE OF GENERAL CARGO

THIS CHAPTER IS ENTITLED "The Stowage of General Cargo," but it is impossible to deal with the stowage of all types of cargo in this single work. In the remaining pages of this chapter we will discuss the stowage of a number of important cargo types. We will also deal with the problem of calculating space consumption using the stowage factor. The discussion will be based on the principles already covered and should serve to illustrate their application. The cargoes selected for discussion are not necessarily any more important than hundreds of others that might have been chosen; however, some selectivity had to be exercised and those covered do bring out a number of interesting points. A full discussion of a large number of commodities will have to await the writing of a book with that objective.

THE STOWAGE OF IMPORTANT CARGO TYPES

The Stowage of Bags

The preparation of the hold for the stowage of bags commences with the laying of a dunnage platform upon which to stow the bottom tier. This platform is primarily for drainage purposes, although in some cases it is equally important to keep bagged cargo from contacting the steel deck. If the ship is equipped with side bilges, the first layer of dunnage should be laid down running athwartships or, preferably, at an angle to the keel. If laid at an angle to the keel, the forward end of the dunnage should be inboard.

If the ship is equipped with drain wells in the after end of the hold, the first tier of dunnage should be laid down running fore and aft. The dunnage should be spaced not more than 1 feet apart.

The second tier of dunnage should be laid at right angles to the first, except that if the first tier is laid diagonally the second tier may be laid either fore and aft or athwartships. For bagged cargoes, the dunnage of the second tier should be spaced not more than 1 inch apart. If the dunnage is too widely spaced, the pressure of the top tiers will cause the bags on the bottom tiers to split.

If ventilation is not a major problem with the commodity in the bags, the dunnage of the second tier should be placed flush together. This eliminates any possibility of the bottom bags splitting and requires very little additional dunnage. If sufficient dunnage is available, the drainage tiers of dunnage should be 2 or 3 inches high for commodities requiring maximum ventilation, such as rice and soy beans. This provides a series of ventilation ducts under the cargo.

The stowage of the bags may be in any one of three ways, depending on the nature of the commodity in the bags. If the commodity requires maximum ventilation, the best stowage is one bag directly on top of the one below, laid with the length fore and aft (see Fig. 5-1a). This stowage will provide small air spaces throughout the stowed cargo block and help in the circulation of air. It is difficult to get longshoremen to do this consistently as the stowage proceeds; it generally requires careful explanation of the need and desirability of care in placing the bags in the hold and the presence of an officer after stowage commences. Stowage in this manner is known as *bag on bag* stowage.

If the commodity does not require maximum ventilation, the best stowage is to place the upper bags between two lower ones, which results in a brickwork style of stowage. This stowage eliminates the spaces between rows and tiers and reduces the broken stowage percentage. If a full hatch is being stowed, it might mean that one complete additional tier can be stowed. This type of stowage is referred to as *half bag* stowage (see Fig. 5-1b).

When stowing bagged cargo in small blocks in which the stability of the block is a factor, it may be advisable to stow one tier of bags fore and aft and the next tier athwartship. This stowage ties the tiers together so that the stowed block is less likely to fall over while working the cargo in port or when the ship is rolling and pitching in a heavy sea. Such blocks should not depend entirely on this cross tiering for their security; they should be shored up or blocked up by adjacent cargo as well. It may not be necessary to cross-tier the bags throughout the stowed block, but simply to do this on the last two rows of the block. Still another way to add to the security of a bulkhead of bagged goods is to place a strip of dunnage along the outside edge of every other tier as the loading progresses vertically. This will tend to tip the bulkhead toward the stowed block or at least to lessen the tendency for the face of the bulkhead to lean away from the stowed block (see Fig. 5-1b).

Although there are exceptions, generally no dunnage is used between tiers of bagged cargoes. Venetian vents are sometimes used *within* a stowed block of commodities needing heavy ventilation.

The only dunnage used besides the drainage floor is vertical dunnage laid against the transverse bulkheads, the sweat battens, and all vertical structural members, such as stanchions, ladders, and ventilator ducts. This vertical dunnage is used to keep the bags from contacting the steel members of the ship. For additional protection and cleanliness, the vertical members may be wrapped with heavy paper and tied with rope yarn.

If the bags contain coffee, cocoa beans, or any other commodity that may leak and must not touch the ship's deck, the bags should be stowed over separation cloths. Any leakage will be caught in the cloth and can be rebagged before being contaminated. The use of these separation cloths is also advisable

Figure 5-1a.
Bag-on-bag method **(top)** for maximum
ventilation and half-bag method **(bottom)**
for maximum use of available cubic.
Note "dog ears" that make it easier for
longshoremen to handle bags (as in **Fig.
3-19a**).

Figure 5-1b. Bag stowage. This is a view of bag stowage extending out into the hatch square for a little more than one section. It is not the best stowage. The bulkhead has been carefully built vertically and looks fairly stable; however, by running every other tier of bags along the bulkhead face with their lengths athwartship and tying the bulkhead bags into the stow, a much more stable bulkhead could have been made. The effort to do this would have been no more than that of building the bulkhead as shown here. Almost all of the bags in the bulkhead are running longitudinally and are built up half-bag style. Thus, these bags are more or less a unit and can more easily fall away from the rest of the stowage in really heavy weather. Of course, if other cargo will always be bearing against this bulkhead or if no bad weather is encountered, no damage will be done. However, cargo should not be stowed so that a good out-turn depends on so many uncertain factors, especially when there is no difference in the amount of effort required. *Courtesy of U.S. Maritime Commission.*

when stowing bagged commodities over other cargoes. The most efficient covering for this purpose is made of burlap. The burlap comes in strips about 4 feet wide, which must be cut to reach the entire distance across the stowed block with enough slack to enable tucking them down the sides of the ship about 2 feet. These cloths should never be stretched tightly over the cargo, but rather should be left with some slack.

Hooks used on some bags will result in tears that allow the contents to leak out. On loosely woven bags a hook can be used without tearing the bag. The hook will slip through the fibers and out again without actually leaving a hole for the contents to leak through. The commodity must be large enough to allow the use of such bags, such as cocoa beans. If a bag is tightly packed and heavy (over 100 pounds), there is little doubt that the longshoremen will use hooks on it. They cannot get a grip on such a bag with their hands and to handle it they are forced to use a hook. If the shipper packs the bags with corners tied to form a place for the longshoremen to grab, known as *dog ears* (see Fig. 5-1a), hooks will not be used as readily. Paper bags of cement or plaster are very vulnerable to the hook, but they are often small enough and light enough to allow the longshoremen to lift them easily. Every effort should be made to prevent hooks being used on such cargoes. A hook with several small slightly curved prongs known as a *bag hook* may be issued to longshoremen handling fiber bags if it is desired that they not use their larger cargo hooks. This will help reduce hook damage in some cases. The bag hook should not be used on paper bags.

In the outboard tiers, bags may be stowed athwartships or placed on end, providing the vertical dunnage cannot be used. The reason for placing the bags athwartships is to present only the relatively small surface at the end of the bag to possible damage from contact with the frames. Standing the bags on end presents a surface to the sweat battens that is too large to protrude through them and is a device that may be used in lieu of vertical dunnage. If the dunnage is available, it should be used.

The bags must not be allowed to rest on the edges of the sweat battens, stringers, upper ends of vertical dunnage, or other surfaces that might be present along the periphery of the hold. If they rest on these surfaces, they will be torn as the cargo settles during the voyage.

In spite of all precautions, some bags will be torn in almost every shipment; hence, it is important to use separation cloths as mentioned above to catch leakage. If the contents that leak out are caught in the separation cloths and rebagged, they are known as *ship fills*. If the contents are not caught but allowed to reach the deck of the ship or dock and are swept up and rebagged, they are known as *sweepings*. Ship fills or sweepings are distributed to the consignees having that type of cargo in the hold in proportion to the total amounts they had originally. Ship fills may be handled by the consignee in the same manner as the rest of the original shipment. Sweepings must be condemned as unfit for eating and either used for the oil content or re-exported.

The Stowage of Bales

In stowing bales, a drainage floor is prepared as described for bags. Vertical dunnage is not as important in the wings as with bags, but it should be used against transverse bulkheads and vertical structural members in the manner described for bags. Bales contain either unprocessed fibers or strands of a commodity or a flat material shipped in layers. Examples of the former are cotton, sisal, jute, wool, and manila. Examples of the latter are cotton piece goods, tobacco, skins, and dry goods.

Bales are generally parallelepiped in shape (see Fig. 5-2). If they contain fibrous commodities, they may be placed in the ship on their flats, edges, or crowns and no harm will come to them. They stow more securely, however, if stowed on their flats in a fore and aft direction. All cargo should be stowed to conform with the shape of the ship unless there is a good reason for not doing so. One good reason for deviating from continuous flat stowage in the case of bales is to use up as much of the cubic as possible in the compartment. Therefore, it is important to measure the hold clearance vertically and stow the bales so that the top of the last tier will come as close as possible to the underside of the beams. It may be that all the bales should be on their flats or edges on all but the last tier, which may have to be placed on their crowns.

Figure 5-2. Bales of cotton being loaded. Bales do not need to be stowed on their flats because of their contents. These bales, however, are mostly stowed on their flats.

If the contents of the bale are in layers, the bales in the first tier are laid down on the dunnage platform on their flats. The outboard bales in each tier should be placed on their edges so that their flats will be presented to the sweat battens. This precaution is necessary to lessen the damage in case of chafage. If the bales chafe or become wet on their flats, only one or two layers will be damaged. If the edges or ends are damaged, every item in the bale is affected. After the bales in the periphery are stowed, it is not necessary to stow the remainder on their flats. In fact, the remaining distance should be measured and the bales should be stowed so that the greatest amount of space is consumed by the cargo and there is a minimum of lost space over the last tier. The bales that bear against stanchions and vertical ventilation ducts should be placed with their flats against these members with dunnage between them and the structural members.

Some of the fibrous commodities may present a danger of fire. Two apparent causes of fires in such commodities are: (1) spontaneous heating until the kindling point is reached, resulting in *spontaneous combustion;* and (2) sparks caused by friction of metal bands used on bales against steel parts of the ship. The first cause of fire can be eliminated by making certain that all bales are dry when stowed and that they remain that way. They must also be free from oil. The second cause can be eliminated by making certain that dunnage always stands between a bale and the metal parts of the ship. In 1978 a cargo hold of cotton bales caught fire in this manner owing to the lack of dunnage between the bale bands and the ship's stanchion.

Carelessness in the use of matches and smoking in the hold is undoubtedly the cause of some fires. Sparks from electrical fixtures in the hold or carelessly placed cluster lights are also responsible for some fires. These causes, however, are simple safety violations and not a direct result of the stowage.

When baled commodities are received, exceptions should be taken if the bands holding them together are broken or missing, if the covering is ripped off and part of the contents is exposed, or if the covering is hanging from the bale in loose strands. The cotton bale, for example, is supposed to have at least three-quarters of its surface, including the ends, covered by burlap or other suitable cloth covering. The bands are spaced about 8 inches apart. During the handling process from the warehouse to the ship, some bands may be broken and the covering ripped and tattered. If this happens, the possibility of fire from all sources mentioned above is increased.

The Stowage of Cardboard Cartons

The dunnage platform on which the stowage of cardboard cartons commences is the same as for bags except that the spacing of the second tier may be up to 4 inches. The stowage of cartons may start at the centerline and proceed outboard, or vice versa. Probably one of the most important points to make about the stowage of cartons is the care needed to maintain the level in the wings. As the stowage proceeds outboard in the lower holds, care must be taken not to stow a carton beyond the level portion of the tank tops. That is, a row should not be stowed upon reaching a point where the next carton, when placed in position, will rise above the level of the rest of the tier. In place of this carton, dunnage must be laid to fill in the triangular space on the outboard side. The next tier can then be stowed. This procedure must be used in the wings until all of the curvature has been stowed under.

The cartons are placed in the hold so that each carton rests on two cartons below it. This results in stowage that is known as *brick fashion* stowage. The dunnage in the wings should be placed against the sweat battens in a vertical position. Dunnage should also be used to separate the cargo from the transverse bulkheads and vertical structural members. If the vertical dunnage is not used in the wings, some of the cartons may become hung up on the sweat battens and as the ship works in a heavy seaway the side of the carton will be sheared off from chafing and super-imposed weight from above.

The need for dunnage floors between cartons in deep lower holds is explained in chapter 3 as part of the section "Protecting the Cargo."

The tiers must be kept level. This requirement is important. Dunnaging in the wings is one of the ways that this is accomplished. Obstructions in the compartment require care in the use of dunnage to keep the tiers level.

The Stowage of Crates

The term *crates* as used here refers to wooden containers that are built as a framework with open sides and tops. These crates are generally stiffened by the use of diagonal pieces, but are, for the most part, open so that the contents are exposed. Crates without diagonal stiffeners are insufficient for ocean transportation. Refrigerators, stoves, and light machinery are shipped in crates. The bottoms are solid, with well-built foundations for supporting the contents. The crate is a poor container, because it lacks strength and lacks protection for the contents. Crates require a layer of dunnage between every tier. The dunnage may be spaced up to about 4 inches apart. If a shipment consists entirely of crates, the best place to stow it is in the 'tweendecks. Top tiers in the lower hold are suitable, providing, of course, that the contents of the crates are not liquid. If a shipment of crates is stowed in the lower hold and it is necessarily placed on the tank tops, the height to which it is stowed should be limited to 12 feet or about half the depth of the lower hold. Cargo stowed over these crates should be lightweight merchandise.

Because of the dunnage layer between each tier of crates, it is not necessary to stow them brick fashion. This is an advantage because it means that in the wings the crates will rise vertically without the stepping in and out resulting from brick fashion stowage.

The Stowage of Cases

The word *case* as used here refers to a wooden box that is sheathed to form a tightly closed container. A wide variety of commodities are shipped in cases. Not only refrigerators, stoves, automobiles, and machinery, but also paints, drugs, beverages, and foodstuffs are shipped in cases. Uniform-sized cases may be stowed brick fashion in the same way as cardboard cartons without the dunnage floors between tiers in the bottom of lower holds. The wooden case depends on its contents for part of its strength, as do all containers, but unlike the cardboard carton, dampness will not weaken it.

Depending entirely on the contents, cases and cartons may at times be placed on their ends or edges if this procedure will facilitate the stowage without endangering the cargo. Another important point to make with respect to the stowage of cases and cartons is that when their length is twice as long or approximately twice as long as their width, security of the stowed block is obtained by placing one tier with the length fore and aft and the next tier with the length athwartships. The pattern of the stowage would be as in brick fashion stowage, but the stepping in and out of the outboard edges would be avoided. This is the manner in which such items are usually stowed, because most cargoes are not constructed with a square base. In some cases the direction of the cargoes in any one tier will be changed so that the division of the commodity is staggered.

Most of the comments above refer to shipments of crates or cases of uniform size. If a cargo lot consists of a number of variable sizes, the stowage precautions include some additional points. First of all, those cargoes with the heaviest items should be stowed in the lower tiers. Secondly, a smaller crate or case must never be stowed within the perimeter of a larger one below it without dunnage to support the upper crate. Such dunnage should extend from at least one side of the lower case to the other, but preferably the dunnage should extend over two or more cases. The upper crate or case is best stowed over two lower ones.

As the stowage of variable-sized crates and cases proceeds, the longshoremen should note the variations in height of the top of the stow and use dunnage to level off small or large sections, whichever is possible.

The use of dunnage in the stowage of such cargo should be extensive. Piling additional cargo on top of irregular platforms of cargo in the lower tiers invites heavy crushing damage. The crates and cases may be fitted together in much the same manner as a set of odd-size blocks, but in so doing the probability that uneven pressures will cause failure of containers of cargo and damage to contents is greatly increased. The use of ample amounts of dunnage to fill in slight steps and to floor off large sections is mandatory for the safest stowage. The lack of such dunnage is improper stowage.

The Stowage of Casks

The word *cask* refers to a type of container. The words *barrel, puncheon, pipe, butt,* and *tun* refer to sizes of the cask type of container. The term "barrel" is often used to mean all containers of the cask type. The actual amount of liquid contained in the various types of casks varies widely depending on the type of liquid being carried and the trade in which it is being handled. To give some idea of the relative sizes of a few of the more common casks and the names used, the following table has been prepared:

Cask	Capacity in U.S. Gallons
1 barrel	31½
1 hogshead	63
1 pipe	126
1 butt	126
1 tun	252

It must be emphasized that these volumes are not universal. For example, the English barrel of beer has a volume of 36 U.S. gallons whereas the 31 1/2 gallons shown in the table is the volume of a barrel of wine. A butt of beer in England has a volume of 108 gallons, whereas a butt of wine has 126 gallons. The volumes of the various casks are so variable that there is little point in trying to remember any of them. When concerned with the stowage of such items, the officer should be certain he/she determines correctly the volume of the cask listed on the manifest or bill of lading before calculating the space required to stow it.

The U.S. gallon is the equivalent of the English wine gallon, $231 in.^3$; the Imperial gallon consists of $277.418 in.^3$ or 1.2 U.S. gallons; and one U.S. gallon is equal to 0.8331 Imperial gallons.

Because of the frequency with which the term "barrel" is used when speaking of the capacity of tank ships, it should be pointed out that the barrel used in the petroleum industry has a volume of 42 U.S. gallons.

The stowage of cask type containers is the same whether they are barrels or tuns, except that the height limitation is less as the container grows larger. There are also two broad categories of casks. There is the wet or tight cask made of oak. The construction of this type of cask must be done with great care. The scarfed joints of the staves must be precisely cut and the staves must narrow from the bilge out to the head with great precision (see Fig. 5-3). This cask is used to ship beer, wine, spirits, and olives. The aluminum cask is now utilized much more extensively than the tight wooden cask.

The other type of cask is the dry or slack type cask. This type is usually made of softer wood than the former, fir being widely used. The joints and other construction details do not require the care and precision of the tight cask. This type of container is used to ship flour, cement, and other dry products.

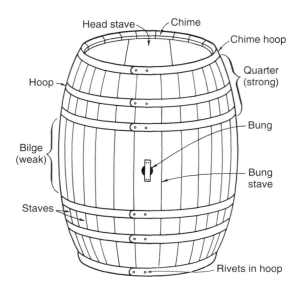

Figure 5-3. The nomenclature of a cask. Note that the bung is in line with the rivets on the hoops and that the head staves are vertical when the bung is up.

The weakest part of the cask, whether wooden or of aluminum construction, is the bilge. The weight should never be placed on this part of the cask when it is stowed. The strongest part of the cask is the quarter. The stowage of wet or tight casks, if in small lots and when there is no need to overstow them with heavy cargo, may be on end with a layer of dunnage between the tiers. The same stowage should always be given to the dry or slack cask. When stowing casks on end, the most important things to remember are to protect the chimes of the lower tiers by using strips of dunnage between tiers and to prevent excessive weights by limiting the weight of cargoes stowed over the casks. In most lower holds it is possible to stow barrels about seven tiers high. This height is too great if barrels are stowed on end; six tiers is the maximum. This type of stowage may open up the seams of the casks, beginning along the bilges. The lower tiers of casks will leak first because they will be supporting the most weight.

When carrying large numbers of the wet or tight casks, or when the best possible stowage is desired, the casks should be stowed as follows. The cask is laid in the ship with the length running fore and aft and in regular athwartship rows. The bilge of the cask is raised off the deck by dunnage at least 2 inches thick laid under the quarters. The cask is secured in position to some extent by the use of small wedges placed on either side of each barrel at both ends. If dunnage and wedges are not used, a more elaborate and safer method is to use *quoins* (Fig. 5-4). These are chocks or supports cut to fit the curvature of the cask at the quarters and raise the cask vertically to clear the bilge from the deck. This type of stowage results in what is sometimes referred to as *bilge free* stowage.

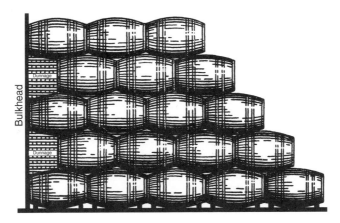

Figure 5-4. The use of quoins. The quoins are placed under the first tier at the quarters of each cask.

In the wings, great care must be given to wedge the outboard cask securely into position with dunnage and bracing. Assuming that we are starting the stowage in the after part of the hold, the next cask forward must be precisely in line with the adjacent cask. Their chimes should fit together. One must not be inboard or outboard of the other nor higher or lower. As the stowage proceeds longitudinally, the curvature of the hull in the entrance or run of the ship will make it necessary to drop a cask from the outboard longitudinal rows and fill in with dunnage. The longitudinal rows should be precisely in line fore and aft.

The second tier should be stepped one half the length of the cask away from the bulkhead against which the bottom tier was stowed and a half diameter athwartship. No dunnage need be used between the first and second tiers. The movement of the second tier forward and athwartships will place the bilge of the second cask over the intersection of four lower casks and the quarters of the upper cask will rest on the quarters of the lower cask. Hence, the bilges of the upper casks will be free without the use of dunnage (see Fig. 5-5).

Before stowing the third tier, dunnage should be placed in the space between the bulkhead and the chime of the second cask. This dunnage should be installed to support the quarter of one end of the third cask while the other quarter is supported by the second cask. Thus the stowage proceeds upward. It is of great importance to stow the bottom tier securely and to pay careful attention to dunnaging the wings and ends of the hold.

The curved intersection of two casks is known as the cantline of the stowed cargo. Hence, this system of stowage is referred to as *bilge and cantline.* However, the casks are stepped one half of their lengths fore and aft, which gives the more descriptive phrase *bilge and cantline half-cask stowage.* If the casks are stowed bilge and cantline *full cask,* the bilges would not be free without additional dunnaging. Full-cask stowage is easier, however, because it obviates the need for the dunnage at the ends of every other tier. It may be used safely if the casks are empty.

a　　　　　　　　　　　　　　　　b

Figure 5-5. Stowage of casks. **(a)** The stowage of the first tier with dunnage on the sides and one end as necessary, with all bungs up. The safety of the entire stow depends on this first tier. These casks are resting on athwartship pieces with bilges raised off the deck and quoins to keep them secure. **(b)** The stowage after the second and third tiers have been stowed, with dunnage being used to chock and fill in. All of the upper casks rest in the cantlines of the lower casks, with four lower casks supporting an upper cask. *Courtesy U.S. Navy.*

The bung on a cask is placed at the bilge in line with all the rivets holding the hoops together. The rivets and bung are always along a side stave in line with the direction of the head staves. Hence, if the end staves are vertical, the bung is pointing either directly up or directly down. A glance to see if the rivets are on top will tell whether the bung is down or up. The bung should always be up in stowage.

If the casks are properly stowed in this bilge and cantline half-cask style with the bung up, the stowage results in what may be described as *bung up and bilge free* stowage. However, this phrase tells *only the result* of proper stowage, not the method.

Occasionally, shipments of casks will be in two or three sizes. If it is desired to give these shipments the best possible stowage, they should be stowed bilge and cantline half-cask style with necessary modifications. It may be necessary to use dunnage and wedges between tiers to give proper support and security when smaller casks are stowed on top of larger ones. Also, instead stepping the third tier back against the bulkhead, it may be expedient to continue upward forming a pyramid, with dunnage and bracing or suitable filler cargo being used to fill in the space left between the casks and the bulkhead. It is recommended that pyramiding be avoided by providing a platform of dunnage for stepping the third tier back against the bulkhead.

The Stowage of Cylinders

Flammable and nonflammable compressed gases are shipped in steel bottles commonly referred to as *cylinders*. These containers are under pressures of 2,000 lb/in.[2] and over. They must be handled carefully and stowed securely to preclude disastrous accidents.

Cylinders may be stowed on deck (see Fig. 5-6) or under deck, but the distance from the side of the ship is regulated. Also, certain cargoes must not be in the same hatch with flammable gases. In general, such gases should not be stowed with cargoes that are liable to give off heat.

Cylinders should be stowed on their bilges in a fore and aft position; the second tier should rest in the cantlines of the lower tier, reversing the direction of the ends in each tier. They should be placed over dunnage and, inasmuch as the cargo is fore and aft, the dunnage should be laid diagonally if the cylinders are stowed on deck with only one tier being used. When stowed below deck, two tiers of dunnage should be laid, with the first tier fore and aft or diagonal and the second tier athwartships. For on-deck stowage, 2-by-4 dunnage spaced every 4 inches is suitable.

Figure 5-6. Cylinders stowed on deck. *Courtesy of Joe Liotta Art & Design.*

Cylinders are shipped in three forms with respect to the way the inlet valves are protected. They are equipped with a screw cap cover or a dished head or they are boxed. The inlet valves must be protected during shipment by one of these three forms.

Under certain conditions, it may be more convenient to stow cylinders standing up instead of lying down bilge and cantline style, for example, when clear deck run is lacking or is at a premium and needed for other deck cargoes. Standing cylinders on end is permissible only when extremely sturdy racks are built out of 2-inch lumber and thoroughly lashed down with wire rope, chain, or steel strapping with turnbuckles on every turn over the stowed block. The clear deck run can be saved by building these racks just forward of or abaft the hatches and well inboard to clear the deck run. If it can be prevented, however, cylinders should not be stowed on end. They are long, narrow, and extremely unstable. They stow very naturally in a fore and aft bilge and cantline fashion, and that is the way they should be placed if possible.

When stowed in the bilge and cantline manner, they must be securely lashed, braced, and tommed. Tomming, of course, is only possible when they are stowed in the 'tweendecks. Tomming is not necessary if the cylinders are extremely well lashed, but if there is any doubt as to their security, it is recommended that plans be made for setting in some toms. Tomming is also not necessary if sufficient heavy cargo is stowed over the cylinders and this cargo is well secured.

When handling cylinders, it is important that the valves be protected as much as possible in addition to the protection afforded by caps or construction. At a pier in New York in 1952, a sling load of cylinders was carelessly discharged from a hold. One cylinder's cap was extending beyond the edge of the platform sling and was struck a blow sufficiently strong to break the cap and the valve. The cylinder immediately took off in flight, propelled like a rocket by the expelling of the gas under pressure. Fortunately it went up instead of down. It spent itself rapidly, but not before it had gained enough velocity to carry it down the waterfront and land it on the roof of a pier warehouse two piers from where it took off. This gives an idea of the power and potential danger in these charged cylinders.

As mentioned before, these cylinders are under pressures of 2,000 lb/in.^{2} and over at normal temperatures. If the temperature rises alarmingly because of fire, direct sunlight on a tarpaulin lying next to them, heating copper concentrates, or other possible causes incident to water transportation, the pressures will be increased. It is quite possible for the pressure to be raised so high that the cylinder will blow a safety plug or, if that fails, that the entire cylinder will blow up. This emphasizes the need for preventing an undue rise in temperature. If carried on deck, cylinders should have dunnage between them and any tarpaulins over them to provide circulation of air. They should never be stowed near cargoes likely to heat in stowage. If fire breaks out, these cylinders should be jettisoned if they are in danger of being affected by the heat. The latter action would be especially important if the cylinders contained hydrogen or other flammable gases. Such an action would be for the safety of the ship and all the other cargo on board.

The Stowage of Drums

Drums may be stowed directly on the deck of a ship if stowed below the weather deck; however, a single layer of dunnage to provide better drainage and to offer more friction in case of heavy rolling is strongly recommended. Drums are stowed on end with the end bung up and packed as closely together as possible. If the distance athwartships allows stowage of an integral number of drums plus a fraction of one, they should be spaced at regular intervals instead of being close together, except for the end drum. The next row should be set in the oversized cantlines formed by the above action. The third row should again be set tightly into the cantlines (vertical) of the second row, and so on. This eliminates the need for any bracing or additional dunnaging in the wings, providing the wings are vertical themselves. If the wings have curvature, the triangular space in this part of the stowage should be filled in with filler cargo, bracing, or dunnage. Dunnage stripping should be placed between every tier. It is not necessary to use solid dunnage floors. Two strips of dunnage over a single row of drums is sufficient. These two strips will tie the stowed cargo block together, spread the weights satisfactorily, and prevent bending of the drum chimes.

In the wings, plenty of dunnage should be used to fill in the space left between the last outboard drum and the ship's side if there is curvature such as is found in the entrance and run of the vessel. A level must be provided for laying the dunnage strips for the next tier of drums (see Fig. 3-21). The drums are usually the 55-gallon size, and the height to which they can be stowed depends on their contents and their construction specifications. On most ships, this height limitation is naturally enforced by the limit of vertical drift in the lower holds. Four tiers is the maximum height that such drums can possibly be stowed in most 'tweendeck compartments. This particular drum is usually stamped with the letters "S.T.C." on the head, meaning "single-trip container" and usually "single trip with flammables." Such containers are often used a second time for the shipment of vegetable oils.

The stowage position for drums on the ship is often limited because of the contents. There are also a number of commodities that cannot be in the same hold. These will be discussed later.

The Stowage of Reels

What is mentioned hereafter with respect to reels also applies to any heavy cylindrical object, such as a millstone. The stowage of such items should always be on their sides unless they are light enough to be capsized easily by one or two men. The type of reel envisaged here is the extremely heavy reel with some type of cable on it, sheathed and generally marked to be rolled in one direction only. Such a reel should always be stowed with its axis running athwartships (see Fig. 5-7). Thus, the curvature is fore and aft. This requirement is simply to lessen the possibility of the reel exerting sufficient force to break its lashings during heavy and continuous rolling in a seaway. A ship will roll, pitch, and yaw in a seaway, but the rolling motion will be the most violent. The reel could work loose with long periods of continual stress due to extended bad weather. It might chafe lashings in two or pulverize blocking cargo. This may happen when the reel is stowed with the axis in either direction, but the probability is less with the axis athwartships.

The safest level at which to stow reels is in the lower holds. This is because the rolling motion is not as violent here as in the upper decks. The reels should be blocked in place with 8- by 8-inch balks on both sides. It is preferable to have the timbers cut to fit the curvature of the reel. The timbers should be tied together by nailing 2- by 6-inch battens between them. Besides this chocking, the reel should be braced, shored, and lashed into position. If suitable cargo is available, the reel may be blocked in with cargo. Some examples of suitable cargoes are bales of wood pulp, rags, hay, or certain types of lumber. Cargoes that cannot stand some chafing without being damaged should never be used. If suitable cargo for stowing around the reel is not available, a bulkhead of dunnage should be provided against

b.

Figure 5-7.
(a) Excellent stowage of a 21-ton heavy reel cable. The reel was 9 feet wide by 11 feet in diameter and is stowed athwartship in the lower 'tweendeck. It was chocked by 8x12" blocks, cut to fit thecurvature of the reel. Heavy shores and braces were used to secure the reel.
(b) The completed securing in the upper 'tweendeck. Supporting timber around the reel prevents any shifting athwartships or fore and aft.

a.

which other cargoes can be stowed adjacent to but safely protected from the potentially dangerous reel. Reels should be given about 6 inch clearance by such bulkheads.

Reels generally are well marked with precautionary measures that the shippers want taken to protect the contents. One of the most important of these, often seen on sheathed reels, says to be careful when using nails to build bracing or shoring around the reel. Some of the cable contained on these reels is enclosed in a tube that is filled with a gas to cut down corrosion and general deterioration. If the cable exterior is punctured by a nail, the entire reel is ruined, and this will result in a very costly claim. This type of damage would almost certainly be adjudged improper care and custody. Arrows are stenciled on the hub of the reel to indicate which way it should be rolled.

The Stowage of Uncased Automobiles

Automobiles that are shipped in the assembled form may be divided into two broad categories: the new car and the secondhand car. There is little difference in the actual stowage of the two types, although there is more preparation required and possibly more potential danger when carrying old cars.

One of the points needing emphasis when discussing the handling and stowage of this commodity is the importance of checking very carefully for exceptions. Here again, the older car will give the most trouble, because there are more dents, scratches, and broken parts to take exceptions on. Many companies provide forms with various views of an automobile on which marks can be made to point out accurately where deficiencies are found. In addition, written statements are made regarding the extent of the deficiencies.

Cars may be stowed in any of the 'tweendecks, facing in any direction that allows the greatest use of the available cubic. If carried in the lower holds on the tank tops, they preclude the use of all the clearance over them. Unless the space is not needed, they should never be stowed on the tank tops.

If cargo is stowed to within 7 feet of the beams in the lower hold, leveled off, and covered with at least two layers of crisscrossed 1-inch dunnage without spacing and a third dunnage layer of 2-inch deals, automobiles may be stowed over this platform. The lost space is practically eliminated.

Automobiles are sometimes safely carried on deck. If carried on deck, they should be lashed securely on top of the hatches and provided with protective light canvas covers. Even if the weather is fair during the voyage, paint from the sailors working aloft might ruin the finish of a car. Stowage on deck should be avoided if the ship is a full-scantling type and loaded to her marks. Such a ship is likely to be extremely wet on deck.

The best method of securing automobiles is by the use of the Peck & Hale type of adjustable cable. It is not as convenient, but they may be attached to chains stretched athwartships and secured by the use of frame clamps and turnbuckles. This would be the only possible way to use these cables to secure automobiles that are stowed over cargo in the lower holds on a platform of crisscrossed dunnage.

Without these adjustable fittings, a large amount of 4- by 4-inch and 2- by 4-inch lumber must be on hand to secure the automobiles. Two, 4- by 4-inch balks are cut to fit in front of and behind the front and rear tires. The balks should be long enough to extend beyond both sides of the car about 6 inches Two, 2- by 4-inch battens are then cut to run the length of the car on each side from the forward balk to the after balk. The 2-by-4s are nailed down securely to all the 4-by-4s. This forms a chock in which the automobile will ride. In addition, some lashings should be attached for greater security. The lashings are needed if the car is not new because the springs may not be compressed. The spring action during heavy weather may cause the auto to move out of its cribbing unless it is lashed. The brakes should be set and the car placed in park.

Automobiles should not be stowed closer together than 6 inches, nor should they be stored closer than 6 inches to any obstruction in the hold. The clearance overhead should also be 6 inches. The possibility of a heavy sea causing the car to rise above its stowed level is greater, of course, if it does not have its springs compressed. It is advisable when setting up any lashings that tend to place a downward strain on the car's frame to have several men stand on the bumpers. The weight of the men will compress the springs and the lashings will be tighter and hold the car down much better.

Prior to loading the automobiles, they should be prepared for stowage. Preparation includes disconnecting the battery terminals and draining the gasoline tank and radiator. All removable items should be taken off and locked in the trunk of the car; this includes hub caps, outside rear view mirrors, and search lights.

After stowage, each car should be secured by one of the methods mentioned above. The windows should be closed and the doors locked. The keys for all the cars should be collected and placed in the custody of one officer. The officer accepting the keys will be required to sign a receipt for them, and when he/she releases them to a member of the agent's office in the port of discharge, he/she should obtain a signed receipt. Each key is identified by a key number, the make and model of the car, and a bill of lading number.

Under older cars, it is advisable to spread a few thicknesses of heavy paper to catch any oil drippings from the crankcase or transmission. Finally, cars should be covered with lightweight canvas covers if there is any possibility of heavy dust from other cargoes during any stage of the voyage. These covers fit over the entire automobile and reach the deck. They are coveted items and should be issued and checked very carefully. When the cars are discharged, these covers should be gathered up, folded, and stored away in a locked compartment to be discharged at the ship's home port. The chief officer may have to sign a receipt for them when they are provided at the loading port, and he/she should be sure to obtain a receipt when delivering them after the voyage is completed.

The Stowage of Deck Loads in General

During World War II there was so much cargo waiting on every dock that ships began carrying more and more on deck. On occasion, the deck loads were so large that the amount of cargo was almost equal to the cargo that would have been stowed if the ship had been provided with an additional 'tweendeck space. Besides the tremendous call for deadweight, some of the built-up units that were shipped had to go on deck because they would not fit anywhere else on the ship. Units that are shipped on deck are those that are not permitted below because of their dangerous characteristics, those that will not fit below, those that if placed below consume a tremendous amount of cubic and can be safely exposed to the weather, and those that are difficult to stow below and can be carried safely on deck. Large deck loads are less frequent when cargo offerings are light.

The two principal concerns of the ship's officers when deck cargo is carried are: (1) the security of the cargo, and (2) the accessibility of the equipment needed to operate the ship safely.

Providing security for the cargo begins with making thorough plans about how the cargo is to be lashed, braced, and shored. A scale drawing of the ship's deck and a scale model of the cargo enable greater accuracy when making such plans. The details of such plans should include the sizes and number of all braces, the under-deck shoring, the number and positions of all pad eyes, and the cribbing required between the load and the deck. If pad eyes are not numerous enough or are placed so that they afford poor leads for the lashings, it is an easy matter to have them relocated. All this should be done long before the cargo is scheduled to be loaded. After the cargo is placed on the ship as per the plan, the lashings and bracings should be installed as directed by the chief officer. The chief officer should not hesitate to insist on a different arrangement of additional lashings if dissatisfied. Lashings and bracing should be applied with the assumption that during the first night at sea the ship will pass through a full hurricane. Using this philosophy, the ship will generally be stowed safely.

Keeping the equipment accessible is a matter of marking off with chalk everything that should be left clear for working the ship. The things to be left clear are the bilge sounding pipe openings, cleats, fair-leads, reach rod valve control wheels, bitts, fire hydrants, and fire hose racks. Large clearances should be indicated and the words "KEEP CLEAR" printed on deck. To insure that these notices are respected, the ship's officers should be on deck when preparations commence. Furthermore, at least one officer should be on deck throughout the actual process.

The type of lashing should be either chain with pear links, pelican hooks, and turnbuckles; wire rope with shackles, clamps, and turnbuckles; or steel strapping with turnbuckles. Manila or other fiber rope lashings should not be used except for frapping purposes during heavy weather or emergency use in general. Fiber rope will stretch and loosen in time, and so many turns are required for strength that setting up such lashings is a long and arduous task.

The place of stowage of deck cargoes is dictated by the nature of the container and the cargo. For example, uncased automobiles should be stowed on top of the hatch and preferably on the hatch just abaft the midship house for greatest protection. Carboys of acid should be placed on the after deck as far inboard as they can be bunched. As mentioned before, drums of flammable liquids must all be placed on the same side of the ship. A 65-foot motor launch may fit in only one or two spots on the ship's deck; hence the choice of where to stow it is automatically dictated.

SHORING UP A DECK

When the deck load is excessive, the main deck may have to be shored up. Shoring will be required whenever the deck load is greater than 350 lb/ft² on the average ship. The shoring up of the main deck may not have to go farther than the 'tweendeck; however, if the load is excessive, the shoring will have to extend all the way down to the tank tops. It is a mistake to load a ship so that shoring is required in all hatches. This stiffens the hull girder and places stresses where the naval architect that designed the ship did not intend them to be concentrated. The possible result in extremely heavy weather is structural failures in the deck or bottom plating.

The size of the shoring depends on the total strength needed. For loads up to 120 lb/ft², 12- by 12-inch balks spaced at 6-foot intervals should be used. This means that such shores would be under every other beam on the average ship and that about two rows would be needed between the hatch carling and the side of the ship. The spacing between the hatch carling and the side of the ship should be such that the three divisions thus formed are approximately equal. If the load is actually equal to 1,200 lb/ft² over the area it rests on, shores would be required all the way to the lower hold. This is because the 'tweendeck load capacity is seldom over 700 lb/ft². It should be obvious that smaller shores can be used if the spacing between them is reduced or the load is less than 1,200 lb/ft².

The shores are placed in position so that the lower end rests on a 6- by 12-inch *stringer* running longitudinally. The upper end bears against a *header* that runs longitudinally under all the beams. The shores are cut slightly shorter than the distance between the header and the stringer and any slack is removed by driving soft *wood* wedges between the lower end of the shore and the stringer. Fishplates are used on both sides of each shore at the upper and lower ends. The fishplates are made of 2- by 12-inch planks cut about 24 inches long and securely nailed to the shores and the stringer and header. The space above the header, between it, and the deck above should be filled with 4-inch timbers cut to fit. This means that the width of this beam filler piece will be equal to the outside measurement of the beam. The length will be equal to the distance between the beams. These pieces offer additional support of the deck plating under the load and prevent the beams from tipping. Figure 5-8 shows this arrangement of shores in a 'tweendeck.

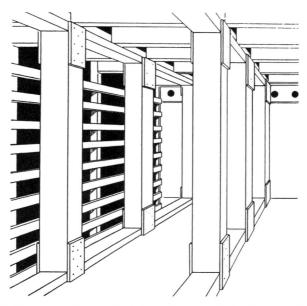

Figure 5-8. Shoring up the main deck from the 'tweendeck. *Courtesy of U.S. Navy.*

THE STOWAGE OF LUMBER

Lumber in sawed form is shipped in full loads from several parts of the world, the largest exporting volume being from the Pacific northwest coast of America. The lumber shipped falls into two broad categories: (1) deals, battens, and boards, which are the smaller pieces, such as the 2- by 4-inch batten and the 1- by 8-inch board, used for light construction work; (2) balks, flitches, and squares, which are the larger timbers, such as the 6- by 10-inch flitch and the 16- by 16-inch square, used for heavy construction work or intended for resawing at the country of destination for use in light construction work.

In the European trades timber is measured in standards of 165 ft³, while in the North American trades 192 ft³ is the average. In other trades the amount can be 216 ft³, that is, a cube 6 feet by 6 feet by 6 feet.

Some timber shipping terms include:

A shipping ton	42 ft³
A load	50 ft³
A load (untrimmed)	60 ft³
A stack	108 ft³
A St. Petersburg and Baltic standard	165 ft³

Lumber is shipped in loose board lots and also in packaged lots. Packaged lumber is not a new idea. Full shiploads of lumber in standard-sized units were carried on the Pacific coast before 1930. Packaged shipments are now carried on the intercoastal route between the west and east coasts of the United States. The package unit has been standardized by one major lumber carrying company at 2 feet high by 4 feet wide. The lengths in any one package are all the same (see Fig. 5-9).

The two most important problems in the stowage of lumber are the protection of the higher grades of lumber and stowage so as to combat tenderness in the ship. The first of these requisites is met by keeping the surfaced and kiln-dried lumbers in the wings, using fiber rope slings, being careful not to stain the lumber, using no hooks on milled or surfaced lumber, and taking other common-sense precautions.

The means used to combat tenderness in the lumber carrier, not including the obvious method of eliminating or drastically limiting deck loads (which would cut into the ship's earning power) are three in number: (1) Place the heaviest woods in the lower holds, (2) Distribute lumber types so that those stowing most compactly per unit of weight are in the lower holds, and (3) Pack the ship's frame spaces.

The lumber below decks, if in loose lots, is stowed piece by piece and packed in carefully by the longshoremen. Uneven surfaces are dunnaged with lath, and the broken stowage is reduced by using *ends* as filler cargo. Ends are pieces of lumber less than 6 feet in length with the same cross section as the rest of the shipment. Once a lot is stowed, it is marked off with rope yarn or by painting stripes across the top of the block. Arrowheads are used to indicate a change in vertical direction of the stowed cargo.

Figure 5-9. Weyerhaeuser lumber units on the pier in Vancouver, B.C., ready for loading. The unit wrap is made from 100 percent polyethylene. Some wraps are made with paper backing to prevent condensation under the wrap. *Courtesy the* Westwood Rainier, © *2004, Weyerhaeuser Company. All rights reserved.*

A lumber deck load is always found on ships carrying full or large amounts of lumber. While the deck load is being started, an officer should be on deck continuously, and the building of the deck load should be watched all during the process. The sides of the load and the ends must be shaped to afford the least resistance to heavy seas. The deck load must also be stowed in accordance with the basic requirements for deck loads in general, the provisions of the International Maritime Organization (IMO) Code of Practice for Ships Carrying Timber Deck Cargoes, and the regulations of the International Convention of Load Lines.

The deck load is secured by use of ¾-inch chain spaced not more than every 10 feet. The lower ends of the lashings are shackled to pad eyes; the upper ends are brought together approximately amidships and secured by the use of turnbuckles, pear links, and slip hooks. For maximum security, the deck load should be solid from side to side where it is possible to build it like this. The height should not impede navigational visibility in any way. Safe access to crew members with guard lines or rails and life lines should be provided in accordance with the IMO Code. As a general rule the quantity stowed on deck should not be more than one-third of the weight of timber carried.

Lumber shipped in packaged lots is packed into the ship with surprisingly little lost space by filling the bigger voids with loose pieces as necessary. The technique of stowing packaged lumber in the hold with the use of the forklift truck is clearly depicted in Figures 5-10 to 5-12.

Figure 5-10. Loading packaged lumber aboard ship. The endless slings are 21 feet long and have a safe working load of 5 m/t (measurement tons). *Courtesy the* Westwood Rainier, © *2004, Weyerhaeuser Company. All rights reserved.*

Figure 5-11. Longshoreman guiding the units of lumber into the hold. Slings are left with the units to facilitate rapid discharge. *Courtesy the* Westwood Rainier, © *2004, Weyerhaeuser Company. All rights reserved.*

The trend in stowage of the increasing tonnages of timber being traded internationally is toward unitization of timber handling.

Since deck timber cargoes are mostly in packaged form, there is a need to ensure that: (1) the packages are securely bound such that they are in "solid" form; (2) a level surface of dunnage provides a secure foundation; (3) in general, stowage is in a fore and aft direction to assist proper and adequate athwartship lashing arrangements; and (4) provisions are made for the tightening of the lashings. Figure 5-13 shows a vessel designed for the carriage of lumber departing with a full deckload.

The calculations relative to the amount of lumber that will go into a given space and the inverse of this problem are presented in the section dealing with stowage factors.

STOWAGE OF REFRIGERATED CARGO

Preparation of the Refrigerated Space

Preparing the refrigerated cargo space to receive cargo includes some special steps in addition to the steps required with regular general cargo spaces. The specialized nature of this preparation is evident from the discussion that follows.

Figure 5-12. Newsprint being loaded aboard the *Westwood Rainier*.

Figure 5-13. The *Westwood Rainier* sailing with a full load bound for Japan.
Courtesy the Westwood Rainier, © *2004, Weyerhaeuser Company. All rights reserved.*

CERTIFICATION OF SPACES

When loading any cargo on a ship, in any compartment, the shipowners may call in a surveyor to have the space certified as being in all respects in good condition and ready to receive the cargo. This survey is frequently made in the case of refrigerated spaces. Whether any cargo survey is made is entirely at the option of the shipowner; most large companies do have surveys made before and after stowage and during the stowage of cargoes. These surveys may not be costly, depending on the type of survey being made.

The survey of the spaces of a refrigerated ship includes the parts of the refrigeration system plus the insulation and equipment in the actual compartment. The machinery survey includes tests to insure that:

1. All controls are reacting properly.

2. Correct pressures can be maintained on both sides.

3. The system is fully charged.

The survey of the insulation of the compartment in an inspection of this type is superficial. Little more than a visual check to determine whether the insulation has any breaks in it can be made; a check of insulation plugs and their condition is also made. The coils of the evaporator should be carefully tested for leaks. The interior of the reefer space must be adequately equipped with gratings and battens to protect the inside surface of the insulation sheathing. The space must be exceptionally well cleaned and all drains clear; a reefer compartment will be equipped with two to four drains instead of only one. Surveys of machinery and insulation are made by the American Bureau of Shipping and similar organizations. Surveys of the actual cargo stowage are made in the United States by the National Cargo Bureau.

CLEANLINESS OF THE SPACES

Although the cleanliness of the space is mentioned as a requisite for stowage for practically every item that may be stowed on a ship, nothing requires a greater degree of cleanliness than the reefer space. Improperly cleaned spaces may cause heavy mold to develop on commodities despite optimum conditions of temperature, humidity, and air motion. Fungus growth and rotting may be caused on fruits and vegetables infected by imperfectly cleaned spaces; however, it should be understood that the appearance of such damage on chilled or cooled products is not proof that the space was improperly cleaned. The product can be infected during its handling prior to loading in such a way that out-turn will show the same effects that it would if infected by unclean conditions in the reefer compartment. In fact, the most frequent cause of infected fruit is improper handling prior to stowage on the ship. The point to be made here is that damage can be caused by an improperly prepared space, damage that can be eliminated only by effective cleaning. If the fruit shows evidence of being unclean or of already having developed mold or disease spots of any kind, thorough exceptions should be taken and written up for submittal to the claims department. To make this cleaning procedure completely practicable is a problem for the shipowner. A recommended procedure is as follows:

1. Remove all gratings and sweep up the compartment.

2. Any residue from past cargoes that cannot be removed by sweeping must be scraped off or washed off the interior surface.

3. Spray the interior with a light antiseptic solution that will kill mold spores and bacteria or at least tend to retard their growth. Such a spray must not be so powerful that it will leave odors behind that might taint the cargoes to be loaded. There are many such solutions; three are given here:

   a. A solution of ½ pound of chloride of lime to 3 gallons of water.

   b. One-quarter teaspoon of high test hypochloride (HTH) to 3 gallons of water. HTH is very powerful and the solution must be made carefully and tested by smelling the mixed solution. If the odor of chlorine is too strong, the solution is too strong. Do not allow the powder to lie around; if the powder in full strength comes in contact with dunnage, the dunnage should be condemned.

   c. A solution of sodium hypochlorite. This solution is made by adding sodium hypochlorite to fresh water, but it should also be very weak. The recommended strength is 0.8 percent, made by adding 0.8 pound of sodium hypochlorite to 99.2 pounds of water. If spraying or washing thoroughly is not possible, the next best step is to wipe down the interior, including the gratings, with rags or hand swabs that have been dampened in the solution.

4. Replace the gratings after washing them with one of the above solutions and allowing them to dry in the sun. If they cannot be allowed to dry, wipe them off as much as possible.

The interiors of reefer spaces are usually sheathed with surfaced tongue and groove spruce, pine, or fir plywood in such a manner that the cleaning is made easier than that of general cargo spaces. All frame spaces are eliminated, corners are coved, edges are chamfered, and the entire surface is painted with several coats of a high-grade varnish. The finish on the inside should not be allowed to deteriorate; revarnish the interior at least annually.

It should be understood that a thorough cleaning may not be necessary every time the spaces are to be prepared for a new reefer cargo. However, if in the judgment of the master or mate of the vessel the space is dirty and needs such a cleaning, the recommended procedure is as described. The exact procedure to be followed should be carefully outlined by the shipowner's operating department and incorporated in the company manual. With some cargoes, such as chilled meats, the cleaning should be frequent and thorough. The final decision rests with the ship's master or mate, a company shoreside refrigeration expert, or with the cargo surveyor retained to survey the cargo space as ready for loading a given reefer cargo.

PRECOOLING

Besides the above preparations, there is also the matter of *precooling* the compartment before loading commences. There are many procedures that may be followed to insure that the space is ready when the cargo is ready. The important thing is to have the ship's chief engineer notified well in advance of the need for the space to be at the temperature specified. Such notification should be given to the chief engineer at least 24 hours prior to the actual loading of the commodity. This officer will then place the refrigeration machinery in operation and commence to pull the temperature down. During this period, all of the dunnage that will be needed to stow the cargo securely should be stacked in the compartment in such a way that its heat load can be picked up easily along with that of the interior of the space. Considerable damage may be caused by using warm dunnage between the containers of refrigerated cargoes. Precooling of cargo spaces is universally required: precooling of the cargoes is not. Bananas are never precooled before stowage.

TEMPERATURE RECORDS

Hourly recordings of the temperatures maintained in all reefer spaces are made and logged in the engineering log book. These temperatures are read at a remote station. The refrigeration engineer simply has to close an electrical circuit including a galvanometer set to read degrees of temperature instead of ohms of resistance. The electrical circuit is closed by pressing a button at the centrally located recording station. On other installations the refrigeration engineer must make periodic rounds of all spaces and read a recording thermograph on the outside of each refrigerated compartment. On modern ships, there is nearly always a recording thermograph regardless of the method used to obtain periodic temperature readings during the voyage. This thermograph chart can be used by the shipowner to ascertain whether the ship's operating personnel actually do maintain temperatures as requested. In the case of claims, these same charts can be used to prove that the temperatures required were, in fact, maintained.

A portable type of recording thermograph is frequently used. These can be secured in a centrally located position in the space at the beginning of the voyage and removed by properly designated personnel just prior to discharging.

RECEIPT AND CARE

The stowage of refrigerated cargoes is a task that requires careful attention to many details on the part of the ship's officers. The officers must be with the cargo from the time the cargo is received on the dock until it is safely stowed on the ship. Refrigerated cargo, commonly referred to as reefer cargo, requires the time of two officers during some phases of its receipt and care.

INSPECTIONS

All cargoes should be observed by the ship's officers as they are received by the dock force and as they are loaded on the vessel. In the case of refrigerated cargoes, this observation should take the form of a continuous inspection of the cargo to ascertain whether there is any evidence that would make it doubtful that the cargo could stand the voyage. The form of this evidence will be presented in the context of this and the following sections; it is important to note, however, that the officer who is not aware of what to look for cannot protect the shipowner's interest or his/her ship's interest regardless of how conscientious his/her inspections may be. The ship's officer's check should be a double check following inspection by the receiving clerk's staff or a specially appointed company expert. Regardless of the number and type of inspections made by dock force personnel, the master of the vessel should require a thorough inspection by at least one of his/her officers, who should submit a written report to him. The written report is an excellent educational device for the junior officers and it will tend to make the officer pay greater attention to what he/she is actually doing. The need for writing about what he/she finds and evaluating it will also build up in him an accurate vocabulary concerning the damaged conditions found.

The inspection commences when the refrigerated cargo is received on the pier. At this time a ship's officer must carefully inspect the containers as they appear in the connecting carrier. The connecting carrier will be either a refrigerated railroad car or truck. Infrequently some leafy vegetables are carried to a ship that have only been iced before leaving the hinterland and have been transported in an unrefrigerated truck. Such facts should be noted and included in a report to the master and claims department. If there are outward signs of improper handling or evidence of any type that might cause the cargo to be suspect, exceptions should be taken. If conditions warrant, the cargo may be rejected. Inspection by simply observing the containers in their connecting carrier is not sufficient. Individual units of the commodity, such as an apple or a pear, should be picked out of the lot and sampled. They should be cut in half to inspect for brown heart or other signs of internal decay. They should be tasted and smelled carefully. Many troubles, such as soggy decay in apples, manifest themselves in the condition of the flesh only, without any external symptoms. The appearance of the skin should be checked for signs of mold, freezer burn, scald spots, or other diseases that may be common to the particular type of fruit in question. The types of diseases and their symptoms are so numerous that they cannot be covered completely here. It is strongly recommended that just prior to receiving a given type of refrigerated commodity, a reference should be consulted to ascertain possible sources and manifestations of troubles. Finally, if the product is supposed to be precooled, an appropriate thermometer should be inserted into the pulp of the commodity and its temperature taken. Such thermometers are ordinary in their construction except for a strong steel tip that makes it possible to insert the instrument into a chilled quarter of beef or a green and firm apple or pear. It is important to note this temperature and either reject the shipment or take exceptions if the temperature is not down. The need for this is twofold: (1) If not precooled, the commodity will have ripened much faster than it should have since being harvested, and it may not be able to last the voyage. Most fruits will not keep well under cold storage conditions unless they are precooled within 24 hours of being picked. (2) The requirement of cooling the commodity after stowing on the ship may be more than the refrigeration system of the ship can handle in the time allowed. In this case, even if the commodity could stand the voyage if brought down to proper temperature, the trouble lies in the fact that the temperature cannot be reached and maintained by the facilities on hand. In this instance also, there is danger of losing the entire shipment. The fact that pulp temperatures were taken and a record of the temperatures should be included in a log book entry. These temperatures are required for any refrigerated product that is supposed to be at some specific low temperature when arriving at the ship.

The operating departments of some companies require that refrigerated products be inspected by a competent surveyor and a report made to the company claims department. Fresh fruit shipments out of the United States should be inspected by a representative of the U.S. Department of Agriculture. If the shipment is found suitable, the inspector will issue an inspection certificate that certifies that the shipment is clean and contains no disease. In many foreign ports such a certificate must be on hand before the shipment can be landed.

When inspecting refrigerated cargoes as received, frozen or otherwise damaged fruit should be set aside. This fruit must not be mixed with fruit in good condition. Damaged fruit mixed with sound and healthy fruit may be the cause of the entire shipment going bad.

STOWAGE

The basic principle to be followed when stowing refrigerated products is to build suitable air channels throughout the stowed cargo block. There are a few exceptions to this general requirement, which will be mentioned later. Baskets and bulge-top fruit cases can be stowed so as to provide excellent air passageways without using dunnage expressly for this purpose. Dunnage used with such containers serves the purpose of binding the load together for more secure stowage. The size of the strips of dunnage used varies considerably from one ship or one company to another: 1×2, 1×1, $\frac{1}{2} \times 1$, and the common building lath of $3/8 \times 1\frac{1}{2} \times 48$ have all been used extensively (see Fig. 5-14). In placing the containers in stowage, take care to see that the contents of the crates do not take the weight of the succeeding tiers, but that the crate supports this weight. Crates that have cleats at the ends only should be stacked in the reefer compartment one on top of the other with dunnage running at right angles to the cleats between every tier. If these crates are staggered in the recognized brick fashion used on many ordinary cargoes, the load will be taken up by the contents, which will become bruised and damaged.

Crates that have a supporting transverse member dividing the crate into two equal parts, and are provided with a center cleat, can be safely loaded in the brick fashion. Brick fashion stowage, of course, makes for a more securely stowed cargo block. Vertical air channels can be provided by placing pieces of dunnage between the rows on their forward and after sides. Crates of citrus fruits, melons, apples, and similar products are packaged in containers with bulged

Figure 5-14. Ship's reefer hold. Note the many laths used to space the crates and permit air circulation. Laths and the crates are always stowed in the direction of the flow of air.

tops. Such containers can be stowed on their ends with the bulged tops together. This arrangement provides ample air channels, and the crate, rather than the contents, will carry the weight of top tiers. It is recommended that stacking no more than five tiers high be allowed with this type of container, with possibly a sixth tier lying longitudinally with the bulge up; this arrangement will aid in tying the entire stowed block together.

Refrigerated Cargo Types

The commodities received for refrigerated stowage are numerous, and increasing every year. Most of these are well known and include meats, fish, poultry, dairy products, fruits, and vegetables. It is impossible, in this limited discussion, to set forth formally precise methods of handling and stowing each commodity type that may be classified as refrigerated. Not only is our space limited, but the methods used in any one instance may vary from nation to nation, trade route to trade route, company to company, and even from ship to ship. Thus far there has been no effort on the part of any group, whether specifically interested in the welfare of the shipping industry or otherwise, to investigate thoroughly and determine the true merits and problems of extant practices found within the marine industry. Shipper, consignee, shipowner, consumer, and underwriter alike would benefit from research leading toward a determination of the best practices.

Apples, grapes, and pears are the fruits shipped in the greatest amounts in partially refrigerated vessels and offer some interesting problems. Bananas are carried almost exclusively on one type of ship and on one trade route. The methods used in handling and stowing bananas are interesting and reflect how efficient the process can become when the efforts of all interested parties are coordinated. Meat carriage is done on a large scale only in the merchant marines of nations other than the United States, principally on British ships.

Types of Refrigerated Ships

There are four classes of refrigerated ships: (1) *the all-refrigerated chilled meat carriers,* (2) *the all-refrigerated frozen meat carriers,* (3) *the all refrigerated cool air fruit carrier, and* (4) *the general refrigerated carrier* designed to accommodate many types of refrigerated commodities at temperatures from below 0 to 55°F. To be most efficient, each of these types should be specially designed for the purpose to which it is going to be put. In practice, however, compromises must be made because refrigerated cargoes are carried on these carriers on only one leg of the voyage. Such compromises are made so as to accommodate general cargoes. For the purposes of discussion, an outline of the major points of each type will be sufficient.

ALL-REFRIGERATED CHILLED MEAT CARRIER

The all-refrigerated chilled meat carrier was the first type of refrigerated carrier developed. A consignment of chilled meat stowed in a compartment cooled with ice was shipped from the United States to Great Britain in 1875.Beef can be carried in chilled condition for not much more than 35 days. The temperature is generally between 28.5°F and 29.5°F. The shipowner does not specify the temperature to be maintained; this is the responsibility of the shipper of the commodity regardless of the class of refrigerated cargo involved. The relative humidity in a compartment of chilled beef should be between 88 and 92 percent. Air velocities within the compartment should be maintained at approximately 32 ft/minute. Chilled beef is hung from meat rails in such ships in 'tweendecks that are approximately 6 feet 6 inches in depth or greater, at increments of 3 feet. If the depth of the hold is greater than 9 feet 6 inches, more than two tiers of beef quarters will have to be carried. The space on older ships is cooled by brine coils that are suspended between the meat rails on the overhead and coils secured to the sides and ends of the compartment. In such compartments deck gratings are unnecessary. The brine piping should be extensive so that higher brine temperatures can be maintained and the average temperature within the compartment still kept at the desired level with only slight variation.

The temperature of the compartment should not be allowed to fluctuate more than 0.5°F below and above the specified carrying temperature.

In compartments containing chilled beef, the weight of the cargo is carried by the overhead. If the deck above is used to carry commodities stowed on the deck in the ordinary manner, the deck must be able to handle the greater deck load. The meat carried in this manner packs in at approximately 125 ft³/ton. The meat must not hang too freely, nor must it be packed in too tightly. If it is too loose, it will suffer some damage from striking adjacent structural members or other meat during violent rolling or pitching in a seaway. If it is packed too tightly, it will be damaged by crushing stresses exerted throughout the stowed block during the voyage, and it may also suffer because of the reduced air flow around the meat. (A good air flow is necessary for a good out-turn.) Because of the necessity of maintaining an even temperature level, and since it is easier to maintain uniform temperature levels in small compartments, an ideal chilled meat carrier would have a number of smaller compartments rather than a few large compartments.

ALL-REFRIGERATED FROZEN MEAT CARRIER

The all-refrigerated frozen meat ship does not require the limited height in the 'tweendeck spaces and lower holds that is necessary in the chilled meat carrier. The stowage required for frozen beef is shown in Figure 5-15. An ordinary cargo vessel can be converted into a frozen meat carrier by properly insulating the spaces and installing coils within the compartments or constructing cold air bunker rooms and ducts. This is because the meat can be stowed to a height limited only by the depth of the compartment. On a ship designed and built for the purpose of carrying only frozen meats, the simplest and most economical installation is wall coils. However, for more versatility the use of cooled recirculated air is called for.

Because of the extremely low temperatures maintained in the frozen meat compartments (0 to 10°F), the insulation must be more effective and is generally

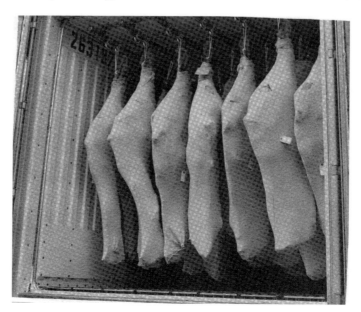

Fig. 5-15. Hanging beef correctly stowed with carcasses positioned bone to bone and meat to meat.

thicker than on a ship constructed for the carriage of chilled or cooled cargoes only. No outside air is allowed to enter the frozen meat compartment once the cargo has been stowed. Any air brought in from the outside would deposit its moisture content on the cooling coils and necessitate frequent defrosting or decrease the general efficiency of the cooling system. For the purpose of maintaining a constant temperature throughout the compartment, the air within is agitated with blowers, but the insulation plugs are caulked and an effort is made to prevent the entrance of outside air. The temperatures maintained in a frozen meat compartment should be 0°F or less. The reason for this is that although the freezing point of meat is 27°F, pork will turn rancid after 2 months at 15°F, and beef, lamb, and veal will turn rancid after 3 months. The needs for some degree of safety when transferring the product from one carrier to another and for prevention of thawing in high-temperature pockets are why the maximum temperature should be below 0°F.

ALL-REFRIGERATED COOL AIR CARRIER

The all-refrigerated cool air carriers differ greatly from both of the other all-refrigerated types mentioned above. For one thing, the cooling is done entirely by recirculating cool air through the cargo spaces after it has been passed over a bank of coils with cold brine in them. In general the refrigeration machinery, such as the compressor, evaporator coils, brine tanks, condenser, and receiver, is located amidships in or near the machinery spaces. The cold brine is piped to a compartment where large fans capable of handling 15,000 to 25,000 cubic feet of air per minute (cfm) blow air over the coils in which the brine is contained. The air is cooled to the desired dry bulb temperature level and sent through ducts to be discharged in the refrigerated spaces. There are numerous variations in the arrangement of the units and methods used in recirculating the cool air type of refrigeration installation. The sizes of the units vary; in smaller installations, direct expansion coils may be used instead of the brine coils; and the air may be recirculated by means of a cold air diffuser or by use of a periphery duct.

GENERAL REFRIGERATED CARRIER

The refrigerated general cargo carrier is a ship that has some part of her total cubic capacity devoted to refrigerated cargo. There is a great variance of opinion as to how much refrigerated space a general carrier should have to make her a versatile carrier. Of course, the run in which the ship operates would have a major influence in fixing this figure. For a carrier to be truly a *general* carrier she must have *some* provision for the carriage of refrigerated products. The amount of partial refrigeration space runs all the way from the 1,000- or 2,000-ft^3 portable, wall-coil reefer boxes up to 90,000 ft^3. Vessels with 70,000 ft^3 of reefer space are examples of adequate provision for refrigerated cargoes if and when they are available.

Fig. 5-16. Stowing fresh fruit in a refrigerated compartment. Burlap covered battens with air space protect fruit contact with frost covered brine pipes. *Courtesy of Joe Liotta Art & Design.*

In the partially refrigerated general carrier the reefer boxes are located in the 'tweendeck areas. Thus, when not in use as reefer spaces, they can be used for general dry cargo of the packaged type without much loss in efficiency. If ingress to the hatchway around the boxes can be obtained via a side port opening, the inconvenience of loading dry cargo into the confined spaces of a reefer box is reduced to a minimum. The lower hold can be worked continuously with loading through the side ports using roller conveyors (see Fig. 3-1 and 8-28).

Factors Involved in the Safe Handling and Stowage of Low-Temperature Cargoes

DRY BULB TEMPERATURE

The proper maintenance of the dry bulb temperature level within a reefer space is not the only factor affecting the condition of refrigerated cargoes at the discharging port. But the temperature level is, of course, of primary importance when carrying hard-frozen cargoes. The exact temperature to be maintained for a good out-turn varies with the type of commodity, the species of the commodity, the length of the voyage, and the authority establishing the temperature range. The first three factors are fairly obvious; the fourth is placed on the list because the authors noted a wide variance in suggested temperatures at which to carry a given commodity when consulting various lists published by different authorities. In many cases the recommended temperatures were the same, but the point is that such lists (see Table 5-1) must be used as guides only and not as hard and fast rules. In addition to the three important variables mentioned above in regards to the temperature levels to be maintained, there is one more. *This is the stage of ripeness of the fruits and vegetables when picked.* The shipper of the commodity specifies the carrying temperature and the limits of temperature variation during the voyage; however, all ship's officers should have a general knowledge of the factors involved in deciding the carrying temperature and should check the specified temperature against the temperature listed in some authoritative text.

TABLE 5-1
Recommended Temperatures for Commodities

Group	Temperature		Products
	(°F)	(°C)	
1	32-34	0-1.1	apples, apricots, berries (not cranberries), cherries, nectarines, peaches, pears, persimmons, plums, prunes, pomegranate, quinces, grapes*$_2$
2	56-60	13.3-15.6	bananas, grapefruit (AZ & CA), mangoes, papayas, tomatoes (mature green)
3	36-41	2.2-5.0	cantaloupes, cranberries, lychees, oranges*$_3$ (FL & TX)
4	50	10.0	avocados, eggplant, grapefruit (FL & TX), muskmelons, tomatoes, pineapple, (not with avocados), watermelons
5	40-55	4.4-12.8	beans (snap), cucumbers, eggplant, lemons (green), limes, oranges (CA & AZ), potatoes, pumpkin, squashes, watermelons, water chestnuts
6*$_1$	32-34	0-1.1	artichokes, asparagus, beets, carrots, escarole, grapes*$_2$, lettuce, mushrooms, parsnips, peas, rhubarb, spinach, sweet corn, watercress
7*$_1$	32-34	0-1.1	broccoli, brussel sprouts, cabbage, cauliflower, celery, horseradish, kohlrabi, leek, onion (green), radishes, rutabagas, turnips
8	55-60	12.8-15.6	ginger, sweet potatoes

*1 Compatible with Group 7 (or 6) except for grapes and mushrooms.

*2 If grapes have been fumigated with sulfur dioxide, they are non-compatible with other products.

*3 If oranges are fumigated with biphenyl, they are non-compatible with other products.

Courtesy of Sealand.

CONDITION OF ATMOSPHERE

The condition of the atmosphere in the reefer space is another factor affecting the condition of the cargo when discharged. Controlling the atmosphere means regulating the amount of carbon dioxide (CO_2) and oxygen in the reefer space. The technique is successful when the total amount of these two gases equals 21% of the total atmosphere in the space. All fruits continue to respire (ripen) after being picked, and the end products of this process are CO_2, water vapor, and heat. It has been established that respiration is diminished not only by lowering the temperature, but also by reducing the amount of oxygen and allowing the CO_2 to accumulate. The percentage of CO_2 can be controlled by ventilating when the concentration becomes too great, but this technique is possible only when the total amount of these two gases is 21%. To obtain a concentration of oxygen less than that which can be obtained by ventilation, it is necessary to absorb excessive amounts of CO_2 by passing the atmosphere of the space through a solution of strong sodium hydroxide or potassium hydroxide. Control by ventilation then becomes possible when the amounts of CO_2 and oxygen have been brought to a total of 21%, such as 8% CO_2 and 13% oxygen. To determine the amount of each it is necessary only to obtain the percentage of CO_2 and subtract from 21. If the initial concentration was 4% oxygen and 6% CO_2, it would be impossible to obtain this ratio except by the absorption technique as mentioned above. To understand this it is necessary to understand that CO_2 is produced in a volume equal to that of the oxygen consumed.

The principal advantage of using a controlled atmosphere is the ability to keep the fruit in storage for longer periods with less deterioration or for the same periods as before the use of controlled atmospheres but at higher temperatures. Another advantage is the reduction in the rate of mold growth in atmospheres high in CO_2 concentration.

Marine cargo refrigeration practice does not yet include the controlling of storage atmospheres beyond the introduction of air by ventilation to prevent the concentration of CO_2 from becoming too high. With respect to how much changing of the air is required in a given reefer space loaded with a certain cargo, no exact answer can be given. The air change rate may vary from a complete air change every minute, or a change of 2 or 3% of the total capacity of the space (unloaded) every minute. This applies only to those products that are carried above their freezing points and are therefore producing CO_2.

Installations for the storage of identical products ashore in many cases call for treatment completely different from that for storage on board a ship. For example, apples in storage ashore may not be ventilated at all, although the apple may suffocate and suffer a diffuse browning of the skin known as "apple scald" if the CO_2 content becomes too great. Over-accumulation of CO_2 is avoided by circulating the storage atmosphere through a washer or "scrubber" filled with a 30% solution of sodium hydroxide. In such an installation, a gastight compartment must be available and all the commodities must respond in the same way to the concentration of CO_2 maintained. On board ship it is impractical to consider such an expensive installation. It would be difficult to obtain shipments that would entirely fill a compartment and much space would thus be lost. Probably the deciding factor is that the technique of controlling the atmosphere to such a fine degree is primarily for the purpose of retaining products in storage for many weeks or months, whereas on the ship the prime objective is to retain them in good condition for a relatively short period and deliver them in that condition to the consignee of the shipment at the port of discharge. Three weeks on board the ship would be a long time. Ship operators plan the loading of refrigerated products on the last day in port and make it a point to arrange for the receipt of such cargoes the day the ship arrives in the port of discharge; hence the time in storage on aboard the ship is usually only the length of the voyage. Under some conditions of operation, however, it may be considerably longer.

RELATIVE HUMIDITY

The relative humidity of the storage atmosphere must be maintained at an optimum level in a reefer space to obtain a good out-turn of the cargo. This factor is closely allied to the problem of controlling the condition of the atmosphere, but it is important enough to deserve a separate entry on our list of factors involved in the safe handling of reefer cargoes. The relative humidities recommended are high for practically all commodities; the exceptions are chocolate candies and dried egg products. The humidity level in a reefer space carrying fruit above its freezing temperature is of the greatest importance. Before and after fruit is picked it is ripening and this ripening process causes the fruit to give off water vapor, as mentioned before. But before being picked, additional water is available to the fruit to replace that given up in respiration during ripening. When this source of water is removed by picking, the ripening process, with its accompanying release of water, must be slowed down. The loss of water vapor is largely a function of the vapor pressure of the water in the ambient air in which the fruit is stowed. Hence, there is the need for a large amount of absolute humidity, which results also in a high percentage of relative humidity, inasmuch as the vapor pressure of the ambient air varies directly as the absolute humidity. Theoretically then, it appears that 100% relative humidity would be the most desirable. This, however, is not so, because at this humidity the water vapor released from the fruit would condense on the skin of the fruit as free moisture and cause conditions that would promote other forms of disease and mold growth. On the other hand, many products are not carried at humidities that are the best for prevention of moisture loss, because that relative humidity level within the compartment in which the commodity is stowed would be too high for the control of mold growth on the containers and on the fruit itself. Actually, the relative humidity used is a compromise between that level which would allow such a rapid discharge of moisture that the skin of the fruit would shrivel and that level which would entirely control moisture loss. If the relative humidity is maintained at too high a level, mold will develop, the skin of the fruit will become slimy, bacterial growth will be promoted, and in general the out-turn will be poor. If the relative humidity is too low, the moisture loss will be excessive, resulting in loss of weight, shriveling and discoloration of the skin, and again a poor out-turn.

Control of Relative Humidity

The control of the relative humidity in refrigerated spaces on board a ship is not precise. Under shipboard conditions it is especially difficult to maintain during the period when the sensible heat load of the product is being stabilized. During this period, generally referred to as the *pull-down period*, the difference between the temperature of the circulating air as it enters the reefer space and as it leaves is at a maximum. This period should not be more than 72 hours. Conditions of the storage atmosphere should be stabilized within that time, which is short enough that little damage should occur as a result of low average relative humidities. That low relative humidities would exist is evident when it is noted that if the incoming air is at 40°F at nearly 100% relative humidity, and the outgoing air is at 45°F. Due to the rise in temperature, there is a 17% drop in the relative humidity, taking it down to 83%. This relative humidity would be increased, of course, by some water vapor picked up by the air from the cargo in storage. Whether the amount picked up would be sufficient to bring the relative humidity up to a suitable level is not certain. On the other hand, once the reefer space temperature level has been stabilized and the incoming air is at 40°F at nearly 100% relative humidity and the outgoing air is at 42°F, the relative humidity at the outlet end will be 93%, which means that the average relative humidity in the reefer space will be very high, and especially so if additional water vapor is picked up from the ripening fruit. In the case of frozen products the relative humidity would be even higher, for the temperature rise of the circulating air would be less. It is evident that with frozen products a two-temperature brine coil system is necessary to prevent the relative humidity from being constantly too high. With products that give off some vital heat and continue to ripen within the refrigerated compartment, the best control of the relative humidity is obtained by operating with a low mean effective temperature differential. The dry bulb temperature within the compartment can be maintained at correct levels under a low mean effective temperature differential by having a correspondingly large area of coils and operating with low air velocities. (The mean effective temperature differential referred to is that between the temperatures of the refrigerant in the coils and of the medium to be cooled.)

AIR MOTION

The rate of air movement within the reefer space also has its effect on the condition of the refrigerated cargo at the out-turn. Air velocities are stated in feet per minute (fpm). The recommended exact rate of air flow within the reefer space depends on the commodities stowed in it. The velocity may range from 30 to 100 fpm. Products requiring precooling to the proper storage level in the reefer space require a greater rate of air flow. Products that have high vital heats need greater velocities than those with no or low vital heats. Although products can be damage by too high or too low an air velocity, it is difficult to obtain exact data concerning the optimum rate for a given type of cargo. The effects of too great a velocity are similar to those of too low a relative humidity; discoloration, excessive moisture loss, and shriveling of skin on fruits; and, of course, a loss of weight. Too low a velocity will produce effects similar to those of a high relative humidity, such as mold growth, slime on surfaces, and some diseases in fruits that cause a loss of flavor or texture or both.

The rate of air flow within a space can be calculated very easily if the volume output of the fans moving the air and the cross-sectional area of the path along which the air must pass are known. Knowing the two values mentioned, we immediately have:

$$V = R \times A \qquad R = \frac{V}{A}$$

where

R = the velocity of the air in fpm.

V = the volume of the fan output (cfm).

A = the cross-sectional area of the air path.

Basic Considerations When Stowing Cargo in These Spaces

When stowing refrigerated cargoes, the principal precaution is to allow adequate space between the tiers and rows. Adequate space is provided by using common building lath for dunnage. The possibility of improper stowage is greater when stowing a partial load in such spaces. Partial loads in compartments using periphery ducts for air distribution should be spread out over the deck area of the compartment, with good spacing between the vertical piles, that is, good horizontal spacing. The air flow here is out from the duct slit and downward to the deck, flowing under the gratings to the outlet. If the cargo is piled up in a block anywhere in the space, the air flow passes over the cargo and then downward and to the outlet. Thus, the air bypasses the cargo block and the interior of the block is not properly cooled, which may result in a poor out-turn.

In a space fitted out with a cool air diffuser unit but without ducts, the best way to stow a partial load is to build it up as high as feasible across the compartment at the end where the outlet louver is located. The cargo must not be at the opposite end from the outlet louver. If it is stowed here, the air flow will naturally follow the course of least resistance, and after leaving the outlet blower the air will drop and return directly to the outlet louver, having penetrated the cargo hardly at all.

The general principle to be followed in all partial loadings of refrigerated spaces is to avoid stowing cargo so that the air flow will bypass the cargo and flow directly to the outlet, rather than being forced through the cargo block. Obviously, there must be no deviation from general good stowage principles when meeting this special requirement.

THE STOWAGE FACTOR

Stowage Factor Defined

The *stowage factor* is defined as the number of cubic feet required to stow 1 ton of a given cargo. It is a value that is used to answer two very important questions: (1) When given a certain amount of cargo, what is the amount of space that will be consumed in stowing it? (2) When given a certain volume of space, what is the number of tons, units, or pieces that will go into the space? These two questions or ones related to them are continually coming up during the voyage of every ship, especially when the plans are being made for stowing the ship, whether with a full load or simply a few hundred tons.

These questions cannot be answered precisely, because the actual amount depends on the broken stowage resulting when the cargo is stowed. This latter value varies greatly. We will use the following equation when calculating broken stowage:

$$L = \frac{V - v}{V} \times 100$$

where

L = the percentage of broken stowage.

V = the volume consumed in stowing the cargo.

v = the volume of the cargo stowed in V.

Lists of stowage factors should not be used without great care. If the list fully describes the containers and gives other particulars so that there is no doubt that the listed item is the same as the item being considered for stowage, there is little danger of a serious mistake. It is recommended, however, that unless the list is one made personally by the officer using it and relates to a particular trade route and commodity type, current data should be obtained for the commodity in question. Then, a trustworthy stowage factor should be calculated prior to any attempts to estimate space or tons as in the above two typical questions.

Calculating the Stowage Factor

The stowage factor is simply the specific volume of the commodity expressed in units of cubic feet per ton. The stowage factor is equal to the cubic feet per 2,240 pounds; hence, if we divide 2,240 by the density of the commodity we obtain the stowage factor. Density is defined as the pounds in 1 ft^3 for our purposes. We can express these facts as follows:

$$f = \frac{2{,}240}{D}$$

where

    f = stowage factor.

    D = density of the commodity in pounds per cubic foot.

    2,240 = the number of pounds in 1 long ton.

However, data concerning cargo are not often received in terms of its density. More often the measurements of the container and its gross weight are available. Of course, we can calculate the density from these data, but why not express the equation for the stowage factor as one operation instead of two separated operations. This equation would be:

$$f = \frac{2{,}240 \times v}{w}$$

where

    v = volume of the container.

    w = gross weight of the container in pounds.

When handling grain, information concerning the cargo is often given in terms of pounds per U.S. bushel. Since the volume of the U.S. bushel is 1.2445 ft^3, the equation for the stowage factor of grain is:

$$f = \frac{2{,}240 \times 1.2445}{w}$$

$$f = \frac{2{,}787.6}{w}$$

where

    w = weight in pounds per U.S. bushel.

When handling other bulk commodities such as ores, sulfur, and sugar, the only way that the stowage factor can be obtained is by weighing a known volume of the substance. A level bucketful can be used, or a box built with a volume of exactly 1 ft³.

Obviously, it is not necessary to have the weight of a single container with its volume. The volume and gross weight of the entire shipment or of any part of the shipment can be used to calculate the stowage factor. Such data are given on the ship's manifest and on the bills of lading. Volume and weight information are readily available during all the phases of the cargo operation. The use of such data obviates the need of looking elsewhere for the information.

Using the Stowage Factor

The stowage factor is used to answer the questions mentioned above, and always with some estimated value for broken stowage percentage. The best way to illustrate the use of the stowage factor in conjunction with the broken stowage percentage is to present some general equations and then some numerical examples.

When given a certain volume of space (V), a cargo with a stowage factor (f), and an estimated broken stowage percentage (L), we find the tons, (T), that will fit into the space as follows:

$$T = \frac{V \times (1 - L)}{f} \tag{1}$$

When given the same data and instead of the tons (T) we want to know the number of pieces (P) that will fit into the given space, we change the denominator of the right-hand side of the equation to equal the volume of a single container (v); hence:

$$P = \frac{V \times (1 - L)}{v} \tag{2}$$

When a given number of tons of a certain type of cargo are to be stowed, we find the space that they will occupy by the following equation:

$$V = \frac{T \times f}{(1 - L)} \tag{3}$$

If the number of pieces is given instead of the tons, the space required would be:

$$V = \frac{P \times v}{(1 - L)} \tag{4}$$

There are times when it is convenient to combine the stowage factor with an estimate of broken stowage and express the result as a known value. We will define such a value F as the ratio of f to $(1 - L)$; thus:

$$F = \frac{f}{(1 - L)} \tag{5}$$

Note then that the following statements are true:

$$T = \frac{V}{F} \qquad \text{and} \qquad V = T \times F \tag{6}$$

NUMERICAL EXAMPLES

EXAMPLE 1:

Given: A hold with a bale cubic of 60,000 ft³. A cargo consisting of cases weighing 400 pounds and measuring 2.5 feet by 2 feet by 2 feet to be stowed. Estimated broken stowage: 10%.

Required: The number of tons that can be stowed in the hold.

Solution: Solving for the stowage factor of this cargo:

$$f = \frac{2{,}240 \times 10^*}{400} \qquad * (2.5 \times 2 \times 2)$$

$$f = 56$$

After finding the stowage factor, we use equation 1 to find the answer to our problem:

$$T = \frac{60{,}000 \times 0.9}{56}$$

$$T = 964 \text{ tons}$$

EXAMPLE 2:

Given: The same data as for Example 1.

Required: The number of cases that could be stowed in the hold.

Solution: Using equation 2:

$$P = \frac{60{,}000 \times 0.9}{10}$$

$$P = 5{,}400 \text{ cases}$$

EXAMPLE 3:

Given: 500 tons of a cargo with a stowage factor of 50. Estimated broken stowage: 25%.

Required: The amount of space required to stow this cargo.

Solution: Using equation 3:

$$V = \frac{500 \times 50}{0.75}$$

$$V = 33,333 \text{ ft}^3$$

Note that the accuracy of such solutions depends entirely on the officer's guess as to the broken stowage that will result from the actual stowage operation. An officer in a given trade route can increase the accuracy of his/her estimations of broken stowage by maintaining records of the broken stowage that resulted in a number of specific cases. These records should be incorporated into a tabulation of average broken stowage percentages resulting with the most common cargoes carried on the route in question and in particular sections of the ship. Where longshore gangs are maintained as units, this fact should be noted also, because longshoremen's operations constitute a variable and some interesting facts may come to light. Without such records, the estimates of a given officer will not increase notably in accuracy. With such records, the estimates are based on facts and should become very accurate as time passes. If the estimate does prove highly inaccurate, the officer at least knows that there must be some good reason and can start checking into the facts. One observation gives some basis for judgment, but the basis becomes more trustworthy as the observations increase in number and are averaged.

Loading Full and Down

Once an officer fully understands the above stowage factor ideas, he/she can solve for the amounts of two different kinds of cargoes that must be loaded to obtain a full and down condition. Variations of the basic problem are more practical than the type of problem presented in most books on cargo stowage. The basic problem deals with choosing the exact amounts of two cargo types that will place the ship down to her maximum legal draft and at the same time fill up her internal volume. A good example of where this problem is met in the industry is at certain ports of Portugal where cork and pyrites are loaded. One of these is definitely a measurement cargo and the other a weight cargo. A measurement cargo is one that stows at or above a stowage factor of 40. Generally the freight charges for such cargoes will be based on measurement tons equaling 40 ft³ each.

Without using specific values, let us look at the elements of the problem. We would always know four things: (1) the total free space available for stowing the cargo, (2) the cargo deadweight of the ship as she goes on the loading berth, (3) the stowage factor of the heavy cargo, and (4) the stowage factor of the light cargo. When solving these problems we will use a stowage factor that has been combined with a broken stowage factor; the resulting value is what we have called F. What we are trying to determine is how many tons of light cargo and heavy cargo must be loaded to put the ship full and down.

For a general solution let us write down the following factors: Let V equal the free space available. Let T equal the cargo deadweight available. Let s equal the stowage factor (broken stowage combined) of the light cargo. Let b equal the stowage factor (broken stowage combined) of the heavy cargo. These are all known factors. Let X equal the tons of light cargo and Y equal the tons of heavy cargo that must be loaded to put the ship full and down. The latter values are unknown.

It is obvious that to put the ship down, the total of X and Y cannot be more or less than T. Hence we write:

$$X + Y = T \tag{7}$$

We also note that the product sX equals the space that will be occupied by X and that bY equals the space occupied by Y. The sum of sX and bY must be equal to V to have the ship full. Hence we write:

$$sX + bY = V \tag{8}$$

The two equations above constitute a set of simultaneous equations; that is, we have two equations with two unknowns. We can solve for one of the unknowns and then insert the known value in either equation and solve for the second unknown. There are several ways of going about the first solution. The easiest method follows. Start with equations 1 and 2. Multiply equation 1 by one of the coefficients of equation 2 and rewrite the set. We do this using the coefficient s:

$$sX + bY = V \tag{9}$$

$$sX + sY = sT \tag{10}$$

Subtracting equation 10 from equation 9 we obtain:

$$bY - sY = V - sT$$

Factor out Y on the left-hand side and solve for Y:

$$(b - s)Y = V - sT$$

$$Y = \frac{V - sT}{b - s}$$

After solving for Y the value of X can be found easily.

The general solution of the problem given above is presented for purposes of providing a thorough explanation. It is not recommended that the reader try to memorize the formula derived, but rather the *method* used. Any given problem can be reasoned out more easily if the general idea is clear.

NUMERICAL EXAMPLE

Given: A ship is loading pyrites with $F = 14$ and cork with $F = 254$. She has 453,000-ft^3 bale capacity and 8,000-ton cargo deadweight available.

Required: How many tons of pyrites and how many tons of cork must be loaded to put the ship full and down?

Solution: Always write down the meaning of the symbols used. Let X equal the tons of cork, and Y the tons of pyrites. Then we have:

$$X + Y = 8,000$$

$$254X + 14Y = 453,000$$

Multiply the top equation by 14 and subtract the result from the bottom equation:

$$
\begin{array}{rcr}
254X + 14Y & = & 453,000 \\
-\ 14X - 14Y & = & -112,000 \\
\hline
240X & = & 341,000
\end{array}
$$

$$X = 1,421 \text{ tons}$$

$$Y = 8,000 - 1,421$$

$$Y = 6,579 \text{ tons}$$

LOADING FULL AND DOWN WITH REQUIRED TRIM

A problem related to the above deals with the question of how much of two kinds of cargo must be loaded in the end hatches of a ship during the final stages of loading to get the ship full and down with a required trim. This problem is best illustrated by an example.

NUMERICAL EXAMPLE

Given: A Mariner class ship with free space in the number 1 main deck space equal to 16,000 bale cubic. This space has its center of gravity 60 feet from the forward perpendicular. This is expressed as L.C.G.–F.P. = 60 feet. Free space is also available in the number 7 second deck equal to 29,000 bale cubic. This space has L.C.G.–F.P. = 416 feet. The ship's tipping center is 264 feet from the F.P. The deadweight remaining is equal to 900 tons. The trim is presently 4 inches by the head. The $MT1$ equals 1,522.

Two cargoes remain to be loaded: (1) wolfram concentrates in double cloth bags with $F = 14$, and (2) India tea in packages with $F = 86$.

Required: The number of tons of wolfram and tea that must be loaded in the number 1 and number 7 spaces to put the ship full and down with a trim of 6 inches by the stern.

Solution: The most direct approach is to solve first for the number of tons of the combined cargoes that must go forward and aft. Thus, let $X =$ tons aft; let $Y =$ tons forward. Obviously, then:

$$X + Y = 900$$

This is one equation of a set of two needed to solve for one of the unknowns. The second equation is obtained by working with the trimming moments needed to obtain the desired trim. The forward space is (264–60) or 204 feet forward of the tipping center. Hence, the forward trimming moment is equal to 204Y. The after space is (416 –264) or 152 feet aft of the tipping center. Hence, the after trimming moment is equal to 152X. Note that the trim in the beginning is 4 inches by the head and that the desired trim is 6 inches by the stern. This means that we must change the trim, through our loading of the cargo, a total of 10 inches. Since the ship is now down by the head and we want it to be down by the stern, we note that the after trimming moment must be in *excess* of the forward trimming moment. It must be in excess a sufficient amount that the difference yields a net trimming moment aft that will give the ship a total change of trim of 10 inches. This can be expressed mathematically as follows:

$$\frac{\text{Excess of moment aft}}{MT1} = 10 \text{ in.}$$

Or:

$$\text{Moment aft} - \text{Moment fwd.} = MT1 \times 10$$
$$152X - 204Y = 15,220$$

This is our second equation with the two unknowns. Multiply the first equation by 204 and then *add* the result to the second equation to eliminate Y. Solve for X, then for Y.

$$
\begin{array}{rl}
152X - 204Y = & 15,220 \\
204X + 204Y = & 183,600 \\
\hline
356X \quad\quad = & 198,820
\end{array}
$$

$$X = 558 \text{ tons aft}$$
$$Y = 900 - 558$$
$$Y = 342 \text{ tons fwd.}$$

With this information, we proceed to solve for the exact amount of wolfram and tea forward and aft by using the same technique as was employed in the problem involving the loading of pyrites and cork. This time we know the same elements. Let us work with the forward end first. Note that we know that a total of 342 tons will go in the forward space and that the space is equal to 16,000 ft³. Hence we can write: Let A = tons of wolfram fwd.; let B = tons of tea fwd. Obviously, then:

$$A + B = 342 \text{ tons}$$
$$14A + 86B = 16,000 \text{ ft}^3$$

Multiply the first equation by 14, and subtract the result from the second equation:

$$\begin{array}{rr} 14A + 86B = & 16,000 \\ -14A - 14B = & -4,788 \\ \hline 72B = & 11,212 \end{array}$$

B = 156 tons of tea fwd.

A = 186 tons of wolfram fwd.

In a similar manner, we solve for the distribution in the after space. Let W = the tons of wolfram aft. Let T = the tons of tea aft. Then:

By multiplying the first equation by 14:

$$\begin{array}{rrr} W + T & = & 558 \\ \hline 14W + 86T & = & 29,000 \\ -14W - 14T & = & -7,812 \\ \hline 72T & = & 21,188 \end{array}$$

T = 294 tons of tea aft

W = 264 tons of wolfram aft

This particular problem may arise during the last day of loading. If the problem does not entail both full and down conditions, only a partial solution with respect to the weight distribution for trim will be required. The holds involved do not necessarily have to be the end holds, but if a specific change in trim is to be obtained, the holds must be on opposite sides of the ship's tipping center.

Stowage Factors Used with Lumber

The stowage factor of general cargo has been defined as the number of cubic feet required to stow one ton of cargo. It was also pointed out that the stowage factor never varied and should always be used in conjunction with an estimated broken stowage value. It must be emphasized that these foregoing remarks were in reference to the stowage of ordinary dry cargo. These ideas are changed somewhat when dealing with lumber.

The stowage factor for lumber is defined as the number of cubic feet required to stow 1,000 board feet of lumber. The symbol for 1,000 board feet is *M*.

One thousand board feet will occupy 83⅓ ft³ if there is no broken stowage. But there is always some broken stowage as the lumber is stowed in the ship. There will be more broken stowage in the end holds than in the mid ship holds. With shipments that have large lots of uniform lengths, such as those found on the intercoastal run of the United States, the average broken stowage will be between 20 and 25%. Poor stowage might raise this percentage to 30%, whereas excellent stowage will lower it to below 20%. On shipments of lumber of varied lengths and many sizes, such as are found in foreign trade, the broken stowage will probably run between 25% and 30%.

When considering stowage factors for lumber, the estimate of broken stowage is included. As a general average figure in the problems discussed in this book, we will assume the stowage factor of lumber to be 110 ft³/*M*.

In practice, the ship's officer should keep a record of the stowage in various compartments of his/her ship. From these data, he/she will be able to judge the broken stowage with accuracy. With a reliable stowage factor, we can estimate the space that is required to stow any given shipment of lumber. If given the size of the compartment, we can calculate the number of pieces of any given type of lumber required to fill the space.

Board Feet in a Shipment

To use the stowage factor for lumber, it is necessary to know the number of board feet of lumber in a shipment. A board foot is defined as the amount of lumber in a piece 1 inch thick and 1 foot square. The number of board feet in any given piece of lumber may be found by this equation:

$$\text{Board feet} = \frac{T \times W \times L}{12}$$

where

T = thickness in inches.

W = width in inches.

L = length in feet.

To find the number of board feet in a shipment, all we have to do is multiply the number so obtained by the number of pieces in the shipment.

THE DECIMAL CONVERSION FACTOR

When lumber is surfaced, the thickness and widths are reduced. Therefore, when a 2- by 4-inch piece is received by the ship, it may be only be $1\frac{5}{8}$ by $3\frac{5}{8}$ inches. This fact introduces an error in stowage calculations unless it is taken into account. The number of board feet in any given shipment is reduced when the rough sizes are reduced. To find the true amount of lumber in such a shipment, multiply the gross amount of the lumber by the ratio of the finished cross-sectional area to the rough cross-sectional area. This ratio is called the *decimal conversion factor* (dcf). For a 2×4 finished to $1\frac{5}{8}$ by $3\frac{5}{8}$ inches the decimal conversion factor would be:

$$\text{dcf} = \frac{1\frac{5}{8} \times 3\frac{5}{8}}{2 \times 4} = 0.7363 = 0.74$$

To use this factor, always round off the figure to the nearest two decimal places. If it reads exactly 50 in the third and fourth places, then raise it to the next highest figure.

With use of the conversion factor, the calculation of the amount of lumber is first done based on the rough sizes; the amount thus obtained is called the *gross measurement*. Multiplying the gross measurement by the conversion factor, we obtain the *net measurement*. We always consider the net measurement when calculating stowage requirements.

TWO GENERAL EQUATIONS: SPACE AND PIECES

Two equations are used continually by the supercargo when checking and planning the stowage of lumber. One equation, for the space requirements of stowing a given shipment, is:

$$\text{Space} = \frac{T \times W \times L \times P \times 110 \times \text{dcf}}{12,000}$$

where

    Space = the space required to stow the shipment.

    T = thickness in inches.

    W = width in inches.

    L = length of the lumber in feet.

    P = total pieces in the shipment.

    dcf = decimal conversion factor if there is a difference between rough (nominal) and finished (standard) size.

    110 = the assumed stowage factor of sawed lumber.

12,000 = the product of 12 and 1,000, the 1,000 being
        used to convert board feet into *M*s.

The second equation, derived from the first, is used to solve for the number of pieces that can be stowed in a given compartment, knowing the type of lumber available:

$$P = \frac{\text{Space} \times 12{,}000}{T \times W \times L \times P \times 110 \times \text{dcf}}$$

It is recommended that the reader learn the reasoning involved in deriving the equation rather than memorize the equation itself.

STOWAGE OF LOGS

Solving for the space for stowage of logs and the inverse problem is approached in the same way as for sawed lumber except that the number of board feet is found by using a *mean* diameter to find the cross-sectional area and a different stowage factor is used. If the logs are all the same length, use 135 as the stowage factor; if they are of various lengths, use 150.

CHAPTER 6

STOWAGE OF HAZARDOUS CARGO

T HE QUANTITY AND DIVERSITY OF hazardous materials transported on cargo vessels has increased significantly in recent years. Industry is continually developing different compounds and chemicals as our technologies demand them. As these commodities come on the market, they appear on our bookings for transportation, necessitating the development of safe methods of transporting them.

Regulations for the transport of hazardous cargoes are increasing apace with the above-mentioned trends, with various regulatory bodies drawing up and enforcing them. In the United States, the Materials Transportation Bureau of the Department of Transportation (DOT) formulates the regulations and the Coast Guard is responsible for their enforcement. The only exception is bulk cargoes, for which the Coast Guard is solely responsible.

The international companion to these regulations are those of the International Maritime Organization (IMO) which come in the International Maritime Dangerous Goods Code (IMDG Code).

The increase in hazardous cargoes makes it more necessary than ever for the ship's officer to be thoroughly familiar with the hazards involved in transporting these cargoes and the regulations governing their transportation on his/her vessel.

HAZARDOUS MATERIAL REGULATIONS

T hese regulations are contained in 49 *Code of Federal Regulations* (CFR) 100–185, *Hazardous Materials Regulations* (HMR). This is a lengthy and complicated publication. It contains regulations for transportation by air, rail, and highway as well as by water. Some sections apply to all modes, whereas others are limited to one. The 49 CFR allows carriers of hazardous materials by vessel to use the International Maritime Dangerous Goods Code as long as they also conform to the requirements listed in section 171.12 and 176.11. Many sections contain a great deal of material that does not concern the ship's officer and a few items that are very important to him/her. The only way to make oneself really familiar with all the regulations is to go through the whole book, picking out those items that apply.

With this in mind, the following summary is not intended as a substitute for the CFR publication, but only as a guide to its use.

Part 171—General Information, Regulations, and Definitions

DEFINITIONS AND ABBREVIATIONS

This section should be read over for applicable items, and then referred to as needed when reading other parts.

INCIDENTS

These sections require that immediate notice be given the Department of Transportation of any incident involving hazardous materials that involves any of the following: a person killed, injuries requiring hospitalization, damage exceeding $50,000, damage to or suspected contamination involving radioactive material or etiologic agents, or any other situation that in your judgment should be reported. This notice must be given by telephone. The notice must contain the name of the reporter; name and address of owner; phone number of reporter; date, time, and place of incident; extent of injuries; class, name, and quantity of hazardous material involved; type of incident; nature of hazardous material involvement; and whether a continuing danger to life exists. A written report must them be made on DOT Form 5800.1 within 30 days of the incident.

Part 172—Hazardous Materials Table and Hazardous Materials Communications Regulations

Part 172 consists of the hazardous materials table (see Table 6-1) and the instructions for its use. Each officer should be familiar with the use of this table and should refer to it when any hazardous material is to be loaded. All sections referred to in the table should be read when looking up an item, because additional information and requirements may be found in them.

SUBPART C: SHIPPING PAPERS

The preparation of these is not the responsibility of the ship's officer, but improper manifests and the like can cause problems, particularly on homebound loadings. The book should be referred to if you are in doubt about the documentation of any shipment.

TABLE 6-1
Hazardous Materials Table

§ 172.101 HAZARDOUS MATERIALS TABLE

Symbols	Hazardous materials descriptions and proper shipping names	Hazard class or Division	Identification Numbers	PG	Label Codes	Special provisions	Packaging (§173.***)			Quantity limitations		Vessel stowage	
							Exceptions	Non-bulk	Bulk	Passenger aircraft/rail	Cargo aircraft only	Location	Other
(1)	(2)	(3)	(4)	(5)	(6)	(7)	(8A)	(8B)	(8C)	(9A)	(9B)	(10A)	(10B)
	Accellerene, see p-Nitrosodimethylaniline.	....			....		....	....		....	....		
	Accumulators, electric, see Batteries, wet etc.	....						....	....		....	....		
D	Accumulators, pressurized, pneumatic or hydraulic (containing non-flammable gas).	2.2	NA1956		2.2		306	306	None ..	No limit	No limit	A	
	Acetal	3	UN1088	II	3	T7	150	202	242	5 L	60 L	E	
	Acetaldehyde	3	UN1089	I	3	A3, B16, T20, T26, T29	None	201	243	Forbidden	30 L	E	
A	Acetaldehyde ammonia	9	UN1841	III	9		155	204	240	200 kg	200 kg	A	34
	Acetaldehyde oxime	3	UN2332	III	3	B1, T8	150	203	242	60 L	220 L	A	
	Acetic acid, glacial or Acetic acid solution, with more than 80 percent acid, by mass.	8	UN2789	II	8, 3	A3, A6, A7, A10, B2, T8	154	202	243	1 L	30 L	A	
	Acetic acid solution, not less than 50 percent but not more than 80 percent acid, by mass.	8	UN2790	II	8	A3, A6, A7, A10, B2, T8	154	202	242	1 L	30 L	A	
	Acetic acid solution, with more than 10 percent and less than 50 percent acid, by mass.	8	UN2790	III	8	T8	154	203	242	5 L	60 L	A	
	Acetic anhydride	8	UN1715	II	8, 3	A3, A6, A7, A10, B2, T8	154	202	243	1 L	30 L	A	40
	Acetone	3	UN1090	II	3	T8	150	202	242	5 L	60 L	B	
	Acetone cyanohydrin, stabilized	6.1	UN1541	I	6.1	2, A3, B9, B14, B32, B76, B77, N34, T38, T43, T45	None	227	244	Forbidden	30 L	D	25, 40, 49
	Acetone oils	3	UN1091	II	3	T7, T30	150	202	242	5 L	60 L	B	
	Acetonitrile	3	UN1648	II	3	T14	150	202	242	5L	60L	B	40
	Acetyl acetone peroxide with more than 9 percent by mass active oxygen.	Forbidden			....		....	....		....	....		
	Acetyl benzoyl peroxide, solid, or with more than 40 percent in solution.	Forbidden			....								
	Acetyl bromide	8	UN1716	II	8	B2, T12, T26	154	202	242	1 L	30 L	C	40

49 CFR Ch. 1

SUBPART D: MARKING

You should be familiar with Sections 172.300 through 172.338. They give detailed requirements for the markings that must appear on packages containing hazardous materials. Violations of these could lead to confusion in emergencies and are readily apparent to Coast Guard boarding officers.

SUBPART E & F: LABELING & PLACARDING

Sections 172.400 through 172.560 give requirements for label and placard placement, number of labels, and so forth. Ship's officers should read these sections carefully and refer to them if in doubt about any package or container.

SUBPART G: EMERGENCY RESPONSE INFORMATION

Sections 172.600 through 172.606 prescribes requirements for providing and maintaining emergency response information during transportation and at facilities where hazardous materials are loaded for transportation, stored incidental to transportation, or otherwise handled during *any phase* of transportation.

SUBPART H: TRAINING

Sections 172.700 through 172.704 prescribes requirements for training hazmat employees. Each carrier must ensure that its employees involved in the transportation of hazardous materials are trained in accordance with this subpart. The record of training required by 172,704(d) must be kept on board the vessel while the crewmember is in service on board vessel.

Part 173—Shipper's General Requirements for Shipments and Packagings

SUBPARTS A AND B

These subparts give general requirements, many of which are not applicable to carriage on ships. However, the following sections at least should be read:

173.2a   Classification of a material having more than one hazard

173.21   Prohibited packing

173.26   Quantity limitations

173.29   Empty packages, portable tanks

173.32   Qualification maintenance and use of portable tanks

SUBPARTS C THROUGH N

These subparts contain detailed requirements for specific commodities listed in the hazardous materials table and define the various classes. The material should at least be skimmed over; it could be useful if you encounter commodities with which you are not familiar or that appear to be hazardous but are not classed as such on your loading list.

Part 176—Carriage by Vessel

This part applies directly to seagoing cargo vessels. Part 176 is divided into Subparts A through O. Subparts A through D cover general operating requirements, as well as general handling, stowage, and segregation requirements. Subparts E through F cover special requirements for transport vehicles and barges. Subparts G through O cover detailed requirements for specific classes of hazardous materials. Every deck officer should be thoroughly familiar with the entire part, as the ship is responsible for compliance. Certain especially important sections are quoted or referred to here, but this text cannot take the place of a thorough study of this part by each officer.

EXCEPTIONS

Note that although shipments may comply with IMO regulations for marking, listing, and so forth, they must still be loaded and stowed in accordance with the regulations in this section.

Dangerous Cargo Manifest

a. The master of a vessel transporting hazardous materials or his/her authorized representative shall prepare a dangerous cargo manifest, list, or stowage plan. This documentation must be kept in a designated holder on or near the bridge. It must contain the following information:

1. Name of vessel and official number.

2. Nationality of vessel.

3. Shipping name of each hazardous material on board, as given in the hazardous materials table, or the "correct technical name," as given in the International Dangerous Goods Code published by IMO. When the shipping name of a material is an "N.O.S." entry, this entry must be qualified by the technical name of the commodity in parentheses, for example, "Corrosive Material, N.O.S. (Caprylyl Chloride)."

4. The number and description of packages (barrels, drums, cylinders, boxes, etc.) and the gross weight for each type of packaging.

5. Classification of the hazardous material in accordance with either (i) the hazardous materials table or (ii) the IMO Dangerous Goods Code.

6. Any additional description required by sections 172.201 through 172.203 of this subchapter.

7. Stowage location of the hazardous material on board the vessel.

b. The hazardous material information on the dangerous cargo manifest must be the same as the information furnished by the shipper on the shipping order or other shipping paper, except that the IMO "correct technical name" and the IMO class may be indicated on the manifest as provided in paragraphs (a)(3) and (a)(5) of this section. The person who supervises the preparation of the manifest shall insure that the information is correctly transcribed, and shall certify the truth and accuracy of this information to the best of his/her knowledge and belief by his/her signature and notation of the date prepared.

c. The master or licensed deck officer designated by the master and attached to the vessel shall acknowledge the correctness of the dangerous cargo manifest, list, or stowage plan by his/her signature.

d. Each carrier who transports or stores hazardous materials on a vessel shall retain, for one year thereafter, a copy of the dangerous cargo manifest, list, or stowage plan, and shall make that manifest or list available for inspection in accordance with Section 176.36(a)(b) (see Tables 6-2 and 6-3).

EXEMPTIONS

"If a hazardous material is being transported by a vessel under the authority of an exemption and a copy of the exemption is required to be on board the vessel, it must be kept with the dangerous cargo manifest." Since in most cases a copy of an exemption must be on the vessel, copies of all such papers should be put with the dangerous cargo manifest in its proper location.

TABLE 6-2
Dangerous and Hazardous Cargo Manifest

DANGEROUS AND HAZARDOUS CARGO MANIFEST

VESSEL _____ OFF.NO VOYAGE NATIONALITY _____ PORT PREPARING MANIFEST _____ SIGNATURE ____

PORT CALL: 1

PROPER SHIPPING NAME	HAZARD CLASS	UN NUMBER	PACKING GROUP	GROSS WEIGHT (KGS) PACKAGING	NUMBER AND TYPE OF PKGS.	CONTAINER NUMBER	STOWAGE	ORIG. LOAD PORT	RELAY PORTS	DEST. PORT
ETHYLENEDIAMINE FLASH POINT TEMP.: 43 C EMERGENCY PHONE: (800) 424-9300 EMS : F-E , S-C	8 (3.3)	UN 1604	II	15372	78 DRMS	GSTU228045-7	11 0582	SPQ		HSN
*RQ ETHYLENEDIAMINE FLASH POINT TEMP.: 43 C EMERGENCY PHONE: (800) 424-9300 EMS : F-E , S-C	8 (3.3)	UN 1604	II	15372	78 DRMS	NOSU247406-3	11 0982	SPQ		HSN
COMBUSTIBLE LIQUIDS, N.O.S.(CONTAINS SULFURIZED ISOBUTYLENE) FLASH POINT TEMP.: 88 C EMERGENCY PHONE: 800-424-9300 EMS : 3-07	CL	NA 1993	III	20285	1 TNK	UTCU413407-1	09 0782	SPQ		HSN
COMBUSTIBLE LIQUIDS, N.O.S.(CONTAINS SULFURIZED ISOBUTYLENE) FLASH POINT TEMP.: 88 C EMERGENCY PHONE: 800-424-9300 EMS : 3-07	CL	NA 1993	III	20194	1 TNK	UTCU458001-0	09 0982	SPQ		HSN

APPROVED _____
MASTER/DESIGNATED DECK OFFICER

INSPECTIONS

Section 176.39 requires that an inspection of spaces containing hazardous materials be made after loading and every 24 hours thereafter. The fire detecting system need not be inspected daily, but must still be inspected after heavy weather. In addition, an inspection is required immediately before entering a U.S. port. The section does not restrict this to entering from foreign waters, so an inspection is required before each port on the coast. All of these inspections must be entered in the deck log.

NOTIFICATION

Section 176.48 requires that the nearest District Commander USCG be notified when a "fire or other hazardous condition" exists and there are hazardous materials on board. Notification is also required when any hazardous material is lost or jettisoned. These notifications are separate from the ones to the DOT required in (b). When an incident occurs during transportation in which a hazardous material is involved, a report may be required (see section 171.15 and 171.16 of this subchapter).

TABLE 6-3
Dangerous Cargo Manifest

DANGEROUS CARGO MANIFEST

PAGE: 52 OF 55

COMPANY NAME:
COMPANY ADDRESS:

NATIONALITY:	VESSEL:	VOYAGE:
DATE OF LOADING:	LOAD PORT: USNFK NORFOLK	DISCHARGE PORT: NLROT ROTTERDAM
		FINAL DESTINATION: NLROT ROTTERDAM
CAPTAIN NAME:		OFFICIAL NUMBER:

SHIPPING/TECHNICAL NAME	IMO FLSHP	UNNO	PACKG GROUP	WEIGHT (KGS)	PACKAGING NUMBER/TYPE	SHIPPER NAME EMERGENCY PHONE	MAR POL	CONTAINER NUMBER	STOWAGE	EMS BOOKING
CORROSIVE LIQUID BASIC ORGANIC NOS (CONTAINS SODIUM MERCAPTOBENZOTHIAZOLE)	8	3267		20411	1 TNK	HYUNDAI CORP 7035273887	NO	BVIU2170079	0906082	F-A S-B 002073378
CORROSIVE LIQUID BASIC ORGANIC NOS (CONTAINS SODIUM MERCAPTOBENZOTHIAZOLE)	8	3267	III	20411	1 TNK	HYUNDAI CORP 7035273887	NO	BVIU2170090	0505082	F-A S-B 002073378
CORROSIVE LIQUID, BASIC, ORGANIC, N.O.S. (CONTAINS SODIUM MERCAPTOBENZOTHIAZOLE)	8	3267	III	20411	1 TNK	HYUNDAI CORP 7035273887	NO	ICSU0280938	1106082	F-A S-B 002073378
CORROSIVE LIQUID BASIC ORGANIS NOS (CONTAINS SODIUM MERCAPTOBENZOTHIAZOLE)	8	3267	III	20411	1 TNK	HYUNDAI CORP 7035273887	NO	TABU2201202	1109082	F-A S-B 002073378
CORROSIVE LIQUID, BASIC, ORGANIC, N.O.S. (COTNAINS SODIUM MERCAPTOBENZOTHIAZOLE)	8	3267	III	20411	1 TNK	HYUNDAI CORP 7035273887	NO	TABU2201218	0506082	F-A S-B 002073378

NAME/SIGNATURE OF PREPARER: DATE PREPARED: 2004/

SUPERVISION

Section 176.57, paragraphs (a) through (d) require that the handling and stowage of hazardous materials be supervised by a ship's officer. This makes it necessary for a mate to be *on deck* at all times when this cargo is being worked.

General Stowage Requirements for Hazardous Materials

Hazardous materials must be stowed in a manner that will facilitate their inspection during the voyage and their removal from a potentially dangerous situation, including fire. Each package marked "This side up" must be stowed so as to remain in the position indicated during transportation.

ON-DECK STOWAGE OF BREAKBULK HAZARDOUS MATERIALS

a. Packages containing hazardous materials must be secured by enclosure in boxes, cribs, or cradles and by proper lashing with wire rope, strapping, or other means, including shoring, bracing or both. Lashing of deck cargo is permitted if pad eyes are used to attach the lashings. Lashings may not be secured to guard rails. Bulky articles must be shored.

b. Packaging susceptible to weather or water damage must be protected so that it will not be exposed to the weather or to sea water.

c. Not more than 50% of the total open deck area may be used for the stowage of hazardous materials except Class 9 material.

d. Fireplugs, hoses, sounding pipes, and access to these must be free and clear of all cargo.

Figure 6-1. Four drums of lube oil stowed on deck at the forward starboard side of the number 2 hatch are classified as a flammable liquid, UN class 3.1. Requirements for stowage from Title 49 172.101 state that these drums must be stowed on deck, separated by 10 feet from other hazardous materials, or belowdecks away from heat.

e. Crew and passenger spaces and areas set aside for the crew's use may not be used to stow any hazardous material.

f. A hazardous material may not be stowed within a horizontal distance of 25 feet of an operating or embarkation point of a lifeboat.

g. Hazardous materials must be stowed so as to permit safe access to the crew's quarters and to all parts of the deck required in navigation and necessary working of the vessel.

h. When runways for use of the crew are built over stowed hazardous materials, they must be constructed and fitted with rails and lifelines so as to afford complete protection to the crew when in use.

OTHER SECTIONS OF CONCERN TO THE SHIP'S OFFICER

Section 176.78 gives comprehensive and detailed requirements for the use of forklifts. Their strict enforcement would require the ship's officers to observe forklift use closely. Note that paragraphs (g)(8) and (9) require that each truck be equipped with a fire extinguisher or that one must be kept in the space the truck is working. The ship's firefighting system must also be kept "ready for immediate use."

Figure 6-2. On the port side of the number 2 hatch on deck are two cylinders of tri-n-hexyl aluminum, also known as isopentane. This commodity is a UN flammable liquid, class 3.1, and thus must be stowed either on deck or belowdecks away from other flammable materials.

Section 176.83 consists of two tables, explanations and definitions that together set forth segregation requirements. This whole section should be understood thoroughly and the tables used whenever hazardous material is to be loaded. These requirements are in addition to any others (see Tables 6-4 and 6-5).

Subparts G through O give detailed requirements for the handling and stowage of each class of hazardous material. Some of these, such as the construction of magazines, will rarely apply to your vessel. Others will be commonly encountered and ship's officers must be conversant with them. Some of the more important sections are mentioned here, but the material should be read over.

Section 176.105(a) requires that class A or B material be loaded last in any one port and that other explosives not be worked at the same time as other cargo.

Section 176.115(a)(2) states: "An explosive may not be stowed nearer than 25 feet in a horizontal plane to the crew quarters."

Section 176.125 states: "A deck load over which explosives must be passed may not exceed the height of the hatch coaming, bulwark, or 3 feet, whichever is greater."

Section 176.205(7) requires fire screens on the weather ends of all vent ducts from compartments containing compressed gases, and paragraph (8) prohibits compressed gases from compartments with gooseneck type vent heads.

Section 176.205 requires that poisons be stowed away from quarters and any vents serving them. It also states that a package having both poison gas and flammable gas labels must be segregated as a flammable compressed gas.

Section 176.800 says that corrosive materials must be stowed so as to be readily observable, and prohibits their stowage above any combustible substance. It also prevents the stowage of corrosive material above a compartment containing cotton or fibers.

Section 176.900 requires that a tweendeck containing cotton or fibers be closed with "hatch covers, tarpaulins, and dunnage," and requires that hatches containing cotton or fibers be closed when not being worked unless a fire watch is kept in the hold. It also requires that cotton or fibers be segregated as flammable solids that may not be stowed with other flammable solids or with any combustible liquid. If cotton or fibers are stowed in the same hold or compartment with rosin or pitch, they must be separated by dunnage or noncombustible cargo. Where large amounts are involved, the rosin or pitch must be floored off with two layers of (2.54 cm) dunnage and the cotton or fiber stowed above them.

FIRE PROTECTION REQUIREMENTS

Fire protection requirements are involved with shipment of any hazardous material. Whenever such material is to be worked, "No Smoking" signs must be posted in the vicinity, the fire hose at each hold must be led out and fitted with an all-purpose nozzle and pressure maintained on the fire line, and two 15-pound foam or dry-chemical fire extinguishers must be placed in the vicinity of each hatch. A copy of the Hazardous Cargo Manifest and Vessel Fire Plan should also be readily accessible (ship's bridge, cargo office, gangway access) in case of fire or an emergency.

TABLE 6-4
Segregation Tables for Freight Containers and Transport Units

Segregation Tables for Freight Containers and Transport Units

▬▬ Segregation Table for Freight Containers	• Table 176.83(f) sets forth the general requirements for segregation between freight containers on board container vessels.
▬▬ Segregation Table for Trailerships	• Table 176.83(g) sets forth the general requirements for segregation between transport units on board trailerships.

TABLE § 176.83(B)—GENERAL SEGREGATION REQUIREMENTS FOR HAZARDOUS MATERIALS
[Segregation must also take account of a single secondary hazard label, as required by paragraph (a)(6) of this section.]

Class	1.1 1.2 1.5	1.3	1.4 1.6	2.1	2.2	2.3	3	4.1	4.2	4.3	5.1	5.2	6.1	6.2	7	8	9
Explosives, 1.1, 1.2, 1.5	(*)	(*)	(*)	4	2	2	4	4	4	4	4	4	2	4	2	4	X
Explosives, 1.3	(*)	(*)	(*)	4	2	2	4	3	4	4	4	4	2	4	2	2	X
Explosives, 1.4, 1.6	(*)	(*)	(*)	2	1	1	2	2	2	2	2	2	X	4	2	2	X
Flammable gases 2.1	4	4	2	X	X	X	2	1	2	X	2	2	X	4	2	1	X
Non-toxic, non-flammable gases 2.2	2	2	1	X	X	X	1	X	1	X	X	1	X	2	1	X	X
Poisonous gases 2.3	2	2	1	X	X	X	2	X	2	X	X	2	X	2	1	X	X
Flammable liquids 3	4	4	2	2	1	2	X	X	2	1	2	2	X	3	2	X	X
Flammable solids 4.1	4	3	2	1	X	X	X	X	1	X	1	2	X	3	2	1	X
Spontaneously combustible substances 4.2	4	3	2	2	1	2	2	1	X	1	2	2	1	3	2	1	X
Substances which are dangerous when wet 4.3	4	4	2	X	X	X	1	X	1	X	2	2	X	2	2	1	X
Oxidizing substances 5.1	4	4	2	2	X	X	2	1	2	2	X	2	1	3	1	2	X
Organic peroxides 5.2	4	4	2	2	1	2	2	2	2	2	2	X	1	3	2	2	X
Poisons 6.1	2	2	X	X	X	X	X	X	1	X	1	1	X	1	X	X	X
Infectious substances 6.2	4	4	4	4	2	2	3	3	3	2	3	3	1	X	3	3	X
Radioactive materials 7	2	2	2	2	1	1	2	2	2	2	1	2	X	3	X	2	X
Corrosives 8	4	2	2	1	X	X	X	1	1	1	2	2	X	3	2	X	X
Miscellaneous dangerous substances 9	X	X	X	X	X	X	X	X	X	X	X	X	X	X	X	X	X

Numbers and symbols relate to the following terms as defined in this section:
1—"Away from."
2—"Separated from."
3—"Separated by a complete compartment or hold from."
4—"Separated longitudinally by an intervening complete compartment or hold from."
X—The segregation, if any, is shown in the § 172.101 table.
*—See § 176.144 of this part for segregation within Class 1.

SEGREGATION

Segregation requirements for a hazardous material and any incompatible package can be determined from Tables 6-4 and 6-5. Comparable guides for stowage and segregation of hazardous cargo on board conventional (breakbulk), container, and roll-on/roll-off vessels can be found in the IMDG Code (Volume 1, Part 7) as well. (See Tables 6-6 through 6-10.)

TABLE 6-5
Segregation Tables for Freight Containers and Transport Units

Segregation Tables for Freight Containers and Transport Units

▬ Segregation Table for Freight Containers	• Table 176.83(f) sets forth the general requirements for segregation between freight containers on board container vessels.
▬ Segregation Table for Trailerships	• Table 176.83(g) sets forth the general requirements for segregation between transport units on board trailerships.

TABLE 176.83(F)—SEGREGATION OF CONTAINERS ON BOARD CONTAINER SHIPS

Segregation requirement	Vertical				Horizontal					
	Closed versus closed	Closed versus open	Open versus open		Closed versus closed		Closed versus open		Open versus open	
					On deck	Under deck	On deck	Under deck	On deck	Under deck
1. "Away from"	One on top of the other permitted.	Open on top of closed permitted. Otherwise as for open versus open.	Not in the same vertical line unless segregated by a deck.	Fore and aft ...	No restriction	No restriction	No restriction	No restriction	One container space.	One container space or one bulkhead.
				Athwartships ..	No restriction	No restriction	No restriction	No restriction	One container space.	One container space.
2. "Separated from".	Not in the same vertical line unless segregated by a deck.	As for open versus open.	Not in the same vertical line unless segregated by a deck.	Fore and aft ...	One container space.	One container space or one bulkhead.	One container space.	One container space or one bulkhead.	One container space.	One bulkhead.
				Athwartships ..	One container space.	One container space.	One container space.	Two container spaces.	Two container spaces..	One bulkhead.
3. "Separated by a complete compartment or hold from".	Not in the same vertical line unless segregated by a deck.	As for open versus open.	Not in the same vertical line unless segregated by a deck.	Fore and aft ...	One container space.	One bulkhead	One container space.	One bulkhead	Two container spaces.	Two bulkheads.
				Athwartships ..	Two container spaces.	One bulkhead	Two container spaces.	One bulkhead	Three container spaces.	Two bulkheads.
4. "Separated longitudinally by an intervening complete compartment or hold from".	Prohibited	....	....	Fore and aft ...	Four container spaces.	One bulkhead and four container spaces*.	Four container spaces.	Two bulkheads.	Four container spaces.	Two bulkheads.
				Athwartships ..	Prohibited	Prohibited	Prohibited	Prohibited	Prohibited	Prohibited.

*Containers not less than 6 meters (20 feet) from intervening bulkhead.
Note: All bulkheads and decks must be resistant to fire and liquid.

49 CFR

SPECIFICATIONS FOR HAZARD LABELS

For the classes in the IMDG Code, labels are provided that denote the hazard by means of colors and symbols. The class number should appear in the bottom corner of the labels, except that, in the case of labels for class 5, it is the sub-class number, i.e. 5.1 or 5.2, which should appear. The labels for packages should not be less than 4 inches by 4 inches (100 mm by 100 mm) except in the case of packages which, because of their size, can only bear smaller labels.

SPECIFICATIONS FOR PLACARDS

A placard should (a) be not less than 10 inches by 10 inches (250 mm by 250 mm), (b) correspond to the label for the class of the dangerous goods in the cargo transport unit with respect to color and symbol, and (c) display the number of the class as appropriate in the lower half, as required for the label, in digits not less than 1 inch (25 mm) high.

TABLE 6-6
IMDG Segregation Table

IMDG

Segregation table

The following table shows the general provisions for segregation between the various classes of dangerous goods.

SINCE THE PROPERTIES OF SUBSTANCES, MATERIALS OR ARTICLES WITHIN EACH CLASS MAY VARY GREATLY, THE DANGEROUS GOODS LIST SHALL ALWAYS BE CONSULTED FOR PARTICULAR PROVISIONS FOR SEGREGATION AS, IN THE CASE OF CONFLICTING PROVISIONS, THESE TAKE PRECEDENCE OVER THE GENERAL PROVISIONS.

SEGREGATION SHOULD ALSO TAKE ACCOUNT OF A SINGLE SUBSIDIARY RISK LABEL.

CLASS		1.1 1.2 1.5	1.3 1.6	1.4	2.1	2.2	2.3	3	4.1	4.2	4.3	5.1	5.2	6.1	6.2	7	8	9
Explosives	1.1, 1.2, 1.5	*	*	*	4	2	2	4	4	4	4	4	4	2	4	2	4	X
Explosives	1.3, 1.6	*	*	*	4	2	2	4	3	3	4	4	4	2	4	2	2	X
Explosives	1.4	*	*	*	2	1	1	2	2	2	2	2	2	X	4	2	2	X
Flammable gases	2.1	4	4	2	X	X	X	2	1	2	X	2	2	X	4	2	1	X
Non-toxic, non-flammable gases	2.2	2	2	1	X	X	X	1	X	1	X	X	1	X	2	1	X	X
Toxic gases	2.3	2	2	1	X	X	X	2	X	2	X	X	2	X	2	1	X	X
Flammable liquids	3	4	4	2	2	1	2	X	X	2	1	2	2	X	3	2	X	X
Flammable solids (including self-reactive and related substances and desensitized explosives)	4.1	4	3	2	1	X	X	X	X	1	X	1	2	X	3	2	1	X
Substances liable to spontaneous combustion	4.2	4	3	2	2	1	2	2	1	X	1	2	2	1	3	2	1	X
Substances which, in contact with water, emit flammable gases	4.3	4	4	2	X	X	X	1	X	1	X	2	2	X	2	2	1	X
Oxidizing substances (agents)	5.1	4	4	2	2	X	X	2	1	2	2	X	2	1	3	1	2	X
Organic peroxides	5.2	4	4	2	2	1	2	2	2	2	2	2	X	1	3	2	2	X
Toxic substances	6.1	2	2	X	X	X	X	X	X	1	X	1	1	X	1	X	X	X
Infectious substances	6.2	4	4	4	4	2	2	3	3	3	2	3	3	1	X	3	3	X
Radioactive material	7	2	2	2	2	1	1	2	2	2	2	1	2	X	3	X	2	X
Corrosive substances	8	4	2	2	1	X	X	X	1	1	1	2	2	X	3	2	X	X
Miscellaneous dangerous substances and articles	9	X	X	X	X	X	X	X	X	X	X	X	X	X	X	X	X	X

Numbers and symbols relate to the following terms as defined in this chapter:
1 – "Away from"
2 – "Separated from"
3 – "Separated by a complete compartment or hold from"
4 – "Separated longitudinally by an intervening complete compartment or hold from"
X – The segregation, if any, is shown in the Dangerous Goods List
* – See subsection 7.2.7.2 of this chapter

IMDG Code, encompassed in 49 CFR

TABLE 6-7
Segregation of Packages On Board Breakbulk/Conventional Vessels

BREAKBULK /CONVENTIONAL VESSELS

7.2.2   Segregation of packages

7.2.2.1   Applicability

7.2.2.1.1   The provisions of this subsection apply to the segregation of:

   .1   packages containing dangerous goods and stowed in the conventional way;

   .2   dangerous goods within cargo transport units; and

   .3   dangerous goods stowed in the conventional way from those packed in such cargo transport units.

7.2.2.2   Segregation of packages containing dangerous goods and stowed in the conventional way

7.2.2.2.1   *Definitions of the segregation terms*

   Legend

     (1)   Reference *package* . . . .

     (2)   *Package* containing incompatible goods . . . .

     (3)   Deck resistant to fire and liquid . . . .

   NOTE: Full vertical lines represent transverse bulkheads between cargo spaces (compartments or holds) resistant to fire and liquid.

  .1 *Away from:*
Effectively segregated so that the incompatible goods cannot interact dangerously in the event of an accident but may be transported in the same compartment or hold or *on deck*, provided a minimum horizontal separation of **3 metres, projected vertically**, is obtained.

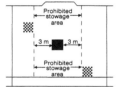

  .2 *Separated from:*
In different compartments or holds when stowed *under deck*. Provided the intervening deck is resistant to fire and liquid, a vertical separation i.e. in different compartments, may be accepted as equivalent to this segregation. For *on deck* stowage, this segregation means a separation by a distance of **at least 6 metres horizontally**.

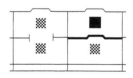

  .3 *Separated by a complete compartment or hold from:*
Either a vertical or a horizontal separation. If the intervening decks are not resistant to fire and liquid, then only a longitudinal separation, i.e. by an intervening complete compartment or hold, is acceptable. For *on deck* stowage, this segregation means a separation by a distance of **at least 12 metres horizontally**. The same distance has to be applied if one package is stowed *on deck* and the other one in an upper compartment.

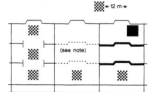

Note: One of the two decks must be resistant to fire and to liquid.

  .4 *Separated longitudinally by an intervening complete compartment or hold from:*
Vertical separation alone does not meet this requirement. Between a package *under deck* and one *on deck*, a minimum distance of 24 metres, including a complete compartment, must be maintained longitudinally. For *on deck* stowage, this segregation means a separation by a distance of **at least 24 metres longitudinally**.

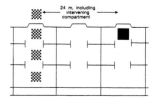

IMDG Code, encompassed in 49 CFR

TABLE 6-8
Table of Segregation of Freight Containers On Board Container Ships

Table of segregation of freight containers on board container ships

SEGREGATION REQUIREMENT	VERTICAL				HORIZONTAL					
	CLOSED VERSUS CLOSED	CLOSED VERSUS OPEN	OPEN VERSUS OPEN		CLOSED VERSUS CLOSED		CLOSED VERSUS OPEN		OPEN VERSUS OPEN	
					ON DECK	UNDER DECK	ON DECK	UNDER DECK	ON DECK	UNDER DECK
"AWAY FROM" .1	ONE ON TOP OF THE OTHER PERMITTED	OPEN ON TOP OF CLOSED PERMITTED OTHERWISE AS FOR OPEN VERSUS OPEN		FORE AND AFT	NO RESTRICTION	NO RESTRICTION	NO RESTRICTION	NO RESTRICTION	ONE CONTAINER SPACE	ONE CONTAINER SPACE OR ONE BULKHEAD
				ATHWART-SHIPS	NO RESTRICTION	NO RESTRICTION	NO RESTRICTION	NO RESTRICTION	ONE CONTAINER SPACE	ONE CONTAINER SPACE
"SEPARATED FROM" .2	NOT IN THE SAME VERTICAL LINE UNLESS SEGREGATED BY A DECK	AS FOR OPEN VERSUS OPEN	NOT IN THE SAME VERTICAL LINE UNLESS SEGREGATED BY A DECK	FORE AND AFT	ONE CONTAINER SPACE	ONE CONTAINER SPACE OR ONE BULKHEAD	ONE CONTAINER SPACE	ONE CONTAINER SPACE OR ONE BULKHEAD	ONE CONTAINER SPACE	ONE BULKHEAD
				ATHWART-SHIPS	ONE CONTAINER SPACE	ONE CONTAINER SPACE	ONE CONTAINER SPACE	TWO CONTAINER SPACES	TWO CONTAINER SPACES	ONE BULKHEAD
"SEPARATED BY A COMPLETE COMPARTMENT OR HOLD FROM" .3				FORE AND AFT	ONE CONTAINER SPACE	ONE BULKHEAD	ONE CONTAINER SPACE	ONE BULKHEAD	TWO CONTAINER SPACES	TWO BULKHEADS
				ATHWART-SHIPS	TWO CONTAINER SPACES	ONE BULKHEAD	TWO CONTAINER SPACES	ONE BULKHEAD	THREE CONTAINER SPACES	TWO BULKHEADS
"SEPARATED LONGITUDINALLY BY AN INTERVENING COMPLETE COMPARTMENT OR HOLD FROM" .4	PROHIBITED			FORE AND AFT	MINIMUM HORIZONTAL DISTANCE OF 24 METRES	ONE BULKHEAD AND MINIMUM HORIZONTAL DISTANCE OF 24 METRES*	MINIMUM HORIZONTAL DISTANCE OF 24 METRES	TWO BULKHEADS	MINIMUM HORIZONTAL DISTANCE OF 24 METRES	TWO BULKHEADS
				ATHWART-SHIPS	PROHIBITED	PROHIBITED	PROHIBITED	PROHIBITED	PROHIBITED	PROHIBITED

* CONTAINERS NOT LESS THAN 6 METRES FROM INTERVENING BULKHEAD.

NOTE: ALL BULKHEADS AND DECKS SHOULD BE RESISTANT TO FIRE AND LIQUID.

IMDG Code, encompassed in 49 CFR

SPECIFICATIONS FOR THE MARINE POLLUTANT MARK

For the purposes of implementing Annex III of the International Convention for the Prevention of Pollution from Ships, 1973, as modified by the Protocol of 1978 relating thereto (MARPOL 73/78), a special marine pollutant mark has been developed. This mark should be triangular in shape. The symbol, letters, and border must be black and the background white, or the symbol, letters, border, and background must be of a contrasting color to the surface to which the mark is affixed (CFR 49 Section 172.322[e][1][2]). See Figure 6-3.

For packages, the triangular shaped mark should have sides of at least 100 mm except in the case of packages which, because of their size, can only bear smaller marks. For cargo transport units this dimension should be not less than 10 inches (250 mm).

TABLE 6-9
Table of Segregation of Cargo Transport Units
On Board Open-Top Container Ship

Table of segregation of cargo transport units on board open-top container ships

SEGREGATION REQUIREMENT	VERTICAL				HORIZONTAL					
	CLOSED VERSUS CLOSED	CLOSED VERSUS OPEN	OPEN VERSUS OPEN		CLOSED VERSUS CLOSED		CLOSED VERSUS OPEN		OPEN VERSUS OPEN	
					ON DECK	UNDER DECK	ON DECK	UNDER DECK	ON DECK	UNDER DECK
"AWAY FROM" .1	ONE ON TOP OF THE OTHER PERMITTED	OPEN ON TOP OF CLOSED PERMITTED / OTHERWISE AS FOR OPEN VERSUS OPEN		FORE AND AFT	NO RESTRICTION	NO RESTRICTION	NO RESTRICTION	NO RESTRICTION	ONE CONTAINER SPACE	ONE CONTAINER SPACE OR ONE BULKHEAD
				ATHWART-SHIPS	NO RESTRICTION	NO RESTRICTION	NO RESTRICTION	NO RESTRICTION	ONE CONTAINER SPACE	ONE CONTAINER SPACE
"SEPARATED FROM" .2	NOT IN THE SAME VERTI-CAL LINE	AS FOR OPEN VERSUS OPEN	NOT IN THE SAME VERTI-CAL LINE	FORE AND AFT	ONE CONTAINER SPACE	ONE CONTAINER SPACE OR ONE BULKHEAD	ONE CONTAINER SPACE	ONE CONTAINER SPACE OR ONE BULKHEAD	ONE CONTAINER SPACE AND NOT ABOVE SAME HOLD	ONE BULKHEAD
				ATHWART-SHIPS	ONE CONTAINER SPACE	ONE CONTAINER SPACE	TWO CONTAINER SPACES	TWO CONTAINER SPACES	TWO CONTAINER SPACES AND NOT ABOVE SAME HOLD	ONE BULKHEAD
"SEPARATED BY A COMPLETE COMPARTMENT OR HOLD FROM" .3				FORE AND AFT	ONE CONTAINER SPACE AND NOT ABOVE SAME HOLD	ONE BULKHEAD	ONE CONTAINER SPACE AND NOT IN OR ABOVE SAME HOLD	ONE BULKHEAD	TWO CONTAINER SPACES AND NOT ABOVE SAME HOLD	TWO BULKHEADS
				ATHWART-SHIPS	TWO CONTAINER SPACES AND NOT ABOVE SAME HOLD	ONE BULKHEAD	TWO CONTAINER SPACES AND NOT ABOVE SAME HOLD	ONE BULKHEAD	THREE CONTAINER SPACES AND NOT ABOVE SAME HOLD	TWO BULKHEADS
"SEPARATED LONGITUDINALLY BY AN INTERVENING COMPLETE COMPARTMENT OR HOLD FROM" .4	PROHIBITED			FORE AND AFT	MINIMUM HORIZONTAL DISTANCE OF 24 METRES AND NOT ABOVE SAME HOLD	ONE BULKHEAD AND MINIMUM HORIZONTAL DISTANCE OF 24 METRES*	MINIMUM HORIZONTAL DISTANCE OF 24 METRES AND NOT ABOVE SAME HOLD	TWO BULKHEADS	MINIMUM HORIZONTAL DISTANCE OF 24 METRES AND NOT ABOVE SAME HOLD	TWO BULKHEADS
				ATHWART-SHIPS	PROHIBITED	PROHIBITED	PROHIBITED	PROHIBITED	PROHIBITED	PROHIBITED

* CONTAINERS NOT LESS THAN 6 METRES FROM INTERVENING BULKHEAD.

NOTE: ALL BULKHEADS AND DECKS SHOULD BE RESISTANT TO FIRE AND LIQUID.

IMDG Code, encompassed in 49 CFR

Figure 6-3. Marine pollutant mark (49 CFR Section 172.322[e][1][2]).

TABLE 6-10
Table of Segregation of Cargo Transport Units
On Board Ro-Ro Ships

Table of segregation of cargo transport units on board ro-ro ships

SEGREGATION REQUIREMENT		HORIZONTAL					
		CLOSED VERSUS CLOSED		CLOSED VERSUS OPEN		OPEN VERSUS OPEN	
		ON DECK	UNDER DECK	ON DECK	UNDER DECK	ON DECK	UNDER DECK
"AWAY FROM"	FORE AND AFT	NO RESTRICTION	NO RESTRICTION	NO RESTRICTION	NO RESTRICTION	AT LEAST 3 METRES	AT LEAST 3 METRES
.1	ATHWART-SHIPS	NO RESTRICTION	NO RESTRICTION	NO RESTRICTION	NO RESTRICTION	AT LEAST 3 METRES	AT LEAST 3 METRES
"SEPARATED FROM"	FORE AND AFT	AT LEAST 6 METRES	AT LEAST 6 METRES OR ONE BULKHEAD	AT LEAST 6 METRES	AT LEAST 6 METRES OR ONE BULKHEAD	AT LEAST 6 METRES	AT LEAST 12 METRES OR ONE BULKHEAD
.2	ATHWART-SHIPS	AT LEAST 3 METRES	AT LEAST 3 METRES OR ONE BULKHEAD	AT LEAST 3 METRES	AT LEAST 3 METRES OR ONE BULKHEAD	AT LEAST 6 METRES	AT LEAST 12 METRES or ONE BULKHEAD
"SEPARATED BY A COMPLETE COMPARTMENT OR HOLD FROM"	FORE AND AFT	AT LEAST 12 METRES	AT LEAST 24 METRES + DECK	AT LEAST 24 METRES	AT LEAST 24 METRES + DECK	AT LEAST 36 METRES	TWO DECKS OR TWO BULKHEADS
.3	ATHWART-SHIPS	AT LEAST 12 METRES	AT LEAST 24 METRES + DECK	AT LEAST 24 METRES	AT LEAST 24 METRES + DECK	AT LEAST 36 METRES	PROHIBITED
"SEPARATED LONGITUDINALLY BY AN INTERVENING COMPLETE COMPARTMENT OR HOLD FROM"	FORE AND AFT	AT LEAST 36 METRES	TWO BULKHEADS OR AT LEAST 36 METRES + TWO DECKS	AT LEAST 36 METRES	AT LEAST 48 METRES INCLUDING TWO BULKHEADS	AT LEAST 48 METRES	PROHIBITED
.4	ATHWART-SHIPS	PROHIBITED	PROHIBITED	PROHIBITED	PROHIBITED	PROHIBITED	PROHIBITED

NOTE: ALL BULKHEADS AND DECKS SHOULD BE RESISTANT TO FIRE AND LIQUID.

IMDG Code, encompassed in 49 CFR

CHAPTER 7

PROPER CARE FOR THE CARGO: VENTILATION OF CARGO HOLDS

ELEMENTS OF THE PROBLEM

THE BODY OF KNOWLEDGE COVERED by this chapter would probably be more accurately described as the air conditioning of cargo holds; however, through common usage on ships through the years, the term ventilation is now used to indicate the steps taken to prevent damage to cargoes from condensed moisture within the cargo holds. One good reason for this is because until about 1938 the only technique used was ventilation. The technique was ventilating, but air conditioning was being accomplished. The control offered by the choice of either ventilating or not ventilating is often not sufficient to prevent condensation under conditions encountered at sea. It was left for a shipper of products suffering from improper air conditioning at sea to recognize this need on ships first. Thus, Mr. Oliver D. Colvin, president of Cargocaire Engineering Corporation, was the first to take positive action toward giving ship's officers full control of the phenomena that cause condensation to appear on the ship's hull or cargo. His investigations into the reasons why his canned milk shipments suffered damage by rusting ultimately resulted in the development of a dehumidifier coupled with a forced air ventilation system.

The simple psychrometric principles and the exact methods used to minimize condensation are the topics of this chapter. It has been observed that in the past a number of ship's officers have failed to recognize the need for correct ventilating procedures. Part of the cause of this is their failure to make themselves cognizant of the simple physical principles that would enable them to fully understand the problem with which they are dealing. As a result, the general opinion among many officers with years of experience is that the best thing to do always is to see that the cargo holds are given the maximum amount of air possible. Under some conditions this is the exact opposite of what should be done.

Fundamental Objective of Ventilation

Ventilation has the single objective of preventing moisture damage to cargo that results from condensation within the cargo holds. Since the condensation comes from the air, it seems logical that before discussing the matter further we should learn something about the composition of air and about what other types of airborne damage there are besides moisture damage. Because air is everywhere and because of our intimate association with it, we all accept it as a highly commonplace substance and take for granted that we know all there is to know about it. As implied above, damage caused by condensation is only one of several forms of airborne damage. Components of air other than water vapor also may cause damage to cargo. These will also be dealt with briefly in this chapter; however, it must be emphasized that the only effective and practicable method of combating moisture damage is through air conditioning by whatever means is at our disposal. Other airborne damage types must be eliminated by other techniques, not because air conditioning would not be effective, but because it would not be practicable.

Composition of Air

The principal components of air and their amounts are as follows: nitrogen, 78.03%; oxygen, 20.99%; argon, 0.93%; carbon dioxide, 0.03%; and neon, helium, krypton, hydrogen, xenon, ozone, and radon, 0,02%. These amounts are for the total air of the Earth's atmosphere. It must be pointed out that air near the Earth's surface contains some additional substances and that all of these amounts will vary to some degree. The additional substances are dust, water vapor, and—under certain conditions—accidental components. In a ship's hold, these accidental components are vapors from commodities stowed in the closed space.

Sources of Airborne Damage to Cargo

Nitrogen acts simply as a diluter. It is a very stable gas and does not readily react with other substances so as to produce any problem in the protection of the ship or cargo. Argon, carbon dioxide, and the remaining gases either do not appear in the air at the surface of the Earth or appear only as traces and consequently offer no problem.

Oxygen is a powerful chemical agent and readily combines with other substances. It is well known that oxygen is necessary for combustion; however, within cargo holds it causes more subtle damage through the process of corrosion. It is important to note that moisture must be present also in order for corrosion to take place. A highly practical corrosion preventative measure would be to remove the moisture from the air in areas where it is possible to do so.

Dust exists in all air to some extent. Dust particles are so small that they float through the air for some time before falling to rest. Dust particles average about 0.5 microns (2×10^{-5} inches) in diameter. Excessive dust can cause considerable damage to cargo. This is an obvious fact and one of the first recognized by students of cargo stowage. It should also be recognized that protection from this airborne damage is not possible by ventilation. Protection from dust damage is obtained primarily by careful planning of the stowage so that dusty cargoes are loaded first and discharged last or segregated from cargoes that may be damaged by dust. The classical example of a dusty cargo is Portland cement, but there are many others, such as sulfur, bauxite, coal, copper concentrates, guano, nitrates, and ores of all kinds. Protection from dust for cargoes stowed in the same compartment and at the same level can be obtained by erecting a dust-tight bulkhead. This is ordinarily necessary only when a dusty cargo must be handled while delicate goods are stowed in the vessel. The damage caused by dust is known as *contamination.*

Accidental components of air in the hold are the fumes or vapors from liquids, gases, or solids stowed therein. The damage caused by this means is known as *tainting* damage. The vapors of turpentine can cause tea to taste of turpentine. Rubber can give a heavy, pungent, and characteristic odor to silk goods stowed in the same hold. Tainting of this sort will result in damage claims. Protection against tainting damage can be obtained only by segregation, and usually the segregation should provide a space for at least one cargo hold between a highly odorous and a very delicate cargo. Temporary vapor-tight bulkheads are not practicable in the way that temporary dust-tight bulkheads are.

Of all the components of air, water vapor is the most variable in amount, from only a trace in the air over a desert far from any large body of water to as much as 4% by volume under extremely humid conditions. It is contributed to the air by evaporation from water surfaces, soil, and living tissues. Water vapor may also be contributed to air by transfer from hygroscopic substances, and in fact this the source of the water vapor that causes most of the trouble in a closed hatch. This transfer differs from transfer by evaporation; the controlling factors will be discussed later. The amount of water vapor that a given air sample can hold varies directly with the temperature of the air. We commonly speak of moist and dry air with the implied meaning that the atmosphere takes up vapor much as a sponge takes up water, but the fact is that the vapor occupies space without regard to the other gases. At any given temperature the same amount of vapor can be diffused through a vacuum as through an equal space occupied by air. In other words, the amount of vapor that can occupy a given space depends *entirely* on the temperature. This amount is approximately doubled with each increase of 20°F within the ordinary ranges experienced in the free air. Thus, if the temperature is raised from 0 to 80°F, the capacity of a given space for moisture is increased almost 16 times.

TERMS OF PSYCHROMETRY

Relative Humidity

When air contains all the water it can hold at a given temperature, it is said to be *saturated.* When the dry bulb temperature of saturated air is decreased, the air will reject some moisture in the form of what is known as condensation. When the dry bulb temperature of saturated air is increased, the air will cease to be saturated and will immediately have the ability to hold more water vapor. The ratio of the amount of water vapor actually in the air to the amount that would be in the air if the air were saturated is known as the *relative humidity.*

Specific Humidity

Specific humidity is defined as the weight of water vapor per unit of weight of dry air. In engineering work it is generally given as grains of water per pound of dry air or pounds of water vapor per pound of dry air.

Absolute Humidity

The amount of water in air may be expressed in terms of units of weight of water vapor per unit of volume of dry air. *Absolute humidity* is the term used to describe this unit. In engineering work, absolute humidity is expressed as pounds of water vapor per cubic foot of dry air or grains of water vapor per cubic foot of dry air. The psychrometric chart (Fig. 7-1) may be used to determine absolute humidity by first obtaining the specific humidity and then dividing by the volume per pound of dry air. This latter value is also found on the psychrometric chart.

Dew Point

Dew point is defined as that temperature below which the air will be unable to retain the moisture it presently contains. The dew point of any given air sample is entirely dependent on the absolute humidity. The reader should note that under constant barometric pressure, the dew point also varies directly with the specific humidity. This last relationship is reflected in the way that you read the dew point and specific humidity from the psychrometric chart, which is constructed assuming a standard barometric pressure of 29.92 inches of mercury.

Wet Bulb Temperature

Heat causes water to acquire the properties of a gas. When applied to a water surface, heating results in part of the water turning into vapor. The heat that is expended in this process, which is called evaporation, is rendered latent or imperceptible so far as temperature effects are concerned until the vapor is again condensed into visible water particles. When this happens, the heat reappears. This explains why evaporation from a moist surface has a cooling effect, and it logically follows that the more rapid the rate of evaporation, the faster the heat will become latent and the greater the cooling of the surface from which the heat is drawn will be. The wet and dry bulb hygrometer measures the relative humidity based on the principle that the rate of evaporation is directly proportional to the relative humidity of the surrounding air.

To most seamen the wet and dry bulb hygrometer is a familiar instrument; however, a few comments concerning it are in order. It consists of two thermometers mounted close together. The bulb of one is covered with a wick that is dampened just before reading it or kept constantly dampened if mounted on a bulkhead in a permanent location. The wet bulb thermometer will register the dry bulb temperature reduced by the cooling effect of the rate of evaporation. The rate of evaporation, of course, depends on the relative humidity. This is the most accurate method in use for arriving at the relative humidity and dew point of the air, providing the wick is clean, there are no artificial heat sources affecting the thermometers, and there is a light flow of air over the wick to wipe away the high humidity air film that will develop around the bulb in dead air. If any one of these requisites is violated, the relative humidity and dew point read will be in error. In the absence of any air flow, the wet bulb reading will be too high; the reader should be able to see quite readily the direction of the error in the resulting relative humidity in such a case.

Wet Bulb Depression

The wet bulb temperature will always be either equal to or less than the dry bulb reading. The difference between the wet bulb and dry bulb reading is called the wet bulb depression. The wet bulb depression obviously will vary directly with the relative humidity. It will be zero when the air is saturated. The relative humidity may be read from Table 7-1 if data from a wet and dry bulb hygrometer are employed.

Vapor Pressure and Saturated Vapor Pressure

When water enters the air by evaporation, it acts as another gas in the mixture of gases that composes the air. This water vapor exerts a pressure in all directions that is independent of the pressure of all the other gases in the mixture. This is known as the *vapor pressure* of the air, and varies directly with the amount of vapor per unit of volume of dry air, that is, the absolute humidity. This pressure is commonly expressed in inches of mercury and its value contributes to the total length of the barometric column. The maximum vapor pressure under conditions of constant temperature and pressure occurs when the air is saturated. Every change in air temperature or pressure changes the *saturated vapor pressure.*

The table in the upper left-hand corner of the psychrometric chart (Fig. 7-1) gives the saturated vapor pressures for temperatures between 20 and 84°F at a barometric pressure of 29.92. Note that the temperature column headed "Wet Bulb Temperature" can be entered with the dew point or dry bulb if the air is saturated, because they are all equal under this condition.

The vapor pressure of air depends on the amount of water vapor per unit of volume of air, but so do the absolute humidity and the dew point. It is important to note and remember that the vapor pressure is an indirect measure of the absolute humidity, specific humidity, and dew point. This fact is of importance when studying the basis of the moisture equilibrium chart (see Figures 7-3 and 7-4).

TABLE 7-1
Relative Humidity Tables*

Difference in Dry and Wet Bulb Readings (°F)

	0	1	2	3	4	5	6	7	8	9	10	11	12
30	100	89	78	67	57	47	36	26	17	7			
35	100	91	82	73	65	54	45	37	28	19	12	3	
40	100	92	84	76	68	60	53	45	38	30	22	16	8
45	100	92	85	78	71	64	58	51	44	38	32	25	19
50	100	93	87	80	74	67	61	55	50	44	38	33	27
55	100	94	88	82	76	70	65	59	54	49	43	39	34
60	100	94	89	84	78	73	68	63	58	53	48	44	39
65	100	95	90	85	80	75	70	65	61	56	52	48	44
70	100	95	90	86	81	77	72	68	64	60	55	52	48
75	100	95	91	87	82	78	74	70	66	62	58	55	51
80	100	96	92	87	83	79	75	72	68	64	61	57	54
85	100	96	92	88	84	80	77	73	70	66	63	60	56
90	100	96	92	88	85	81	78	75	71	68	65	62	59
95	100	96	93	89	86	82	79	76	72	69	66	63	60
100	100	97	93	90	86	83	80	77	74	71	68	65	62

Difference in Dry and Wet Bulb Readings (°F)

	13	14	15	16	17	18	19	20	21	22	23	24
30												
35												
40	1											
45	13	7	1									
50	22	16	11	6	1							
55	29	24	19	16	10	6	1					
60	34	30	26	22	18	14	10	6	2			
65	39	35	31	28	24	20	17	13	10	6	3	
70	44	40	36	33	29	26	23	19	16	13	10	7
75	47	44	40	37	34	31	27	24	21	19	16	13
80	51	47	44	41	38	35	32	29	26	23	20	18
85	53	50	47	44	41	38	36	33	30	28	25	22
90	56	53	50	47	44	41	39	36	34	32	29	26
95	58	55	52	49	47	44	42	39	37	35	32	30
100	59	57	54	51	49	47	44	42	39	37	35	33

Dry Bulb reading (°F)

* Relative humidity readings taken as percentage. *Example*: What is the relative humidity of air with a dry bulb temperature of 70 and a wet bulb temperature of 60? An swer: 55%.

Equations for Calculation of Relative, Specific, and Absolute Humidity

Relative humidity can be expressed as a ratio of two masses or two pressures:

$$RH = \frac{A}{A_s} = \frac{e}{e_s}$$

where

A = existing absolute humidity.

As = absolute humidity if saturated.

e = vavpor pressure.

es = saturated vapor pressure.

Specific humidity is obviously a ratio of the weight of water vapor in the air to the total weight of the air expressed in the appropriate units. It is also the ratio of the vapor pressure to the total barometric pressure multiplied by a constant. The value of the constant depends on the units used for expressing the specific humidity. The constant is 4,500 if the specific humidity is expressed in units of grains per pound.

$$W = \frac{\text{Weight of vapor}}{\text{Weight of air}} \qquad W = K\frac{e}{p}$$

where

W = specific humidity.

e = vapor pressure.

p = total air pressure.

K = constant (value depends on units of W).

Absolute humidity is equal to the ratio of the weight of water vapor in the air to the volume of the air sample being considered. Inasmuch as we always obtain the specific humidity from a psychrometric chart based on a pound of dry air, we can find the absolute humidity by dividing the specific humidity by the volume of one pound of dry air.

$$A = \frac{\text{Weight of vapor}}{\text{Volume of air}} \qquad A = \frac{Ke}{pv}$$

where

v = volume of one pound of dry air and the other symbols are the same as those in the equation for specific humidity.

The density of dry air is greater than the density of air mixed with water vapor. This fact sometimes comes as a mild surprise to the reader who is accustomed to considering moisture as always adding weight to the dry form of the substance. But water vapor, which acts as just another gas in the total mixture of gases in the air, is actually lighter than the mixture in its dry state; hence, any addition of moisture makes the total mixture have less mass per unit of volume.

HOW TO USE THE PSYCHROMETRIC CHART

The psychrometric chart, Figure 7-1, is a development of the Carrier Corporation. Whereas tables may be used to solve problems involving psychrometric data, the use of a chart makes the process easier and faster. Inasmuch as it is necessary to have a thorough understanding of the amounts of moisture involved in changing the various psychrometric values of air, it is desirable for the reader to become familiar with the use of this psychrometric chart and the notations that appear on it.

Definitions, Abbreviations, Symbols

*Dry bulb temperature: **DB***. Temperature of air as registered by an ordinary thermometer.

*Wet bulb temperature: **WB***. Temperature registered by a thermometer whose bulb is covered bv a wetted wick and exposed to a current of rapidly moving air.

*Dew point temperature: **DP***. Temperature at which condensation of moisture begins when the air is cooled.

*Relative humidity: **%RH***. Ratio of actual water vapor pressure in air to the pressure of saturated water vapor in air at the same temperature, expressed as a percentage.

*Specific humidity: **W***. Moisture content of air in terms of weight of water vapor in grains or pounds per pound of dry air.

*Absolute humidity: **A***. Moisture content of air in terms of weight of water vapor in grains or pounds per cubic foot of air.

Enthalpy: ***h***. Total heat. A thermal property indicating the quantity of heat in the air above an arbitrary datum, in Btu per pound of dry air.

Vapor pressure: ***e***. The pressure exerted by the water percent vapor contained in the air, in inches of mercury.

Volume (as used in psychrometrics): ***v***. Cubic feet of the mixture per pound of dry air.

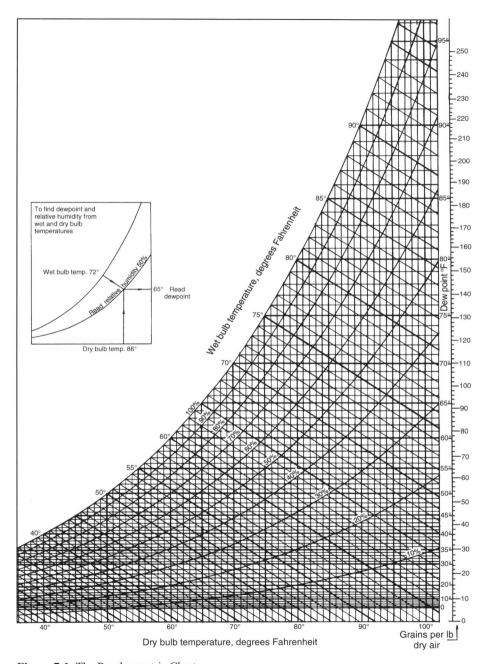

Figure 7-1. The Psychrometric Chart.

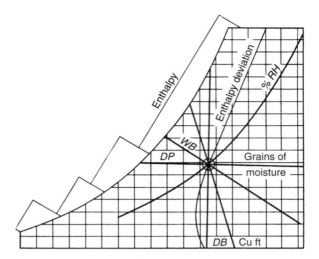

Figure 7-2. Items read from the psychrometric chart.

Pounds of dry air: The basis for calculations, this value remains constant during all psychrometric processes.

The dry bulb, wet bulb, and dew point temperatures and the relative humidity are related in such a fashion that if two of these properties are known, all other properties shown in Figure 7-2 may be read from the chart. When air is saturated, dry bulb, wet bulb, and dew point temperatures are identical. The enthalpy of air for any given condition is the enthalpy at saturation corrected by the enthalpy deviation due to the air not being in a saturated state. Our only interest in the enthalpy value as found on the chart is that it is needed to investigate the approximate heat load involved when renewing the air in a refrigeration system requiring the addition of fresh air from time to time. Not being burdened with the necessity of making precise calculations along these lines, we will not concern ourselves with the enthalpy of added or rejected moisture given on the chart. The sensible heat factor also appearing on the chart will not be used in any of our calculations, and therefore an explanation of this value will be omitted.

NUMERICAL EXAMPLE

Reading the properties of air.

Given: DB = 70°F. WB = 60°F.

Required: %RH, DP, volume (*v*), specific humidity (*W*), absolute humidity (*A*), and enthalpy (*h*).

Solution: Locate point of intersection on the chart of the vertical line representing 70° *DB* and the oblique line representing 60° WB. All values are read from this point of intersection.

Interpolate between relative humidity lines on 70°F *DB* line; read *RH* = 56%.

Follow horizontal line left to saturation curve; read *DP* = 53.6°F.

Interpolate between lines representing cubic feet per pound of dry air, read
v = 13.53 feet

Follow horizontal line all the way to the right; read the specific humidity,
W = 61.4 grains/lb.

Divide 61.4 by 13.53 to obtain absolute humidity of 4.54 grains/ft.

HYGROSCOPIC MOISTURE TRANSFER

"Hygroscopic" Defined

The word *hygroscopic* is an adjective implying the ability to absorb moisture in the form of a gas. Hence, hygroscopic moisture is moisture absorbed by a substance capable of absorbing water vapor in the gaseous form. Not all substances are capable of this. A substance capable of absorbing hygroscopic moisture is known as a hygroscopic substance. Hygroscopic substances include all substances of an organic nature, such as all grains, wood and wood products, cotton, wool, sisal, jute, paper, sugar, and other products of animal or vegetable origin. Examples of nonhygroscopic substances are all metals and glass products.

Factors Controlling Hygroscopic Moisture Transfer

Hygroscopic moisture leaves the hygroscopic substance and enters the ambient air in a manner that is similar but not identical to the transfer of free moisture to the air. Moisture in the liquid state will leave the parent body and enter the air as a gas so long as the ambient air is not saturated. The speed of evaporation depends on the relative humidity of the ambient air and the temperature of the water. Evaporation will continue even if the water temperature is lowered to the freezing point or below. When water vapor enters the air from ice without passing through the liquid state, the process is known as sublimation rather than evaporation. The important point is that either process, evaporation or sublimation, will continue if the ambient air has a *RH* of less than 100%.

Hygroscopic moisture will leave its parent body if the vapor pressure within the substance exceeds that of the ambient air. This warrants some discussion. The hygroscopic moisture within a hygroscopic substance will possess a vapor pressure somewhat similar to the vapor pressure at the surface of liquid water or on the surface of a block of ice. For any given substance this vapor pressure varies as the *moisture content* of the substance and the *temperature* of the substance. A given combination of moisture content and temperature will produce different vapor pressures in different commodities. It has already been pointed out that the water vapor in the air also has a vapor pressure, which is dependent upon one thing only, namely, the moisture content of the air. Recall that the dew point is also dependent on only this one thing.

It was said above that the hygroscopic moisture will leave the substance if the vapor pressure of the ambient air is less than the vapor pressure of the substance. It follows that if the two vapor pressures are equal there will be no transfer of water vapor. Under these conditions the air and substance are said to be in *moisture equilibrium.* Although it may not seem logical, nevertheless it is true that if the vapor pressure of the air is greater than that of the substance, the water vapor will "flow" back into the substance.

Significance Within the Ship's Hold

If a hygroscopic commodity in a ship's hold has a moisture content and temperature such that the resulting vapor pressure is greater than that of the air in the hold, water vapor will leave the commodity and enter the air until the vapor pressure of the air builds up to the vapor pressure of the commodity, the vapor pressure of the commodity falls to that of the air, or the vapor pressure of the air will rise and that of the commodity will fall until they meet at some common midpoint. If we constantly ventilate the hold with this low-vapor-pressure air, we rule out the first possibility; the air passing through the hold will continue to remove water vapor from the commodity. The student is apt to jump to the conclusion that the latter procedure will, in fact, lower the vapor pressure of the commodity to that of the air. Although it is true that the commodity's vapor pressure will be lowered, it will not be lowered an appreciable amount unless the process is continued much longer than the longest passage made by any modern ship, or air with a much lower vapor pressure than that found at sea is used.

On the other hand, if the hatch is not ventilated for any reason, the possibility of the vapor pressure of the air building up to that of the commodity does exist; in fact, this is what will happen under such conditions. It must be pointed out that under no circumstances will the vapor pressure of the commodity fall to meet that of the air. This can be demonstrated clearly by a numerical example that will be given later.

THE MOISTURE EQUILIBRIUM CHART

Use of Moisture Equilibrium Charts

The moisture equilibrium chart, which is illustrated by Figures 7-3 and 7-4, can be used to determine the dew point temperature that the air surrounding a hygroscopic commodity will have when in moisture equilibrium with that commodity.

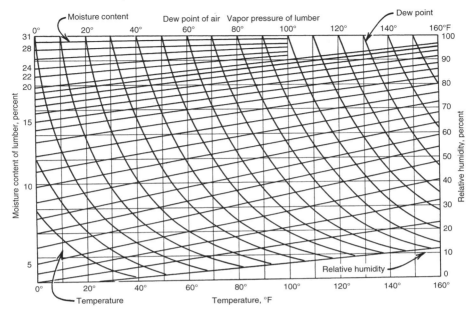

Figure 7-3. Moisture equilibrium diagram of lumber for determining the vapor pressure of lumber from its moisture content and temperature. *Courtesy Cargocaire Engineering Corp.*

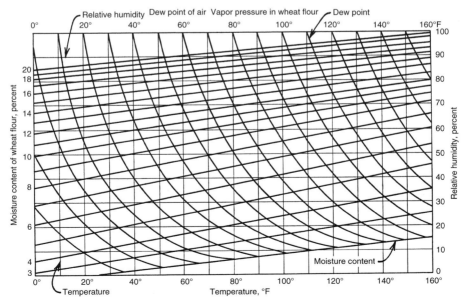

Figure 7-4. Moisture equilibrium diagram for wheat flour (approximate). *Courtesy Cargocaire Engineering Corp.*

Recall that for any given moisture content of the air the water vapor in the air will have a certain vapor pressure; also recall that for every vapor pressure value there is a corresponding dew point value. Inasmuch as there is a one-to-one correspondence, if we choose any vapor pressure $x1$ there will be a corresponding dew point value $y1$ and a corresponding specific humidity $z1$. Hence, if we know any one of these values, we always can find the other two, providing, of course, that we have suitable tables or a suitable psychrometric chart.

It was noted above that all hygroscopic commodities have vapor pressures depending on the commodity's *moisture content and temperature.* (Moisture content of a commodity is expressed as a percentage by weight. If the moisture content of lumber is given as 25%, it means that for every 100 pounds of lumber there are 75 pounds of dry wood fiber and 25 pounds of water in the form of hygroscopic moisture.) The vapor pressure comparison is the criterion used to tell whether hygroscopic moisture is being absorbed by the commodity or by the air or if the air and the commodity are in moisture equilibrium. But vapor pressure can be stated in terms of dew point temperatures. The moisture equilibrium charts give the vapor pressure of the commodity in terms of the dew point temperature that air with an equal vapor pressure would possess. This is done because we are interested in knowing final dew points rather than vapor pressures; that is to say, the resulting dew point has more meaning than the resulting vapor pressure.

The charts can be entered with the air's relative humidity and dry bulb temperature to obtain the dew point of the air. If the *dew point corresponding to the vapor pressure in the commodity* is equal to the air's actual dew point, moisture equilibrium will exist. Note the expression, "dew point corresponding to the vapor pressure in the commodity." Hereafter, in this book, this long and somewhat awkward expression will be replaced by the expression, *commodity's dew point.* It should be clear, however, that the commodity itself cannot have a dew point as defined earlier.

If the commodity's dew point is greater than the air's dew point, moisture will leave the commodity and enter the air. If the dew point relationship is reversed, the flow of moisture will be reversed.

It should now be apparent that if a commodity with a high moisture content is stowed in a nonventilated hold, the dew point in that hold will be high. If the exact moisture content and temperature of the commodity are known, the exact level that the dew point will reach within the hold can be obtained from a moisture equilibrium chart. Before this can be demonstrated by means of a numerical example, the method of reading a moisture equilibrium chart must be explained.

The moisture equilibrium chart has the following data recorded upon it: the commodity's moisture content, dry bulb temperature, and vapor pressure (given in terms of dew point); and the air's *RH, DB,* and DP. Entering any two known factors for the commodity, the third can be read from the chart; the same is true in the case of the air.

EXAMPLE 1: Reading the moisture equilibrium chart.

Given: Lumber with a moisture content of 20% and a temperature of 70°F.

Required: The commodity's dew point.

Solution: Locate the point of intersection between the vertical dry bulb temperature line for 70°F and the oblique moisture content line for 20%. Interpolate between curved lines to the dew point scale. Read 66°F as the commodity's dew point.

EXAMPLE 2: Reading the moisture equilibrium chart.

Given: Air with an *RH* of 70% and a *DB* of 70°F.

Required: The DP of the air.

Solution: Locate the point of intersection between the DB temperature line for 70°F and the horizontal line for a *RH* of 70%. Follow a curved line to the dew point scale. Read 60°F as the air's DP.

EXAMPLE 3: Estimating the reaction between cargo and air.

Given: The data from Examples 1 and 2.

Required: What will the dew point be in an unventilated hold loaded with the lumber of Example 1 if, when secured, the air's dew point was as given in Example 2?

Solution: From the discussion about hygroscopic moisture transfer, it should be clear that the hatch will eventually have a dew point of 66°F. In other words, the hatch would have a dew point precisely as dictated by the commodity.

The proof of the truth of the last statement is demonstrated in the following section.

CONTROL OF STORAGE ATMOSPHERE BY THE COMMODITY

Closed Container Hypothesis

In view of the laws controlling the transfer of hygroscopic moisture and the factors controlling vapor pressures in air and in hygroscopic materials, this hypothesis can be made: The characteristics of the air in a closed container are controlled by the temperature and moisture content of a hygroscopic material within the container if the weight of the material is *much greater* than the weight of the air. We show below that this hypothesis is true, using a hypothetical example, and comment upon the significance of such facts for the proper care and custody of cargo on a ship.

The closed container we will have in mind is a nonventilated, well secured ship's hold. That the weight of the material is very much greater than the weight of the air involved will be quite obvious on comparing them in our hypothetical case or under actual conditions on board ship.

Assume: A hold of 80,000 grain cubic. Sixty thousand (60,000) cubic feet is consumed in stowing 600 tons of jute. The jute has a temperature of 80°F and a moisture content of 10%. When the hold is secured, the air has a *DB* of 80°F and *RH* of 90%.

To illustrate the reaction between the air and the jute and arrive at a proof, we must accept certain basic laws of psychrometry. These laws are as follows:

1. Water vapor will always flow from an area of high vapor pressure to an area of low vapor pressure.

2. Water vapor pressure in air depends on moisture content.

3. Vapor pressure in a hygroscopic commodity depends on two factors, namely, (1) the moisture content and (2) the temperature of the commodity.

4. Vapor pressure, dew point temperature, and specific humidity all vary directly with one another and have corresponding values.

To prove the hypothesis we must resort to a quantitative analysis of a given problem. We will use the assumed data given above to illustrate the reaction between the jute and the air. Note that the assumed data are typical of arrangements on a ship.

Proof: On the moisture equilibrium chart for jute, locate the point of intersection between the temperature line for 80°F and the moisture content line for 10%. Read the commodity's dew point as 62°F.

On the psychrometric chart locate the point of intersection between the 90% relative humidity line and the vertical *DB* temperature line for 80°F. Read the following data from this point of intersection: $DP_1 = 76.8°F$; $W_1 = 140$ grains/lb; $v_1 = 14.05$ ft³/lb of dry air.

Laws 1 and 4 above tell us that under the initial conditions, water vapor will flow from the air into the jute. This initial reaction will continue until one of three possible things occurs:

1. The vapor pressure of the air has fallen to the vapor pressure of the commodity.

2. The vapor pressure of the commodity has risen to the vapor pressure of the air.

3. The vapor pressure of the commodity has risen and that of the air has fallen so that they come to equilibrium at some intermediate level between their initial vapor pressures.

In effect, the hypothesis says that possibility (1) will take place. If a quantitative study of the reaction proves this to be true, then we will have proved the hypothesis.

Our quantitative study amounts to a comparison of the quantities of moisture involved. Initially the jute contains $(600 \times 0.1) = 60$ tons of hygroscopic moisture. Sixty tons is equal to 94.08×10^7 grains. The air contains 140 grains/lb of dry air, and there are $(20,000/14.05) = 1,423$ lb of dry air in the hold. The total moisture in the air of the hold amounts to $(1,423 \times 140) = 199,220$ grains.

We have already noted that initially some of the water vapor will leave the air and enter the commodity. The question we must now answer is how much? The only thing that can stop the flow of moisture is the attainment of equal vapor pressures by the air and the commodity. It is obvious that due to the enormous difference between their moisture contents, even if all the water in the air left it and entered the commodity, the latter's moisture content would be practically unaffected on a percentage basis. This means that its vapor pressure would also be practically unaffected. It is evident then that possibility (1) of the three mentioned above, will take place.

To make this more evident, let us examine the final conditions of the air and the commodity assuming the air is brought to a dew point of 62°F.

At a DP of 62°F and DB of 80°F, we read the following: $W_2 = 83$ grains/lb of dry air. Assuming the same amount of dry air, we find that moisture equilibrium will be reached when the total amount of moisture in the air is $(83 \times 1,423) = 118,109$ grains. Thus it is seen that the amount of moisture that would have to leave the air to make the dew point fall from 76.8 to 62°F is $(199,220 - 118,109) = 81,111$ grains.

This 81,111 grains would, of course, be absorbed by the jute. The factors affecting the jute's vapor pressure would not be appreciably changed by the absorption of 81,111 grains. The jute already contains 940,800,000 grains at 10% moisture content. Adding 81,111 grains would change the percentage only slightly, to 10.0007%.

Under the final conditions in the hold, a commodity's vapor pressure will be the same as at the beginning of the reaction, but the DP of the air will have been lowered from 76.8°F to 62°F.

Significance of the Hypothesis

The significance of the above fact for proper care and custody of cargo is that it offers a complete explanation of the following items to the ship's officers:

1. Why it is possible to restrict all ventilation without danger of moisture damage if hygroscopic commodities are shipped sufficiently dry.

2. Why it is desirable that hygroscopic commodities have low moisture contents.

3. Why stowage of hygroscopic commodities adjacent to a warm bulkhead can cause high-dew-point storage conditions.

4. Why the upper 'tweendecks is the most likely place for heavy condensation.

5. Why *continuous* proper ventilation is necessary for dew point control.

The hypothesis is also significant because it offers an explanation of the causes of continuous heavy condensation and certain other types of moisture damage problems. Finally, it illustrates the extent of the control that the ship's officer has in meeting practical ventilation needs on a ship under operating conditions.

Determining Moisture Content

Much has been said above about the importance of the moisture content of hygroscopic commodities with reference to the problem of moisture damage in a ship's hold. We discuss briefly below the methods used to ascertain moisture content.

WEIGHT DIFFERENCES

One method for determining moisture content consists of weighing a known volume of the commodity. This sample of the commodity is then placed in an oven and heated to 212°F for about 3 hours. This should remove all the moisture from the sample. The sample is again weighed. The difference between the two weights is equal to the weight of the moisture in the original sample. To obtain the percentage moisture content, divide the weight of the moisture removed from the sample by the original weight of the sample and multiply the quotient by 100. Given as a mathematical equation, this is:

$$\frac{W_1 - W_2}{W_1} \times 100 = \% \text{ M.C.}$$

where

W_1 = original weight of commodity sample.

W_2 = dry weight of commodity sample.

If the dry densities of the commodities are available, there is no need to dry the sample in the oven. Instead, after carefully weighing the sample, calculate its density and determine the moisture content from these data in a manner similar to that outlined above.

THE MOISTURE METER

Another system for measuring moisture content involves the use of a device that measures the resistance to an electric current as it passes through a sample of the

Figure 7-5. Moisture meter provides instantaneous determination of moisture content of lumber within a limited range. In use, the needles in the handle are driven into the board. The rheostat (selector) is then adjusted until the needle on the milliammeter is vertical. The moisture content of the board is then read directly from the dial on the rheostat. A modification of this instrument is used for determining the moisture content of grain.

material tested. A galvanometer registers the resistance, but instead of indicating voltage or amperage, the dial is calibrated to read percentage of moisture by weight. Since the scales have to be calibrated from empirical data for every commodity type, a different instrument is needed for every commodity. The principal differences between such instruments are the calibration of the scales and the method used to insert into the commodity the electric terminals over which the electric current passes. Figure 7-5 shows the electric moisture meter for the instantaneous determination of moisture content of lumber within the range of 7 to 24%.

MEASURING HYGROSCOPIC TRANSFER

A third method of measuring moisture content is based on the premise that the condition of the air in an enclosed space is controlled by the condition of any hygroscopic material contained in the space. We have already proven that this premise is reasonable.

This method requires a container several cubic feet in capacity capable of being hermetically seated and fitted with a psychrometer. The psychrometer must be so fitted that measurements of the inside air can be taken after the air and commodity have reached moisture equilibrium without allowing any admixture with outside air. The important data obtained from this experiment are (1) the dew point of the inside air and (2) the dry bulb temperature of the commodity (same as that of the air). Since we know that the air's dew point results from the commodity's temperature and moisture content, we can use a moisture equilibrium chart to obtain the moisture content of the commodity.

NUMERICAL EXAMPLES

Obtaining moisture content by allowing moisture equilibrium to be reached.

Given: Some wheat grains are spread thinly on a screen within a hermetically sealed container. After 6 hours, a wet bulb thermometer on the inside of the container reads 65°F and a dry bulb thermometer reads 70°F. It is assumed that the wheat and air are in thermal equilibrium.

Required: Moisture content of the wheat.

Solution: On a psychrometric chart locate the point of intersection between the vertical dry bulb line and slanting wet bulb line. Follow horizontally to the left and read the dew point as 62.3°F.

On the moisture equilibrium chart, locate the intersection point of the curved dew point line and the vertical dry bulb line. Now read the grain moisture content on the oblique line to the left, 13%.

Of the three methods mentioned, the electric moisture meter is the most practical for use by ship or dock personnel interested in making spot checks on moisture contents. The principal advantage of this method is the speed with which a check can be made. The disadvantage is the reliance that must be placed on the correct operation of a delicate instrument. It is necessary to check and calibrate such an instrument frequently to make certain it is giving true readings.

Moisture Contents in Practice

Although it is evident that more moisture content information would in some instances contribute to better out-turns of shipments, there are numerous occasions wherein the shipowner receives no information concerning the moisture contents of hygroscopic cargoes as they are shipped. When the moisture content is known, the information may not be passed on to the officers of the ship or to any dock force personnel. In some cases, even if the information were passed on, its significance would not be understood.

The moisture contents of grain, seeds, nuts, and pulses are of considerable importance, and sometimes shippers of these products are required to certify the moisture content of such items. When the moisture content of grain is sufficiently low, this item is almost completely dormant, it may be kept in sealed containers for years even if heated to abnormally high temperatures. For example, barley may be heated to approximately 200°F without losing its germinating power or undergoing any decomposition. This is a valuable property to have in grain, especially when loaded in a ship's hold, but it is lost when the grain is damp. As the moisture content rises in grain, it ceases being dormant and commences to respire. Respiration is a complicated series of biological and chemical changes influenced by conditions within and without the substance. These changes or processes are frequently referred to as germination, fermentation, turning rancid, sprouting, and so on. The end products of these processes are water vapor, carbon dioxide, and heat.

There is no clear and definite moisture content level below which grain may be considered dormant and above which it respires; however, all grain may be considered practically dormant at moisture contents below 10%. Under normal conditions of storage on land, where ambient temperatures change slowly, the following moisture contents are generally considered safe for several months' storage: soy beans, 16%; maize, 14.5%; wheat, 14%; rice, 12%; and flax seed, 11%.

With higher moisture contents than those stated, the rate of respiration increases rapidly. See Figure 7-6 for the respiration rates of rice and sorghum grains at 100°F. This diagram uses the amount of carbon dioxide produced in 24 hours as an indication of the respiration rate. It also illustrates the difference between the respiration rates of white rice (also milled or polished rice) and rough rice (also known as brown rice), which explains the great difference between the stowage techniques used with the two types of rice.

Table 7-2 gives the moisture contents of a number of commodities as they are shipped in practice as determined by S. J. Duly of London. It should be interesting to the ship's officer that in most cases he/she receives these commodities with moisture contents that are at the limit of the safety level, or, as with Danubian maize, well above it. Hence, it is evident that anything that may cause an increase in moisture content during the voyage is likely to cause some damage to grain cargoes.

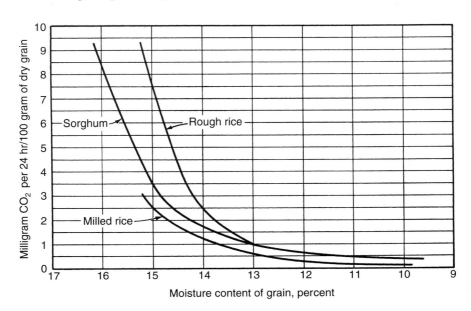

Figure 7-6. Respiration of grain as a function of its moisture content. Temperature of grain, 100°F; length of test, 96 hours.

TABLE 7-2
Average Moisture Contents of Common Hygroscopic Materials

Material	Moisture Content, Percent	Material	Moisture Content, Percent
Cacao	8–10	Textile fibers	
Cereals		Cotton	8–11.5
Maize (plate)	11–14.4	Jute	12–17
Maize (Danubian)	17–19.5	Silk	11
Rye (Polish)	17.19	Wool, raw	9.5–20
Wheat	10–14	Hides and skins	
Coffee	8.5–10.6	Dry	14–20
Dried fruits		Dry salted	14–20
Dried apricots	0.28	Wet salted	40–50
Prunes	24–28	Tobacco leaf	
Raisins	17–28	Usually	12–13
Sultanas	18–19	Range	9.5–17
Oil seeds		Timber	
Copra	3.4–5.6	Kiln dried	11–16
Cotton seed	7.1–9.5	Air dried	16–24
Ground nuts	4.4–5.6	Unseasoned	over 30
Linseed	5.9–12.1	Wood pulp	
Soya	7.9–12.1	Kraft (sulfate)	10–20
Tea	6–8	Bleached chemical	10–20
		Unbleached chemical	10
		Mechanical	50–55

The Effects of Hot and Cold Bulkheads

The effect of a heated bulkhead, deck, or overhead on a hygroscopic commodity is to raise the vapor pressure of the commodity and thereby do one of two things: (1) drive moisture out of the commodity into the ambient air, or (2) diffuse moisture from the heated zone of the cargo to the cooler zone.

If the moisture is driven into the ambient air, it must be removed by powerful air currents or the dew point will climb until heavy condensation appears on the overhead. When this condensation is heavy enough to drip back down on top of the cargo, it may cause heavy damage. This is a description of the daily cycle in the upper 'tweendecks of a ship in tropical or summer climes when the ship's ventilation system cannot remove the moisture-laden air before the evening drop in temperature. Sudden drops in temperature brought about by squalls can also cause condensation.

It is quite obvious by now that if the initial moisture content is low enough, heat sources will have no effect. Unfortunately, cargoes are not usually shipped with extremely low moisture contents; we must rely on reliable ventilation equipment properly operated.

If bulk grain is loaded in a space where one of the bulkheads is considerably warmer than the others, the hygroscopic moisture will diffuse from the heated area toward the cool area. This can cause no trouble if the moisture content is low; however, if it is bordering on the critical level of about 14%, the cool grain will receive moisture that will drive its percentage above 14%. At the higher level, the grain may heat and deteriorate. This could be an indirect cause of damage to grain (see Fig. 7-7).

If grain is loaded in a hold in such a way that it comes against an extremely cold steel plate, such as the ship's side in the winter or a poorly insulated reefer bulkhead, the vapor pressure is lowered. Moisture will then diffuse from the warmer zones to the cold zones; thus, the percentage moisture content in the cold zone goes up (see Fig. 7-8). This will cause a localized damage area, probably only a few inches thick, against the steel plate. The higher moisture content may cause the grain to heat, sprout, and spoil. During discharging, the spoiled grain will tend to adhere to the metal.

LIMITING DAMAGE DUE TO HOT OR COLD BULKHEAD

The extent of damage caused by hot or cold bulkheads will vary as (1) the temperature difference between the bulkhead and the cargo, and (2) the nature and condition of the grain cargo. If the cargo is prone to spontaneous heating, as, for example, are soy beans, the sudden increase in moisture content will cause an increase in the respiration of the cargo. This latter change will augment the effect of the hot bulkhead. It is obvious that this entire chain of events and the resulting damage can be made less likely by conditioning (drying out) the cargo before shipment. Some protection may be obtained by insulating boiler room

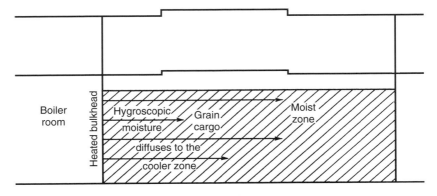

Figure 7-7. Effect of a heated bulkhead on adjacent cargo.

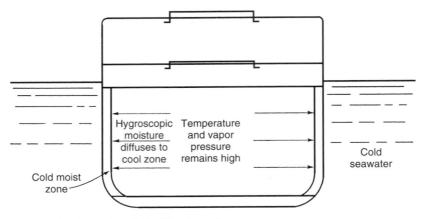

Figure 7-8. Effect of a cold bulkhead on adjacent cargo.

bulkheads and similar places. A slow increase in temperature will not produce effects as damaging as does sudden heating.

Ventilation by Natural Means

Most general cargo ships built today are equipped with supply fans, or supply and exhaust fans, for ventilating purposes. The change from the old cowl vent to some method that would guarantee a continuous supply of air, when needed, was long past due when it arrived.

In contrast to the uncertain capacity of the cowl vent system, a forced system will consistently deliver 4,000 to 10,000 cfm of air, depending on the capacities of the fans and ducts in the system. Used intelligently, such a system can eliminate as much as 80% of all condensation. The remaining 20% can be eliminated if the ship is equipped with a dehumidifier and connecting ducts that are used correctly.

Damage to Cargoes Caused by Moisture

Damage to grain, seeds, nuts, and pulses from moisture has been discussed earlier. The moisture causes a deterioration of the commodity through accelerated respiration, which eventually results in partial or complete loss of such cargoes. The moisture that causes such damage may be free moisture dripping onto the cargo from the deckhead, the hygroscopic moisture already present when the cargo was shipped, or hygroscopic moisture acquired during the voyage.

Other hygroscopic commodities and nonhygroscopic commodities in packages may be damaged by heavy stains from dripping condensation. This type of damage may not materially affect the product itself, but damages may be claimed on the basis of some reduction in salability of the product.

Cargoes of metal products may be heavily damaged by moisture condensing directly on the commodity and causing stains or corrosion.

Some special damage types exist, as in the case of refined sugar. If refined sugar is allowed to absorb hygroscopic moisture and it subsequently releases this moisture, it will become caked. If excessive caking occurs, damages may be claimed; under correct conditions, caking need not occur.

Eliminating Moisture Damage

Ways and means of reducing the detrimental effects of condensation are outlined below. Some of the systems or techniques in use are not very effective, and others are very expensive: the ship operator should investigate all methods with great care. The ship's officer should be aware of all methods and attempt to make them as effective as possible.

AIR CONDITIONING HOLDS

Proper air conditioning of the ship's holds can eliminate all of the moisture damage due to condensation on the ship or cargo and some of the damage caused by hygroscopic moisture. It should be noted that in the case of refined sugar *proper air conditioning* means the closing off of all circulation in the hold.

Stevedores and other practical cargo handlers have for many years practiced certain basic precautions against moisture damage that do not include ventilation. They have found from experience that they cannot rely on ventilation methods. Whether this situation continues depends entirely on the equipment placed on ships of the future and the knowledge of the officers who use the equipment.

DUNNAGING

The most common technique used for minimizing moisture damage is the thorough dunnaging of cargo so that (1) it cannot touch any metal, (2) drainage is provided beneath the cargo, and (3) ventilation air channels through it are provided. This protective measure is necessary whether or not suitable air conditioning systems are present.

COVERING TOP TIERS

The top tiers of cargo are sometimes covered with a moisture-repellent material, such as a tarpaulin or plastic, to prevent dripping condensation from striking the cargo. The idea here is to catch such moisture and direct it into the frame spaces, where it will fall and eventually find its way into the bilges.

One bad feature of this technique is that the air may become so moist below the covering that heavy condensation will occur there, especially if ventilation with low-temperature air is taking place over the top of the covering. If this happens, the corrective measures could actually be the cause of more damage than would have occurred if nothing had been done.

HERMETICALLY SEALING CONTAINERS

In some cases, shippers of products that are of a nonhygroscopic nature, but may be easily damaged by condensation, pack their products in hermetically sealed containers with small bags of a desiccant sealed within the package. The reaction between the trapped air and the desiccant is such that the dew point of the air is reduced to a level at which no condensation can possibly occur on the metal parts; furthermore, the moisture content of the trapped air is so low that the contents can remain in the package for years without rusting or other forms of corrosion. The material used to wrap the contents must be capable of shedding free moisture from the outside also.

COATING EXTERIORS

Some products with a highly polished finish are coated with a thin protective covering applied like paint. This covering prevents corrosion and may be removed by wiping the surface with a rag soaked in a paint thinner or specially designed product.

DEW POINT CONTROL

Importance of Dew Point Control

All of the means used to protect cargo from moisture damage resulting from condensation on cargo or hull are unnecessary if the dew point of the air in the ship's hold is kept below the temperature of the cargo and the hull or deckhead. Control of the dew point should be the basis of all our thinking on and efforts toward minimizing moisture damage in the hold.

It has been pointed out that successful dew point control with natural ventilation systems is quite impossible. Forced ventilation systems give some measure of protection. They will fail when the outside air has a moisture content that is higher than that of the air in the ship's hold. When this occurs, the outside air should not be brought in for ventilating purposes. If ventilation is stopped, the dew point inside the hold may climb to the level of the outside air. In other words, control is lost. In periods of heavy fog, rain, or mist, ventilation with outside air should be stopped. This action also brings about a loss of dew point control.

Control of the dew point is only complete when the ship is equipped with a device capable of manufacturing an adequate supply of low-dew point air, which is mixed with *recirculated air* in the closed holds; this should be done only when it becomes technically impossible to keep the holds opened to the outside air.

Such a device is called a *dehumidifier.* How a dehumidifier is integrated with a forced ventilation system to afford complete mechanical control of the dew point is the topic of a later section.

Basic Rules for Ventilating

If there is a single guiding rule that may be used for ventilation, it is as follows: *When the dew point of the outside air is lower than or equal to the dew point of the air in the hold,* ventilate. *When the dew point of the outside air is greater than the dew point of the air in the hold,* do not ventilate.

Hard and fast rules can sometimes lead us into difficulties because of particular changes that may take place in outside atmospheric conditions; also, the rule stated above assumes that the operator has sufficient and trustworthy instruments for obtaining the data needed for making a decision. Because of these considerations, *four general rules* for four specific situations are given below. It is important to understand that these rules should be used only as guides.

1. HYGROSCOPIC CARGOES GOING FROM A COLD TO A WARM CLIMATE

This is not a critical situation. There is little danger of ship's sweat, although there may be the possibility of cargo sweat. Without instruments to check the condition of the air in the holds, a ship's officer could never be certain that he/she was doing the correct thing. After battening down, it is advisable to keep a close check on the condition of the air in the holds and the outside air. In all probability, it will not be necessary to ventilate initially. At first, the inside air will probably have a dew point that is lower than that of the outside air. The dew point will probably climb upward gradually, but until the inside dew point is higher than the outside dew point there is no purpose in ventilating.

2. HYGROSCOPIC CARGOES GOING FROM A WARM TO A COLD CLIMATE

As a ship proceeds from a warm climate to a cold climate, it will experience a gradual drop in atmospheric dew point as well as a drop in dry bulb temperature. Under these conditions, a danger of heavy condensation on the ship's hull and top decks exists. The air in the below deck spaces will be receiving large quantities of moisture from the hygroscopic commodities, and unless constant and vigorous ventilation is maintained, heavy condensation is certain.

3. NONHYGROSCOPIC CARGOES GOING FROM A COLD TO A WARM CLIMATE

Under these conditions, the temperature of the cargo being loaded will usually be much lower than the dew point of the air through which the ship will pass as it proceeds into warmer climes. It will be necessary to keep the outside air out of the hold; hence, ventilation should be stopped. If ventilation is maintained during the voyage, condensation will occur on the cargo.

Not ventilating will protect the cargo during the voyage, but unless the cargo temperature rises above the dew point of the air at the port of discharge, there will be condensation on the products when they are discharged. However, some damage will have been prevented. If the nonhygroscopic cargoes are steel products, they might be badly rusted if soaked with condensation all during the voyage.

The possibility of large masses of steel rising in temperature during a voyage of only a few weeks is small. Few data concerning heat transfer through cargoes in a ship's hold have been gathered; however, the heat transfer is known to be slow. There will be a rise of about 1°F per day per 25° temperature differential between the cargo and the outside or sea temperature. A cargo of steel products 40° colder than the sea temperature warm up to the sea temperature in about 20 days, according to Colvin, Hahne, and Colby.

4. Nonhygroscopic Cargoes Going from a Warm to a Cold Climate

The possibility of trouble in this situation is remote. There is no possibility of cargo sweat, because the cargo is warm and will remain warm during the voyage. Hull sweat can occur, but the slightest ventilation will prevent this.

Mechanical Control of the Dew Point

All mechanical dew point control systems (as differentiated from simple forced ventilation systems) require three distinct *divisions* of equipment. For maximum control under all conditions, all three divisions are necessary. These divisions are:

a. *The hold fan and duct system:* This acts primarily as a forced ventilation system. It maybe designed with a forced supply and natural exhaust or vice versa; the most efficient systems have a forced supply and a forced exhaust.

b. *The instrumentation:* This is the means of gathering data from which the operator is able to make intelligent decisions concerning what to do with the system. This division will be explained later in greater detail, but it should be mentioned here that these instruments measure the moisture contents of the air in the holds and the outside air. With reliable information, the operator can judge accurately how to set up the system. With incorrect information or no information, the system may be used to cause more condensation than would result without the use of the system at all.

c. *The dehumidifier:* This is a machine for removing moisture from the air by adsorption or absorption. Air thus dried is injected into the recirculated air stream within the hold.

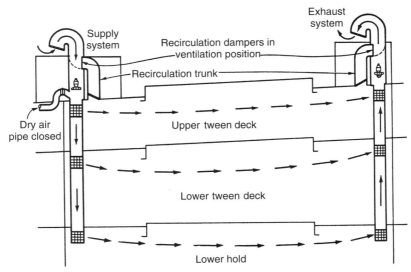

Figure 7-9. Hold fan and duct system, showing air flow when set on ventilation. *Courtesy Cargocaire Engineering Corp.*

The axial flow fans used at each hatch should have a rated capacity of 6,000 cfm. The outlets in the holds should be fitted with volume controls, which are adjusted when the system is installed. These volume controls must not be tampered with; otherwise the correct volumes will not be sent to the individual spaces. The duct system should be designed to split off portions of the total 6,000 cfm being delivered in proportion to the number and sizes of the holds to which they are destined and route them to these spaces. In other words, a hold of three divisions vertically (Fig. 7-9) would have the 6,000 cfm delivered in units of 2,000 cfm to each of the spaces. In each space there would be three outlets mounted in a fore and aft direction. Each of these outlets would deliver an equal amount of air.

If the dew point of the outside air is lower than or equal to the dew point of the inside air, the system should be set up to ventilate. If the outside dew point is greater than the inside dew point, the system should be set up to recirculate and add dry air (see Figs. 7-10 and 7-11). To obtain maximum penetration of the cargo by the air stream, the cargo must be stowed with great care and with particular provision for vertical and horizontal air channels through the stowed block.

NEED FOR ADDING DRY AIR WHILE VENTILATING

When the outside dry bulb temperature is falling rapidly and the system is already on ventilation, the dehumidifier should be put into operation and the dry air used to increase the differential between the hold air dew point and the temperature of the ship's hull. This is a special case, but should be understood so that condensation may be prevented under such conditions.

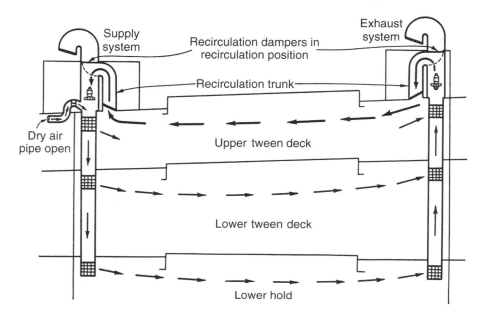

Figure 7-10. Hold fan and duct system, showing the air flow when set on recirculation and adding dry air. *Courtesy Cargocaire Engineering Corp.*

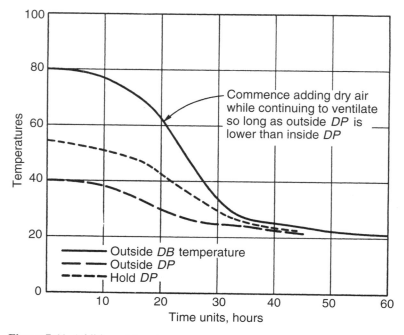

Figure 7-11. Addition of dry air.

On runs from South America to the United States during the winter on the east coast, there occurs an excellent example of the conditions described above. When ships leave the Gulf Stream and pass by Cape Hatteras northbound, the dry bulb temperature may fall 40° within 12 to 24 hours. If precipitation does not occur, the system may remain on ventilation. The differential between hull temperature and inside dew point temperature will decrease until there may be less than a degree difference. The addition of dry air to the ventilation air stream may increase the differential so that in the event of further temperature drops or complications, condensation will not occur. See Figure. 7-11 for a graphic illustration of the above discussion.

NEED FOR RECIRCULATION WITHOUT ADDITION OF DRY AIR

The only time that recirculation of the air in the holds should be maintained without the addition of dry air is when it is desired to raise the temperature of cold nonhygroscopic cargoes stowed below the upper 'tweendeck level. Here is the situation envisioned: The lower hold contains steel products that have been loaded at a very low temperature. Unless the temperature of these products is raised to a level above the dew point of the air at the port where they are to be discharged, they will become wet with condensation when the hatches are opened.

During the voyage, the upper 'tweendecks may reach a temperature above 100°F, while below the water line the steel will remain cold. The steel's temperature will rise, but very slowly, and it may not rise enough to prevent condensation from the cause mentioned above. To obtain some heat transfer to the cargo of steel, the air within the hold may be recirculated without the addition of dry air. Adding dry air will do no harm, but it will accomplish nothing. There is no object in operating the dehumidifier unnecessarily. To make this arrangement more effective, the only upper 'tweendeck outlets and intakes on the ducts should be covered. Do *not* cover the recirculation trunk openings.

INSTRUMENTATION

Instrumentation with sensors in each cargo hold records the dew point on a recorder graph in the chart room or wheel house. With the outside dew point also recorded, the mate will be able to determine whether to ventilate or recirculate.

The hand-aspirated, sling, or digital psychrometer is used to obtain wet and dry bulb temperatures. A sling psychrometer (Fig. 7-12) is a device consisting of two thermometers (wet bulb and dry bulb) that is rapidly whirled and with the use of tables yields the relative humidity and dew point. When taking a reading with the psychrometer, the wick of the wet bulb is wet thoroughly with distilled water using an eye dropper. Do not allow excessive water to remain over the wick. The instrument should be held at arm's length when taking readings

Figure 7-12. (a) Sling Psychronometer. **(b)** Whirling in air to obtain Wet Bulb and Dry Bulb readings.

and the operator's hand should not be near the metal cover, which should be closed over the bulbs. This prevents the readings from being affected by the operator's breath and body heat. The wet and dry bulb readings are used with a psychrometric chart or suitable tables to determine the dew point.

Probably the greatest weakness in the total system for mechanically controlling the dew point in the hold of a ship lies in the instrumentation. On some ships the system has been maintained in good order and the results are good. However, the system requires a considerable amount of attention to be kept in good operating order. It takes time also to obtain the psychrometric information necessary for the operator to make correct decisions as to the proper setting. For these reasons, the instrumentation has often been neglected. As a result, many ships equipped with excellent and expensive mechanical dew point control systems have failed to use them correctly. If these systems fail to check condensation from any cause, it is probably due to improper operation by the ship's personnel. These machines are constructed according to the laws of physics, and if operated intelligently, they will prevent condensation.

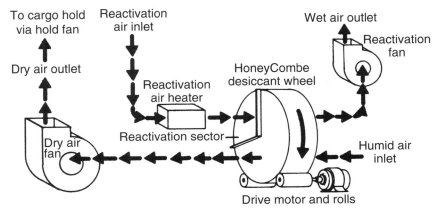

Figure 7-13. Air flow diagram. Desiccant or drying agent in HoneyCombe unit is continuously reactivated or dried by stream of hot air moving through the smaller reactivation section of the slowly rotating desiccant wheel. *Courtesy Cargocaire Engineering Corp.*

DEHUMIDIFIER

Removing wet air and adding dry air to the cargo hold is done by the dehumidifier. The wet air or humid air from the cargo hold is pulled into the humid air inlet (Fig. 7-13) through a cleanable filter and through the HoneyCombe desiccant wheel, which removes the moisture. The dry air leaves the dehumidifier via a motor-driven fan and is ducted to the suction side of the main hold fan. Here it mixes with weather air (if on Ventilation) or with recirculated hold air (if on Recirculation), and the mixture is ducted to the cargo hold.

Reactivation air comes from the weather, passes through a filter, is heated by steam or electricity, and enters the reactivation sector of the desiccant wheel. The desiccant (usually silica gel) is continuously reactivated or dried as the wheel slowly rotates through a stream of hot air supplied by an air heater.

SUMMARY AND CONCLUSION

Moisture damage or sweat damage probably ruins more cargo each year than any other form of oceanic shipping hazard. This is partly because sweat, or condensed moisture, is so prevalent a condition in the ordinary vessel's cargo holds, and partly because so many commodities are susceptible to damage by moisture. Textile goods are discolored and mildewed, metals and machinery are rusted, food stuffs of many sorts are rendered unpalatable, fibers and grains are heated and fermented, woods of some kinds are stained, and many minerals and chemicals are dissolved or changed in chemical composition. Scores of other commodities too numerous to mention are likewise susceptible to sweat damage.

The Carriage of Goods by Sea Act of 1936 states that the carrier is responsible for making the holds in which goods are carried fit and safe for their reception, carriage, and preservation. The carrier, however, is not responsible for damage to cargo arising out of such causes as "acts of God," "perils of the sea," and "Inherent vice of the cargo." The formation of sweat on the ship's structure or the cargo is the result of natural laws (see Fig. 7-14) and can be prevented; therefore the carrier is often found liable for cargo damage resulting from sweat.

Ship sweat, the most common source of moisture damage to cargo, is condensation dripping from the overhead (see Fig. 7-15). The extent of damage depends, of course, on the vulnerability of the commodity and the length of time that the condensation has been dripping before the hatches are opened. Ship sweat or condensation on the ship's structure is a result of the steel becoming cooled to below the dew point of the air in the holds through contact with cold air, rain, or sea water. This causes the air to release its moisture, which condenses on the overhead and on the ship's sides.

Cargo sweat is next in importance as a source of damage, and is the result of condensation of moisture on the cargo itself, usually metal products. Cargo sweat occurs when cargo is loaded cold and stored in a hold where its temperature will rise very slowly. After reaching warmer weather, moisture evaporates from other cargo, lumber in packing cases, dunnage, and cartons, raising the dew point of the surrounding air above the temperature of metal cargo, causing condensation to form on them. This process may take place even though the hold is kept tightly sealed throughout the voyage. If the hold is ventilated with moist, tropical air, the condition will be greatly aggravated.

Figure 7-14. Visible moisture vapor emanating from the cargo.

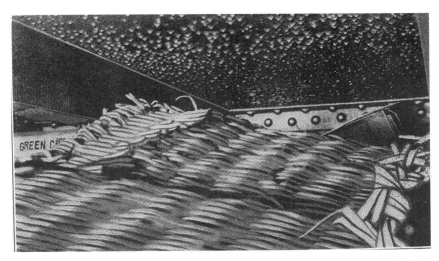

Figure 7-15. A typical example of ship sweat where condensation forms on the underside of the weather deck. Note the mats which protect the cargo.

Thus, it is evident that if the dew point of the air in the holds can be kept below the temperatures of the hull and cargo at all times, no condensation will form. This dew point control is accomplished by means of dehumidification systems.

The whole economic structure of the shipping industry depends on cargo delivered in good condition. The person primarily responsible for good cargo out-turn is the ship's officer. The ship's officer must observe appropriate temperatures. A case illustrating the lack of observing temperatures and non compliance with the basic rule for carrying nonhygroscopic cargo from cold to a warm climate is displayed in Figure 7-16. The voyage of the M/V *Tupungato* carrying steel coils from Huachipato, Chile, to New Orleans was one where the ship's officers constantly ventilated with outside air. The outside dew point increased daily on the northbound voyage and through the Panama Canal. As a result the steel coils were heavily damaged by cargo sweat which is illustrated in Table 7-3.

For the ship's officer a cargo ventilation log should be maintained on general cargo vessels. Such a log (see Table 7-4) should include the taking of temperatures at least twice a day. Minimal temperatures to be recorded are outside air and dry, wet bulb, and dew point temperatures. For each cargo hold the dry bulb and dew point temperature has to be taken. It is important to note with only wet and dry bulb readings the dew point temperature can be obtained from psychrometric chart or appropriate tables.

The ship's officer must then compare dew points (cargo hold and outside) in order to comply with the basic and general rules for ventilation. Only then can he or she properly protect the cargo which the carrier is responsible for.

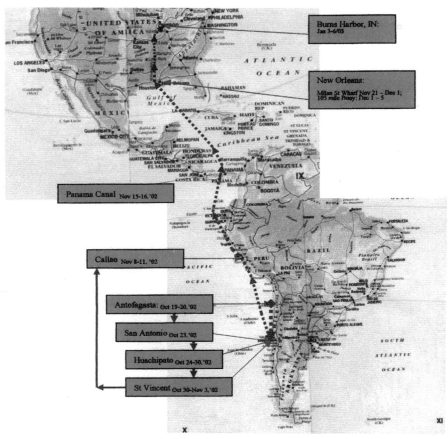

Figure 7-16. Approximate route of steel coils shipped from Huachipato, Chile, to New Orleans and then by barge to Burns Harbor, Indiana. *Courtesy of Kingsley, Kingsley, and Calkins, Hicksville, New York.*

TABLE 7-3
M/V *Tupungato* Ventilation Log Readings

2002 Date	Time	Temp o'f VSL above W/L outside RH%	DB°	Temp Ship Below W/L Sea Temp°	Outside Dew Point°	Inside Dew Point°	Cargo Temp Day/Night AVG°	Ship Sweat	Cargo Sweat	Ship Loc.	Rem.
10 Nov	1800	68	75	68	63	63	60	No	No	In Port	In Port Callao Peru Loading
11 Nov	0600	90	64	63	61	61	60	No	No	At Sea	At sea en route Panama Open Vents
	1800	82	70	66	63	63	60	No	Yes	At Sea	At sea en route Panama Open Vents
12 Nov	0600	81	68	82	63	63	60	No	Yes	At Sea	At sea en route Panama Open Vents
	1800	75	75	70	67	67	60	No	Yes	At Sea	At sea en route Panama Open Vents
13 Nov	0600	82	72	68	66	66	60	No	Yes	At Sea	At sea en route Panama Open Vents
	1800	70	82	75	71	71	60	No	Yes	At Sea	At sea en route Panama Open Vents
14 Nov	0600	84	77	73	72	72	60	No	Yes	At Sea	At sea en route Panama Open Vents
	1800	78	86	81	78	78	60	No	Yes	At Sea	At sea en route Panama Open Vents
15 Nov	0600	84	79	75	73	73	60	No	Yes	At Sea	At sea en route Panama Open Vents
	1800	79	88	82	79	79	60	No	Yes	At Sea	At sea en route Panama Open Vents
16 Nov	0600	84	81	77	77	77	60	No	Yes	Panama Canal	Transit Panama Canal Open Vents
	1800	73	91	84	81	81	61	No	Major Sweat	At Sea	At sea en route Nola Open Vents
17 Nov	0600	85	84	80	79	79	61	No	Major Sweat	At Sea	At sea en route Nola Open Vents
	1800	78	86	81	76	79	61	No	Major Sweat	At Sea	At sea en route Nola Closed Vents
18 Nov	0600	78	86	79	76	79	61	No	Major Sweat	At Sea	At sea en route Nola Closed Vents
	1800	85	82	79	77	79	61	No	Major Sweat	At Sea	At sea en route Nola Closed Vents
19 Nov	0600	77	81	75	73	73	61	No	Yes	At Sea	At sea en route Nola Open Vents
	1800	84	77	73	73	73	61	No	Yes	At Sea	At sea en route Nola Open Vents
20 Nov	0600	75	75	70	66	66	61	No	Yes	At Sea	At sea en route Nola Open Vents
	1800	68	75	69	63	63	61	No	Yes	At Sea	At sea en route Nola Open Vents
21 Nov	0600	81	64	61	58	58	61	No	No	In Port	Arrive Nola
	1800	66	72	64	57	57	61	No	No	In Port	

TEMPERATURE AND CARGO VENTILATION LOG

MV. ALEXANDRIA

VOYAGE ODESSA – NEW HAVEN

DATE/TIME	AIR TEMPERATURE DRY	WET	HOLD No.1 DRY	WET	REL	DEW	HOLD No.2 DRY	WET	REL	DEW	HOLD No.3 DRY	WET	REL	DEW	HOLD No.4 DRY	WET	REL	DEW	HOLD No.5 DRY	WET	REL	DEW	HOLD No.6 DRY	WET	REL	DEW	REMARKS
25/124 08.00	20	18	(17)	18	–	:	16	22	20	:	13	22	20	:	19	22	21	–	20	22	20	–	19	26	24	–	VENTILATION OF 12 No 2-3-4-5-6 Holds
16:00 27/08	24	21	(19)	23	19	:	17	24	21	:	19	21	01	:	15	24	21	:	19	24	21	–	19	26	24	:	VENTILATION OF No 6 Hold
08.00	20	18	(17)	21	15	:	16	21	18	:	16	21	18	–	16	12	20	1	19	23	01	–	20	28	23	–	23 No 6 Hold
16:00 28/09	23	20	(18)	22	20	:	19	23	21	:	20	23	21	:	20	23	21	–	20	24	21	–	19	28	23	–	VENTILATION OF 20 No 4-5-6 Holds
08:00	23	20	(18)	24	20	:	18	25	21	:	19	24	01	:	19	25	22	:	20	25	22	:	20	30	24	:	VENTILATION OF 20 No 1-2-3-4-5-6 Holds
16.00 29/09	24	21	(19)	25	21	:	19	25	20	–	17	25	20	–	17	25	22	:	20	25	21	–	19	29	24	–	VENTILATION OF 24 No 2-3-4-5-6 Hold
08:00	24	21	(19)	24	21	:	19	25	21	:	19	24	21	:	19	25	22	:	20	25	21	–	19	27	25	–	VENTILATION OF 22 No 1-6 Holds
16:00 30/09	30	24	(21)	27	22	:	19	27	22	:	19	26	23	–	22	26	23	:	22	28	24	–	22	32	25	–	VENTILATION OF 22 No 3-4-5-6 Hold
08:00	25	21	(15)	24	21	:	19	25	24	:	19	26	23	–	21	25	22	:	21	25	21	–	19	29	25	–	VENTILATION OF 23 No 4-6 Holds
16:00 1/10	28	23	(20)	28	25	:	24	27	24	:	23	27	24	:	23	28	25	:	24	28	25	–	24	30	26	–	VENTILATION OF 24 No 1-2-3-4-5-6 Hold
08:00	23	20	(18)	22	20	:	19	23	21	:	20	23	21	:	20	24	22	:	21	24	21	–	21	28	25	–	VENTILATION OF 24 No 1-2-3-4-5-6 Holds
16:00	25	22	(20)	23	23	:	22	26	22	:	20	24	24	:	23	24	24	:	23	25	25	–	23	26	–	VENTILATION OF 24 No 1-3-4-5-6 Holds

Signed: ....   C.H.I.E.F. OFFICER.

All temperatures in Celsius

CARGO VENTILATION LOG

Date / Time	Temp of VSL above W/L outside RH % DB°	Temp Ship Below W/L Sea Temp	Outside Dew Point	CARGO HOLDS										Remarks
				#1		#2		#3		#4		#5		
				DB	DP	DB	DP	DB	DP	DB	DP	DB	DP	

DB Temp. in hold is also the Cargo temperature

Indicate which holds are ventilated an if so to eliminate or reduce the possibi of cargo or ship sweat.

CHAPTER 8

MARINE MATERIALS
HANDLING EQUIPMENT

THE PURPOSE OF THIS CHAPTER is to describe the methods and equipment used to load and unload ships. Included with the presentation of extant practices is a discussion of the limitations of each and precautions on their use.

SHIP'S EQUIPMENT

The Married Fall System

A common rig still found on some merchant ships for the purpose of loading and discharging cargo is the *married fall* system. This rig is sometimes referred to as the *yard and stay* or *burton* system. The last two names are used most often among seafarers. In this rig, one of the ship's booms is guyed so that its outer or upper end is over the hatch and the other boom so that it is over the dock. The block plumbing the hatch was sometimes secured to the mast's stay and the block over the dock was frequently secured to one of the ship's yards. Thus the dock boom is still called the yard boom and the hatch boom is called the stay boom. The falls rove through the blocks attached to these booms are given the same names respectively. Hence, the designation *yard and stay* system.

The practice of using two booms, as seen in Figure 8-1, in which both booms are *fixed,* originated on the west coast of the United States during the late 19th century. The swinging boom is used today only when handling loads considered beyond the capacity of the fixed rig. On most ships it is not safe to burton a load on fixed rigging if it exceeds 3 tons; however, if the guys are carefully positioned, the parts are large enough, or a *safe* rig such as the Ebel rig (discussed later) is used, then heavier loads may be burtoned. (To *burton* a load is to move it athwartship.)

The stay fall is an up-and-down fall, the yard fall pulls the load across the ship. Actually, both falls carry the load across the ship, and it is only after the athwartship movement is complete that either the yard or the stay fall takes the entire load, depending on which way the load is moving. The fall on the dock boom often is referred to as the burton, whereas the fall on the hatch boom is known as the hatch or up-and-down fall. This is so despite the fact that during

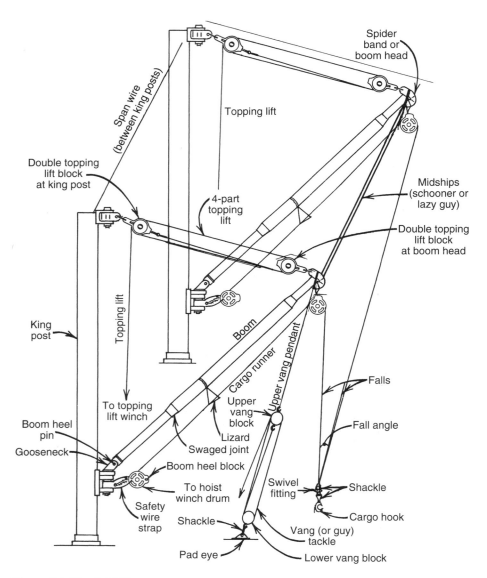

Figure 8-1. Married fall system.

loading the hatch fall also carries the load across the ship. It is evident, then, that a confusing array of terms exists for speaking about this rig. The fall over the dock may be termed the dock fall, the burton fall, or the yard fall; likewise, the fall over the hatch may be referred to as the hatch fall, the up-and-down fall, or the stay fall. Inasmuch as the use of the dock and hatch terminology results in the least possible confusion, these are the terms that will be used in this discussion.

The booms of Figure 8-1 are able to pivot in two planes. The vertical movement of each boom is controlled by the topping lift. The transverse movement of the boom is controlled by the outboard or working guy and the midship or schooner guy. The midship guy is also known as the spanner guy, schooner guy, or lazy guy. At the lower end of the boom, a fitting known as the gooseneck allows movement in the two directions mentioned.

The cargo fall leads from the winch drum directly to the heel block mounted below the gooseneck fitting. The gooseneck and heel block generally make up a single assembly. The fall then leads up the boom through lizards or fair-leads to the head block and then to the cargo hook.

Topping Lift Rigging

All modern ships are fitted with this *topping lift winch.* Some of these winches are made so that they can lower or top with the boom loaded; others cannot handle a loaded boom. If the topping lift winch is not designed to handle a loaded boom but an attempt to have it do so is made, the excessive torque required of the winch will cause a large rise in current through the motor's armature; this will result in a safety device breaking the circuit and an automatic braking mechanism being applied. This prevents the excessive current from burning out the armature. If the circuit breakers fail to operate, the armature will be burned out and a great deal of expense will be incurred on account of repairs and lost time.

Guying Systems

As can be seen from Figure 8-1, there are two distinct systems for guying the fixed booms of the yard and stay rig. It is necessary to find a place down on deck to secure the inboard guy. This brings additional gear to a location already overly crowded, impairing the safety of the working area. The load on the cargo hook is always between the heads of the two booms or directly under one of them; therefore, there is little or no stress on the inboard or midship guys. Thus the lightweight midship guy is quite sufficient, and it is placed aloft out of the way.

The outboard guys are often referred to as the working guys because they are the guys that are under the greatest stress. The stresses on the guys appear when the load is being transferred athwartships (burtoned) or when it is being supported anywhere between the two boom heads. An analysis of the stresses on the falls and guys is made later. It is important for all officers to know how to keep these stresses at a minimum.

PREVENTERS

In addition to the regular outboard guy on the fixed boom, an additional wire may be attached to the head of each boom and led to the deck to act as a *preventer guy.* This preventer guy is made of ⅝- or ¾-inch wire rope. It may be completely of wire or have a tail spliced onto the lower end so that the part used to secure the preventer will have more flexibility than the wire itself. These tails are made of 4-inch, three-strand manila rope or ¾- to 1-inch chain. If they are made of manila, they are susceptible to being cut by plates or other items being handled; if made of chain, they are less vulnerable to damage. Quite frequently the regular guy and preventer are set up in such a fashion that the regular guy takes all the load and the preventer is supposed to take a stress only in case the regular guy parts. *This is not a safe practice;* the net result is that when the regular guy parts, the preventer parts also. The ship's officers must make certain that the load is being carried equally by the regular guy and the preventer. The safest procedure is to make both the regular and preventer guy secure as close together as possible and to equalize the stress on all parts. It follows also that it would be more sensible to have one guy rigged so as to have the strength of the ordinary guy plus the preventer.

The preventer is a constant source of trouble and in many cases fails when the regular guy fails. In the records of the Accident Prevention Bureau of the Waterfront Employers of San Francisco, only one case is recorded in which the preventer held after the regular guy parted. In this particular case, the preventer was not made secure properly, and when the boom started to swing the preventer took up the strain gradually until the wire became jammed on the cleat and the boom's swing was checked. Because of this problem, the functions of the regular guy and the preventer have been combined in the vang guy.

SPOTTING THE GUYS

When securing the outboard guys to the deck after topping the booms, consideration should be given to the location of the lower end of the guy with respect to the stress that will be placed on it when under a load and with respect to the possibility of jackknifing.

Guy failures account for the great majority of cargo gear breakdowns. Bending of the boom due to too much compression caused by the component of thrust from fall, guy, and topping lift is the second most important cause of breakdowns. A number of very practical points relative to the task of positioning guys for greater safety are presented in the following section. These factors should be common knowledge to all deck officers and longshoremen.

Maximum Stresses

It is well known that tight-lining of the falls causes extremely heavy stresses on the guys. Undoubtedly, a question may arise in the minds of many officers as to the magnitude of the stress when the falls are tightlined with an empty hook. Because of the limitation placed on the power of the winch, the stress on the guys depends entirely on the fall angle when the winch is pulling its maximum.

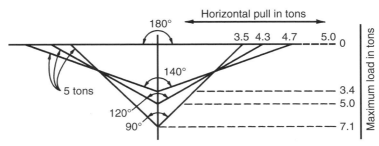

Figure 8-2. Maximum stresses.

Figure 8-2 indicates the maximum load that a pair of 5-ton winches can lift to various fall angles and the corresponding horizontal pulls between the heads of the booms. It is, of course, this *horizontal pull* that puts the stress on the guys. The horizontal pull will be at a maximum when the winches are pulling against each other with an empty hook, and with 5-ton winches would be equal to 5 tons. Thus, an empty hook is potentially more dangerous than a heavily loaded one.

When 5-ton winches are holding a 5-ton load at a fall angle of 120°, the horizontal pull is 4.3 tons. The stress on each fall under this condition would be 5 tons also; thus, it can be seen that this is as high an angle as these winches can possibly lift such a load.

Topping or Jackknifing of Booms

Topping or jackknifing of booms can have very serious and costly results. Although the extreme conditions under which a boom will or will not top are well known, the dividing line, or *danger point,* is not well known. Experiments with a model such as those carried out with respect to guy stresses have established the line of demarcation between jackknifing and not jackknifing and a means of locating this danger point on board ship.

When the two booms are at different heights, which is usually the case, their respective tendencies to top are different. The fall leading upward from the lower to the higher boom will tend to lift the lower boom. For this reason the working guy of the lower boom must be placed closer to the heel than is necessary for the higher boom. The working guy of the lower boom must be so placed that a line of sight (dotted line in Fig. 8-3) from the pad eye to the head of the higher boom will pass beneath the lower boom somewhere ahead of the gooseneck of the lower boom. If the line of sight is behind the heel of the lower boom, the boom will definitely top. If the line of sight passes above the boom but ahead of the heel, the boom will top until it reaches this line of sight and then it will stop.

Because the higher boom is being somewhat pulled down by the fall, its guy need not be as close to the heel as that of the lower boom and the line of sight from the pad eye to the head of the lower boom may pass behind the heel of the boom. However, the working guy at the height of the gooseneck must be

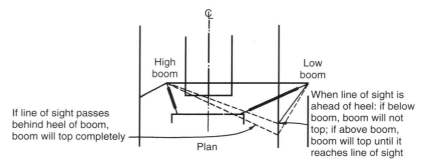

Figure 8-3. Jackknifing conditions.

ahead of the line of sight between the gooseneck of the higher boom and the head of the lower boom. If the high boom's working guy is behind this line of sight at the height of the gooseneck, the boom will top.

Summary of Discussion of Guy location

Several important facts that all officers should keep in mind when their ship is working cargo have been pointed out in the above discussion. These are summarized below.

1. The closer the heel of the boom is to the rail, the greater the stresses on the guys and booms for the same fall angle.

2. The increased drift obtained by spacing heels widely may not fully compensate for the increased stress on the guys.

3. When a boom is angled outboard from the fore and aft line through its heel, the stress on the guy decreases as it is moved back of the heel. The practical amount of this movement is limited by the critical point for jackknifing.

4. When a boom is on the fore and aft line through its heel or swung inboard from this position, the stresses on the guy and the boom are least when the guy is in line with the fall or at right angles to the boom when viewed from above. Under most conditions, there will be little difference in the amount of stress at these two positions of the guy.

5. Depending on the spacing of the heels, the stress on the working guy of the hatch boom at a fall angle of 120° may be as much as 4 ½ times the weight of the load. Improper leads of guys can increase these stresses considerably.

6. At any given fall angle the stress on the guys will vary directly with the weight of the load, but the *maximum* stress that can be placed on a guy in any given cases is determined by the capacity of the winches, not by the weight of the load. In fact, the lighter the load, the greater the maximum possible stress.

Additional Conclusions

1. Excessive stresses caused by faulty rigging of the gear cannot be safely compensated for merely by the use of preventers or by otherwise increasing the strength of the guys. To use this method of compensation may cause the boom to fail.

2. The smallest stresses are produced (because of increased drift and good guy angles) on gear with widely spaced king posts when the head of the hatch boom is well toward the centerline of the ship and the working guy is at right angles to the boom in the plan view.

3. Since the pull of the fall along the boom makes up a large percentage of the total compression on the boom, maximum benefits are obtained by doubling the fall rather than putting the winch in low gear when heavy weights or lack of drift makes either necessary.

CALCULATION OF STRESSES

Calculation of Stresses Using Vectors

It is often convenient to be able to solve for the stress placed on a given part of the ship's rigging by graphic methods. We will discuss here vectorial methods for doing this.

The physical quantities of length, time, and mass can be described quite nicely by using numbers with appropriate units, such as 9 feet, 9 minutes, and 9 pounds. These numbers are known as scaler units. However, when dealing with a physical quantity that has a number *plus* a *direction* related to it, it is more convenient to use vector quantities. Vector quantities are represented by properly *directed* lines the lengths of which represent the *magnitudes* of the vector quantities.

When a number of forces are acting upon a body in various directions, the total force and the direction of that force can be calculated by adding the various vector quantities. The single force thus calculated is known as the *resultant force.* If the resultant force is zero, then the body will remain at rest. For example, when a cargo hook is suspended between two booms with two falls and a loaded pallet attached to it, we know that the resultant of all these forces is equal to zero because the hook is not moving. It is at rest. Furthermore, it is obvious that the upward forces taken alone must produce a resultant force precisely equal to the downward forces. Therefore, if we have a known weight on the hook, we know that the falls are pulling so that they produce an upward resultant equal to the weight in suspension. With this information we can solve for the stress on each fall. Alternatively, if we are given the stress on each fall, we can calculate the resultant force itself.

One of the most common methods of calculating the resultant force is known as the parallelogram method. In the problems occurring in our study of the stresses on the parts of cargo rigging, we will ordinarily know one force (the load on the cargo hook) and be seeking the value of two forces acting to oppose the given force. These two forces will be the stresses on the two cargo falls. We will also deal with stresses on topping lifts, compression on booms, and approximate stresses on guys. Figure 8-4a shows a weight being suspended by two falls AC and CB with a fall angle of 120°. The weight is suspended at C. We know that the forces acting in the direction of A from C and in the direction of B from C are holding the weight in suspension.

The forces involved may be drawn as shown in Figure 8-4b. F_1 and F_2 are opposed to the weight W; thus, F_1 and F_2 are creating the resultant R that opposes W. To solve for the stress on F_1 and F_2 by the parallelogram method, R is drawn opposite to W equal to W. In this example let W equal 3 tons. Then R and W would each be drawn 3 units long. We start from any convenient point O. From the point O we draw F_1 parallel to CA and F_2 parallel to CB. Next, the end of the vector R is connected to the vectors F_1 and F_2 so as to form a parallelogram. Then the lengths of F_1 and F_2 from O in the chosen units give the stresses acting on the two parts. In this case, F_1 equals 3.2 tons, and F_2 equals 2.7 tons.

If the values of F_1 and F_2 and the direction in which they acted from the point O had been known first, the resultant force R could have been found by reversing the process.

Trigonometrical Solution

The values of the resultant or the forces can be found by using trigonometry when the angles a, b, and r are known (see Fig. 8-4c). These angles would be known because the directions of the forces and the resultant are known. In the above example, angle b is 50° and angle a is 70°. Thus, with R equal to 3 we can set down these elements in the diagram shown by Figure 8-4c. By the law of sines we have:

$$\frac{A}{\sin a} = \frac{R}{\sin r} \quad \text{and} \quad \frac{B}{\sin b} = \frac{R}{\sin r}$$

where

$A = F_1$

$B = F_2$

$a = 70°$

$b = 50°$

$r = 60°$

$R = 3.$

Since $\sin 70° = 0.94$, $\sin 60° = 0.87$, and $\sin 50° = 0.77$:

$$A = \frac{3 \times 0.94}{0.87} = 3.24 \qquad B = \frac{3 \times 0.77}{0.87} = 2.65$$

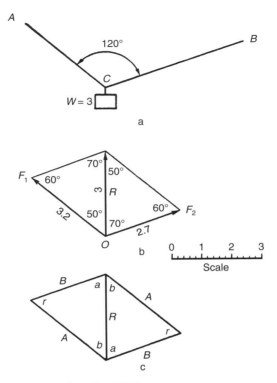

Figure 8-4. Fall angle of 120°.

The slight differences in values arrived at by graphic and mathematical methods are due to the inability to read the units on the measuring instrument to the third significant figure in the graphic method.

NUMERICAL EXAMPLE

Given: Two falls are attached to a 1-ton lift and they both make an angle with the vertical of 60°.

Required: The stress on each fall using the parallelogram method.

Solution: Figure 8-5 illustrates the situation as a vector diagram.

The answer is obtained graphically as 1 ton.

Effect of Fall Angle

It is important that the reader note that with both falls making an angle of 60° with the vertical, the stress on each fall is equal to the load being suspended.

By making a diagram as shown in Figure 8-6, it can be seen that as the angle between the falls increases above 120°, the stress on each fall goes above the weight being suspended, and that as the angle between the falls decreases below 120°, the stress on each fall goes below the weight being suspended. This is true when both falls make equal angles with the vertical. The lowest stress possible is equal to one-half the weight being suspended, and occurs when the angle between the falls is equal to zero. The stresses on both falls will be equal only when both falls make the same angle with the vertical.

In Figure 8-7a it can be seen that although one fall makes an angle of only 60° with the vertical, it is supporting a stress greater than the weight being suspended; this is because the other fall is making an angle with the vertical that is greater than 60°. Note that the fall with the *least angle* from the vertical carries the *greatest* percentage of the total load. Figure 8-7b shows the result of decreasing the angle on the right side until it is 15° less than 60° rather than 15° greater. Now the load on the fall making an angle of 60° with the vertical is less than the weight being supported; note also that the stress on the other fall, which is making an angle with the vertical of less than 60°, is greater than the stress on the first fall. An analysis of these facts points up the great importance of limiting the drift between the hook and load while increasing the drift from the head of the boom to the deck of the ship.

Figure 8-7a and b shows the variation of stress on each fall as the angle between the falls and the angle that each makes with the vertical vary.

The following conclusions can be drawn from this brief discussion: (1) The drifts should be such that the angle that each fall makes with the vertical will never be more than 60°. This is of special importance when the load being hoisted is equal to the safe working load of the fall. (2) The rig and slings used should be set up so that the angle each fall makes with the vertical is as small as possible.

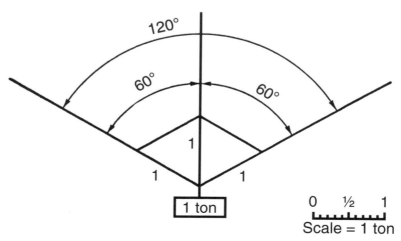

Figure 8-5. Fall angle of 120° with a 1-ton weight.

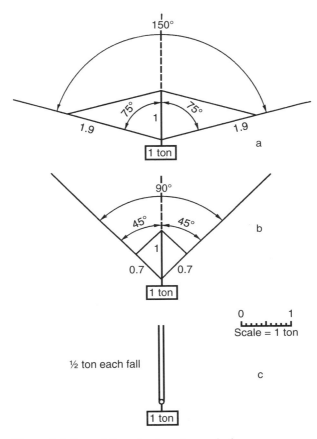

Figure 8-6. Same fall angles from the vertical.

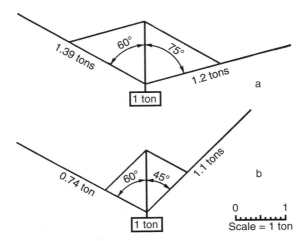

Figure 8-7. Different fall angles from the vertical.

WORKING WITH ABOVE-NORMAL LOADS

Limiting Factors

The limit on the weight of the load that is safe when working with any cargo handling rig is dependent on the size and type of wire being used for the fall. (The type of tackle is a factor also, but this is discussed separately under the discussion of doubling up.) In this section, reference is to the single whip as normally used with the yard and stay system. Although the fall is the limiting factor when initially hoisting the load on the up-and-down lift, it should be remembered that the guys may be the limiting factor when burtoning the load across the deck. The guys are thrust into the role of a limiting factor whenever they are not positioned properly or whenever the drift between the hook and the bottom of the load is excessive. We will consider only the fall as a limiting factor in this section. Table 8-1 on breaking strengths is presented for reference when considering the rigging of any given gear. Equations for finding breaking strengths should be used only when tabulated data are unavailable.

A single strand of ⅝-inch, 6 × 19, plow steel wire rope has a breaking stress of 12.9 tons, and a ¾-inch wire has one of 18.5 tons. Many ships now use improved plow steel wire rope, for which the following breaking strengths are: ⅝-inch, 14.9 tons and ¾-inch, 21.2 tons. From these figures, it is evident that improved plow steel wire rope is about 1.15 times stronger than plow steel. This is an increase of 15%. The fiber core is used almost universally for the running and standing rigging on merchant ships.

Running Rigging and Safety Factors

When determining *safe working loads* for running rigging, a safety factor of at least 5 should be used. This gives safe working loads of 3 tons for the ⅝-inch improved plow steel and 4 tons for the ¾-inch improved plow steel wire rope of 6 ×19 construction with fiber cores. (The ton referred to in this discussion is the ton of 2,240 lb.) The safety factor of 5 may seem excessive, but it must be remembered that this is the factor only when the line is new. During normal use with shipboard rigs, the wire rope is subjected to treatment that will reduce its original breaking stress rapidly.

Boom Ratings

Tests of fully rigged cargo gear are made by the American Bureau of Shipping and equivalent authorities in other countries. These tests have become necessary since various nations began enforcing regulations relative to tests and periodic inspections of cargo handling gear as recommended by the

TABLE 8-1
Wire Rope Breaking Strengths[*]

Rope Diameter, in.	Improved Plow Steel	Breaking Strengths, in long tons Plow Steel	Mild Plow Steel
½	9.5	8.3	7.3
⅝	14.9	12.9	11.2
¾	21.2	18.5	16.0
⅞	29.7	25.0	21.7
1	37.3	32.5	28.2
1⅛	47.0	40.8	35.5
1¼	57.7	50.2	43.6
1⅜	69.3	60.3	52.5
1½	82.1	71.4	62.1
1¾	110.7	96.4	83.6
2	142.8	124.1	108.0
2¼	178.5	155.4	

[*] The data presented in this table apply to 6 × 19 classification ropes with fiber cores either preformed or nonpreformed. For the breaking strengths of galvanized ropes, deduct 10% from the strengths shown. For wire strand cores and independent wire rope cores, add 7½% to the listed strengths.

International Labor Convention of 1932. Without proper gear certification, ships are subject to delays in many ports of the world in order to undergo tests and inspections locally.

The rules of the American Bureau of Shipping specify standards to be complied with for certification of the ship's cargo gear and maintenance of that certification. These standards also apply to the upkeep of chain and wire slings and certain other loose gear used during the longshore operations. Periodic annealing of wrought iron gear is required, and all blocks, wire, and loose gear should be furnished with certificates of testing by the manufacturer. The American Bureau of Shipping specifies a safety factor of 4 for all gear.

After the gear is installed, the complete assembled rig is tested by swinging of live proof loads of amounts greater than the rated capacities in the presence of a surveyor. The live loads are required for the rating of newly built ships. On satisfactory completion of such tests, the heels of the booms are stamped with the safe working loads and the date. It should be remembered that this test is given to the gear used as a swinging boom, but that the boom is almost always used in a fixed position. This fact changes the stresses on all parts and should be kept in mind and investigated by the ship's officers using various diagrams of the gear and its arrangement on their particular vessel.

Gear Certification

The surveyor issues a certificate covering the proof loads and angle at which each boom is tested. This certificate, together with all manufacturer's certificates regarding loose gear, is inserted in the Ship's Register of Cargo Gear. This register has pages for entering certification data for the original proof loads, the annual surveys, and the surveys every 4 years, when the proof loads have to be applied again. Pages are also available for recording the annealing of all wrought iron gear. This simple bookkeeping process provides evidence of the condition of the cargo gear and the maintenance given it.

The American Bureau of Shipping rules require that new ships be furnished with a diagram showing the arrangement of the assembled gear and indicating the approved safe working load for each component part of the gear. With these diagrams, replacements for loose gear may be ordered to suit the safe working loads.

For the certification of cargo gear on existing ships, the use of spring or hydraulic balances to register the proof loads required to be applied to the assembled rig is permitted. Figure 8-8 show such test arrangements. In an actual 5-ton design, the thrust load in the boom and the tension loads in the topping lift and cargo falls are calculated under the application of the safe working load of 5 tons and of a test proof load of 6¼ tons at the cargo hook.

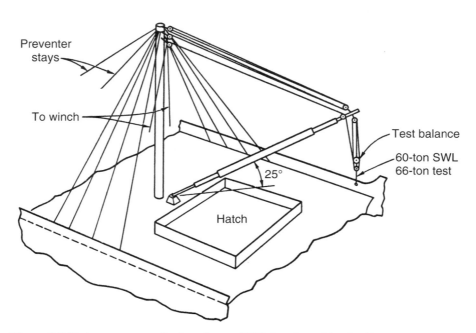

Figure 8-8. Test arrangements for 5-ton boom. (SWL is safe working load.)

Doubling Up

Whenever the load to be hoisted by the yard and stay rig exceeds the safe working load of the rigging, some alternative rig should be employed that will increase the safe working load. The safety factor of 5 is recommended when arriving at safe working loads with running rigging. Using the alternative rigs discussed in the following sections is known as *doubling up.* If the wire fall has just been renewed and the mate is confident of the skill of the winch drivers, he/she may not require doubling up for loads close to the limit. For example, if the mate considers a safety factor of 4 to be sufficient, he/she might permit hoisting a 3¼-ton load with a ⅝-inch plow steel wire rope. The doubling up process is slow and costly, and freight rates generally reflect the cost of handling heavy items. It is often a great temptation to attempt the loading of items whose weights are just over the limit of the regular gear. Because of the risk involved, the practice of overloading the gear should be discouraged.

YARD AND STAY WITH GUN TACKLES

When one is forced to double up with a swinging boom, the time required to transfer the load from the dock to the ship or vice versa is greatly increased. This increase in time can be cut down by using systems that retain the advantages of fixed booms rather than changing to a live boom operation. This is especially important when a large number of loads just over the safety limit are to be handled. One of the easiest methods of augmenting the load limit of the gear is to rig both booms with gun tackles. This requires two additional 14-inch cargo blocks, four shackles, and two cargo falls that are double the length of the regular falls (see Fig. 8-9).

The first step is to run the old fall off the winch drum. Next, the new fall is placed on the winch drum and led up to the head block via the heel block. The fall is then rove through the traveling block and the standing part is secured to the spider band at the head of the boom. This is done with both booms. The added traveling blocks should have beckets on them to permit the attachment of a common ring or separate swivels of a standard cargo hook assembly. The booms have to be lowered to the deck to make this conversion. When the booms are topped again, the rig is ready to handle cargo with fixed booms under the standard yard and stay system (see Fig. 8-10). If the booms are 5-ton booms with ⅝-inch improved plow steel wire rope falls, the load limit should be kept at 5 tons. If the booms are 10-ton booms with a ¾-inch wire fall, the load limit should be kept to 8 tons. The greatest danger point with this rig are the guys. The guys should be checked carefully, and the positions chosen to give the least strain to the guys. Slings should be applied carefully so that a minimum of drift is allowed between hook and load. In this way the hook will not have to be hoisted an excessive

Figure 8-9.
Doubling up of the yard and stay with gun
tackles. Note the small chain between the
tops of the blocks, which prevents the slack
block from toppling over and fouling itself.

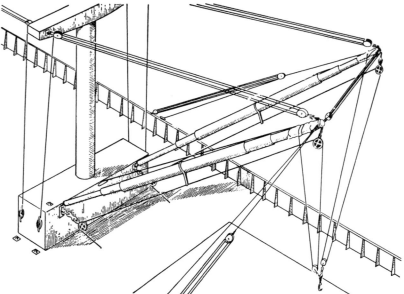

Figure 8-10. Typical yard and stay system rigged with gun tackles on each boom. If the head
block has no becket, the runner should be secured with two round turns to the boom itself
about 4 feet back from the head. The eye splice at the end of the runner is shackled to the link
band at the head of the boom. The turns around the boom must be started from the inside to
prevent chafing against the runner leading from the head block to the heel block in operation.
If 5 tons are burtoned with this rig, every possible precaution must be taken to
ensure minimum guy stresses and equal strain on all parts. *Courtesy U.S. Navy.*

distance above the deck and the angle between the falls can be kept to a minimum, thus relieving the strain on the guys. The angle between the falls should be kept below 120°.

The Heavy-Lift Boom

Almost all ships are equipped with at least one *heavy-lift* or *jumbo boom.* As can be seen from the above discussion, when the weight of the unit to be taken aboard is above 3 tons, one of the doubling up rigs can be used. By using these one may avoid using the jumbo rig, which is very slow in operation and may require an hour or more to prepare for use. However, when the weight of the unit goes above the safe working load of any of the doubling up rigs, there is nothing left to do from the standpoint of safety but rig the jumbo boom. Now and then, for expediency, loads exceeding the safe working load will be taken on board with the conventional gear. Such practices may prove to be very costly instead of economical.

The heavy-lift boom is usually shipped in a pedestal mounted along the ship's centerline. There are usually two ratings for its capacity; the lowest is without a preventer stay being rigged. The maximum rating is with the preventer stay rigged. The preventer stay is a large wire rope that is normally carried unrigged on the mast supporting the jumbo rigging. Two stays are generally used.

With this rig, four men operating the two guy winches, the purchase, and the topping lift can control the boom. The capacity of a given rig on a given ship is stated on the ship's capacity plan or on a blueprint showing the plan and elevation views of the rigging.

Handling a heavy lift requires careful planning. The method of slinging the load up must be considered carefully. In many cases a sling weighing several tons may be required to lift a load weighing 40 or 50 tons. The weight of the sling must always be considered when calculating the total load on the boom. If a load of 24 tons is to be hoisted and the sling weighs 3 tons, it is necessary to rig the preventer stays even though the load being lifted is less than the rated capacity of the boom without preventers rigged.

The chief officer should be advised of the method being used to hoist, stow, and secure a given heavy lift, and should make it his/her business to be on hand during the rigging and handling of all heavy lifts. If he/she finds it impossible to be on hand, he/she should designate another officer to observe the operations. The importance of officer supervision is even greater when the ship is not operating in her home port.

When using the heavy-lift boom, the load should be taken up only a few inches at first and held steady. All rigging should be checked while the load is held suspended in this position. Then the load can be hoisted very slowly. At no time should there be any attempt to rush the process. If any particular part of the procedure can be said to be more dangerous than any other, it is when the load is being lowered and it becomes necessary to stop the lowering. If this is done with a jerky motion or too suddenly, the stresses on the gear may be raised to a dangerous level and contribute to the failure of some part of the rigging. The stresses can be raised also by hoisting the load too rapidly. Hoisting and lowering of heavy lifts should always be carried out slowly and carefully.

At single-rigged hatches, where it is necessary to lead the guy hauling parts to winches at the next hatch, care must be taken to assure that drivers of the guy winches can see the signal man clearly. There have been several cases in which the guys parted because one guy winchman heaved while the other was either heaving or holding fast.

When slewing the jumbo boom, it should be at the lowest position possible for easy operation. The boom should not be slewed when topped so as to reach the hatch area immediately in front of the pedestal. The forces applied to the guys place great strains on the gooseneck, pedestal, and pacific iron when the boom is so high. At lower positions it rotates more easily.

All of the parts of the heavy-lift rigging should be carefully stowed away or secured in the rigged condition when not in use. Because of the tremendous weight of the blocks and hooks used, the gear is not generally stripped and secured. The boom is topped as high as it can go, and the purchase and topping lift are secured by lashings after slushing them down with grease. Generally a collar is provided aloft in which the boom is secured. The large blocks are secured by using short wire pendants and turnbuckles. It is also important that the gooseneck and pin of the jumbo boom (as of all booms) be kept well lubricated.

Stuelcken Boom

The wishbone type Stuelcken heavy-lift boom (see Figure 8-11a) is becoming a common sight on modern merchant vessels. These booms have capacities ranging up to 525 tons. The Stuelcken boom on the typical merchant vessel has a capacity of about 80 tons. A heavy-lift boom has yet to be designed that improves upon the features of this boom. Several variations exist in the means of moving the boom from one hatch to the other. The Stuelcken rig (see Fig. 8-11b) consists of a centrally located swinging boom supported by two king posts (usually inclined outboard at their tops). Each king post is fitted with a swivel head from which a multiple-purchase topping-slewing tackle is led to pivots at the boom head to prevent twisting of the tackle. Four winches are utilized: two for hoisting the load and two for each of the topping tackles. The boom is raised by both topping winches and swung by hauling on one topping winch and paying out on the other. The chief characteristic of Stuelcken rig is that the boom head, when fully raised, can be flopped forward (or

Figure 8-11a. Seventy-ton Stuelcken boom. *Courtesy Blohm + Voss AG.*

aft) between the king posts, allowing the boom to work the adjacent hatch. This shift of working positions takes 3 to 5 minutes, without rerigging. The forked boom head prevents fouling of the tackle when the boom is moved between the king posts to the opposite side.

In addition to its main advantage of working adjacent hatches, the advantages of the Stuelcken rig are its greater lifting capacity, its requirement for less deck gear, and the increased speed of the cargo hook. The typical 60-ton Stuelcken boom has a hoisting speed of 20 fpm and light hook speed of 45 fpm. The Stuelcken rig is designed for fast loading, unloading, and spotting of heavy cargo and thus far is the ultimate in shipboard heavy-lifts.

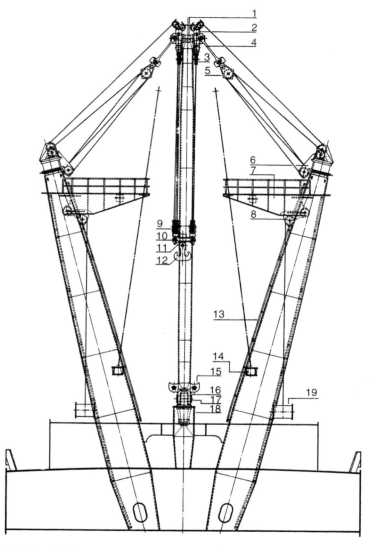

1. Derrick head fitting
2. Pendulum block fitting with guide rollers
3. Upper cargo blocks
4. Connecting flats
5. Lower span block
6. Span swivel
7. Cross tree
8. Inlet for the hauling part
9. Lower cargo blocks
10. Connecting traverse
11. Swivel eye for flemish hook
12. Flemish hook
13. Ladder
14. Gooseneck pin socket
15. Fastening device for lower cargo block
16. Heel fitting
17. Derrick pin
18. Gooseneck and gooseneck pin socket
19. Winches

Figure 8-11b. Parts of the Stuelckenmast. *Courtesy Blohm + Voss AG.*

Modifications of the Married Fall

Wing and Wing

Rigging the hatch boom over the offshore side of the vessel while the dock boom remains over its conventional spot on the pier apron is known as *wing and wing* rigging. It is a simple variation of the regular yard and stay rig used when loading or discharging deck loads and its use is necessary when handling loads on both sides of the ship.

The House Fall

At some ports, a number of piers are equipped with a cargo block made secure on a steel structure on the face of the dock shed in such a way that a fall rove through it plumbs the dock apron. The structure may be a steel outrigger or a short boom stepped on the side of the building. Such an arrangement is used mostly on piers with very narrow aprons, which are in some cases less than 3 feet wide. They are also very convenient on piers with two decks. The fall used with this rig is furnished by the pier, because the regular fall on the ship is too short. The house fall may lead to the ship's winch via proper fair-leads or, in some cases, to a winch on the pier. The hatch boom with its fall is used as it is normally. Figure 8-12 is a diagram of this type of rig.

The advantages of the house fall are as follows:

1. On piers with very narrow aprons, it eliminates the possibility of fouling the head of the dock boom against the face of the dock shed.

2. It provides a steady spotting area under the permanently installed block on the dock.

3. On piers with second decks, it may provide the only means of working the second deck platform, because of the limited drift of the ship's booms. When the ship is deeply loaded and the booms are short, the drift over the second deck landing platform may be reduced to only a few feet if the ship's booms are used.

4. If the house fall block can be made fast at a sufficient height, it becomes possible to work extremely wide aprons with a spotting point at the dock shed doorway or at any one of as many as three railroad spurs. When working with booms, the dock boom must be lowered to a dangerously small angle from the horizontal to work the third track.

Split Fall Rig

Two variations of the split fall rig will be described. Essentially, it consists of unmarrying the yard and stay falls so that they can work independently.

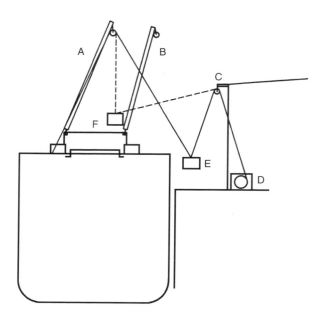

Figure 8-12. The house fall rig. The house fall may be led from block C to a dock winch D as shown or to a ship's winch at the foot of boom B. When the load is in position F, the operator of the winch of boom A is in control of the load and has a good view of it. Boom A should be used for the ship's fall, because its working guy is rigged to handle the stress of burtoning.

In one rig, the two booms are guyed loosely; we will describe this one first. The dock boom is guyed so that it plumbs a point on the dock, and is allowed to swing inboard so that it plumbs another point slightly inboard on the stringer plate. The hatch boom is guyed tightly. Obviously, this type of rig is easier to set up if inboard guys are used on both booms instead of the midship guy.

The rig operates as follows, assuming a discharging operation: The single fall of the hatch boom brings up a load and a man stationed on deck pulls the load outboard just enough to allow it to be landed on the deck of the ship. The hook is removed from the load and it goes below for another load. In the meantime, the dock fall is hooked onto the load on deck. A strain is taken and the load slides outboard. The dock boom, being guyed loosely, swings inboard as far as its working guy will allow it. This brings the dock boom over the stringer strake of deck plating. The winch driver hauls away on the fall, dragging the load under the boom, where he/she stops it momentarily before hoisting it clear of the deck. The man on deck pushes the load outboard and the load is landed on the dock. When loading, the steps are reversed.

In another arrangement of almost the same type, the two booms are guyed tightly in a fixed pattern. The point plumbed by these booms in both split fall arrangements must be only a few feet clear of the ship's side and the hatch coaming.

In this system, again assuming a discharging operation, the hatch boom brings a load up and stops. The winchman holds the load with the hook about level with the top of the hatch coaming. The man on deck takes the hook of the dock fall and puts it on the sling. Now both falls work together and take the load on deck or out over the dock, at which point the hatch fall is released. The load is landed with the dock fall while the hatch fall goes below for another load.

As can be seen, the only difference between the two methods of using the split fall is that in the first system the load is moved across the ship by being pushed or pulled manually or being dragged with one fall. In the second system the load is burtoned by temporarily married falls.

With longshoremen trained in the use of the system and with certain types of cargoes, the split fall rig has proved faster than the married fall system. When handling baggage stowed in deep lower holds on passenger ships, it is quite likely to be more productive than the yard and stay system. Full cooperation of the longshoremen is mandatory, of course.

Yard and Stay Jury Rig

This rig utilizes two booms with a single winch. The hatch fall is the regular wire rope, but the dock fall is a four-stranded 4-inch manila line. The wire fall is made fast to the winch drum as it would be ordinarily. The manila line, however, is worked on the winch gypsy head by a man known as the *burton man*. To describe its use, let us assume that we are discharging. First the load is hoisted from the hold as with the regular rig. The manila line *A,* of course, is married to the cargo hook along with the hatch fall *B*. To retrieve the slack on this line, the burton man *C* takes one round turn on the gypsy head and hauls away. Thus, when the load is above the hatch coaming, the manila line is quickly removed from the gypsy head and three turns are taken in the opposite direction to the turns on the winch drum. Now, as the winch driver slacks away on the wire fall, the burton man hauls away on his/her line. This action burtons the load across the deck, and if the load was taken up to the right height the manila line will have all the weight of the load while the wire fall will be completely slack. At this point the wire is slacked off a little more by surging the manila line on the gypsy head. When sufficient slack has been obtained, the winch is stopped and the burton man slacks off on his/her line until the load is landed gently on the dock.

When a load is taken aboard, the burton man lifts the load and then surges his/her line and slacks off while the wire burtons the load across the deck until the hatch is plumbed. Once the wire has all the weight, the burton can be removed from the gypsy head and the load landed in the hold.

A description of this system makes it seem a good deal more difficult to use than it is. A skillful seaman is needed to handle the manila line, but this is not difficult with a small amount of practice. The author has used this system on tankers to discharge and load drums of lubricating oil at the small dry cargo hatch forward and remember it as being surprisingly efficient. It is a system that may be placed into use on any ship when a winch breaks down or in a similar emergency.

The Farrell Rig

The first real improvement in many years in the yard and stay system of rigging the ship's gear for burtoning cargo was advanced by Captain V. C. Farrell about 1947. This improvement over the conventional gear consists of placing the heels of the outboard guys or vangs and the heels of the booms on a common axis (making them coaxial). The greatest usefulness from this rig is obtained by also installing topping lift winches and placing the hauling part of a twofold topping lift through a lead block secured near the ship's centerline. With this setup, all that must be done to top or lower the boom is to press the button controlling the topping lift winch. There is no need to tend the guys. The boom head will move along a straight line parallel to the centerline of the ship.

Once the guys have been secured to the short vang posts and pulled tight and the fall has been made clear in the normal manner, one man can hoist all the gear on a ship in less than an hour. If this is done while at sea, the falls must be run up on the winch drums and pulled tight with the cargo hook secured amidships or the falls crossed and shackled into pad eyes to keep the gear from breaking loose as the ship rolls. The latter procedure is necessary regardless of the system used to guy the gear.

With willing and able longshoremen and winch drivers, the full advantage of this rig may be realized. One set of gear may be used to service two spotting points on the ship. With fingertip control of the topping lift winch, the winch driver can alternately top up and lower the boom so as to spot a point first at one end of the hatchway and then one at the opposite end. Hence, without having to wait for the spot to be cleared each time, the hook can continue to work.

Opening or closing hatches with beams or pontoons takes much less time because of the ease and speed of positioning the hatch boom over the exact spot necessary to pick up the beam or pontoon. This may be done without having to pull the hook into line with a guide line.

Figures 8-13 and 8-14 show the slight change that is necessary to rig the conventional gear with the Farrell rig. The erection of the vang posts is all that is necessary if the ship already has topping lift winches.

Data gathered during a carefully observed voyage showed that the hatch served by the Farrell improved burtoning gear handled 39% more cargo per hour than one served by a pair of booms rigged in the conventional manner. The anomalous situation of more cargo per hour passing through the single-rigged hatch than through the double-rigged one came about via a combination of the diminishing returns experienced with double ganging and the fact that cargo handling requirements were sometimes such that it would not have paid to activate both sets of booms on the double-rigged hatch.

The advantages experienced with the Farrell gear included a 70% reduction in the time required to open and close the hatches and an 80% reduction in the time required to place the booms in operation or secure them for sea. The

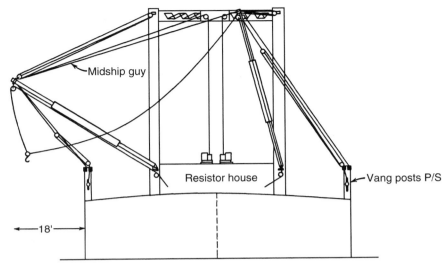

Figure 8-13. Elevation of the Farrel rig port and starboard.

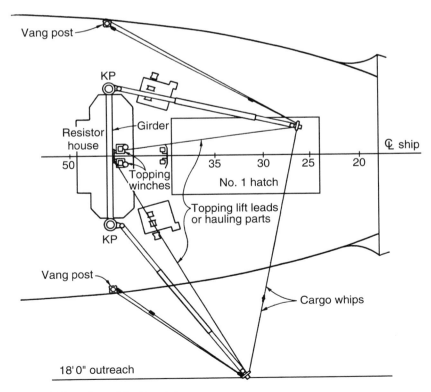

Figure 8-14. Plan view of the Farrel rig.

increased spotting ability, it is believed, reduces cargo damage, and the gear in general is *safer* than gear that does not employ topping lift winches.

The Ebel Mechanical Guy Rig

This rig was devised by F. G. Ebel, Senior Naval Architect, Maritime Administration. It was installed on the *S.S. Schuyler Otis Bland,* a prototype ship designed prior to the Mariner type ships. The cargo handling gear on this ship represents an outstanding improvement over the conventional rig.

Although the married fall system is an efficient system for transferring a great variety of cargo types from shore to ship and back again, there are three outstanding disadvantages to the conventional method of setting this rig up. These are:

1. Maximum load limitations

2. Lack of spotting ability

3. Dangers involved

For reasons that become quite clear after studying the section covering stresses on fixed cargo booms, the load that can be safely burtoned on the regular rig is limited to about 50% of the rated boom capacity. The strength of the working guys usually is the limiting factor. Being designed for hand operation, the working guys are generally made of light equipment and rove off with manila line. If designed to handle larger loads, their size would make them unwieldy. As a result, it has been the custom to expect to rig the fixed boom as a swinging boom when loads become greater than 3 tons. Swinging boom operation is very slow, and thus it is very costly to load units over 3 tons. Although it would be economical to handle some cargo in units over 3 tons from all other standpoints, this limitation reduces the overall efficiency of the cargo handling gear.

The second disadvantage was partially overcome by the Farrell arrangement. This is the lack of flexibility of the usual burtoning gear due to the boom heads being fixed in position over the pier and hatch. This, of course, makes it necessary to bring all cargo directly under the boom head that is going to hoist it and to haul it away from a fixed point of deposit under the boom that lowers it. Changing the positions of the boom heads with the unimproved rig entails the use of several men and considerable time, and is dangerous.

The third disadvantage of the old system is the probability of gear failures. Many longshoremen have not the slightest idea of the safest point at which to secure the guy when setting the gear for work. Consequently, if a competent officer is not present to check on the location of guys, excessive stresses may be incurred, with disastrous results. The guys are usually made as light as possible, and after a little use they become weak and fail when loads near the limit are hoisted. Because of the time and trouble involved in converting the fixed boom to a swinging boom, there is a temptation on the part of officers to attempt hoisting loads just a little over the safe limit. Careless or inexperienced winch drivers tight-lining a load, spreading the boom heads in the wing-and-wing position when topped very high, and using excessively long slings are additional possible causes of excessive stresses on the guys and booms.

Further dangerous elements with the older rig are the amount of slack line lying about the decks and the necessity to shift the topping lift from cleat to gypsy head and back again when positioning the booms.

The Ebel rig adequately overcomes all three of the above mentioned disadvantages. The gear on the *Bland* was designed:

1. To handle all loads up to the full capacity of the booms (5 and 10 tons) by the burton system.

2. To provide for complete *power positioning* of the unloaded boom.

3. To eliminate all manual handling of lines.

4. To increase safety.

Figure 8-15 shows schematically the arrangement of the topping lift on the 10- and 5-ton booms. Figure 8-16 shows the arrangement of the mechanical guys on the 10- and 5-ton booms. The topping lift is offset inboard at a point near the centerline of the ship to control the swinging of the boom in the outboard direction. The hauling part is led down the inboard side of the king post through a lead block to the drum of one of the small king-post-mounted topping lift winches.

The standing part of the guy is secured to the extreme outboard end of the crosstree. It is run over a sheave at the boom head, down to a sheave at the bulwark, back around the second sheave at the boom head, and back to the crosstree through a lead block; and then led down the outboard side of the king post to the drum of the electric guy winch, which is also mounted on the king post.

With this setup, there is complete mechanical control of the boom. The boom can be lifted from its cradle and swung to any desired position over the hatch or pier with mechanical power. All hand operations are eliminated, and the entire operation is done by one man.

Tests have shown that it takes 1 minute 13 seconds to raise a pair of 5-ton booms from their cradles to the working position. It takes 56 seconds to shift a pair from the working position on one side to the working position on the other side. The 10-ton booms require slightly longer times, 2 minutes 36 seconds and 1 minute 21 seconds, respectively. The winch driver can perform all these shifts without moving from his/her regular operating station. To do the same operation with the conventional gear takes several men 10 to 15 times as long,

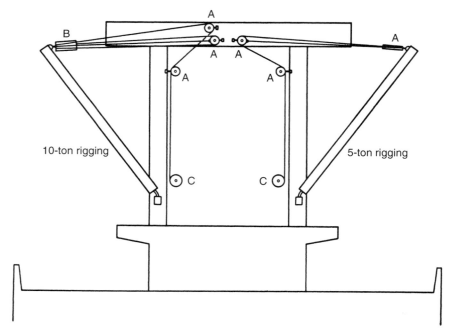

Figure 8-15. A schematic representation of the topping lifts on the Ebel rig. All blocks are single A except for the boom topping lift block on the 10-ton rig B. The hauling part is led to a topping lift winch C, which is controlled from the position where the winches are operated. All blocks have 14-inch sheaves and are rove off with ¾-inch, 6 × 19 improved plow steel wire rope.

and the danger of a boom dropping or a man being injured in handling the lines is ever present.

As mentioned before, with the older method of rigging, the married fall system, there is always the danger of accidental hoisting of the load to greater heights than the gear was designed for. If this happens, the guy stresses become very great, especially when a poor guy location is selected by the longshoremen. The consequence may be a parted guy, a collapsed boom, or a jackknifed boom. All of these failures of the gear will result in damaged cargo and damaged gear, and may result in injury or death to personnel.

The Ebel rig is designed so that the effective guy resultant force keeps the stresses moderate even when handling 5- and 10-ton loads. If the load is hoisted to excessive heights, the dock boom head will rise by *riding up* in the bight of the guy tackle until it reaches a position of equilibrium with the load. While the boom head rises, the load remains almost stationary. Thus, the angle between the two falls is limited to a fixed predetermined maximum, and the overloading of any element is precluded.

When the load is lowered by slacking off on the falls, the boom resumes its original position by *riding down* the bight of the guy. The boom is never free from the tensioned guy; therefore, it cannot drop freely. When burtoning 5 tons,

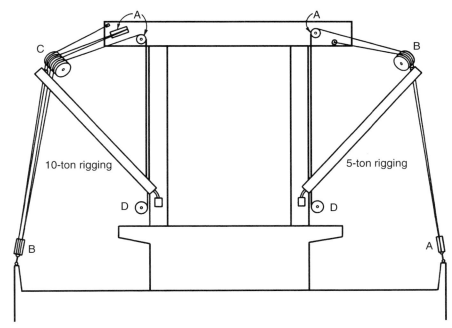

Figure 8-16. Mechanical guys: a schematic representation of the guys on the Ebel rig. All blocks marked with an A are single. B indicates a double block, and C a quadruple block. D marks a guy winch that is controlled from the position where the winches are operated. Note that the standing parts are secured to the crosstrees. All blocks have 14-inch sheaves and are rove off with ⅝-inch, 6 × 19 improved plow steel wire rope.

the minimum height of the married fall above the deck at which the riding up will occur is about 30 feet, and for lighter loads it is higher. This is ample drift to handle almost any load.

Since only one guy location is provided for, it is impossible to locate the guy improperly. When handling loads with the single fall, the maximum load is determined by the size of the fall: With ⅝-inch, 6 × 19 improved plow steel, it is 3 tons, and with ¾-inch wire rope, it is 4 tons. When it is desired to hoist 5- or 10-ton loads by the married fall system, it is necessary to use a multiple purchase, because the winches are generally limited to a single line pull of about 3 tons.

On the *Bland,* two specially designed burtoning blocks have been provided for burtoning loads up to 5 and 10 tons, respectively. They are illustrated in Figure 8-17. The one with single sheaves is for handling loads up to 5 tons with two-part lines. The other, with double sheaves, is for handling 10-ton loads with four-part lines. These blocks are self-overhauling and nontoppling and are equipped with roller bearing sheaves. These blocks prevent the twisting and toppling that sometimes take place when two separate blocks are married for burtoning with a multiple purchase.

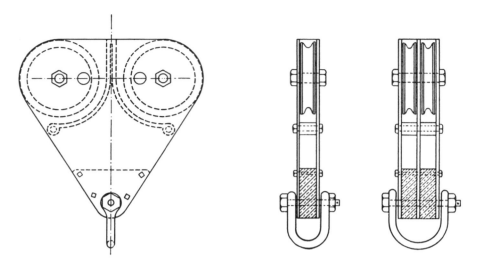

Figure 8-17. Nontoppling blocks. These blocks are used for doubling up the yard and stay rig to be used with fixed booms. Instead of using two separate blocks at the hook, this single, specially built block will suffice.

Additional Methods of Handling Cargo

The Ship's Crane

The question of which is the most efficient, the yard and stay rig or ship's cranes, would appear to be answered in favor of the crane if one were to judge from the number in use at this time.

The factors involved in deciding the merits of one system as compared with another are: (1) initial cost, (2) cost of maintenance, (3) the productivity of the system, (4) the flexibility of the system, and (5) safety. It is evident that in order for anyone to be in a position to say anything conclusive about either gear, they would have to have a modern cost accounting system and industrial engineering organization to obtain the facts on which to base a comparison.

Types of Installations

Cranes on general cargo ships today range from 5 to 100 tons in capacity and most are hydraulically powered (see Fig. 8-18).

Cranes have been installed on either side of and on the centerlines of ships. When they are installed on the centerline, it is with the intention of the one crane being able to work both sides of the ship and one end of two adjacent hatches. This is more economical and weighs less. However, if the crane is on the centerline, it must be much larger to provide ample reach over the side.

Figure 8-18. (a) Five-ton crane between hatches. **(b)** Typical modern multipurpose cargo vessel with twin hatches and twin slewing cranes. *Courtesy Schiller International Corp.*

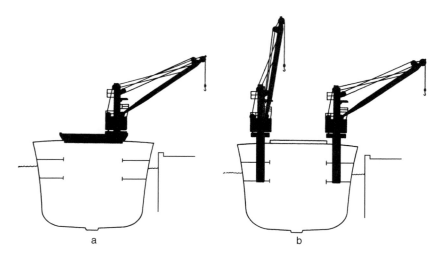

Figure 8-19. Because of the limited radius of the boom on cranes, it is necessary to install them so that an ample reach over the side of the ship is obtained. These sketches illustrate two means of achieving this end. **(a)** The application of a movable crane mount. **(b)** The mounting of two cranes, one on each side outboard of the ship's centerline instead of one on the centerline. *Courtesy Colby Steel and Manufacturing, Inc.*

Cranes are becoming more and more commonplace aboard U. S. general cargo ships. It seems that there are many things in their favor. Figure 8-19 shows two possible installations on large ships.

ADVANTAGES OF THE SHIP CRANE

Spotting area

The crane is able to pick up and drop loads over a greater area than can the yard and stay, which should, under certain conditions, reduce delay time of the hook. Figure 8-20 indicates the working zone of the crane as compared with the working zone of the conventional burtoning gear.

Safety

Cranes are installed without guys and their supports do not include shrouds and stays. All supports are built into the mounts for the cranes. This leaves the decks of the ship clear of numerous lines of running and standing rigging and thereby adds to the safety of operating the ship.

Simplicity of operation

The operator needs only a few minutes of instruction, and one man can prepare or secure the gear in a few minutes.

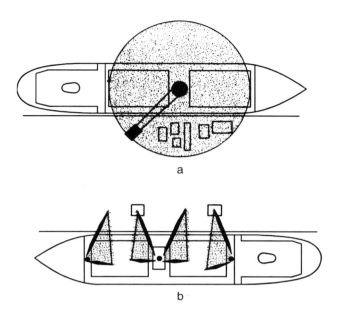

a

b

Figure 8-20. The spotting ability of the crane is graphically compared with that of conventional gear in this sketch. **(a)** The spotting area of the crane is that covered by the shaded section. **(b)** The shaded areas show the spotting areas of the conventional gear. Note that this figure indicates the possibility of one crane doing the work of four sets of gear provided the hook could keep up with the workers in the hold. Although this would not ordinarily be possible, it is conceivable that two cranes could take the place of four sets of gear. *Courtesy of Colby Steel and Manufacturing, Inc.*

DISADVANTAGES OF THE SHIP CRANE

Not only do the above advantages leave little room for argument, but the disadvantages often listed may not truly weigh against the crane. One disadvantage that seems to be at least partially valid is that the crane is not as flexible as the yard and stay. In other words, the crane cannot handle *all* the cargo that the yard and stay can.

Two features of the first cranes placed on ships that proved to be detrimental to speedy operations were (1) the pendulous swinging of the load when the crane was slewed between ship and shore, and (2) the need to adjust the height of the load as a separate operation when luffing the boom. (Luffing the boom means topping or lowering it.)

The first objection was overcome by using two falls leading out over sheaves at the end of the jib instead of a single fall to support the load. The second problem was overcome by designing into the controlling machinery a device that would allow the boom to be luffed while the load remained at a constant height. This is known as *level luffing*. It prevents the load from swinging when the boom level is adjusted and requires much less power when topping the boom with a load on the hook.

SHORESIDE MATERIALS HANDLING EQUIPMENT

In the following sections we will describe the various types of materials handling equipment and comment briefly on those items used most frequently. The changeover from hand-powered equipment to mechanically powered equipment took place from about 1932 to 1941. These years were the years for the first purchases of dock tractors and lift trucks, respectively. The first purchases of powered conveyors and crane trucks were also between these years. The year of the earliest recorded purchase of dock tractors is 1918, and that of lift trucks is 1928. These facts give some idea of the speed with which mechanization takes place along the water front. It can hardly be called rapid.

Hauling and Handling Materials

To reduce the uneconomical use of manpower and thereby bring some degree of efficiency to the marine terminal, there must be a continued effort to reduce the number of handlings of all products carried by the ship and to develop machines to do a given job with the least inefficiency. Efforts along these lines have produced a variety of materials handling equipment. Each has several uses for which it is better fitted than is any other type of equipment. The two broadest classifications into which equipment can be divided are equipment which is best for *hauling* and that which is best for *handling*.

We will define hauling as the horizontal movement of cargo for a distance over 300 feet. Handling is defined as the vertical movement or relatively short (i.e., under 300 feet) horizontal movement of cargo.

TRACTOR-TRAILER COMBINATION AS COMPARED WITH FORKLIFT TRUCK AND PALLET

The best contrast between equipment best suited for hauling and that best suited for handling is between the *tractor-trailer combination* and the *forklift truck and pallet*. The former is essentially a hauling combination, whereas the latter is a handling combination. In many simple operations, the costs can be made much higher than they should be merely by an improper decision regarding the type of equipment that should be used.

THE TWO-WHEELED HAND TRUCK

The common hand truck will remain a useful tool in the handling of cargo no matter how mechanized the total operation may be made. When labor is very cheap, the purchase of mechanized units may not be warranted according to the principle of amortization. The hand truck can be used for the movement of packages too heavy to be moved by hand or to increase the unit load of small packages on occasional short trips. The hand truck can be used also as a pry or lever in much the same way as a crow bar. With two or more men working with hand trucks, a large crate or case may be raised several inches and transported a few feet very slowly. The nose is wedged under the case, the wheels are chocked, and the operator bears downward on the handles. This action raises the case on the nose of the truck, and with two or more trucks at opposite ends the entire case may be raised off the deck and moved slowly in a straight line (see Fig. 8-21).

Two or three men make the best combination for working with the hand truck. With three men, two remain at the loading terminal to load the truck while the third man acts as the mover. With two men, the operator of the truck also helps to load.

The load must be placed on the truck in just the right way to make it easy to transport. If the load is too low on the bed of the truck, the handles are difficult to keep down while pushing the truck. On the other hand, if the load is too high on the bed of the truck, the operator has a difficult time supporting the load while maneuvering the truck. If the load is placed on the bed so that it is well balanced when the truck is tipped backward about 60° from the vertical, surprisingly heavy loads can be handled easily by an experienced man.

The working loads may run anywhere from 200 to 600 pounds depending on the size and type of truck. The trucks are able to support more than it is normally possible to transport on them. Models weighing about 45 pounds have a capacity of 900 pounds, while heavy-duty models weighing 155 pounds have a capacity of 2,000 pounds.

The two-wheeled hand truck is economical only for very short occasional movement of materials, and then only if the cost of labor is extremely low or some special circumstances exist, such as a low volume of movement or limited working room. Two types of hand truck are shown in Figure 8-22. Figure 8-23 shows a method of loading light bulky cases. The operator must experiment a few times to discover the best way in which to load any given container. Care must be taken not to place a fragile case or bag over the nose in such a fashion that the upper containers will damage it.

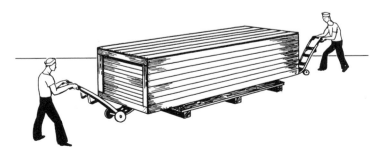

Figure 8-21. Two-wheeled hand truck is used to move large crates and cases.

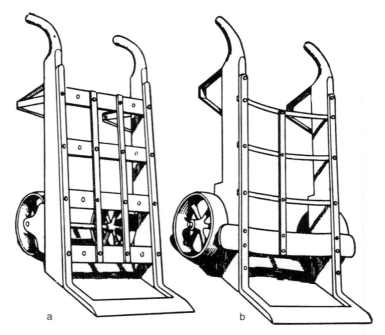

a   b

Figure 8-22. Two types of hand truck: **(a)** Western-style, and **(b)** Eastern-style.

Figure 8-23. With experience an operator of a two-wheeled truck can load surprisingly large loads on the bed. Here, a load of sixteen lightweight cases is loaded on the bed of an Eastern-style, two-wheeled truck. Without experimentation to discover the best way to load such containers, it would have been possible to load only six cases.

THE FOUR-WHEELED PLATFORM HAND TRUCK

This type of truck is also useful today where labor is very cheap or the volume of movement is too low to warrant the purchase of powered equipment. It is much faster and easier to use this truck than it is to use the two-wheeled type when working cargo to and from the pier apron on marine terminals. The loads can be made up on the platform of the truck within the pier shed and transported directly to the hook on the apron where the load is hoisted aboard. If the load is too heavy for one man, two may be used. The same method applies to discharging. The load can be landed on the bed of the truck and immediately moved away to clear the spot for the next load. If the two-wheeled hand truck is used, the spot is blocked until the hand truck is loaded after the load is landed on the pier. The use of the platform truck thus eliminates an additional handling and reduces the costs and the damage to the cargo.

Four-wheeled platform hand trucks also find use in ship's holds for moving loads between the hatch square and the wings. The load is landed on the bed of the truck and pushed to the wing or built on the bed in the wing and pushed out to the square. It is necessary to lay down a roadway of light steel plates or dunnage boards over which the truck can pass easily.

THE TRACTOR-TRAILER COMBINATION

For hauling purposes the tractor and trailer combination is excellent. One important requisite for the efficient use of this combination is a smooth surface on the pier apron and in the dock shed.

The tractor is a short, highly maneuverable vehicle powered by gasoline with a sheet steel bumper face in front and a trailer-coupling device on the rear. Its primary purpose is to pull a number of trailers on a train. It may also be used for pushing railroad cars along spur tracks and similar work. Most tractors used on marine terminals are equipped with four wheels, and although they may be capable of greater speeds, they should not be driven over 5 mph, especially when hauling a trailer train.

The trailer is actually a special type of four-wheeled platform truck that is able to take heavier loads than the regular platform truck. Trailers are constructed in many ways: some are fitted with four wheels that turn, others with only the two front wheels turnable, and still others with caster wheels. The bed of the trailer averages about 3 by 7 feet and is about 14 inches high. The bed is usually made of hard wood and bound with steel. Sometimes the bed is covered completely with a light steel plate for heavy-duty work.

When pulled as a train by the tractor, the trailers follow in the path of the tractor. One tractor can be used to keep the hook supplied with trailers, either loaded or empty depending on the operation. For example, in loading, the tractor will arrive at the hook on the pier apron with four to six trailers in tow.

Dropping these trailers, the tractor removes the empties and travels to the point on the dock where the cargo originates. Here it drops the empties and picks up a loaded set. It then takes the loaded set to the pier apron again, arriving before the last of the previously loaded set has been emptied. Depending on the length of the haul and the coordination of the entire job, one tractor may be able to keep two or three hooks supplied. A forklift truck should be employed with the tractor-trailer combination to load the trailers or empty them on the dock. No forklift is needed under the hook, because the loads are hoisted from or landed directly on the trailer bed.

Assuming an ideal operation, then, the following would be needed: three trailer trains, one tractor, and one forklift truck. Only four men would be required, assuming all pallets were loaded and stacked on the dock, awaiting this operation. As the distance from the loaded pallets to the pickup point on the pier apron decreased, eventually it would become more economical to do away with the tractor-trailer combination and bring in another forklift. Any given operation must be analyzed carefully on its own merits.

The Forklift Truck

The forklift truck is the most widely used piece of handling equipment. The load is supported on a pallet that is carried on a pair of parallel bars that protrude in front of the truck body itself. These bars or forks are thin and slightly beveled and are attached to the truck by a sturdy frame. Almost all of these trucks used on marine terminals are equipped with hydraulic lifting devices capable of raising loads for high-level tiering. The fork truck may be driven by electricity, gasoline, gas-electric power, diesel engine, or engines using liquefied petroleum gas as a fuel. It is extremely flexible, handling loads on either skids or pallets. It handles some commodities without the use of a pallet, such as rolls of paper, bales, and lumber. Some models are able to stack loads with a 48-inch depth as high as 15 feet. There are many attachments for the fork truck that enable it to handle special commodities without pallets. Figure 8-24 shows some of the different types of attachments.

The Capacity of the Forklift Truck

The capacity that a forklift truck can carry may be stated as a given weight with the center of gravity a given distance from the face of the forks. For example, it may be given as 4,000 pounds at 15 inches. This means that the truck will carry a maximum load of 4,000 pounds with the center of gravity no more than 15 inches forward from the heel of the forks. If the center of gravity is closer than 15 inches the maximum load is still 4,000 lb. If the distance is greater than 15 inches, the maximum load is less than 4,000 pounds. This is explained below.

LOAD-CARRYING POWERED TRUCK

For specialized work a four-wheeled nonelevating platform truck may be used. This type of truck was one of the first mechanized trucks used on marine terminals. Its greatest disadvantage for general cargo work on the marine terminal is quite apparent: the operator must rely on a second device for loading and discharging, and it transports only one unit at a time. Exactly the same function can be accomplished by one trailer with a tractor, and adding two additional trailers removes the necessity of the tractor being tied up at either end of its run; this is a great increase in efficiency. However, use may be found for this type of equipment on certain types of jobs; those that are occasional in nature, require careful control of the load, and include very heavy loads. Some models of powered trucks are capable of carrying 10 tons. The platforms of these trucks may be at variable heights off the deck. Some models have platform heights of between 20 and 24 inches. Lower-platform models have heights of only 11 inches.

The greater the weights that are carried, the more concern there should be about the height of the platform. A worker should lift packages weighing between 150 and 200 pounds no higher than the knee, and then only when he/she is trained to lift properly. Packages of 75 to 100 pounds should be lifted only waist high, although they can be transported at shoulder level if loaded onto the man from shoulder height by helpers. Packages of 25 to 35 pounds may be lifted shoulder high.

HIGH- AND LOW-LIFT ELEVATING PLATFORM TRUCKS

These trucks are designed to pick up loads on skids, transport them, and deposit them without the aid of an assisting device. In other words, they are self-loading and -discharging. The skid is a platform built over side runners or stringers so that there is about 6 to 8 inches clearance under the skid bed. The skid also may be constructed of angle iron with stilts at the four corners.

This type of truck was first introduced in industrial plants about 1915, four years before the first forklift truck was built. The load on this type of truck is carried over the wheels and does not extend out in front of the body. This fact makes it possible to construct the trucks to handle very heavy loads without having to put equally heavy counterbalancing weights at the rear. Some models are capable of handling loads up to 30 tons, but these are obviously not the type of equipment to be found working on the average marine terminal.

The high- and low-lift elevating platform truck represents the first improvement beyond the nonelevating platform truck. It is many times more efficient than the simple load-carrying truck because it is a self-loader and -unloader when used in conjunction with the skid. The terminal time is reduced to a minimum.

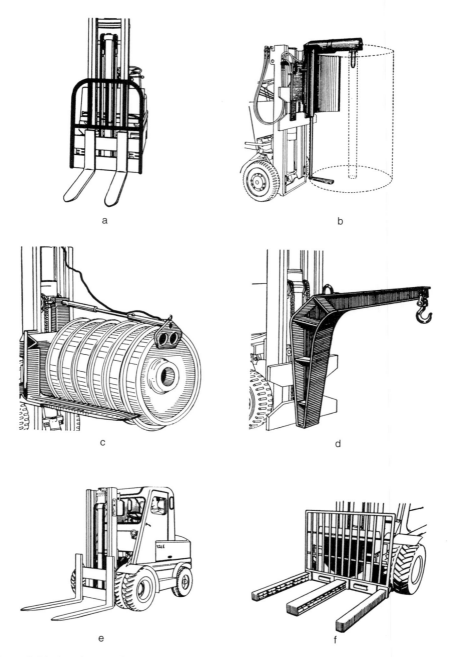

Figure 8-24. Attachments for the forklift truck. **(a)** Load backrest. **(b)** Bartel device for rolls of newsprint. **(c)** Car wheel handling device. **(d)** Gooseneck boom. **(e)** Detachable cab. **(f)** Gripping forks for bricks and cinder blocks.

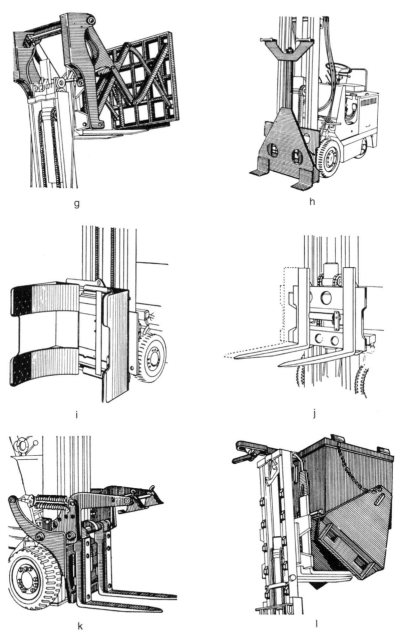

Figure 8-24 (continued). (g) Pallet unloader used with pallet plate eliminates need for pallets. **(h)** Hydraulic crate clamp device. **(i)** Revolving roll clamping device. **(j)** Side shifter attachment for positioning loads to left or right. **(k)** Clamp and fork attachment for handling tin plate safely. **(l)** Bottom dumping hopper.

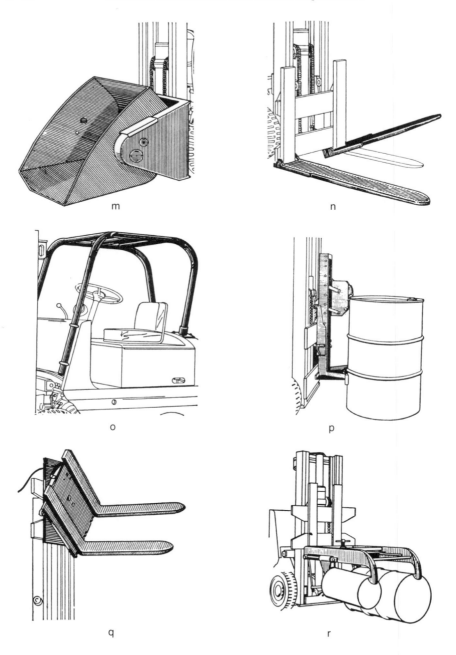

Figure 8-24 (continued). (m) Shovel scoop for handling loose free-flowing materials. **(n)** Fork extensions for handling materials of greater depth. **(o)** Canopy guard. **(p)** Vertical drum handling attachment. **(q)** Revolving forks for dumping skid bins. **(r)** Horizontal drum handling device.

Figure 8-24 (continued). (s) End dump hopper for safe handling of steel scrap, forgings, and so forth. **(t)** Triple lift attachment increases the telescopic range of forklift to 16½ feet. **(u)** Hydraulic clamping device for bales, boxes, drums, and fragile containers. **(v)** Carton clamping device for handling large fragile cartons.

CLAMP TRUCKS

The clamp truck is a type of forklift truck. The forks are replaced by an attachment capable of gripping a container between two arms and raising it off the deck. The truck then transports the item and sets it down where desired. In other words, this device accomplishes all that the forklift truck does, but without the use of a pallet. Figure 8-24u shows a clamp truck picking up a roll of paper. The load may be a single item or in units. If in units, these should be strapped together or carefully stacked and handled with a broad-faced gripping device (see Fig. 8-24v). The containers must be capable of withstanding the pressure of the gripping plates without being damaged.

The development of flexible gripping arms made of gripping steel has made it possible to lift palletless loads of compressed gas cylinders nine at a time, a

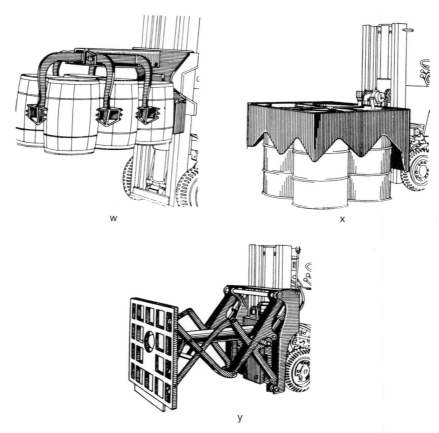

w   x

y

Figure 8-24 (continued). (w) Multiple barrel handling attachment. **(x)** Multiple drum handling attachment. **(y)** Hydraulically operated pusher attachment equipped with ram for pushing off coils of steel, wire, and similar materials. *Courtesy Yale and Towne Manufacturing Co.*

stack of automobile tires, and other such units. The gripping arms can be placed on any lift truck clamp. Each pressure plate is loosely mounted on three spring-steel fingers. This allows the pressure plate to tilt in the direction or directions dictated by the load shape and provides for proper load distribution among the fingers. Further accommodation is permitted by the individual flexing of the fingers. The design of the arm structure is such that as seen from the front, each pressure plate toes in at the bottom. As seen from the top, the pressure plates toe in at the front. These features make it possible to accommodate variations in the size of objects in the load and also to apply a pressure tending to hold the load together. The pressure can be set to suit the load by means of a dial at the operator's position. A high-friction plastic coating bonded to the pressure plate reduces the necessary grab pressure. Capacities run between 1,500 and 2,700 pounds.

CRANE TRUCKS

The crane truck has found considerable use on narrow apron piers in ports. These trucks are able to pick up net slings or pallet sling loads and transfer them with ease. They are popular where the pier structure makes it impossible or inconvenient to utilize the much faster tractor-trailer combinations and/or forklift trucks with pallets. Their terminal time is lengthened because they are not self- loaders or -unloaders, and for the same reason they require extra labor at the terminal within the pier shed.

These trucks find their greatest usefulness when handling certain extremely bulky and awkwardly shaped materials that are best accommodated in a net sling. The boom on these types of trucks cannot be slewed; however, some models incorporate slewing ability into their designs. Because of the limited drift under the boom head and the length of the sling, the boom is fitted with a wide flanged roller on its tip so that the sling with all its parts can be hove up short for transporting the load.

OVERHEAD MONORAILS

Overhead monorails are a means of moving materials about a dock shed of a marine terminal that keeps the deck clear of moving vehicles and utilizes the overhead for roadways. Overhead monorail systems have been used successfully at several piers for over 40 years. At all of these installations, one commodity was continually handled over a fixed route, usually relatively short.

The lack of flexibility of this system is evident. It may be, however, that with additional trackage and suitable methods for switching the trolleys from one track to another from a single control point as well as locally, sufficient flexibility will be incorporated into the overhead monorail system to make its operation not only feasible but highly economical.

FACTORS IN THE DESIGN OF STEVEDORING TRUCKS

Stuffing, stacking, stocking, lifting, breaking out; round loads, square loads, short loads, tall loads; light loads, heavy loads, easy loads, awkward loads—there is probably a greater variety of goods and materials handled in stevedoring than in any other materials handling situation, and as many ways of handling them. Requirements vary from day to day, from ship to ship, and from port to port. No run-of-the-mill, off-the-assembly-line conventional lift truck can handle the immense range of port and stevedore operations.

Maneuverability is exceptionally important in warehouses that are stuffed to capacity, and ships' holds contrive to defeat even the most agile truck. To complicate matters even more, loads are not always neatly stacked on pallets, and forks on a lift truck become useless unless the truck can quickly and readily adapt to the use of one or more attachments.

Stevedore lift truck rated capacities normally range from 6,000 to 70,000 pounds; the need for individual capacities within this broad range will vary with the geographic location of the ports and the range of materials indigenous to these ports. Generally speaking, the popular capacities are 6,000, 8,000, 10,000, 15,000, 20,000, 35,000, 45,000, and 70,000 pounds, with the lower capacities used for stuffing containers and for general terminal work. Medium-capacity trucks handle steel, lumber, and heavier loads, whereas the upper end of the range is used for container handling (see Figs. 8-25 and 8-26).

Ports on the southern Atlantic seaboard are finding that the 8,000-pound truck is being replaced by 10,000-pound pneumatic-tire units that are versatile and maneuverable and can stand the derating encountered when attachments must be substituted for forks. In the Port of Savannah, Georgia, for example, the Clark C500 Y100 is gradually becoming the all-purpose truck for general terminal use; this truck has the agility to work even in ships' holds. It can easily handle loads up to 10,000 pounds with forks, and can carry 8,000 pounds in most instances where an attachment must be employed. These same trucks must be flexible and adaptable enough to handle the assignments of the busy period, which are commonly dictated by the cargo configuration, size, and weight. Forks, roll clamps, bale clamps, carton clamps, rams, side shifters, quick-change couplers, detachable host reels, and other attachments become important handling instruments, and the lift truck with which they work must have the capability to switch devices in minutes as the applications demanded change,

Figure 8-25. Container forklift.

Figure 8-26. 80,000-pound diesel pneumatic tires truck. *Courtesy Clark Equipment Co.*

thereby minimizing idle truck time, which stevedores can ill afford. There is more at stake than the operator's time when a stevedore truck is idle. Many times a whole crew, who do *not* work for minimum wage, are involved.

Conveyors

On the marine terminal, conveyors are used for loading and unloading trucks, railroad cars, and lighters; for loading and discharging the ship through side ports and through the hatches; and for moving cargo to and from the wings in the holds of the ship.

GRAVITY CONVEYORS

Gravity conveyors are either simple wooden chutes or conveyors made of metal and fitted with steel rollers or wheels. The roller or wheel type conveyors come in sections usually about 5 or 10 feet long and in widths of 18 to 24 inches. They may be either steel or aluminum, and are built to withstand rugged usage. The rollers rotate on free-rolling steel ball bearings. The sections are fitted with bars at one end and hook connectors at the other, which makes possible quick setting up and taking down as needed. They are not made for really heavy loads; the weights transported over them should be limited to about ½ ton.

Wooden conveyors, or chutes, as they are called, are somewhat lighter than the steel roller or wheel conveyors. They must be used in place of the steel type with some cargoes, such as explosives. They are built of surfaced hardwood and are sometimes provided with guard rails. In fact, chutes used to handle explosives must have a 4-inch guard rail by law.

Metal chutes built in a spiral have been used successfully to lower case oil and bagged sugar and coffee into a ship's hold by taking advantage of gravity.

POWERED CONVEYORS

Powered conveyors of many types have been used with great success on marine terminals. These may be classified under four broad headings: (1) endless belt, (2) endless pocket or bucket, (3) screw, and (4) pneumatic elevators or air conveyors. No attempt will be made here to lay down rules or guiding principles.

Endless Belt Conveyors

The endless belt conveyor consists of a belt that runs over a drive pulley from which it derives its power. The belt is mounted on a bed in such a manner that a series of wheels take the burden of the load as the load is placed on top of the bed. The underside of the bed is fitted with one or two idler rollers over which the belt passes as it cycles around the bed. Most goods can be sent up inclines as steep as 32° if the belting is made of some good nonslip material. The use of cleats on the belt enables goods to be lifted up a greater incline. These conveyors may be obtained in portable models as well as permanently installed in a fixed position. Figure 8-27 is an illustration of a portable type endless belt conveyor showing some of the names of the parts and the mechanism that allows it to be

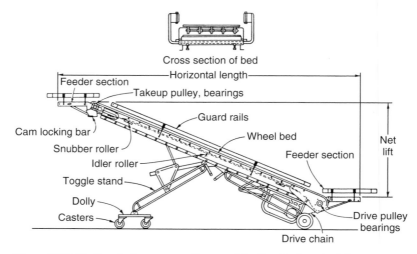

Figure 8-27. Endless belt conveyor. *Courtesy The Rapids-Standard Co.*

adjusted for working at various elevations all the way down to horizontal. These portable models are extremely versatile materials handling tools. They can be used to mechanize the loading of trucks, for loading ships through side ports, for raising cargo from one deck to another where it might be discharged through a side port, and for many similar tasks. When loading ships through the hatches or discharging from side ports where conveyors might be used, gravity types are the most desirable. (Gravity should always be used, if possible.) Figures 8-28 (a) and (b) are portable examples.

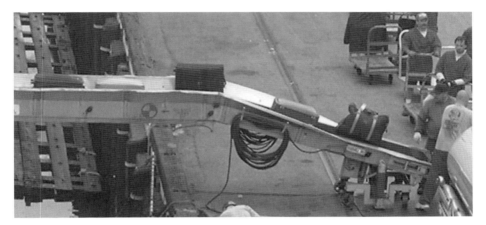

Figure 8-28a. Endless belt conveyor used through a side port. *Courtesy Frederick Kurst.*

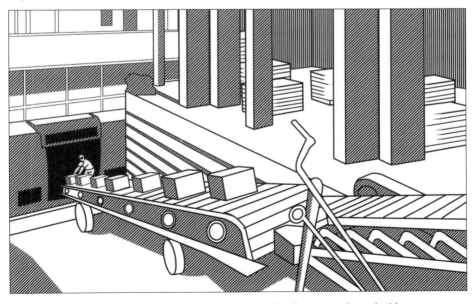

Figure 8-28b. Endless belt conveyor being used for unloading cargo through side port. *Courtesy of Joe Liotta Art & Design.*

Endless Pocket Conveyors

Probably the most intensive users of the endless pocket type conveyor in the marine field are the banana carrying ships. They load and discharge entire loads using conveyors of this.

Air Conveyors

Machines utilizing air suction methods of picking up and carrying materials through a flexible, noncollapsible tube of large diameter are called *air conveyors*. They are used to discharge a number of commodities and there may be wider use of them in the future. Pneumatic elevators for discharging grain fall into this category. They are a conveyor type in the sense that they utilize an air stream as the conveyor belt. Among the commodities that are discharged by air conveyors are bulk copra, grain, and bulk cement. They may be large, permanently installed units or portable units capable of being moved from pier to pier. Floating grain air conveyors (pneumatic elevators) brought alongside the offshore side of the ship are used to discharge full cargoes of grain into waiting barges or coastal steamers at the rate of 250 tons per hour.

Pallets

The pallet, used in conjunction with forklift trucks and, in some operations, with straddle trucks, has become a very important piece of materials handling equipment. The pallet was developed after the platform skid especially for use with the forklift truck. It is far superior to the skid for marine terminal work, for a number of reasons. It is lighter and vertically shorter, and is capable of being quickly and easily tiered without the use of dunnage between each load.

PALLET DEFINITIONS

Before discussing pallets in general, it will be best to define some of the terms that will be used later.

Single Faced: A pallet that has only one deck.

Double Faced: A pallet that has a top and bottom deck.

Reversible: A double-faced pallet with both decks capable of supporting a load.

Two-Way: A pallet that a fork truck may enter from two directions.

Single Wing: A pallet on which the outside stringers are set inboard 4 to 6 inches from the ends of the deck boards of the upper deck but flush with the lower deck boards. This gives a nonreversible double-deck pallet adaptable for use with straddle trucks.

Double Wing: A pallet on which the outside stringers are set inboard an equal distance, about 4 to 6 inches, from the ends of the deck boards of both decks. This is the construction of most stevedoring pallets and allows for the accommodation of the bar and spreader type sling.

Flush: A pallet on which the outside stringers are flush with the ends of the boards of both decks.

Decks: The top and bottom surfaces of the pallet.

Stringers: The separations and supports for the decks, sometimes called "runners."

Chamfers: Beveled edges to permit easy entrance of forks without catching or chipping the end boards.

End Boards: Deck boards on the extreme outside edges of the pallet. These are the most vulnerable parts of the pallet. They should be of the best wood, at least 6 inches in width, and renewed as soon as split.

Drive Screws: Fastening devices for attaching top and bottom deck boards to the stringers. They are either spirally twisted or have annular rings.

SOME PALLET TYPES

There are four basic types of pallets with reference to the type of work for which they are intended. They are the (1) stevedoring, (2) shipping, (3) warehouse, and (4) factory or manufacturing plant pallets. Although this book is mostly concerned with the stevedoring pallet, some comments will be made regarding all four types.

The Stevedoring Pallet

The stevedoring pallet is used to handle cargo on marine terminals, and as such, it receives a good deal of rough treatment. Because of their heavy duty, the stevedoring pallets are made of heavier materials than any of the other types. The stringers are made of 3- by 4-inch or 4- by 4-inch lumber and the deck boards are made of 2-inch-thick deals (nominal size). The end boards should be not less than 6 inches in width and made of no. 1 or 2 grade stock board. The other deck boards may be of random widths not less than 4 inches. The stringers should be 4- by 4-inch material if the length of the pallet is over 6 feet. The fastenings used on stevedoring pallets may be either stove bolts or drive screws 4 inches long with large heads.

The stevedoring pallet must be capable of accommodating a large number of commodity types and sizes and as a result a number of sizes have been used.

For large, bulky packages such as furniture and general household goods, the 4- by 7-foot size has proven convenient. For smaller packages, the 4- by 5-foot size is commonly used.

The Shipping Pallet

The shipping pallet must conserve space and weight as much as possible. It is not loaded, unloaded, and handled as much as the stevedoring pallet and can be made with smaller scantlings throughout. Consideration of the accommodation of the shipping pallet in connecting carriers and in stowage in the ship has led to the use of a few standard sizes that are smaller than the stevedoring pallet. The Navy has indicated that either the 48- by 48-inch or 40- by 48-inch size is the most economical size for palletized loads (see Fig. 8-29a). The latter are the best for transport in the closed truck body, because the truck requires a 40-inch dimension for greatest use of available cubic. If rail transport or truck transport with an open platform bed is used, the 48- by 48-inch pallet is suitable. The average boxcar width is 110 inches, whereas the average truck closed body type has a width of 88½ inches. If the shipping pallet's smallest dimension is 48 inches, two pallet loads cannot be stowed side by side in the closed body truck; this means a great deal of lost cubic during transport. These figures apply only to closed body trucks and boxcars of the United States. When considering transport in other countries, the dimensions of the connecting carriers at the foreign port must be determined for full coordination of the cargo movement. If open flat-bed trucks are used, the 48- by 48-inch pallet can be accommodated. The stringers on the shipping pallet should be of 2- by 4-inch material, whereas the decking should be of only 1-inch boards.

The Warehouse Pallet

The warehouse pallet is used to receive commodities in a warehouse for storage for periods of many months or even years. The materials are palletized as economically as possible, and the pallets are tiered and left in storage. Careful planning of aisle widths and pallet sizes is necessary to obtain efficient use of the available area.

The Factory Pallet

The factory pallet is used to handle special materials in large volume as the material is worked during the manufacturing of some product. Factory pallets must be specially designed in size and strength. It is obvious that in every case a study must be made of the entire procedure and the best pallet determined in the light of the data obtained.

48" × 48" NAVY STANDARD
HARDWOOD PALLET

•

NAILING

a. Use #6 screw gauge x 2½" cement coated or chemically etched drive screw nails or #10 wire gauge x 2½" cement coated or chemically etched annular ring (fetter ring) nails.
b. Boards 3⅝" to 4½" require 2 nails at each bearing point.
   4¾" to 6¾" " 3 " " " " " .
   7" to 9" " 4 " " " " " .
   9⅛" to 11" " 5 " " " " " .
   11⅛" to 12" " 6 " " " " " .
c. Drill deck boards if necessary to prevent splitting.
d. Stagger nails to prevent splitting.
e. Nailing thru notches not acceptable.
f. When a board exceeding 5" nominal width covers a notch, one less nail can be used.

LUMBER

a. Use sound square edge lumber free of decay and free of knots with an average diameter greater than ⅓ of the width of the board. No piece shall contain any defect which would materially weaken the strength of the piece.
b. Use the following woods: white ash, beech, birch, rock elm, hackberry, hickory, hard maple, oak, pecan.
c. Use random width boards 3⅝" or wider, surfaced one side ⅞", hit or miss. Surfaced faces to be exposed faces. All boards on any one face to be of uniform thickness.
d. Space between top deck boards to be 1" min. and 1½" max. Space between bottom deck boards not to exceed 1½" except 11" spaces as noted.
e. Boards must be placed so that each notch is completely covered by a single board of not less than 4" nominal width.
f. Length tolerance plus or minus ¼".
g. Minimum moisture content shall be not less than 12% and the maximum moisture content not to exceed 25% at time of shipment.

•

DEPARTMENT OF THE NAVY
Bureau of Supplies and Accounts

SW RELEASE NO. 52C (Superseding RSX Release No. 52B)

Figure 8-29. (a) U.S. Navy standard pallet.

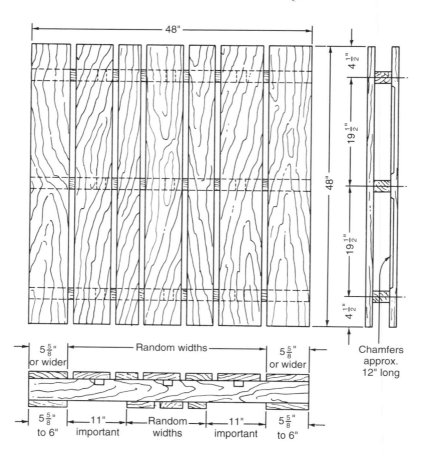

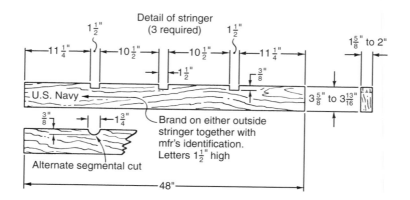

Figure 8-29. (b) U.S. Navy standard pallet.

PALLET PATTERNS

Operations on the commercial marine terminal utilizing the stevedoring pallet do not permit extreme care in building pallet loads. It is sufficient to make certain that the tiers are built up in such a way that one tier ties together with another so that sufficient stability is obtained to keep the load together while it is being transported on the pier.

In the building of loads on pallets for shipment on the pallet, or when the operation makes it possible to exercise care in this matter, greater utilization of the pallet area available can be obtained by building the load in accordance with some definite pattern. When building the pallet load, some items may be allowed to extend beyond the deck of the pallet an inch or so. This may be done with steel drums and cases made of wood. It should be avoided with bagged commodities or cargo in cardboard cartons. Figure 8-30 shows some standard Navy pallet patterns. All possible arrangements on the 48- by 48-inch pallet can be reduced to four basic patterns, which, for the sake of common nomenclature, may be identified as *block, row, pinwheel,* and *brick.*

Block: Square or round containers will always be loaded in this pattern on a 48- by 48-inch pallet. This is the least desirable of all the patterns, in that there can be no cross tiering to tie the load together for stability.

Row: The row pattern is one of the most common and is used with oblong materials for which a multiple of the widths and a multiple of the lengths both approximate 48 inches. An excellent cross tie is provided by placing alternate layers at 90° angles to each other.

Pinwheel: The pinwheel pattern is another widely used pattern for material of an oblong nature that does not readily conform to the row pattern. Cross stacking is easily accomplished by reversing alternate layers. The major objection to this pattern is the fact that there is usually a chimney in the center of the load. This pattern is extremely flexible and can be varied.

Brick: The brick pattern can be used only in a few well-defined instances, namely, with a box whose width is one-half or one-quarter of its length, and whose length is one-half, one-quarter, or one-third of 48 inches. Frequently a box will fit both the pinwheel and the brick pattern. However, when the pinwheel pattern is used, four or eight columns are formed, and this gives less stability to the load.

It must be remembered that these patterns cannot be followed under practical operating conditions on most marine terminals. In the first place, the containers are usually placed on the pallet at the pier for transport to the pier apron only. In the second place, union labor agreements prevent the full utilization of a pallet by limiting the load to a set number of containers or a set height with the last

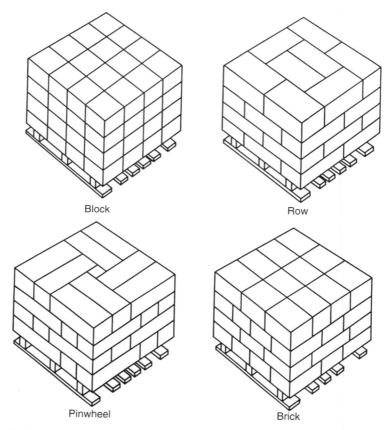

Block   Row

Pinwheel   Brick

Figure 8-30. Basic pallet patterns.

tier frequently used to tie the load together. These pallet patterns are for use on shipping pallets, where space utilization is of importance.

PALLETIZED OPERATIONS TODAY

For the past 40 years containerization has been changing the face of ports throughout the world. A substantial proportion of containerizable cargo, however, has been untouched by the container revolution. In practice these cargoes are not carried in containers either because no container vessel serves the trade concerned or because the port has inadequate container handling facilities.

Uncertain Future

Although it is clear that the pallet is bound to be employed in fruit handling at one stage or another, its full use along the transport chain is still undecided.

Most fruit handling ports are thoroughly in favor of full palletization, since to them it means increased handling efficiency with reduced labor and capital investment costs. Likewise, the advantages to be gained from full containerization from the point of view of the port operator hardly need be spelled out. The variety of vessel types and port facilities in existence, combined with the diverse origins and characteristics of fruit produce, however, prevent any clear resolution of this question in the near future. No doubt unitization methods will be more quickly adopted in the future, especially on those trades to Europe from developed countries, but growth will be less quick in developing countries.

Summary of Advantages of Palletized Loads

1. Less labor required in the handling of palletized materials at all terminals.

2. With palletization, pilferage and damage to individual containers are less possible.

3. Packaging may be eliminated on some products that are palletized properly, resulting in a saving.

4. On some palletized loads, only one or two labels or stencils are required for identification. Without pallets, labeling costs are considerably higher. This is sometimes overlooked as a shipping cost, because labels are applied by a shipping clerk. The cost of preparation of the labels by office help may not be counted into the cost of shipping, of which it is really a part.

5. Less personnel problems are experienced, because fewer men are needed when working with pallet loads. The operation is safer. Fewer men have fewer accidents, and thus insurance premiums should be reduced.

Sling Types

An important part of the materials handling equipment on the marine terminal is the *sling*. As used in this section, "sling" means any device attached to the cargo or its container for the purpose of hoisting it on board the ship. There are many sling types: some might be classified as general slings because they can be used on a large number of container types, and others might be classified as special slings because they are used on only a particular type of container or type of cargo. The choice of sling for any given operation should be made with the objective of maximum safety, minimum delay on the ship and on the dock, and minimum damage to the cargo. Safety is obtained by using slings that give small angles between the parts at the hook and afford an easy and effortless method of attaching and releasing.

Endless Rope or Strap Sling

This is one of the most common slings used (Figs. 8-31 and 8-32). Many ships carry their own supply of these slings when operating in trades in which bagged goods such as coffee or raw sugar are carried in large amounts. For a full loading operation, about 25 slings should be available for every set of gear on the ship. Not all of these will be needed at any one time. However, the mate who doesn't carefully control the number of slings given out will, on some runs, find that many more than 25 per gear will be used. About 8 to 10 slings will keep one gear going; more or less may be required depending on the cycle time of the total operation.

Figure 8-31. Two endless rope slings. Note danger of damaging some of the bags.

Figure 8-32. Endless strap slings are made of polyester.

These slings average about 18 feet in length when made; that is, the rope should be cut in lengths of 36 feet when making them. They should be made out of 3½-inch, three-stranded manila or sisal. When the short splice is completed, there should be no twists in the sling, or they will be difficult to work with. To prevent turns from being worked into the sling as the splice is made, one turn should be thrown out of the sling just before marrying the two ends preparatory to making the splice. This seemingly trivial point is quite important.

The endless fiber rope sling is well adapted to use with bagged goods, if the bags are rough gunnies; bales; tires; single, large, lightweight, but strongly constructed cases; reels of wire; and similar cargoes. This sling should not be used on bags of refined commodities such as refined sugar or flour, nor on bags of cement. Cement bags are unable to withstand the sling pressures; the bottom bags invariably split and spill the contents, causing considerable damage to the cargo plus making a mess of the ship and contaminating other cargo. These slings should not be used for hoisting several small cases or cartons, or for steel products.

THE FIBER ROPE SNOTTER

This is simply a length of rope with an eye splice at each end and generally fitted with a sliding hook. Two of these slings are used on the cargo hook and ride the hook in and out because they are released instantaneously at the end where the load is landed. They are used mainly when handling lumber of the finer grades.

THE WIRE ROPE SNOTTER

This sling is constructed in the same manner as the fiber rope snotter, but it has more uses. Besides being used on lumber of the rougher grades, it is also used on steel products such as pipe, steel rails, and structural steel shapes. Long wire rope snotters without sliding hooks are used to handle some large bulky cases. When used for this purpose, both eyes are placed on the cargo hook and the case rests in the bites thus formed.

THE WEB SLING

This is simply an endless rope sling with a canvas web sewn between the two parts (Fig. 8-33). It is one of the best slings for handling refined bagged products or bagged cement.

Figure 8-33. Web sling.

THE PLATFORM, TRAY, AIRPLANE, OR PALLET SLING

All of these terms are used to describe the wooden platform type sling (Fig. 8-34a). Before pallets were used so widely, this was a simple platform made of 2-inch lumber and fitted with rings at the four corners where four hooks hanging down from a suitable spreader could be engaged. The rings on the platform have now been removed and bars are now used to fit between the upper and lower decks outside of the runner or stringer on the double type pallet. The bars hang from a spreader, which is required to keep sling pressures from bearing against the containers piled on the platform. This is the most widely used sling in ports where forklift trucks are used to handle the pallet. It has always been a popular sling, however. These slings may be used safely for almost all types of cargo, including cartons, crates, cases, bagged goods, cylinders, barrels, drums, carboys, furniture, and short lengths of lumber or pipe. There may be some situations in which the platform sling is used where the web or endless rope sling would actually be better. Such operations might include the handling of some bagged commodities and also of baled goods. The principal reason for the rope slings being superior in these cases is that with them less delay is caused by having to return a number of slings after the landing spot is clogged with empties. An all-metal platform sling is shown in Figure 8-34b.

CHAIN SLING

Chain slings are used when handling heavy concentrated cargoes such as pigs of iron, lead, tin plate, or copper bars. They are safer than wire rope because they stand up better with such heavy loads.

CANT OR CHIME HOOKS

These are used exclusively for hoisting several drums or cask type containers at one time. They are also used for hoisting hogsheads of tobacco but the hook is very broad and offers several inches of bearing surface.

FIBER ROPE NET

The fiber rope net is made of interwoven 2-inch fiber rope in sizes of about 12- by 12-feet square. For loading of some products these nets may be lined with canvas. They are used for bagged goods, mail, single cases, or heavy-duty drums. When lined, they are used for bulk products such as brazil nuts or fertilizer. They should not be used for crates and cases in general, because excessive sling pressures are exerted and damage to the cargo will result. They are also poor slings for lightweight drums for the reason just mentioned, and if used, some leakers are almost certain to develop.

Figure 8-34. (a) Airplane or platform sling. This picture shows the use of spreaders and safety nets to prevent cargo from falling off. *Courtesy Peck and Hale, Inc.* **(b)** All-metal platform sling with two pallets of bagged coffee. Note absence of protective grating due to necessity of providing access to pallets for forklifts.

Figure 8-35. Chime or cant hooks.

Figure 8-36. Unloading bales of paper using a net sling.

WIRE ROPE NET

The wire rope net (Fig. 8-37) has some special uses. One of the most common is for handling rubber bales.

CRATE CLAMPS

The crate clamp is used not only for crates as the name implies, but also on reels of wire cable and rolls of heavy paper. It is an excellent sling for crated

Figure 8-37. Wire rope net sling. Rubber bales are handled in this type of sling.

automobiles and similar containers because it can be applied and released quickly and because with its use there is no accumulation of slings at either end of the hook's travel.

SIDE DOGS

Side dogs are used exclusively for handling steel plates. When plates are extremely long and limber, more than one pair should be used. Even as many as three pair may be required to prevent the bending of the plates.

DOG HOOKS

Dog hooks are similar to crate clamps. The difference is that the dog hook is attached to the bottom of the crate or case and, because, of the dog-leg shape of the hook's shank, they set in place securely. When a strain is taken on the cargo fall, they tend to grip the bottom and will not slip off. They have the advantage over crate clamps in that they are a little less likely to be accidentally released, but they are more difficult to set in place than are crate clamps.

BALE HOOKS

Bale hooks consist of about eight to 10 snotters of 2- or 2½-inch fiber rope spliced into a steel ring. At the lower end of each snotter, which is about 6 to 8 feet long, a hook is attached having a shank of about 8 inches in length. The ring is placed on the cargo hook after the smaller hooks on the several snotters have been engaged on the steel bands of the bales. At least two bands should be engaged on each bale to prevent one band from taking the entire weight and perhaps breaking. Bale hooks cannot be used on bales that are extremely heavy. They are commonly used on wool bales of 200 or 300 pounds each.

BALE TONGS

Bale tongs (Fig. 8-38) are levered tongs similar to ice tongs. They are used to handle cotton bales and make an excellent sling because they can be applied and removed with great speed.

Figure 8-38. Bale tongs hoisting three cotton bales at one time. *Courtesy of Joe Liotta Art & Design.*

Figure 8-39. One type of newsprint sling. *Courtesy of Joe Liotta Art & Design.*

NEWSPRINT SLING

Newsprint is easily damaged by cutting the outer surface or denting the edges of the ends, and the slings for use with this commodity are generally designed to reduce the possibility of this happening, which is high with the endless rope sling. These types of slings are good examples of specialized slings developed because no general sling could be well adapted to handling this commodity (Fig. 8-39). As said before, the endless rope sling is often used for hoisting newsprint, but it is not a good sling for the purpose.

THE PIE PLATE

The pie plate is a circular platform placed in a rope net sling to prevent sling pressures from damaging cargo hoisted in the net. It is an awkward sling and should be avoided if at all possible (see Fig. 8-40).

TRUCK AND AUTO SLINGS

There are a number of designs of slings for handling automobiles that are not crated. Improvised slings generally cause damage of some type to any car hoisted by them. A specially constructed sling with ample spread between the vertical parts should always be used (Fig. 8-41).

Figure 8-40. The pie plate used with a fiber rope net.

Figure 8-41. One type of automobile sling. *Courtesy of Joe Liotta Art & Design.*

U12

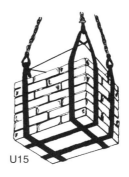

U15

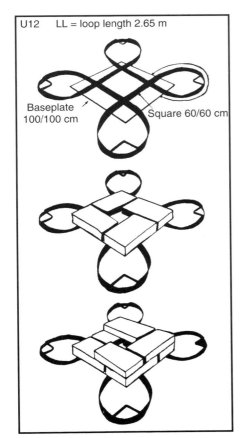

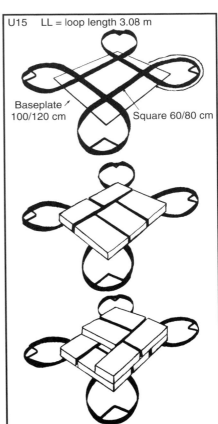

Figure 8-42. The Span Set Unisling is made of synthetic fiber—polyester yarn sealed between two layers of plastic foil. The sling is endless, without a seam, and less dependent on specially shaped lifting hooks. (Note: For woven webbing slings, special hooks are to be used in order to keep the sling flat.) The base plate is welded to the sling and not stitched or clamped. *Courtesy Span Set Unisling.*

Special Slings

On many pieces of machinery and certain odd-shaped units of considerable bulkiness and/or weight, slings will be found attached when the cargo arrives at the pier. Great care must be taken not to allow such a sling to become lost or damaged during the voyage. If it is removed, note carefully how it was attached.

The UNISLING

The Unisling unitizes bags and cartons and is designed for one-way use from the shipper to the consignee. It is made of synthetic fiber, namely, a polyester endless yarn sealed between two layers of polyethylene or plasticized paper. The base plate protects the cargo and ensures quick and easy stacking. The broad, flat bands guarantee a wide bearing area, reducing the risk of cutting bags. Once loaded aboard a vessel, this sling is unhooked and left intact about the cargo (see Fig. 8-43). It thus facilitates unloading at the port of discharge.

Figure 8-43. Similar to the UNISLING, the Marino sling is shown around bags of coffee, ready for discharge.

Stowage Factors of Commonly Carried Breakbulk Commodities

Commodity	Most Common Package(s)	Average Stowage Factor
A		
Abalone	Bags/cases	80/90
Acetate of lime	Drums/casks	80/90
Acetone	Drums/casks	80/90
Achiote (annatto)	Cases	60/64
Acid oil	Deep tank	42
Agar-agar	Bales	70/75
Ajwan seed (ajowan)	Bags	77/80
Alabaster (gypsum)	Bags	43/46
Albumen, dry	Tins in cases	57
Albumen, moist	Tins in cases	46
Alburnum	Bags	57
Alcohol	Barrels/drums	75
Alkanet	Cases	49
Alkyl benzene	Drums/bulk	50/41
All spice (Jamaica pepper or pimento)	Bags	120/130
Almonds	Cases/bags/hogs heads	73/74/120
Aloes	Cases	40
Alum	Cases/casks	53/58
Alumina	Bulk	18/24
Aluminum	Ingots	29
Aluminum ore	Bags/bulk	40/28
Aluminum scrapfoil	Bags/bales	50
Alunite	Bulk	26
Amber	Cases	37
Amblygonite	Bulk	30

Animal meal	Bags	54
Aniseed	Bags	120
Aniseed oil	Tins in cases	50
Annatto	Barrels	91
Antimony oil	Bags/cases/bulk	20/25/18
Apples	Barrels/cases/cartons	95/85/95
Apricot kernels	Bags/cases	85/90
Arachides (monkey nuts)	Cases/bags/unshelled	68/70/100
Arachis oil (groundnutoil)	Barrels/bulk	60/62
Aragoes	Cases	39
Archill	Casks/bales	41/88
Arecanuts (betelnut)	Bags	59
Arrack	Barrels/cases	72/55
Arrowroot	Cases/bags	70/53
Arsenic	Cases/kegs	24/33
Asafetida	Cases	43
Asbestos	Cases/bags	55/120
Asbestos cement	Bags	65
Asbestos ore	Bags	70
Asbestos powder	Bags	83
Asparagus (canned)	Cases	45
Asphalt (devil'sdrugs)	Drums/barrels/bulk	45/50/33
Automobiles	Crates/unboxed	150–300

B		
Bacon	Cases	59
Balata	Bags	57
Balsam copaiba	Kegs/bottles/cases	60/65/55
Bambara groundnut	Bags	67
Bambooblinds	Bales	125
Bamboopoles	Bundles	70
Bambooreeds	Bundles	67
Bamboosplits	Bales/bundles	100/200+
Bananas	Cartons	135
Barbedwire	Reels	58
Barilla	Casks	34
Barjari	Bags	54
Barks	Bales	150

Barley	Bags/bulk	60/54
Basil	Bales	120
Bauxite	Bulk	29
Bdellium	Cases	78
Beans		
Alexandria	Bulk	48
Black	Bags	52
Castor	Bags	60
Cocoa	Bags	78
Dried	Bags	50
Horse	Bags	60
Jarry	Bags	100
Lima	Bags	65
Locust	Bulk	84
Soya	Bulk	50
Beanoil	Cases/barrels/bulk	53/63/39
Bêche-de-mer (trepang)	Bale	143
Beer	Casks/hogsheads/cases/ cartons	55/57/70/75
Beeswax	Barrels/cases	73/68
Belladonna	Bags	93
Benjamin	Bundles	53
Bennin seed	Bags	54
Beryllium ore	Bags	20
Bidi leaves	Bags	250+
Billets	Bags	12
Birie leaves	Bags	250+
Bismuth metal	Boxes/ingots	11/7
Bismuth ore	Bags	31
Bitumen	Barrels/drums	45/50
Blacklead	Kegs	49
Blackwood	Logs	53
Bleaching powder	Drums	78
Blende	Bulk	22
Blood, dried	Bags	43
Bones	Bulk/bags	94/65
Bone grist	Bags	67
Bone manure	Bags	65
Bone meal	Bags	43

Borax	Casks/bags	54/43
Boric acid	Barrels/cases	65/57
Boussir	Bags	65
Bran	Bags	110
Brazil nuts	Bags/bulk	92/83
Bricks	Bulk	25
Bristles	Cases	70
Brunak (poonac)	Bags/bales	79/76
Burlap	Bales	64
Butter	Cases/cartons/kegs/tins	52/54/63/73
Butterfat, dried	Cases	77
Butternuts	Bags	103

C		
Calaba beans	Bags	80
Calaena ore	Bags	17
Camphine	Drums	63
Camphor	Cases (tin lined)	63
Camphor oil	Drums	70
Canada balsam	Casks	53
Canary seed	Bags	53
Canella alba	Bales	130
Canes	Bundles/bales	100/120
Canned goods	Cases/cartons	55/60
Caoutchouc capsicums	Varies	153
Caraway seed	Bags	60
Carbon black (lampblack)	Kegs/bags/paper cartons	117/113/110
Cardamoms	Cases/bags	95/103
Carnarina	Bags	48
Carob	Bulk	87
Carpets (approx.)	Bales/rolls	170/150
Casein	Bags/cases	68/65
Cashew kernels	Cases	70
Cashew nuts	Bags	75–90
Cashew nut oil	Bulk/drums	38/88
Casings	Casks/kegs	73/63
Cassia	Cases/bundles/bales	163/115/160
Cassia buds	Cases	133

Castor oil	Barrels	61
Castor seeds	Bags	83
Catechu (Cutch)	Cases/bags	54/63
Cattle meal	Bags	73
Caustic soda	Drums	34
Caviar	Cases	53
Celery seed	Bags	75
Cement	Casks	42
Cement, boiler	Double bags	64
Cement, color	Drums	63
Cement, Portland	Casks/bulk/drums	38/22/37
Cerasein	Barrels	67
Chalk	Barrels/bulk	43/38
Charcoal (wood)	Bags/bulk	100/180
Chasam (chussums)	Bales	77
Cheese, processed	Cases	57
Chestnuts	Cases/bags	123/190
Chickpeas (grams)	Bags	57
Chicle	Bags	57
Chicory	Bags/tins in cases	58–66/75
Chilies, dry	Bags/bundles	103/225
China bark (cinchona)	Bales	110
China clay (kaolin)	Bulk/casks/bags	39/44/48
China grass (rheafiber)	Pressed/bales	48/70
China root	Cases/bags	94/103
China wood oil (tung oil)	Barrels/tins in cases/bulk	64/57/38
Chiretta	Bundles	350–400
Chrome ore	Bulk/cases	13/16
Chussums	Bales	77
Chutney	Casks	39
Cigars and cigarettes	Cases	175
Cinchona (Peruvian bark)	Bales	140
Cinnabar	Bags	19
Cinnamon	Bundles/cases	135/100
Citron	Bags/cases	70
Citronella	Drums	77
Civet leaves	Bags	240
Clay	Bulk	20

Clover seed	Bags/barrels	53/50
Cloves	Bales	115
Clove oil	Drums	63
Cobalt	Bulk/bags	19/12
Coca	Bags	85
Cochineal	Cases (tin lined)	63
Cocoa (cacao)	Bags/cases	75/88
Coconuts	Bags/bulk	95/98
Coconut cake	Bags/bales	79/76
Coconut, desiccated	Cases	75
Coconut fiber (coir)	Bales	100
Coconut oil	Casks/drums/bulk	67/60/39
Coconut shell, broken	Bags	63
Coffee	Bags	70
Coke	Bulk	70–100
Colocynth	Bales	105
Colombite ore	Bags	21
Colombo root, meal	Bags	95
Colombo root	Bales/bags	100/110
Colza oil (rapeseed oil)	Barrels	61
Colza seed (rapeseed)	Bulk	35
Condensed milk	Tins in cases	45
Copal, gum	Cases	80 (approx.)
Copper	Ingots/barrels	11/14
Copper concentrate	Bulk/bags	/slabs
Copper cuttings	Bales	115
Copper matte	Bulk/bags	17/20
Copper pyrites, yellowsulfur	Bulk	21
Copperas	Casks	55
Copra	Bags/bulk	102/73
Copra cake	Bags	63
Copra expeller pellets	Bulk	63
Copra meal	Bags	83
Coquilla nuts	Bags	63
Coral	Bags	90
Corestock	Crates	140
Coriander seed	Bags	123
Cork	Bales/hard pressed	300–420/220

Cork shavings	Bales/bags	280–300
Corn (maize)	Bulk/bags	48/53
Corn flour	Bags	48
Corozo nuts	Bags	63
Corundum ore	Bags/bulk	43/23
Costusroot	Bags	115
Cotton	Bales	79
Cottonseed	Bulk/bags	64–100
Cottonseed cake	Bales/loose	52/58
Cottonseed oil	Barrels/bulk	61/39
Cotton waste	Bales	150
Cowgrass seed	Sacks	62
Cowrie shells	Bags	47
Cowtail hair	Bales	73
Cream of tartar (argal)	Barrels	63
Creosote	Barrels/drums/bulk	59/60/67
Cubeb (tailed pepper)	Bags	80
Cube gambler	Package	115
Cubic niter–nitrate of soda	Bags	37
Cubic niter–saltpeter	Bags/bulk	37/34
Cudbear	Bales	87
Cumin seed	Bags	80–105+
Curios	Cases	150–180
Currants	Cases	48
Cuttlefish	Cases	150

D		
Damar	Cases/bags	67/65
Dari jowaree	Bags	55
Detergents	Bulk liquid	45
Dhall dal	Bags	50–75
Divi-divi	Bags	117
Dodder (hellweed)	Bags	105
Dogs' droppings	Bags	67
Dog skins	Bales	105
Dogtail seed	Sacks	88
Dom nuts	Bags	55–120
Dragon's blood	Cases	85

Dried blood	Bags	57
Dripping	Casks	73
Dur-dur	Bags	87
Durra	Bags	57

E		
Ebony	Bulk	58
Egg albumen	Cases/crates	95/110
Eggs, desiccated	Cases	74
Egg yolk liquid	Tins in cases	43
Egg yolk powder	Tins in cases	78
Emery	Bags	25
Esparto grass	Bales	130–170
Ethyl hexanol	Bulk	45

F		
Farina	Bags/cases	57
Feathers	Pressed bales	65–90
Feldspar	Bags	35–40
Felt	Rolls/bales	60–150
Fennel seed	Bags	95
Ferromanganese	Bags	16
Fescue seed	Sacks	130
Fiber root	Bales	185
Figs	Cases/baskets	47/50
Firecrackers	Cases	95
Fish manure (meal)	Bales/bags	62/65
Fish oil	Barrels/bulk	58–62/39
Flavin	Cases	44–48
Flax	Bales	85–155
Flax seed	Bags/bulk	60/50
Flour	Barrels/sacks/bags	60/49/45
Fluorine	Cases	85–105
Flourite (fluorspar)	Mats	34
Foggrass seed	Sacks	170
Formaldehyde	Barrels	55–60
Fossilwax	Drums	67
Frankincense	Drums	63

Fruit, dried	Cases	73
Fuller's earth	Bags	40
Furs	Cases, boxes, or bales	100–150
Fustic	Bulk	70–90

G		
Galangal	Bales	95–150
Galena (lead ore)	Bags/bulk	16/13
Galls (gallnuts)	Cases/bags	78–100/83
Gallnut extract	Cases	45
Galvanized iron	Packages/coils	26/30
Gambier	Bales/cases/baskets	97/110/120
Gamboge	Cases	68
Garlic	Bags	95
Garnet ore	Bags	19
Gasoline	Cases/drums	51/63
Gelatin	Cases/bags	65/60
Geneva (Hollands Schiedam)	Cases	60
Gentian root	Bales	123
Ghee	Tins in cases	53
Gingelly (sesame)	Bags	59
Ginger	Cases/casks	73/61
Ginger root	Bags	88
Ginseng	Baskets	115
Glass	Crates	50
Glaxo	Cartons/bags	80/95
Glucose	Cases/barrels	43/47
Glue	Bales/drums/casks/bags	175/120/115/125
Glue refuse	Casks	48
Glycerin	Cases/drums/bulk	42/50/29
Gold slag	Bags	15
Granite	Blocks	17
Graphite (plumbago)	Kegs/cases/bags	49/47/43
Grass cloth	Cases	100–110
Grass seeds	Bags	50–100
Greases	Barrels/drums	55/65
Guano	Bulk/bag	40/43
Guinea corn	Bags	52

Gum, gum resin	Bags	50–65
Gum olibanum (bdellium)	Cases/bales	68/66
Gunny sacks	Bales	50–65
Gutta-percha (gutta)	Bags/cases	85/80
Gypsum	Bags/bulk	44/38

H		
Hair, human	Cases/bales	70/62
Hay	Bales	120–160
Hematite	Bulk	12–15
Hemp	Pressed bales	92–105
Hemp seed	Bags/bulk	70/53
Henequen (sisalhemp)	Bales	90–130
Herbs	Cases/bags	190/120
Herring	Barrels	45–62
Hessians	Bales	50–65
Hominy, chopped	Bags	53–60
Honey	Barrels/drums	47/40
Hoof tips	Bags	90–100
Horns	Loose	100
Horns havings	Bags	150–180
Horse hair	Bales	70–100

I		
Illipe nuts	Bags	63
Ilmenite sand	Bulk	13
Indigo, paste	Casks	77
Indigo, powder	Cases	62
Infusorial earth	Bags	90
Iron, pig	Bulk	11
Isinglass	Casks/bales	91/98
Istle (Ixtle)	Bales	95
Ivory	Bundles/cases	35/57
Ivory nuts	Bags	63
Ivory scrap	Barrels	67

J		
Jaggery	Bags	47
Jarrah wood	Bulk	30
Jarry beans	Bags	100
Jelatong	Cases	73
Jowareedari (jowar)	Bags	54
Juniper berries	Bags	81
Jute	Bales	66
Jute butts	Bales	59
Jute caddles	Bales (pressed)	88
Jute cuttings	Bales	56

K		
Kainite	Bag/bulk	39/36
Kapok	India bale/pressed bale	63/145
Kapok seed oil	Bulk	39
Kauri gum	Bags/cases	70/63
Kerosene	Cases/drums/barrels	51/63/64
Kieselguhr	Bags	52
Kola nuts	Bags	75
Kolai	Bags	57
Kraft liner board	Reels	57
Kyanite	Bulk/bags	20/33

L		
Lac dye	Cases	77
Lamp black (carbon black)	Kegs/bags/cartons	117/113/110
Lard	Cases/pails/tierces	57/73/63
Lard oil	Barrels	63
Latex	Bulk/drums	37/53
Lead concentrates	Bulk	13
Lead, pig	Pigs/ingots	9/11
Lead, sheet	Cases/rolls	21/18
Lead, white	Kegs	26
Leather	Bales/cases/rolls	85/70/up to 200
Lentils	Bags	53
Licorice	Bales	96
Licorice extract	Barrels	63

Licorice extract paste	Cases	47
Lignum vitae	Bulk	27
Lily bulbs	Cases	53
Lime, hydrated (calciumhydrate)	Bags/casks	41/46
Lime, borate of	Bags	52
Lime, cirate of	Bags	83
Lime juices	Cases/barrels	55/75
Linen, flax	Bales	100
Linen, tow	Bales	100
Linoleum	Rolls	70
Linseed	Bags/bulk	59/56
Linseed cake	Bags/bulk	50/55
Linseed oil	Barrels/bulk	67/38
Liqueurs	Bottles in cases	70
Locust beans	Bulk	84
Locust meal	Bags	85
Logs	Bulk	75–130
Logwood	Bundles	90
Lubricating oil	Cases/barrels/drums	47/59/56
Lucerne	Bags	107
Lupin seed	Sacks	65

M		
Macaroni	Cases	85
Mace	Cases/bags	90/73
Madder	Bales	65–80
Magnesite, dead burned	Bulk	25
Magnetite	Bulk	16
Mahogany (acajou)	Logs/boards	28/43
Mail	Bags	100–150
Maize (hominy)	Bulk/bags	48/53
Malt	Bags/tanks	93/67
Manganese ore	Bulk/bags	17/24
Mangrove bark	Bags/bales	77/75
Manioc, mandioca meal	Cases/bags/bulk	90/95/63
Manjeet	Bales	65–80
Manola	Bags	78

Manure	Bags/bulk	40–55/43
Marble	Blocks/slabs/crates	16/19/21
Marjoram	Bales	200–240
Matches	Cases	100–130
Mathieseed (methey)	Bags	95
Mats, matting	Mats/rolls/bales	100–220
Meat meal	Bags	83
Metal borings and cuttings	Bulk	25–50
Methylated spirits	Barrels/drums	73/71
Micatalc	Cases/bags	40/50
Middlings, semitin pollards	Bags	75
Milk, malted	Bottles in cases	93
Milk, powdered	Cartons/cases/bags	63/80/68
Millet durra	Bags	51
Mirabolans	Pockets/bags	71/73
Mirabolan extract	Bags/cases	47/36
Mohair	Bags/bales	250/125
Molasses	Casks/bulk	55/27
Molasses, concentrated	Baskets	41
Molybdenum ore	Bags	20
Monezite	Bags	50
Morocco leather	Rolls/bales/cases	200/100/110
Moss	Bales	300–600
Mother of pearl	Cases	46
Mowa (mowrah)	Bags	65
Mowa or mowrah cake	Bags	59
Musk (musquash)	Bales/cases	100/150
Mustard seed	Bags	56–70
Mustard seed oil	Cases/drums	50/54

N		
Nails	Cases/bags/kegs	30/27/33
Neat's-foot oil	Barrels/drums	61/73
Nickel ore	Barrels/bags/ingots	24/20/12
Niger seed	Bags	63
Niger seed cake	Bags	55
Niger seed oil	Barrels	62
Nitrates	Bags	40

Nutmegs	Cases	60–70
Nuts	Bags	Varies
Nux vomica	Bags	63

O		
Oak	Staves	53
Oakum	Bales/pressed bales	95/73
Oatmeal	Bags	68
Oats, clipped	Bags/bulk	74/66
Oats, unclipped	Bags/bulk	83/76
Ochre puree	Drums/barrels/bags	50/60/80
Oil cakes	Bags	55–70
Oiticica oil	Drums	33
Oleostearin	Bags	68
Olives	Kegs	69
Olive oil	Barrels/drums	60/62
Onions	Cases/crates/bags	80/82/88
Oranges	Cases/cartons	88/63
Orange oil	Barrels/cases	50/70
Orchella	Bales	95
Ores	Bulk/bags	Varies

P		
Paint	Drums	19
Palm kernels	Bulk/bags	55/65
Palm nut oil	Barrels/bulk	59/38
Palm oil	Barrels/bulk	59/39
Paper	Rolls	85
Paper pulp (dry)	Bales	47
Paper pulp (wet)	Bales	54
Paraffin wax	Bags/barrels/cases	53/73/71
Patchouli patch	Bales/bulk	160/400
Peas	Bags/bulk	53/48
Peacake	Bales	51
Peanuts	Bags	63
Pea pulp	Bags	67
Pepper (black)	Bags	86
Pepper (white)	Bags	75

Phormium	Bales	95
Phosphate rock	Bulk	34
Piassaba (piassava)	Bales	105
Pimento	Bags	125
Pineapples	Cases/crates	58/73
Pistachio nuts	Cases/drums	73/63
Pitch	Barrels/bulk	48/33
Plantains	Bunches	130
Plywood	Crates/bundles	77/73
Podophyllum ernodi	Bags	95
Poppy seed	Bags	71
Poppy seed cake	Bags	57
Pork	Tierces	61
Potash	Bags/bulk	37/33
Potash, caustic	Drums	28
Potassium, chlorate of	Kegs	56
Potatoes	Barrels/bags/cartons	73/60/62
Prawns	Bags/cartons	85/100
Preserved meats	Cases	60
Prunes	Casks/cases	55/51
Pumice	Bags	110
Puree, yellow ochre	Barrels	55
Putchok (patchuk)	Bales	135
Pyrethrum flower seeds	Bales	70
Pyrites	Bulk	25

Q		
Quebrache extract	Bags	40
Quebracho	Bundles	70
Quebracho extract	Bags	42
Quercitron	Bales/bags	85/87

R		
Rabbit skins	Bales	170
Raffiagrass	Bales/pressed bales	170/125
Rags	Bales/pressed bales	175/65
Railway iron	Rails/ties	14/45
Raisins	Cases	51

Ramie	Bales/pressed bales	83/53
Rapeseed	Bags	63
Rapeseed cake	Bags	52
Rapeseed oil	Bulk	35
Rattans	Bundles	140
Rattan core	Bales	145
Rattan, split, peeled	Bales	150
Rheafiber	Bales/pressedbales	83/53
Rice, broken	Bags	54
Rice, cargo	Bags	49
Rice dust (boussir)	Bags	65
Rice meal	Bags	67
Rice paper	Cases	83
Rope, coir	Coils	95
Rope, manila	Coils	83
Rope, sisal	Coils	83
Rope, wire	Coils	30
Rope seed	Bags	63
Rosin	Barrels	59
Rubber	Cases/bales/bags/sheets/crepe	69/66/66/
Rubber latex	Bulk/drums	37/53
Rum	Hogsheads/casks/cases	66/70/58
Rush hats	Bales	140
Rutile sand	Bags/bulk	28/20
Rye	Bulk/bags	50/55
Rye grass seed	Sacks	130

S		
Safflower	Bales	68
Safflower oil	Barrels	63
Safflower seeds	Bags	70
Saffron	Cases	72
Sago	Bags	54
Sago flour	Bags	51
Salmon	Tins in cases/barrels	51/47
Salt	Bulk/barrels/bags	50/55
Saltpeter	Bags	37
Samp	Bags	52

Sand	Bulk/cases	19/60
Sandalwood	Bales	117
Sandalwood powder	Cases	95
Sapanwood	Bulk	105
Sardines	Cases	46
Sarsparilla root	Bales	170
Sausage skins	Casks/kegs	73/63
Scheelite ore	Bags	26
Scrap iron	Bulk/bales	35/50
Semolina	Bags	61
Senna leaves	Bales/bags	120/200
Sesame	Bags	59
Shea nuts	Bags	70
Sheepskins	Bales	140
Sheep wash (sheep dip)	Drums	53
Shellac	Lined cases	83
Shells	Cases	46
Shooks	Bundles	97
Shrot	Bags	67
Shumac	Bags	71
Silk cocoons	Bales/pressed bales	215/70
Silk, piece	Cases	120
Silk, punjam	Cases	170
Silk, raw	Bales	105
Silk, waste	Bales/pressed bales	160/60
Silk, waste	Bundles	115
Skins	Bales/pressed bales/loose	150/87/185
Slag, basic	Bags/bulk	30/32
Slates	Loose/cases	19/25
Soap	Cases/kegs	65/43
Soda ash	Barrels/bags	46/43
Sooji (suji)	Bags	93
Sorghum	Bulk	48
Soy	Casks	47
Soya beans	Bulk/bags	50/65
Soya bean cake	Bags/bulk	73/68
Soya bean oil	Cases/barrels/bulk	53/63/39
Spaghetti	Cases	95

Spelter	Ingots	10
Spermaceti	Cases/cartons	65/70
Sponges	Bales/presse dbales	160/120
Starch	Cases/barrels	52/67
Staves	Bundles	98
Stearin	Bags/casks	52/63
Steel	Bars/billets/plates/pigs	14/12/11/11
Straw braid (strawplait)	Bales/cases	215/180
Sugar, dry	Hogsheads/bags/bulk	54/47/43
Sugar, green	Bags/baskets	41/49
Sulfur (brimstone)	Bulk/barrels/bags	31/47/36
Sultanas	Cases	51
Sunflower oil	Barrels	63
Sunflower seeds	Bags	105
Sunflower seed cake	Bulk	59
Superphosphate	Bags/bulk	38/40
Syrup	Barrels/hogsheads	50/44

T		
Talc	Bags	39
Tallow	Barrels/drums/cases/bulk	64/73/46/39
Tamarina	Barrels/cases/bags	43/39/50
Tamarind seed	Bags	65
Tankage	Bags	63
Tapioca, flake	Bags	69
Tapioca, flour	Bags	55
Tapioca, pearl	Bags	63
Tapioca, seed	Bags	63
Tar, coal	Barrels	50
Tar, pine	Barrels	56
Tea	Chests/boxes/cases	105
Tea dust	Boxes	90
Tea shooks	Cases	62
Teak	Boards/logs/planks	77/85/90
Tejpatta	Bales	275
Thyme	Bales	165
Thymol oil	Cases	53
Ties	Creosoted timbers	45

Tiles, bulk	Bulk	40
Tiles, fire clay	Crates	50
Tiles, roofing	Crates	80
Timothy seed	Bags	69
Tin	Ingots	9
Tincal	Casks/bags	55/44
Tin clippings	Pressed bales	39
Tinfoil	Bundles/cases	23/31
Tin ore	Bags	20
Tin plates	Packs/boxes	12/17
Tires	Loose	100
Tobacco	Hogsheads/cases/cartons	190/120/135
Tokmari seed	Bags	57
Tomatoes	Crates/boxes	70/75
Tonka beans	Barrels/boxes	90/70
Tortoise shell	Cases	142
Tow	Bales	100
Tripolite	Bulk	75
Tung oil	Barrels/tinsincases/bulk	64/57/38
Tungsten ore	Bags	17
Turmeric	Bags	83
Turpentine	Barrels/tins in cases/drums	63/55/60
Twine	Bales	65

U		
Umber	Bulk	41
Uranium	Bags	17

V		
Vaionia	Bags/bulk	103/93
Vanadium ore	Bags/bulk	23/25
Vanilla	Cases/bulk	63/53
Varnishes	Cases/barrels	57/63
Vaseline	Barrels/cases	60/53
Vegetable fiber	Bales	175
Vegetable oil	Bulk	39
Vegetable wax	Boxes/bags	46–70/57
Veneers	Crates	135

Vermillion	Cases	45
Vinegar	Barrels	63

W		
Walnuts	Bags	120
Walnut meat	Cases/bags	85/150
Waste	Bales	185
Wattles	Bags	47
Wax	Cases/barrels/bags	53/73/58
Whalebone	Cases/bundles	67/113
Whale meal	Bags	70
Whale oil	Drums/bulk	75/41
Wheat	Bulk/bags	48/53
Whiskey	Barrels/cases	69/63
Whitening (whiting)	Barrels/bags	43/38
Wines	Casks/cases	61/65
Wire, barbed	Reels	58
Witherite	Bulk	19
Wolfram	Bags	17
Wood pulp	Bales	50
Wool	Bales/pressed	58
Wool grease	Barrels/drums	60/64
Wood chips, softwood	Bulk	105
Wood chips, hardwood	Bulk	82

Y		
Yams	Bags or crates	92
Yarrow seed	Sacks	90

Z		
Zinc	Ingots	10
Zinc ash	Bags	40
Zinc concentrates	Bulk/ingots	21/15
Zinc dross	Cases	21
Zinc dust	Cases or drums	23
Zinc, white	Drums or kegs	23
Zircon sand	Bags/bulk	25/30
Zirconium ore	Bags/bulk	20/18

PROBLEMS PERTAINING TO MARINE CARGO OPERATIONS

SECTION 1: VERTICAL WEIGHT DISTRIBUTION OR STABILITY PROBLEMS

Common formulas used:

1. KG or V.C.G. $= \dfrac{\text{Total vertical moments}}{\text{Total weight}}$

2. $GM = KM - KG$

3. Shift of weight: $GG' = \dfrac{\text{Weight } (W) \times \text{Distance } (D)}{\Delta}$

4. Adding or removing a weight: $GG' = \dfrac{W \times D}{\Delta \pm W}$

5. Free-surface correction — use tables provided for type of ship or for individual tank:

$$GG' = \frac{r \times l \times b\,3}{12V}$$

$r = \dfrac{\text{Specific gravity (S.G.) of liquid}}{\text{S.G. of salt water}}$

l = length of tank

b = breadth of tank

$V = \Delta \times 35$

Problem #1

A ship in light condition displaces 2,000 tons, the KG being 10 feet. The KM in the loaded condition is 12 feet. 3,500 tons of cargo are loaded 9 feet above the keel and 400 tons of fuel 15 feet above the keel. Find the GM.

Answer

	W (tons)		V.C.G. (ft)		Moment (ft-tons)
Lt. ship	2,000	×	10	=	20,000
Cargo	3,500	×	9	=	31,500
Fuel	400	×	15	=	6,000
Totals Δ =	5,900				57,500

$$KG = \frac{57,500}{5,900} = 9.74 \text{ ft}$$

$$
\begin{aligned}
KM &= 12 \text{ ft} \\
-KG &= 9.74 \text{ ft} \\
\hline
GM &= 2.26 \text{ ft}
\end{aligned}
$$

Problem #2

A ship displacing 15,000 tons has a *KG* of 30 feet. Two thousand tons of fuel oil is burned from the double bottoms; this mass had a *KG* of 2 feet. What is the ship's new KG?

Answer

$$D = KG \text{ (ship)} - KG \text{ (F.O.)} = 30 - 2 = 28 \text{ ft}$$

$$GG' = \frac{W \times D}{\Delta - W} = \frac{2,000 \times 28}{15,000 - 2,000} = \frac{56,000}{13,000} = 4.3 \text{ ft}$$

New KG = 30 ft + 4.3 ft = 34.3 ft

or

	W (tons)		V.C.G. (ft)		Moment (ft-tons)
	15,000	×	30	=	450,000
	− 2,000	×	2	=	− 4,000
	13,000				446,000

$$\text{New } KG = \frac{446,000}{13,000} = 34.3 \text{ ft}$$

Problem #3

A vessel dis places 16,000 tons and has a KG of 18.5 feet. What will her KG be after 600 tons is loaded into a deep tank, with the center of gravity of the 600 tons at a KG of 10.5 feet?

Answer

$$D = KG \text{ (ship)} - KG \text{ (load)} - 18.5 - 10.5 = 8 \text{ ft}$$

$$GG' = \frac{W \times D}{\Delta \pm W} = \frac{600 \times 8}{16,000 + 600} = 0.3 \text{ ft}$$

$$\text{New } KG = 18.5 - 0.3 = 18.2 \text{ ft}$$

or

W		V.C.G.		Moment
(*tons*)		(*ft*)		(*ft-tons*)
16,000	×	18.5	=	296,000
+ 600	×	10.5	=	+ 6,300
16,600				302,300

$$\text{New } KG = \frac{302,300}{16,600} = 18.2 \text{ ft}$$

SECTION II: LONGITUDINAL WEIGHT DISTRIBUTION OR TRIM PROBLEMS

Common formulas used:

1. $\text{L.C.G.} = \dfrac{\text{Total long. moments}}{\text{Total weights}}$

2. $\text{Change in trim} = \dfrac{W \times D}{MT1}$

3. $\text{Mean sinkage} = \dfrac{W}{\text{T.P.I.}}$

4. Trim lever = difference between L.C.G. and L.C.B.

5. Change in trim = $\dfrac{\text{Trim lever } (GG') \times W}{MT1}$

6. If tipping center is amidships:

Change in draft = $\dfrac{\text{Change in trim}}{2}$

7. If tipping center is not amidships:

Change in fwd. draft = $\dfrac{\text{L.C.F.} - \text{F.P.}}{\text{L.B.P.}} \times$ Change in trim

Then:

Change in trim − Change in fwd. draft = change in draft aft

Problem #1

A ship with an *MT*1 of 1,200 pumps 200 tons of fuel oil from a forward tank to an after tank, a distance of 60 feet. The drafts before the shift were as follows: forward, 23 feet 08 inches; aft, 23 feet 04 inches; and mean, 23 feet 06 inches. What are the total change in trim and the final drafts?

Answer

1. Change in trim = $\dfrac{W \times D}{MT1} = \dfrac{200 \times 60}{1,200}$

= 10 in total change (by stern)

2. Change in draft = $\dfrac{10}{2}$ = 5 in fwd and aft (assuming tipping center is amidships)

	Fwd.	Mean	Aft
Initial draft	23 ft 08 in.	23 ft 06 in.	23 ft 04 in.
Change	− 5 in.	0 in.	+ 5 in.
Final draft	23 ft 03 in.	23 ft 06 in.	23 ft 09 in.

Problem #2

A ship has an *MT1* of 1,000, and 150 tons are loaded 100 feet aft of the tipping center. The drafts before the loading were forward, 19 feet 02 inches; aft, 19 feet 04 inches; and mean, 19 feet 03 inches. The T.P.I. is 50. What is the total change in trim and the final drafts?

Answer

1. Mean sinkage $= \dfrac{W}{\text{T.P.I}} = \dfrac{150}{50} = 3$ in

	Fwd.	Mean	Aft
Initial draft	19 ft 02 in.	19 ft 03 in.	19 ft 04 in.
Sinkage	+ 3 in.	+ 3 in.	+ 3 in.
	19 ft 05 in.	19 ft 06 in.	19 ft 07 in.

2. Change in trim $= \dfrac{W \times D}{MT1} = \dfrac{150 \times 100}{1,000} = 15$ in

3. Change in draft $= \dfrac{15}{2} = 7.5$ in. down by stern

	Fwd.	Mean	Aft
	19 ft 05 in.	(Stays same)	19 ft 07 in.
Change	− 7.5 in.		+ 7.5 in.
Final draft	18 ft 09.5 in.	19 ft 06 in.	20 ft 02.5 in.

Problem #3

A vessel has drafts of 26 feet 10 inches forward and 31 feet 02 inches aft. Her *MT1* is 1,850 ft-tons and her T.P.I. is 68. Find the final drafts if 410 tons are loaded at a point 205 feet abaft the tipping center. Assume tipping center is amid ships.

Answer

1. Mean sinkage $= \dfrac{W}{\text{T.P.I}} = \dfrac{410}{68} = 6$ in.

	Fwd.	Mean	Aft
Before loading	26 ft 10 in.	29 ft 00 in.	31 ft 02 in.
Mean sinkage	+ 6 in.	+ 6 in.	+ 6 in.
	27 ft 04 in.	29 ft 06 in.	31 ft 08 in.

2. Change in trim $= \dfrac{W \times D}{MT1} = \dfrac{410 \times 205}{1,850} = 45$ in.

3. Change in draft $= \dfrac{45}{2} = 22.5$ in. $= 1$ ft. 10.5 in.

	Fwd.	Mean	Aft
Draft	26 ft 16 in.	Stays same	31 ft 08 in.
Change	− 1 ft 10.5 in.		+ 1 ft 10.5 in.
Final draft	25 ft 05.5 in.	29 ft 06 in.	33 ft 06.5 in.

SECTION III: STABILITY AND TRIM PROBLEMS

Problem #1

Given:

	W	V.C.G.	L.C.G.–F.P.
Light ship	10,000 tons	35 ft.	350 ft.
Fwd. cargo spaces	5,000	20	200
Aft cargo spaces	4,000	25	550
Passengers/baggage	500	45	400
Fuel oil and water	2,500	10	300
	22,000 tons		

KM at 22,000 tons = 28.5

*MT*1 at 22,000 tons = 2,200 ft-tons

Mean draft at 22,000 tons = 29 ft 00 in.

L.C.B. is 344.1 ft from F.P.

Free-surface correction = 0.6 ft

Required: Final *GM* and drafts

Answer

Stability

	W	V.C.G.	Vertical Moments
Light ship	10,000 tons	35 ft.	350,000 ft-tons
Fwd. cargo	5,000	20	100,000
Aft cargo	4,000	25	100,000
Passengers/baggage	500	45	22,500
Fuel oil and water	2,500	10	25,000
Δ =	22,000 tons		597,500 ft.tons

$$\text{New } KG = \frac{597,500}{22,000} = 27.2 \text{ ft}$$

$$
\begin{array}{rcl}
KM & = & 28.5 \text{ ft} \\
-KG & = & 27.2 \text{ ft} \\
\hline
GM & = & 1.3 \\
\text{Free-surface correction} & = & -0.6 \text{ ft} \\
\hline
GM & = & 0.7 \text{ ft}
\end{array}
$$

Trim

	W	L.C.G.	Long. Moments
Light ship	10,000 tons	350	3,500,000
Fwd. cargo	5,000	200	1,000,000
Aft cargo	4,000	550	2,200,000
Passengers/baggage	500	400	200,000
Fuel oil and water	2,500	300	750,000
	Δ = 22,000 tons		7,650,000 ft-tons

1. L.C.G. = 7,650,000/22,000 = 347.7 ft

2. L.C.G. 347.7 ft (trim aft) − L.C.B. 344.1 ft = 3.6 ft lever arm

3. 3.6 × 22,000 tons = 79,200 ft-tons

4. 79,200/$MT1$ of 2,200 = 36 in. total change in trim

5. 36/2 = 18 in. = 1 ft 06 in.

6.

	Fwd.	Mean	Aft
Draft	29 ft 00 in.	(Stays same)	29 ft 00 in.
Change	− 1 ft 06 in.		+ 1 ft 06 in.
Final draft	27 ft 06 in.	29 ft 00 in.	30 ft 06 in.

Problem #2

Given:

	W	V.C.G.	L.C.G.–F.P.
Light ship	6,000 tons	30 ft.	300 ft.
Dry cargo	8,000	25	200
Liquid cargo	1,500	20	350
Deck cargo	500	50	300
Fuel oil and water	1,000	15	400
	17,000 tons		

KM at 17,000 tons = 30 ft

$MT1$ at 17,000 tons is 1,700 ft-tons

Mean draft at 17,000 tons = 27 ft 00 in.

L.C.B. at 17,000 tons is 260.2 ft from F.P.

Free-surface correction = 1 ft

Required: *GM* and drafts

Answer

Stability

	W	*V.C.G.*	*Vertical Moments*
Light ship	6,000 tons	30 ft.	180,000 ft-tons
Dry cargo	8,000	25	200,000
Liquid cargo	1,500	20	30,000
Deck cargo	500	50	25,000
Fuel oil and water	1,000	15	15,000
	Δ = 17,000 tons		450,000 ft.-tons

$$\text{New } KG = \frac{450,000}{17,000} = 26.5 \text{ ft}$$

$$
\begin{aligned}
KM &= 30.0 \text{ ft} \\
-KG &= 26.5 \text{ ft} \\
GM &= 3.5 \\
\text{Free-surface correction} &= -1.0 \text{ ft} \\
GM &= 2.5 \text{ ft}
\end{aligned}
$$

Trim

	W	*L.C.G.*	*Long. Moments*
Light ship	6,000 tons	300	1,800,000 ft-tons
Fwd. cargo	8,000	200	1,600,000
Aft cargo	1,500	350	525,000
Passengers/baggage	500	300	150,000
Fuel oil and water	1,000	400	400,000
	Δ = 17,000 tons		4,475,000 ft-tons

1. L.C.G. = 4,475,000/17,000 = 263.2 ft

2. L.C.G. 263.2 ft − L.C.B. 260.2 ft = 3 ft trim lever (trim by stern)

3. Total change in trim = 3 ft × 17,000/1,700 = 30 in.

4. 30/2 = 15 in. = 1 ft 03 in.

5.

	Fwd.	Mean	Aft
Draft	27 ft 00 in.	(Stays same)	27 ft 00 in.
Change	− 1 ft 03 in.		+ 1 ft 03 in.
Final draft	25 ft 09 in.	27 ft 00 in.	28 ft 03 in.

SECTION IV: WEIGHT CONCENTRATION PROBLEMS

Common formulas:

1.
$$t = \frac{v}{V} \times T$$

where

t = tons to be loaded in desired compartment

T = total tons to be loaded

v = compartment volume

V = total volume

All volumes are given as bale cubic.

2. Deck load capacity = $C = \dfrac{\text{tons} \times 2{,}240}{W' \times L'}$ or $\dfrac{\text{(lb)}}{W' \times L'}$

where

W' = width of compartment

L' = length of compartment

3. Height limitation = $h = \dfrac{C \times f}{2{,}240}$

where

C = deck load capacity

f = cargo stowage factor

Note: Deck load capacity is always expressed in lb/ft².

Problem #1: Amount of Weight to Load

What is the number of tons that can be loaded in the upper 'tweendeck (U.T.D.) if 13,000 tons are to be loaded?

Given:

Deck	Bale Cubic
U.T.D	235,130 ft³
L.T.D.	297,452
L.H.	188,056
	720,638 ft³

Answer

$$\frac{v}{V} \times T = t$$

$$\frac{235,130}{720,638} \times 13,000 = 4,242 \text{ tons}$$

Problem #2: Deck Load Capacity

Could boiler plate that covers an area of 8 feet × 40 feet and weighs 100 tons be loaded in the number 4 hold?

Given: American Racer Class number 4 Hold.

Deck Capacity

U.T.D	360 lb/ft²
L.T.D.	528 lb/ft²
L.H.	528 lb/ft²

Answer

$$\frac{\text{Tons} \times 2,240}{W' \times L'} = \frac{100 \times 2,240}{8 \times 40} = \frac{224,000 \text{ lb}}{320 \text{ ft}^2} = 700 \text{ lb/ft}^2$$

The answer is no, unless dunnage is used to increase the area ($W' \times L'$ and thereby reduce the weight per area.

Problem #3: Height Limitation

How high can railroad steel with a stowage factor of 14 be loaded in the number 4 lower hold of the vessel above?

Answer

$$h = \frac{c \times f}{2,240} = \frac{528 \times 14}{2,240} = \frac{7,392}{2,240} = 3.3 \text{ ft}$$

Problem #4: Maximum Use of Available Cubic with Two Cargoes Differing in Density

How high would steel billets with a stowage factor of 12 be stowed in a compartment 14 feet high with a deck capacity of 600 lb/ft² so the rest of the compartments could be filled with bales of cork stowing in at 300 ft³/ton?

Answer

Let

x = cubic feet of cork

y = cubic feet of steel billets

$$\text{Density of cork} = \frac{2{,}240}{300} = 7.47 \text{ lb/ft}^3$$

$$\text{Density of steel billets} = \frac{2{,}240}{12} = 186.67 \text{ lb/ft}^3$$

$$x + y = 14$$

$$
\begin{array}{rrcr}
& 7.5x + 186.7y & = & 600 \\
-7.5 \times (x + y = 14) = & -7.5x - 7.5y & = & -105 \\
\hline
& 179.2y & = & 495 \\
& y & = & 2.76 \text{ ft}^3 \text{ of steel billets}
\end{array}
$$

$$x = 14 - 2.76 = 11.24 \text{ ft}^3 \text{ of cork}$$

The steel billets will be 2.67 ft high and the cork 11.24 ft high.

Problem #5: Maximum Use of Available Cubic with Two Cargoes Differing in Density

Given: Steel billets with a stowage factor of 12 are to be stowed in a compartment 12 feet high with a deck load capacity of 400 lb/ft³. General cargo with an average stowage factor estimated at 160 is to be stowed over the steel.

Required: How high should the steel be tiered to allow the free space over the steel to be filled with the general cargo and not exceed the deck load capacity?

Answer

First solve for the density of the steel billets and the general cargo.

$$\text{Density of the steel} = 2{,}240/12 = 186 \text{ lb/ft}^3$$
$$\text{Density of the general cargo} = 2{,}240/160 = 14 \text{ lb/ft}^3$$

Let
x = cubic feet of general cargo and

y = cubic feet of steel.

Then:

$$x + y = 12$$

$$
\begin{array}{rl}
14x + 186y = & 400 \\
-14 \times (x + y = 12) = -14x - 14y = & -168 \\
\hline
172y = & 232
\end{array}
$$

$$y = 1.35 \text{ ft}^3 \text{ steel}$$

$$x = 10.65 \text{ ft}^3 \text{ general cargo}$$

Therefore, the steel should be tiered 1.35 feet high; thus the general cargo would be 10.65 feet high.

Now, what deck space will be required given 50 tons of steel billets?

$$
\begin{array}{rl}
\text{Tons} \times f = & \text{Total cubic} \\
50 \times 12 = & 600 \text{ ft}^3 \\
\text{Cubic} = & \text{Height} \times \text{Area} \\
600 = & 1.35 \times \text{Area}
\end{array}
$$

Therefore:

$$\text{Area} = \frac{600}{1.35} = 444.4 \text{ ft}^2$$

SECTION V: STOWAGE FACTOR PROBLEMS

Common formulas:

1. $f = \dfrac{2{,}240}{D}$

where

D = density in lb/ft^3

2. $f = \dfrac{2{,}240 \times V}{W}$

where

V = volume in ft^3

W = weight in lb

3. $T = \dfrac{V \times (1 - L)}{f}$

where

L = estimated broken stowage

T = tons

V = volume of space

4. $p = \dfrac{V \times (1 - L)}{v}$

where

p = number of pieces

v = volume of pieces

Problem #1

Given: A hold of 60,000 bale cubic. A cargo consisting of cases weighing 400 lb and measuring 2.5 feet by 2 feet by 2 feet is to be stowed. Estimated broken stowage is 10 percent.

Required: The number of tons that can be stowed in the hold.

Answer

Solving for the stowage factor of this cargo:

$$f = \frac{2{,}240 \times 10^*}{400}$$

$$f = 56$$

$^*10 = 2.5 \text{ ft} \times 2 \text{ ft} \times 2 \text{ ft} = \text{cubic of each case}$

Therefore:

$$T = \frac{60{,}000 \times 0.9}{56}$$

$$T = 964 \text{ tons}$$

Problem #2

Given: The same data as for Problem #1.

Required: The number of cases that could be stowed in the hold.

Answer

$$P = \frac{60,000 \times 0.9}{10}$$

$$P = 5,400 \text{ cases}$$

SECTION VI: BOOM PROBLEMS

Common formulas:

1. Tension on topping lift span $= \dfrac{\text{Length of span}}{\text{Length of mast}} \times W$

2. Thrust on boom $= \dfrac{\text{Length of boom} \times W}{\text{Length of mast}} + \text{S.H.P.}$

3. S.H.P (stress on the hauling part) $=$

$$\frac{(0.1 \times S \times W) + W}{\text{No. of parts at mov. block}}$$

where

    S = no. of sheaves

    W = weight to be lifted

    $0.1 = 10\%$ loss due to friction

Problem #1

Given: A cargo boom is 32 feet long and plumbs a point 25 feet from the foot of a mast. The topping lift span is made fast on the mast 25 feet above the heel of the boom. A gun tackle purchase is being used to lift a load of 12 tons, with the hauling part led through the heel block to the winch at the foot of the boom. (Make an al lowance of 10% of the load for friction.)

Required: Tension on the topping lift and the total thrust on the boom.

Answer

$$\text{Tension on span} = \frac{\text{length of span}}{\text{length of mast}} \times \text{weight} = \frac{25}{25} \times 12 = 12 \text{ tons}$$

$$\text{S.H.P.} = \frac{(0.1 \times S \times W) + W}{\text{No. of parts at mov. block}} = \frac{(0.1 \times 3* \times 12) + 12}{2}$$

$$= \frac{3.6 + 12}{2} = \frac{15.6}{2} = 7.8 \text{ tons}$$

*Includes heel block. (Gun tackle = 2 sheaves + heel block = 3 sheaves.)

$$\text{Thrust on boom} = \frac{\text{length of boom} \times W}{\text{length of mast}} + \text{S.H.P.}$$

$$= \frac{32 \times 12}{25} + 7.8 = (1.28 \times 12) + 7.8 = 15.36 + 7.8 = 23.16 \text{ tons}$$

Problem #2

Given: The height of the mast is 40 feet, the length of the topping lift span is 40 feet, and the length of the boom is 57 feet.

Required: If lifting a 1-ton weight with a twofold tackle, find (a) the tension on the topping lift, and (b) the thrust on the boom.

Answer

$$\text{Tension of T.L. span} = \frac{\text{length of span}}{\text{length of mast}} \times W$$

$$= \frac{40}{40} \times 1 = 1 \text{ ton}$$

$$\text{S.H.P.} = \frac{(0.1 \times 5 \times 1) + 1}{4} = 0.375 \text{ tons}$$

$$\text{Thrust on boom} = \frac{\text{length of boom} \times W}{\text{length of mast}} + \text{S.H.P.}$$

$$= \frac{57 \times 1}{40} + 0.38 = 1.81 \text{ tons}$$

Appendix 3

Stowage of Bulk Grain

Introduction

THIS APPENDIX IS A COMPILATION of information that includes a portion of the International Grain Rules, the regulations of the U.S. Coast Guard which apply to the carriage of bulk grain, recommendations, suggestions, and other information related to loading bulk grain aboard vessels. It is intended as a handy reference for shipmasters, deck officers, surveyors, and others involved with the maritime industry.

The text in this appendix was taken from the 2007 edition of *General Information for Grain Loading*, prepared by the National Cargo Bureau from information obtained from sources which are believed to be reliable and accurate. *The National Cargo Bureau and the authors do not guarantee its accuracy and completeness and do not assume any responsibility or liability for damage which may arise from the use of this appendix or its contents.

The appendix is intended for use by shipmasters and ship operators when engaged in the ocean transport of grain in bulk. It is their responsibility to comply with the mandatory regulations for such carriage as set forth in the International Code for the Safe Carriage of Grain in Bulk (hereinafter referred to as "the Code") if these regulations are applied at the port of loading. It is not intended for use by naval architects or ship designers.

The descriptive material and the amplifying information on the regulations, as contained in this appendix, are not intended as official interpretations but rather as explanations regarding how these regulations are understood by the surveyors of the National Cargo Bureau, which is the agency designated by the U.S. Coast Guard to enforce the provisions of the Code on ships loading bulk grain at United States ports. In all cases where the intent or meaning of any IMO Grain Rule discussed in this appendix is subject to question, resolution must depend solely on the content of IMO publication No. 240E.

* The following pages of Appendix 3 have been reproduced directly from the National Cargo Bureau book, *General Information for Grain Loading*. The original page numbers, starting with page 18, have been retained so that figures or portions of text that are referenced within the book can be found easily.

2007 Revision

NATIONAL CARGO BUREAU, INC.

GENERAL INFORMATION
FOR
GRAIN LOADING

17 Battery Place ■ Suite 1232
New York, NY 10004

National Cargo Bureau, Inc., 1994, Rev. 2007

INFORMATION ON REQUIREMENTS

Application

In accordance with Requirement 1, Regulation 9, Part C, Chapter VI of SOLAS 1974, as amended, and A 1.1 of the Code, the Code applies to, and is mandatory for, all ships which carry bulk grain on an international voyage, including those of less than 500 tons gross tonnage. However, it should be noted that two of the requirements in the Code apply only to ships built after 1 January 1994. One is a requirement pertaining to the provision of a table of Maximum Permissible (Allowable) Heeling Moments (this is discussed in a paragraph, marked with an asterisk, on page 26 of this booklet). The other requirement pertains to the immersion of the deck edge and is discussed in a paragraph beginning on page 25 of this booklet.

As provided for in A 8 of the Code, Documents of Authorization which were previously approved under Regulation 12, Chapter VI of SOLAS 1960, or IMO Resolutions A.184(VI) or A.264(VIII), will continue to be recognized. Existing ships holding such Documents are not required to obtain new Documents of Authorization indicating compliance with the Code. More information on Documents of Authorization is given on page 27 of this booklet.

In the case of vessels registered in the United States, the Code applies to all ships and barges carrying grain in bulk, whether or not engaged on international voyages, except that voyages on inland waters, the Great Lakes, and specified coastal waters are exempted.

Definition of Grain

A 2.1   The term *grain* covers wheat, maize (corn), oats, rye, barley, rice, pulses, seeds and processed forms thereof, whose behavior is similar to that of grain in its natural state.

The term "pulses" includes edible seeds for such leguminous crops as peas, beans or lentils. Nuts such as peanuts in the decorticated form are included. However, undecorticated (unshelled) forms are not included. These requirements apply to saw-delinted cottonseed and acid-delinted cottonseed but not to linted cottonseed. The requirements do not apply to processed grains such as flour or soybean meal, but processing is not the determining criteria. For example, the requirements do apply to rapeseed pellets. In general, when there is a question as to whether or not the requirements apply to an agricultural commodity, the angle of repose (i.e. the natural angle which a freely poured pile will attain with the horizontal) should be carefully measured. If it is 30 degrees or less, the requirements of the Code should be deemed to apply.

Leveling/Trimming

When grain is free-poured into a compartment, it arranges itself into a pile of conical shape. The angle of the surface with the horizontal varies with the specific variety of the grain. This is termed the angle of repose. As long as the pile is static, the surface will remain undisturbed. However, when the grain is in a ship and subjected to the motions of the ship at sea, the surface grain can move in response to this motion, resulting in movement of the center of gravity of the grain mass. This is a grain shift. The off-center weight condition is termed a GRAIN HEELING MOMENT and causes the ship to list. But, if the surface of the grain is leveled, then the ship would have to roll to an angle greater than the angle of repose before the grain would shift. That may require a roll in excess of 23 degrees, for example. Consequently, to minimize the possibility that bulk grain will shift at sea, the IMO Grain Rules require that, after loading, all free grain surfaces be level.

The magnitude of a grain shift depends upon the amount of open space above the grain into which it can move. Thus, when a compartment is filled to the maximum extent possible, the adverse effect of the grain shift (i.e. the grain heeling moment) will be less that if the compartment is partly filled. The Grain Rules recognize this by assuming a 15 degree shift of grain when the compartment is filled as opposed to a 25 degree shift when the compartment is partly filled. Obviously, there is a much greater volume of open space above the grain surface when the compartment is partly filled.

The term "trimming", as generally used in the context of grain loading, refers to the physical act of filling underdeck voids, typically outside the perimeter of the hatch coaming, to the maximum extent possible or practicable. Common methods include spout trimming (slow free-pour with an angled spout or directional spout fitting), hand trimming (shoveling), and use of mechanical trimming machines of various types.

    A 2.2   The term *filled compartment, trimmed*, refers to any cargo space in which, after loading and trimming as required under A 10.2, the bulk grain is at its highest possible level.

This is understood to mean that, in the hatchway itself, the grain is at a height corresponding to the position of the closed hatchcovers or the underside of the hatch beams which either frame or support the hatchcovers. The grain surface must be leveled at this height.

Beneath the deck, outboard and fore and aft of the hatch opening, the grain must be trimmed to the maximum extent possible. Due to the capabilities of many of the machines used for trimming, this is generally to a level slightly above the bottom of the hatch side girders and hatch end beams.

Figure 1 illustrates a transverse section through a filled compartment, trimmed. Figure 2 shows a compartment which appears to be filled, trimmed, but which is not because the spaces outside the periphery of the hatchway were merely free-poured. It is, therefore, filled, untrimmed.

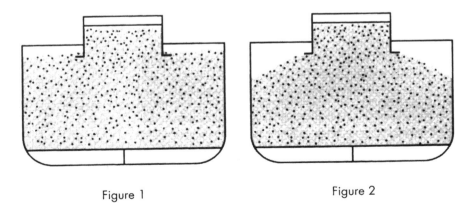

Figure 1   Figure 2

    A 2.3   The term *filled compartment, untrimmed*, refers to a cargo space which is filled to the maximum extent possible in way of the hatch opening but which has not been trimmed outside the periphery of the hatch opening either by the provisions of A 10.3.1 for all ships or A 10.3.2 for specially suitable compartments.

As illustrated in Figure 3, below, the grain does not have to be trimmed if its surface is permanently restrained by grain-tight structure which slopes at an angle of 30 degrees or more. On most bulk carriers this is achieved by the structural design, which includes upper wing tanks extending the lengths of the holds, port and starboard. In accordance with A 2.7, compartments so fitted are termed *specially suitable*. While, in a filled specially suitable compartment, the grain is restrained against shift in the areas to the port and starboard of the hatch opening, it is not similarly restrained forward and aft of the hatch opening. In accordance with A 10.3.2, dispensation may be granted from trimming the ends, provided the compartment is specially suitable and otherwise filled (i.e. the compartment is filled to the maximum extent possible in way of the hatch opening). Such dispensation must be included in the approved grain loading information referenced in the ship's Document of Authorization.

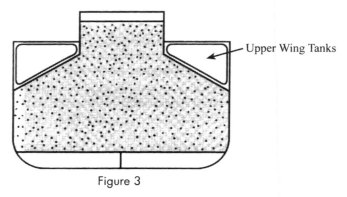

Figure 3

Figure 4 shows a longitudinal section through the centerline of a filled compartment with untrimmed ends. The dashed lines illustrate the relative position of the upper wing tanks detailed above.

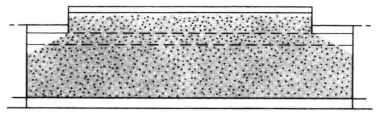

Figure 4

Additionally, the Grain Rules provide that the *filled compartment, untrimmed* status can be applied to compartments which are not specially suitable but, instead, are provided with *feeder ducts, perforated decks or other similar means* which reduce the open volume of space above the free-flowing grain surface so that it is equivalent to that which would be obtained if there were no feeding arrangements and the space was trimmed in the normal manner. Acceptance of this alternative must be included in the approved grain loading information. Figure 5 illustrates a transverse section through a ship with a filled lower hold which does not have to be trimmed because of the use of deck perforations in the tween deck.

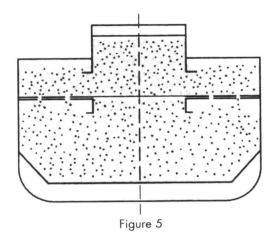

Figure 5

With this type of arrangement, the surveyor will always want to ascertain, before loading commences, that covers, if any, have been removed from all deck openings and/or all feeding ducts are fully open to allow grain to flow through to the space(s) to be fed.

A 2.4   The term *partly filled compartment* refers to any cargo space wherein the bulk grain is not loaded in the manner prescribed in A 2.2 or A 2.3.

Whenever a compartment is not filled then, as required by A 10.6, the grain surface must be leveled to minimize the possibility of a grain shift. It is to be especially noted that there is no such status as *almost filled.* Either a compartment is filled, as prescribed in A 2.2 or A 2.3, or it must be regarded as partly filled. In the former case, the Grain Rules assume a potential shift of 15 degrees. In the latter case, the rules assume the more severe effect of a 25 degree shift. Figures 6 and 7 show examples of partly filled compartments.

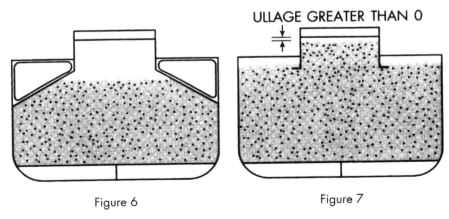

ULLAGE GREATER THAN 0

Figure 6   Figure 7

In addition to filled and partly filled, there is another stowage arrangement which should be mentioned. On multi-deck ships, such as break-bulk or general cargo, A 10.8 permits LOADING IN COMBINATION (also known as common loading). In this type of loading, the hatch covers in the intermediate decks (i.e. the tween-decks), are left in the fully open position. Thus, the grain in way of the vertically aligned hatch openings forms a homogeneous column and void spaces exist only beneath the peripheral decks at each level and, of course, beneath the uppermost, closed, hatch cover. The grain in the peripheral areas must be trimmed to fill the spaces to the maximum extent possible. This procedure completely eliminates the void spaces in way of hatch openings at every level except the uppermost and, therefore, results in a smaller total grain heeling moment than would apply if the tween-deck covers were closed and the filled grain heeling moments at each level were summed.

There are a few caveats concerning the use of this option. The data to calculate the grain heeling moments which apply for this condition must be included in the approved Grain Loading Booklet. The hatch covers in the tween-decks must be in their fully open positions. Also, if they are the retractable type, they must not, when in the open position, restrict the free-flow of grain in the peripheral areas and prevent the attainment of a filled, trimmed, condition. Figure 8 shows a transverse section through a cargo hold which is loaded in combination.

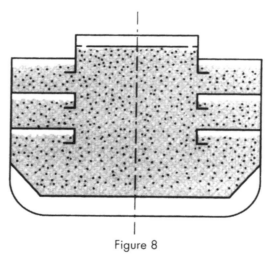

Figure 8

Volumetric Heeling Moments

With the grain in a ship loaded symmetrically and the grain surface(s) leveled, the center of gravity of the grain mass is on the centerline and the ship should be upright. A 7.3 specifically requires the ship to be in an UPRIGHT CONDITION before proceeding to sea. Since the weather, sea, and even operating condition of the ship cannot be fully predicted for the entire duration of a voyage, it is possible that, in spite of the precautions which have been taken, the grain will shift. If this occurs, the center of gravity of the grain mass will move off the centerline of the ship and the distance it moves multiplied by the weight of the shifted grain will create a GRAIN HEELING MOMENT, which will cause the ship to list. The magnitude of this moment depends upon three factors; the angle of shift, the internal geometry of the ship (i.e. the shape of the space into which the grain shifts), and the weight of the grain.

As tedious and lengthy arithmetic is involved in the consideration of the above factors, it is not practical for the ship's officers to attempt to calculate the grain heeling moments for a specific loading condition from first principles. However, since the angle(s) of assumed grain shift and the internal geometry of the ship always remain the same, the naval architect, in accordance with directions set forth in Part B of the Code, can pre-calculate the Volumetric Heeling Moments for the various cargo compartments and the different volumes of grain in those compartments. Of course, a volume multiplied by a distance cannot exert a force. But, a volume of space divided by the Stowage Factor of the commodity which fills that space, equals a weight. So, the regulations utilize the mathematical stratagem of tabulating Volumetric Heeling Moments for each compartment which, when divided by the Stowage Factor (as defined in A 2.6) of the type of grain loaded in the compartment, gives the Grain Heeling Moment. Thus:

$$\text{Grain Heeling Moment} = \frac{\text{Volumetric Heeling Moment}}{\text{Stowage Factor (per A 2.6)}}$$

A Volumetric Heeling Moment, since it represents an abstract concept of a volume multiplied by a distance, has an unusual dimensional unit, namely m^4, as derived below:

$$\begin{array}{ccc} \text{Volume} \times \text{Distance} & = & \text{Volumetric Moment} \\ (m^3) \qquad (m) & & (m^4) \end{array}$$

It becomes a physical moment when divided by the Stowage Factor:

$$\frac{\text{Volumetric Heeling Moment } (m^4)}{\text{Stowage Factor } (m^3/\text{tonne})} = \text{Heeling Moment (tonne-meters)}$$

Stowage Factor

Due to the way it is utilized in grain stability calculations, the term "Stowage Factor" has a different definition from that usually applied in commercial maritime practice. In accordance with A 2.6, Stowage Factor means the volume per unit weight (ft^3/long ton or m^3/tonne) as attested by the loading facility. While this value allows for the interstices between the grain particles, it does not include "broken stowage" (i.e. the space left vacant when the compartment is nominally filled) or compaction. This approach is necessary because the weight of the mass of grain which moves transversely in a grain shift is the actual weight and not a weight reduced by the void spaces which constitute the broken stowage in the compartment as a whole. Loading facilities in the United States usually furnish test weights per bushel. (See page 99 of this booklet for a means of translating this data into the Stowage Factors specified by the Code).

It should be noted that, when calculating the weight of grain which can be stowed in a compartment, and hence the displacement of the ship, the conventional Stowage Factor, which allows for broken stowage and compaction, should be used. Generally, this is based on knowledge of previous loadings of the same ship (or similar type) and the experience of the particular port or loading facility.

In the case of *filled compartments, untrimmed*, the volumetric capacities shown in the Grain Loading Booklet for this condition generally understate the volume(s) of grain that can actually be loaded in the compartment(s). This is because Part B of the Code directs the naval architect to base his calculation on an angle of repose of 30 degrees, whereas the actual angle of repose of the grain may be as low as 22 degrees. Thus, if the tabulated "untrimmed" capacities are used, more grain may be loaded in the "filled, untrimmed" compartments than calculations anticipated. This could result in a deeper draft and/or much less grain than planned in another compartment. This, then, could result in a significantly increased Volumetric Heeling Moment, potentially leading to an unsafe condition. Final trim may also be affected. Unless there is prior experience to rely upon, it is wise to use the "full, trimmed" capacities in initial calculations, rather than the reduced "full, untrimmed" capacities, even though no trimming is intended. Any differences between the initially calculated condition and the final, loaded, condition will then be on the safe side.

Stability Requirements

Once the Grain Heeling Moment has been determined, the response of the ship to this moment (i.e. the resultant angle of heel and the amount of reserve stability remaining) depends upon the hydrostatic properties of the ship with the actual displacement and vertical center of gravity. The Code prescribes the following requirements in these regards:

A 7.1   The intact stability characteristics of any ship carrying bulk grain shall be shown to meet, throughout the voyage, at least the following criteria after taking into account in the manner described in Part B of this Code and, in figure A7, the heeling moments due to grain shift:

    .1   the angle of heel due to the shift of grain shall not be greater than 12° or in the case of ships constructed on or after 1 January 1994 the angle at which the deck edge is immersed, whichever is the lesser;

    .2   in the statical stability diagram, the net or residual area between the heeling arm curve and the righting arm curve up to the angle of heel of maximum difference between the ordinates of the two curves, or 40° or the angle of flooding (θ_1), whichever is the least, shall in all conditions of loading be not less than 0.075 metre-radians; and

    .3   the initial metacentric height, after correction for the free surface effects of liquids in tanks, shall be not less than 0.30 m.

A 7.2   Before loading bulk grain the master shall, if so required by the Contracting Government of the country of the port of loading, demonstrate the ability of the ship at all stages of any voyage to comply with the stability criteria required by this section.

A 7.3   After loading, the master shall ensure that the ship is upright before proceeding to sea.

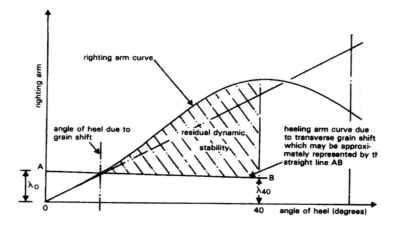

Figure A 7

(1)   Where:

$\lambda_\circ$ = <u>assumed volumetric heeling moment due to transverse shift</u> ;
stowage factor x displacement

λ_{40} = 0.8 x $\lambda_\circ$;

Stowage factor = volume per unit weight of grain cargo ;

Displacement = weight of ship, fuel, fresh water, stores etc. and cargo.

(2)   The righting arm curve shall be derived from cross-curves which are sufficient in number to accurately define the curve for the purpose of these requirements and shall include cross-curves at 12° and 40°.

The first step in determining compliance with these requirements is to calculate the final displacement and vertical center of gravity corrected for the free surface of the liquids on board (KG_V). This is the same calculation that is made for any cargo ship. From the KG_V, the corrected metacentric height (GM) can be calculated and, as required by A 7.1.3, it must be not less than 0.3 meters.

The Volumetric Heeling Moment data for each compartment in which grain is stowed is provided in the approved Grain Loading Booklet. This is used to calculate the Grain Heeling Moment, for individual compartments when different Stowage Factors are involved, or the ship as a whole in the case of homogenous loading. If Grain Heeling Moments are calculated individually, they must be summed to obtain the total Grain Heeling Moment that the Code assumes the ship may be subjected to if the grain shifts; if all of the grain loaded has the same Stowage Factor, it is simpler to sum the Volumetric Heeling Moments and calculate the total Grain Heeling Moment from that sum. The Grain Heeling Moment will cause the ship to heel and A 7.1.1 requires that this heel shall not be greater than 12 degrees. On some ships, with low freeboards, a 12 degree heel could immerse the deck edge, which is a very undesirable condition. Recognizing this, the older version of the Grain Rules recommended that an angle of heel which immersed the deck edge should not be exceeded, even if it was less than 12 degrees. This has been given even greater weight in the Code and it is now a requirement, for ships built on or after 1 January 1994, that it not be exceeded.

The basic means of calculating the angle of heel which will result from an applied heeling moment is to construct a stability curve for the actual displacement and KG_V from the information furnished in the ship's approved Cross Curves of Stability and to superimpose on it a second curve derived from the Grain Heeling Moment as shown in Figure A 7. A method for doing this is explained, beginning on page 52 of this booklet.

Regardless of the initial GM, a ship which is heeled to an angle of 12 degrees could find itself in a very perilous position. To guard against this, the Code requires that a ship, heeled to an angle of 12 degrees, has an adequate reserve of stability. This is a dynamic, rather than static, amount and is specified in A 7.1.2 as a minimum of 0.075 metre-radians of residual area within the boundaries shown in Figure A 7. A method for determining this area is given on page 56 of this booklet.

Angle of Flooding

In some cases, but not all, one of the boundaries of the residual area may be the *Angle of Flooding* (θ_f), which is defined, in A 2.5, as the angle of heel at which openings in the hull, superstructures or deckhouses, which cannot be closed weathertight, immerse. Small openings, through which progressive flooding cannot take place need not be considered as open. Progressive flooding means that adjoining watertight compartments fill consecutively as the trim of the ship changes due to the gradually increasing weight of the flood water. Gooseneck vents or tank overflow pipes are examples of small openings which are exempted in this definition. Figure 9 illustrates the location of an air intake for the main engine, which would establish the angle of flooding. Note that the gooseneck vents at the deck edge do not establish the angle of flooding. Also, it is important to note that the angle changes as the draft of the ship changes. As the draft increases, the angle of flooding (θ_1) decreases.

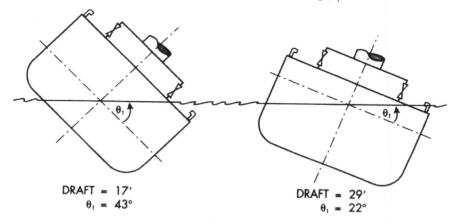

DRAFT = 17'   DRAFT = 29'
θ_1 = 43° θ_1 = 22°

Figure 9

Maximum Allowable Heeling Moments

The construction of a stability curve from the Cross Curves of Stability and the measurements taken therefrom have been eliminated and the calculations necessary to determine compliance with A 7.1 of the Code have been greatly simplified by the use of Tables or Curves of Maximum Permissible (Allowable) Heeling Moments (see A 6.3.2 of the Code). In lieu of calculating the actual GM, angle of heel, and determining the residual area for a given displacement, KG, and total Grain Heeling Moment, and then testing these values against the requirements of the Code, the naval architect pre-calculates the maximum heeling moments which will meet all three of these conditions for combinations of displacement and KG_v (or GM) within the range of the ship's operating conditions. These Maximum Allowable Heeling Moments are then shown in tabular form (or curves) and contained within the ship's approved Grain Loading Booklet. Thus, all the ship's Master has to do is calculate the displacement, KG_v, GM and the total Grain Heeling Moment and then compare it to the Maximum Allowable Heeling Moment shown in the Grain Loading Booklet.

* Tables or curves of Maximum Allowable Heeling Moments are not required for ships built before the Code came into force on 1 January 1994; they are required for ships after that date. (This is one of the few changes in the Grain Rules that were instituted with the inception of the Code). However, most ships now in service have them as there is a considerable benefit to be gained by their use in terms of less time spent calculating and consequently less errors made in the calculations.

Notice that the Code requires, in A 7.1, that the stability characteristics must meet the governing criteria <u>throughout the voyage.</u> Thus, it is not sufficient to check for compliance at the point where the ship completes loading (including bunkering) and departs upon its voyage.

A check must also be made for the arrival condition (i.e. after the changes in displacement and KG_v due to consumption). If the voyage is interrupted by calls at intermediate ports to load or discharge cargo (whether it is grain or not) or to bunker, then the departure and arrival conditions must be calculated for each leg of the voyage. Additionally, if the condition upon arrival at the grain discharge port includes ballast that was not on board at the time of departure, then compliance with A 7.1 at the point at which the ballast was taken must be confirmed. To confirm compliance, it is necessary to calculate the most unfavorable condition that could exist at that time (i.e. a condition in which the KG_v is not yet reduced due to the weight of the pumped-in ballast, but is already corrected for the potential free surface effect caused by the ballast in the tank(s) being filled).

Grain Loading Booklet

A 6.1   Information in printed booklet form shall be provided to enable the master to ensure that the ship complies with this Code when carrying grain in bulk on an international voyage. This information shall include that which is listed in A 6.2 and A 6.3.

A 6.2 and A 6.3 list the specific information that is to be included. However, these details are not the responsibility of the Master. If the Grain Loading Booklet is approved by the Administration or an agency authorized to act on behalf of the Administration, then the content of it shall be deemed to be in compliance with regulation A 6.1. This will be demonstrated by issuance of a Document of Authorization by or on behalf of the Administration in accordance with A 3.1. The Document of Authorization and associated data (including the Grain Loading Booklet) may be drawn up in the language of the issuing country but, if that language is neither English nor French, the text shall include a translation into one of those languages. A copy of the Grain Loading Booklet and any associated plans shall be maintained on board the ship in order that the Master, if so required, can produce them for inspection and use by appropriate authorities at the ports of loading.

Document of Authorization

One of the basic principles of the International Convention for the Safety of Life at Sea, is that member nations will be responsible for the details of compliance with the requirements of the Convention and that other nations will accept, in good faith, that these details have been properly observed. But, each nation retains the right to ascertain that any ship which conducts commerce from its ports has, in fact, been subjected to the promised oversight by its home Administration. In the case of ships carrying grain in bulk, the mechanism for accomplishing this is the Document of Authorization, referenced above and described in A 3.

The Document of Authorization is a certification made by an Administration signatory to the Convention, or by an agency authorized to act on behalf of that Administration, that a specific ship under its registry is capable of safely carrying grain in bulk and that the information in the Grain Loading Booklet, defining such capability, has been reviewed and is approved as being in compliance with the requirements of the Code. Thus, when a ship of a nation which is signatory to the Convention presents itself to load grain at any port of a nation which is also signatory, the information in the approved Grain Loading Booklet will be accepted as being correct and the Booklet will be utilized to determine that the specific stowage arrangement and loading condition for the forthcoming voyage complies with the requirements of the Code. Since over 150 nations are signatory to the Safety of Life at Sea Convention, this means that the Document of Authorization will be accepted at almost every port in the world.

Of course, if a nation is not signatory to the Convention, then member nations would not extend to its ships the benefits of being signatory (i.e. Grain Loading Booklets and Documents of Authorization would not be recognized).

A Ship without a Document of Authorization

Unlike a Trim and Stability Booklet or a Cargo Ship Safety Construction Certificate for example, no International Convention requires that every cargo ship have a Document of Authorization. Instead, this Document is optional for ships, usually bulk carriers, for which it greatly facilitates their operations. The Code provides two options under which, subject to certain limitations, a ship without a Document of Authorization may load grain in bulk:

a)   Under A 3.5

The ship's home Administration must be provided with plans and calculations demonstrating that the proposed stowage arrangement and loading condition comply with the requirements of the Code. The calculations must include derivation of the Volumetric Heeling Moments as well as the calculations demonstrating compliance with A 7.1. The home Administration approves the calculations and the approval must be presented at the port of loading. Alternatively, if the home Administration so authorizes, the authorities at the port of loading may review and approve the calculations prior to permitting loading.

b)   Under A 9

A ship without a Document of Authorization may carry a partial cargo of bulk grain without performing all the detailed calculations required under the option previously described, by utilizing the provisions of A 9. **Note that authority to use this option must be obtained from the home Administration**.

A 9.1   A ship not having on board a document of authorization issued in accordance with A 3 of this Code may be permitted to load bulk grain provided that:

.1   the total weight of the bulk grain shall not exceed one third of the deadweight of the ship;

.2   all filled compartments, trimmed, shall be fitted with centreline divisions extending, for the full length of such compartments, downwards from the underside of the deck or hatch covers to a distance below the deck line of at least one eighth of the maximum breadth of the compartment or 2.4 m, whichever is the greater, except ·that saucers constructed in accordance with A 14 may be accepted in lieu of a centreline division in and beneath a hatchway except in the case of linseed and other seeds having similar properties;

.3   all hatches to filled compartments, trimmed, shall be closed and covers secured in place;

.4   all free grain surfaces in partly filled cargo space shall be trimmed level and secured in accordance with A 16, A 17 or A 18;

.5   throughout the voyage the metacentric height after correction for the free surface effects of liquids in tanks shall be 0.3 m or that given by the following formula, whichever is the greater;

$$GM_R = \frac{L\,B\,Vd\,(0.25\,B - 0.645\,\sqrt{Vd\,B})}{SF \times \Delta \times 0.0875}$$

Where:

L = total combined length of all full compartments (metres)

B = moulded breadth of the vessel (metres)

SF = stowage factor (cubic metres per tonne)

Vd = calculated average void depth calculated in accordance with B 1 (metres – Note: not millimeters)

Δ = displacement (tonnes); and

.6   the master demonstrates to the satisfaction of the Administration or the Contracting Government of the port of loading on behalf of the Administration that the ship in its proposed loaded condition will comply with the requirements of this section.

The factor Vd, average void depth, needed for the calculation required by this option necessitates reference to Part B of the Code, which contains the details needed by naval architects to prepare Grain Loading Booklets. However, tables to calculate Vd are provided on pages 62 and 63 of this booklet together with a rearrangement of the formula in A 9.1.5, intended to make it easier to perform on a calculator.

Implicit in the option under A 9, is the loading condition whereby no standard grain stability calculations are required. If, in accordance with A 9.1.4, all the bulk grain cargo is carried in partly filled holds and secured and the total weight of grain is limited as per A 9.1.1, then there is no GM_R calculation requirement. However, if the Administration imposes a cargo ship stability requirement, then this would still apply.

Additional Grain Stowage Requirements

In addition to trimming to minimize the possibility that bulk grain may shift, A 10 makes other stowage requirements which are necessary to achieve this purpose.

A 10.4 requires that, if there is no bulk grain or other cargo above a lower cargo space containing grain, the hatch covers shall be secured in an approved manner. The need for this is evident when considering that, if the covers are not secured, a shift in the grain below could cause the covers to lift, spilling grain into the upper compartment and thereby generating a Grain Heeling Moment as shown in Figure 10.

See diagram next page ➤

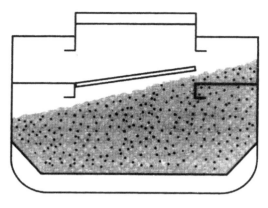

Figure 10

Similarly, A 10.5 requires that when bulk grain is to be stowed on top of closed tween-deck hatch covers which are not grain-tight by design, such covers shall be made grain-tight by taping the joints, covering the entire hatchway with tarpaulins or separation cloths, or other suitable means. It is obvious that if, during the course of the voyage, some of the bulk grain in an upper compartment shifts down to a lower compartment through the joints in the hatch covers, then the void space above the grain in the upper compartment will increase. This will increase the potential Grain Heeling Moment so that the stability calculations, although demonstrating compliance at the start of the voyage, will not indicate the actual condition.

In the case of specially suitable compartments which are filled, untrimmed, in accordance with A 10.3.2, the grain in the spaces forward and aft of the hatchway is disposed at its angle of repose, flowing outward from the lower edges of the hatch end beams. However, if there are bleeder (feeder) holes in the hatch end beams, as shown in Figure 11, the grain flows through the holes, thereby reducing the void space which would be present if the grain flowed only from the lower boundary. Where such holes are provided the tabulated Volumetric Heeling Moment is reduced to credit the smaller void space. Thus, when the hatchway is filled, time must be allowed for bleeding through the bleeder holes to be completed. When bleeding ceases and the hatchway is filled, then loading is complete and the hatch can be closed.

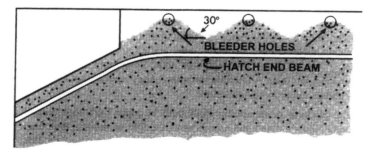

Figure 11

Other Methods of Achieving Compliance

In the event that the calculations for a proposed stowage arrangement do not meet the stability requirements of A 7.1, alternative stowage arrangements should be investigated. If this is not successful, other, usually more costly, alternatives are available as follows:

A.   Ballasting

If there is reserve deadweight (i.e. the proposed loading condition does not bring the ship to its permitted Load Line draft), then taking ballast may be helpful. The ballast should be in the double bottom tanks and the tanks should be filled to eliminate any free surface effect. The addition of weight low down will increase the displacement and lower the KG_V. Generally, this will increase the Maximum Allowable Heeling Moment and that, in turn, may be sufficient to make the proposed stowage arrangement acceptable.

If this alternative is to be used, the ballast must be on board at time of departure. Sometimes, because of dirty harbor water or similar considerations, it is not advisable for the ship to take ballast while at the loading berth. In such cases, the stability calculation should show the ballast on board and the Master must certify that the ballasting will be done en route to sea and will be completed before the vessel departs sheltered waters. This certification may be in the form of a letter, signed by the Master.

This option does not require any special information or endorsement in the Grain Loading Booklet.

B.   Overstowing

If a compartment is partly filled with bulk grain, the Grain Heeling Moment is much greater than it would be if the compartment was filled. The Grain Heeling Moment for a partly filled compartment can be eliminated (i.e. reduced to zero) by securing the slack surface against shifting by overstowing it with bagged grain or with other cargo that will have the similar effect of restraining the grain surface against any movement. A reduction in the total Grain Heeling Moment, achieved by this means, may be sufficient to bring the proposed stowage arrangement within the limits specified in the Maximum Allowable Heeling Moment table.

This option does not require any special information or endorsement in the Grain Loading Booklet.

The specific requirements for overstowing are given in A 16, as follows:

A 16.1   Where bagged grain or other suitable cargo is utilized for the purpose of securing partly filled compartments, the free grain surface shall be level and shall be covered with a separation cloth or equivalent or by a suitable platform. Such platform shall consist of bearers spaced not more than 1.2 m apart and 25 mm boards laid thereon spaced not more than 100 mm apart. Platforms may be constructed of other materials provided they are deemed by the Administration to be equivalent.

A 16.2   The platform or separation cloth shall be topped off with bagged grain tightly stowed and extending to a height of not less than one sixteenth of the maximum breadth of the free grain surface or 1.2 m, whichever is the greater.

A 16.3   The bagged grain shall be carried in sound bags which shall be well filled and securely closed.

A 16.4   Instead of bagged grain, other suitable cargo tightly stowed and exerting at least the same pressure as bagged grain stowed in accordance with A 16.2 may be used.

C.   Saucers

The Grain Heeling Moment may be significantly reduced in a filled compartment by constructing a saucer in the square of the hatchway, as described in A 14. This device is considered to have the same effect as a centerline, grain-tight bulkhead in that it prevents the grain from shifting across the entire breadth of the compartment, as illustrated in Figure 12.

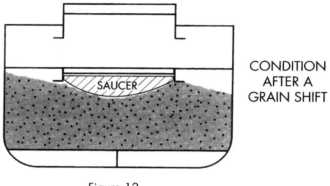

CONDITION AFTER A GRAIN SHIFT

Figure 12

Unless there are grain-tight divisions forward and aft of the hatchway, the effect is limited to the longitudinal length of the saucer. The Volumetric Heeling Moment which applies in a specific compartment when a saucer is fitted must be included in the approved Grain Loading Booklet if this option is to be available for use by the ship.

The specific requirements pertaining to the use and construction of saucers are given in A 14 as follows:

A 14.1   For the purpose of reducing the heeling moment a saucer may be used in place of a longitudinal division in way of a hatch opening only in a filled, trimmed, compartment as defined in A 2.2, except in the case of linseed and other seeds having similar properties, where a saucer may not be substituted for a longitudinal division. If a longitudinal division is provided, it shall meet the requirements of A 10.9.

A 14.2   The depth of the saucer, measured from the bottom of the saucer to the deck line, shall be as follows:

     .1   For ships with a moulded breadth of up to 9.1 m, not less that 1.2 m.

     .2   For ships with a moulded breadth of 18.3 m or more, not less than 1.8 m.

     .3   For ships with a moulded breadth between 9.1 m and 18.3 m, the minimum depth of the saucer shall be calculated by interpolation.

A 14.3   The top (mouth) of the saucer shall be formed by the underdeck structure in way of the hatchway, i.e. hatch side girders or coamings and hatch end beams. The saucer and hatchway above shall be completely filled with bagged grain or other suitable cargo laid down on a separation cloth or its equivalent and stowed tightly against adjacent structure so as to have a bearing contact with such structure to a depth equal to or greater than one half of the depth specified in A 14.2. If hull structure to provide such bearing surface is not available, the saucer shall be fixed in position by steel wire rope, chain, or double steel strapping as specified in A 17.4 and spaced not more than 2.4 m apart.

D.   Bundling of Bulk Grain

Whereas a saucer is formed by a volume of bagged grain or similarly restrained cargo, the same result (i.e. preventing a transverse shift of grain across the entire breadth of the compartment), as illustrated in Figure 12, may be achieved by constructing a single, large bag of bulk grain which fills the hatchway and which is fixed in position by the structural boundaries of the hatchway. This is termed "bundling of bulk grain" and is an acceptable alternative to a saucer. (See illustration on page 58 of this booklet).

The Volumetric Heeling Moment which applies when bundling of bulk grain is used in a specific compartment is the same as that which applies for a saucer used in the same location and, similarly, it must be listed in the Grain Loading Booklet if this option is to be available for use by the vessel.

The specific requirements pertaining to the method "bundling of bulk grain" are given in A 15. It is to be noted that the limitations on its use are the same as those which apply to a saucer and are specified in A 14.1.

A 15   As an alternative to filling the saucer in a filled, trimmed compartment with bagged grain or other suitable cargo a bundle of bulk grain may be used provided that:

    .1   The dimensions and means for securing the bundle in place are the same as specified for a saucer in A 14.2 and A 14.3.

    .2   The saucer is lined with a material acceptable to the Administration having a tensile strength of not less than 2,687 N per 5 cm strip and which is provided with suitable means for securing at the top.

    .3   As an alternative to A 15.2, a material acceptable to the Administration having a tensile strength of not less than 1,344 N per 5 cm strip may used if the saucer is constructed as follows:

        .1   Athwartship lashings acceptable to the Administration shall be placed inside the saucer formed in the bulk grain at intervals of not more than 2.4 m. These lashings shall be of sufficient length to permit being drawn up tight and secured at the top of the saucer.

        .2   Dunnage not less than 25 mm in thickness or other suitable material of equal strength and between 150 mm and 300 mm in width shall be placed fore and aft over these lashings to prevent the cutting or chafing of the material which shall be placed thereon to line the saucer.

    .4   The saucer shall be filled with bulk grain and secured at the top except that when using material approved under A 15.3 further dunnage shall be laid on top after lapping the material before the saucer is secured by setting up the lashings.

.5   If more than one sheet of material is used to line the saucer they shall be joined at the bottom either by sewing or by a double lap.

.6   The top of the saucer shall be coincidental with the bottom of the beams when these are in place and suitable general cargo or bulk grain may be placed between the beams on top of the saucer.

E.   Strapping or Lashing

Partly filled compartments have the greatest Volumetric Heeling Moments because they have large volumes of open space above the grain surfaces into which grain can shift and, also, because the regulations assume a 25 degree shift instead of the 15 degree shift which applies when the compartment is filled. A significant reduction in the total Volumetric Heeling Moment and, consequently, the Grain Heeling Moment can be achieved by completely preventing a grain shift in a partly filled compartment. The Grain Heeling Moment attributable to that compartment would then be reduced to zero. This may be accomplished by fabricating a somewhat costly construction which completely covers the slack grain surface and physically restrains it against any movement which may be generated by the motions of the ship at sea. (See illustration on page 59 of this booklet).

The use of this option does not require any special information or endorsement in the Grain Loading Booklet. The specific requirements pertaining to the details of construction and application are given in A 17:

A 17   When, in order to eliminate heeling moments in partly filled compartments, strapping or lashing is utilized, the securing shall be accomplished as follows:

.1   The grain shall be trimmed and levelled to the extent that is very slightly crowned and covered with burlap separation cloths, tarpaulins or the equivalent.

.2   The separation cloths and/or tarpaulins shall overlap by at least 1.8 m.

.3   Two solid floors of rough 25 mm x 150 mm to 300 mm lumber shall be laid with the top floor running longitudinally and nailed to an athwartships bottom floor. Alternatively, one solid floor of 50 mm lumber, running longitudinally and nailed over the top of a 50 mm bottom bearer not less than 150 mm wide, may be used. The bottom bearers shall extend the full breadth of the compartment and shall be spaced not more than 2.4 m apart. Arrangements utilizing other materials and deemed by the Administration to be equivalent to the foregoing may be accepted.

.4   Steel wire rope (19 mm diameter or equivalent), double steel strapping (50 mm x 1.3 mm and having a breaking load of at least 49 kN), or chain of equivalent strength, each of which shall be set tightly be means of a 32 mm turnbuckle, may be used for lashings. A winch tightener, used in conjunction with a locking arm, may be substituted for the 32 mm turnbuckle when steel strapping is used, provided suitable wrenches are available for setting up as necessary. When steel strapping is used, not less than three crimp seals shall be used for securing the ends. When wire is used, not less than four clips shall be used for forming eyes in the lashings.

.5   Prior to the completion of loading the lashing shall be positively attached to the framing at a point approximately 450 mm below the anticipated final grain surface by means of either a 25 mm shackle or beam clamp of equivalent strength.

.6   The lashings shall be spaced not more than 2.4 m apart and each shall be supported by a bearer nailed over the top of the fore and aft floor. This bearer shall consist of lumber of not less than 25 mm x 150 mm or its equivalent and shall extend the full breadth of the compartment.

.7   During the voyage the strapping shall be regularly inspected and set up where necessary.

F.   Securing with Wire Mesh

This method of reducing the Grain Heeling Moment to zero, by preventing a slack grain surface from shifting, is essentially the same as "Strapping or Lashing" except that the principal restraining force of the transverse cables, spaced every 2.4 meters for the length of the hold, is transmitted to the overall, fabric-covered surface of the grain by means of a stiff wire mesh, of the type used to reinforce concrete, instead of through a deck constructed of dunnage. (See illustration on page 60 of this booklet).

The use of this option does not require any special information or endorsement in the Grain Loading Booklet. The specific requirements pertaining to the details of construction and application are given in A 18:

A 18   When, in order to eliminate grain heeling moments in partly filled compartments, strapping or lashing is utilized, the securing may, as an alternative to the method described in A 17, be accomplished as follows:

.1   The grain shall be trimmed and levelled to the extent that it is very slightly crowned along the fore and aft centreline of the compartment.

.2   The entire surface of the grain shall be covered with burlap separation cloths, tarpaulins, or the equivalent. The covering material shall have a tensile strength of not less than 1,344 N per 5 cm strip.

.3   Two layers of wire reinforcement mesh shall be laid on top of the burlap or other covering. The bottom layer is to be laid athwartships and the top layer is to be laid longitudinally. The lengths of wire mesh are to be overlapped at least 75 mm. The top layer of mesh is to be positioned over the bottom layer in such a manner that the squares formed by the alternate layers measure approximately 75 mm x 75 mm. The wire reinforcement mesh is the type used in reinforced concrete construction. It is fabricated of 3 mm diameter steel wire having a breaking strength of not less than 52 kN/cm^2 welded in 150 mm x 150 mm squares. Wire mesh having mill scale may be used but mesh having loose, flaking rust may not be used.

.4   The boundaries of the wire mesh, at the port and starboard side of the compartment, shall be retained by wood planks 150 mm x 50 mm.

.5   Hold-down lashings, running from side to side across the compartment, shall be spaced not more than 2.4 m apart except that the first and the last lashing shall not be more than 300 mm from the forward or after bulkhead, respectively. Prior to the completion of the loading, each lashing shall be positively attached to the framing at a point approximately 450 mm below the anticipated final grain surface by means of either a 25 mm shackle or a beam clamp of equivalent strength. The lashing shall be led from this point over the top of the boundary plank described in A 18.4, which has the function of distributing the downward pressure exerted by the lashing. Two layers of 150 mm x 25 mm planks shall be laid athwartships centred beneath each lashing and extending the full breadth of the compartment.

.6   The hold-down lashings shall consist of steel wire rope (19 mm diameter or equivalent), double steel strapping (50 mm x 1.3 mm and having a breaking load of at least 49 kN), or chain of equivalent strength, each of which shall be set tight by means of a 32 mm turnbuckle. A winch tightener, used in conjunction with a locking arm, may be substituted for the 32 mm turnbuckle when steel strapping is used, provided suitable wrenches are available for setting up as necessary. When steel strapping is used, not less than three crimp seals shall be used for securing the ends. When wire rope is used, not less than four clips shall be used for forming eyes in the lashings.

.7   During the voyage the hold-down lashings shall be regularly inspected and set up where necessary.

G.   Temporary Longitudinal Divisions

The Grain Heeling Moment in a compartment, in either the filled or partly filled condition, can be significantly reduced by installing, usually on the fore and aft centerline, a longitudinal bulkhead which prevents the grain from shifting across the entire breadth of the compartment. This is an expensive alternative, but it is available for use if the applicable Volumetric Heeling Moment is listed in the ship's Grain Loading Booklet. Obviously, if the grain is loaded on both sides of a longitudinal bulkhead, the stress on the bulkhead will be less than it would be if the grain was loaded on only one side. The Code contains regulations governing the strength of fittings and design of divisions loaded on both sides and on one side only. The requirements for divisions loaded on both sides are simpler and detailed in A 11 and A 12:

A 11.1   *Timber*

All timber used for grain fittings shall be of good sound quality and of a type and grade which has been proved to be satisfactory for this purpose. The actual finished dimensions of the timber shall be in accordance with the dimensions specified below. Plywood of an exterior type bonded with waterproof glue and fitted so that the direction of the grain in the face plies is perpendicular to the supporting uprights or binder may be used provided that its strength is equivalent to that of solid timber of the appropriate scantlings.

A 11.3   *Other materials*

Materials other than wood or steel may be approved for such divisions provided that proper regard has been paid to their mechanical properties.

A 11.4   *Uprights*

.1   Unless means are provided to prevent the ends of uprights being dislodged from their sockets, the depth of housing at each end of each upright shall be not less than 75 mm. If an upright is not secured at the top, the uppermost shore or stay shall be fitted as near thereto as is practicable.

.2   The arrangements provided for inserting shifting boards by removing a part of the cross-section of an upright shall be such that the local level of stresses is not unduly high.

A 11.5   *Composite section*

Where uprights, binders or any other strength members are formed by two separate sections, one fitted on each side of a division and interconnected by through bolts at adequate spacing, the effective section modulus shall be taken as the sum of the two moduli of the separate sections.

A 11.6   *Partial division*

Where divisions do not extend to the full depth of the cargo space such divisions and their uprights shall be supported or stayed so as to be as efficient as those which do extend to the full depth of the cargo space.

A 12.1   *Shifting boards*

.1   Shifting boards shall have a thickness of not less than 50 mm and shall be fitted grain-tight and where necessary supported by uprights.

.2   The maximum unsupported span for shifting boards of various thicknesses shall be as follows:

Thickness	Maximum unsupported span
50 mm	2.5 m
60 mm	3.0 m
70 mm	3.5 m
80 mm	4.0 m

If thicknesses greater than these are provided the maximum unsupported span will vary directly with the increase in thickness.

.3   The ends of all shifting boards shall be securely housed with 75 mm minimum bearing length.

A 12.2   *Other materials*

Divisions formed by using material other than wood shall have a strength equivalent to the shifting boards required in A 12.1.

A 12.3   *Uprights*

.1   Steel uprights used to support divisions loaded on both sides shall have a section modulus given by

$$W = a \times W_1$$

Where:

W = section modulus in cubic centimeters
a = horizontal span between uprights in metres.

The section modulus per metre span W_1 shall be not less than that given by the formula:

$$W_1 = 14.8 \ (h_1 - 1.2) \ cm^3/m$$

Where:

h_1 is the vertical unsupported span in metres and shall be taken as the maximum value of the distance between any two adjacent stays or between a stay and either end of the upright. Where this distance is less than 2.4 m the respective modulus shall be calculated as if the actual value were 2.4 m.

.2   The moduli of wood uprights shall be determined by multiplying by 12.5 the corresponding moduli for steel uprights. If other materials are used their moduli shall be at least that required for steel increased in proportion to the ratio of the permissible stresses for steel to that of the material used. In such cases attention shall be paid also to the relative rigidity of each upright to ensure that the deflection is not excessive.

.3   The horizontal distance between uprights shall be such that the unsupported spans of the shifting boards do not exceed the maximum span specified in A 12.1.2.

A 12.4   *Shores*

.1   Wood shores, when used, shall be in a single piece and shall be securely fixed at each end and heeled against the permanent structure of the ship except that they shall not bear directly against the side plating of the ship.

.2   Subject to the provisions of A 12.4.3 and A 12.4.4, the minimum size of wood shores shall be as follows:

Length of shore (m)	Rectangular section (mm)	Diameter of circular section (mm)
Not exceeding 3 m	150 x 100	140
Over 3 m but not exceeding 5 m	150 x 150	165
Over 5 m but not exceeding 6 m	150 x 150	180
Over 6 m but not exceeding 7 m	200 x 150	190
Over 7 m but not exceeding 8 m	200 x 150	200
Exceeding 8 m	200 x 150	215

Shores of 7 m or more in length shall be securely bridged at approximately mid-length.

.3 When the horizontal distance between the uprights differs significantly from 4 m the moments of inertia of the shores may be changed in direct proportion.

.4 Where the angle of the shore to the horizontal exceeds 10° the next larger shore to that required by A 12.4.2 shall be fitted provided that in no case shall the angle between any shore and the horizontal exceed 45°.

A 12.5 *Stays*

Where stays are used to support divisions loaded on both sides, they shall be fitted horizontally or as near thereto as practicable, well secured at each end and formed of steel wire rope. The sizes of the wire rope shall be determined assuming that the divisions and upright which the stay supports are uniformly loaded at 4.9 kN/m². The working load so assumed in the stay shall not exceed one third of its breaking load.

If the bulkhead is going to be loaded with bulk grain on one side only (usually the case when a temporary, transverse, bulkhead is installed to reduce the length of a compartment), there are additional strength requirements in A 11.2 and A 11.4.3. These have been omitted from the above. Also, further details of construction are given in A 13. These have not been included here as application of this regulation requires a knowledge of structural engineering. If, therefore, it is to be used on a ship, the plans and specifications for the bulkhead must be included in, or be a supplement to, the ship's approved Grain Loading Booklet.

GENERAL INFORMATION ON GRAIN LOADING

ACCEPTANCE OF VESSELS TO LOAD BULK GRAIN AT UNITED STATES PORTS

Certificate of Readiness

A Certificate of Readiness is a document which must be issued by a National Cargo Bureau surveyor before a vessel can load grain at a United States port (see example on page 81 of this booklet). The information presented in the following pages is intended to clarify the requirements for the issuance of the Certificate and thereby help prevent costly delays which might result from failure to meet them.

Document of Authorization

The vessel should have on board a Document of Authorization (see page 27 of this booklet), issued by the Administration of the country of registry or by an agency authorized to issue such documents on behalf of that Administration. The document should accompany and refer to the approved Grain Loading Booklet which is provided to enable the Master to meet the requirements of the International Grain Code.

Change of Registry

When a vessel changes registry, the Grain Loading Booklet must be approved or accepted by the new Administration or an agency authorized to act on behalf of that Administration and a new Document of Authorization issued. Owners and operators are cautioned that such approval is not automatic and may, in some cases, require preparation of a new Booklet to conform to the requirements of the new Administration. Therefore, it is strongly recommended that timely action be taken to obtain such approval or acceptance by the new Administration in order to avoid possible delay when the vessel is presented to load grain.

Seaworthiness

The vessel should have on board valid Cargo Ship Safety Construction and Load Line Certificates.

A Vessel without a Document of Authorization

A vessel which does not have on board a valid Document of Authorization may load grain under the requirements and limitations set forth in A 3.5 or A 9 of the Code (see page 28 of this booklet).

Stability Calculation

A stability calculation, signed by the Master, which demonstrates that the vessel will comply with the stability requirements of the appropriate regulations at every stage of the voyage must be presented to the attending Surveyor before a Certificate of Readiness will be issued. The source information used in preparing the calculation must correspond to that detailed in the approved Grain Loading Booklet. Information on preparation of grain stability calculations is shown in this booklet, beginning on page 49.

Fittings

All grain divisions which are to be utilized for a particular stowage arrangement shall be grain tight, in sound condition, and constructed in accordance with the requirements in A 11 and A 12 of the Code or the design and specifications as included in the approved Grain Loading Booklet, whichever is applicable.

Structural Defects

The boundaries of cargo compartments in which grain is to be loaded shall be structurally intact and free of leaks. Deficiencies which may affect seaworthiness or the satisfactory carriage of the grain may have occurred after issuance of the Cargo Ship Safety Construction and Load Line Certificates. If such deficiencies are found, they will be brought to the attention of the Master and evaluation or repair to the satisfaction of the ship's Classification Society shall be required before a Certificate of Readiness to load grain can be issued.

PREPARING A SHIP FOR LOADING GRAIN

Compartments scheduled to be loaded must, in every respect, be fit to receive grain. The following suggestions are offered for personnel in charge of preparing a ship for loading grain:

CLEANLINESS. It is essential that all spaces intended for grain be thoroughly clean (i.e. free of previous cargo residues and other contaminants, free of odor and free of loose rust or paint scale). Particular care must be taken to clean the overhead beams, ledges and the underside structure of steel hatch covers.

BILGES. Bilges and/or drain wells must be cleaned and then securely covered with burlap or other suitable material which is grain-tight but not watertight. Bilge suctions and sounding pipes must be clear. Tween-deck scuppers must be made grain-tight.

MOISTURE. Compartments in which grain is to be loaded should be dry. Consideration should be given to wooden structures, such as ceiling landing pads, bilge limber boards and grain fittings, where water may become trapped in or behind the structures/fittings.

INFESTATION. A thorough inspection of the grain compartments should be made for any signs of insect or rodent infestation. This applies particularly to vessels which have previously carried grain cargoes. Any indication of infestation will be cause for rejection by government inspectors or their representatives, who may then require fumigation or extermination prior to acceptance.

STRUCTURAL INTEGRITY. Cargo compartments must be structurally sound. Cement boxes over holes or cracks affecting the watertight integrity are not permitted. Bulkheads below the main deck must be watertight. Manholes on double bottom tanks under grain holds should be inspected for tightness and, if necessary, the tanks should be tested by pressing up. Weather deck hatch covers should be inspected for watertightness and, if necessary, hose tested.

SHEATHING OF HOT BULKHEADS. Fire-room and engine room bulkheads, which are subject to temperatures of 110° F (43.3° C) or above and are adjacent to holds in which bulk grain is stowed, should be sheathed. Sheathing is also required whenever bulk grain is stowed adjacent to the bulkhead of a tank in which a heated liquid is carried.

DEEP TANKS. When grain is to be loaded in deep tanks, the ballast filling lines and heating coil lines must be blanked in the tanks or engine room. Where deep tanks are not fitted with drain wells or covered bilges, the bilge suctions should be adequately boxed.

WING TANKS. When grain is to be loaded into wing tanks, precautions should be taken against the entry of water through ballast filling lines, overboard discharge valves, deck vents, deck manholes and any other openings. Ballasting of wing tanks is to be avoided when grain is carried in the cargo holds.

ELECTRICAL WIRING. Wiring and electrical equipment buried in bulk grain constitute a significant fire hazard. Unless essential to the underway operation of the ship, all electrical circuits in grain compartments must be disconnected or defuzed.

PRECAUTIONS WHILE LOADING A GRAIN CARGO

The grain regulations are predicated on cargo spaces being as full as possible and well trimmed. Constant supervision and inspection by ship's officers is required to ensure that this is done. Proper trimming can be ascertained by frequent sighting through trimming hatches and access manholes. When loading dusty cargoes, it may be necessary to interrupt loading periodically to allow the dust to settle sufficiently to inspect the trimming. When trimming machines are used, the throwing distance should be kept to a minimum. Poor trimming is difficult and expensive to correct.

TRIMMING HATCHES. When tween-decks and lower holds are loaded in combination, trimming hatches and access manholes must be left open. When the tween- decks and lower holds are loaded separately, these openings must be closed.

SEALING OF TWEEN-DECKS. When a tween-deck is loaded separately from a lower hold, the tween-deck must be sealed to prevent the settling of grain into the compartment below.

SECURING HATCH COVERS OF FILLED COMPARTMENTS. If there is no bulk grain or other cargo above a filled compartment of a tween-deck vessel, the hatch covers shall be secured in an approved manner, having regard to the weight of the covers and permanent arrangements provided for securing such covers.

ELECTRICAL FIRES. During loading operations serious fires, or even explosions, can be caused by faulty electrical circuits in cargo compartments and by portable cargo lights left unattended in grain compartments. All electrical circuits in grain compartments must be disconnected or defuzed and portable lights must be removed when not in use.

LOAD LINES. A Certificate of Loading will not be issued if the vessel is loaded deeper than her seasonal marks, after correction for density. In all cases, the applicable freeboard, as shown on the Load Line Certificate, will govern. The Certificate of Loading becomes void if, at any stage of the voyage, the vessel is at a draft deeper than her appropriate seasonal marks.

If, in order to remain within a certain Load Line Zone, the vessel must follow an indirect route to her destination, the stability calculation should indicate this fact and there should be sufficient fuel and water on hand for the intended voyage. No allowance will be permitted for pumping out residual ballast after departure.

GREAT LAKES LOAD LINE REGULATIONS. All ships loading at U.S. ports on the Great Lakes must comply with the U.S. Coast Guard Great Lakes Load Line Regulations. 46 CFR §45.9 states as follows:

(a) For the purposes of the law and regulations prohibiting submergence of load lines (46 U.S.C. 88c; 46 CFR 42.07-10) the marks assigned to vessels holding international load line certificates apply during the following seasons:

(1) Vessels assigned freeboards as new vessels under the International Load Line Convention, 1966 -
  (i) Winter - November 1 through March 31;
  (ii) Summer - April 1 through April 30 and October 1 through October 31;
  (iii) Tropical - May 1 through September 30.

(2) Vessels assigned freeboards as existing vessels under the International Load Line Convention, 1966 -
    (i)   Winter - November 1 through March 31;
    (ii) Summer - April 1 through April 30 and October 1 through October 31;
    (iii) Tropical - September 16 through September 30;
    (iv) Tropical Fresh - May 1 through September 15.

(b) Except for hopper dredges operating at working freeboards in accordance with subpart C of part 44 of this chapter, the Assigning Authority may not allow for lesser freeboards.

Note that there is no provision for a vessel loading in the Great Lakes to utilize Fresh Water Allowance and submerge any of the applicable marks accordingly. This means that a ship loading in the Great Lakes in April, for example, will not reach Summer Displacement – loading must stop when the Summer <u>Marks</u> are reached.

The governing regulations for the above example can be found in 46 CFR §42.07-10 as follows:

(c) When a vessel is in fresh water of unit density, the appropriate load line may be submerged by the amount of the fresh water allowance shown on the applicable load line certificate. Where the density is other than unity, an allowance shall be made proportional to the difference between 1.025 and the actual density. **This paragraph does not apply to vessels when navigating the Great Lakes.**
(Emphasis added)

(d) When a vessel departs from a port situated on a river or inland waters, deeper loading shall be permitted corresponding to the weight of fuel and all other materials required for consumption between the port of departure and the sea. **This paragraph does not apply to vessels when navigating the Great Lakes.**
(Emphasis added)

LIST. A Certificate of Loading will be issued only if, after completion of loading and prior to departure, the vessel is upright or is listed no more than one degree.

TRIM BY THE HEAD. If, at the completion of loading, the vessel is trimmed by more than one-half percent of the Length Between Perpendiculars (0.005 x LBP) by the head, a Certificate of Loading will be issued only if the Master furnishes a statement that he considers it safe to proceed in this condition.

LONGITUDINAL STRENGTH. Longitudinal strength is not regulated by the International Grain Code. Should longitudinal strength become a concern to the surveyor, the ship's Master shall satisfy the surveyor that the longitudinal strength of the ship is not impaired.

WEATHER-DECK HATCH COVERS. Precautions should be taken to prevent the leakage of water into grain cargoes through the joints of metal weather-deck hatch covers, such as may be caused by the working of the vessel in heavy weather. Sealing of these joints by tape or other means is recommended, particularly with respect to the forward hatches.

OVERHEATING OF DOUBLE BOTTOM TANKS. Precautions should be taken to prevent damage to grain cargoes by overheating of double bottom or other fuel tanks. Engineer officers should be advised regarding this hazard.

CARRIAGE OF BULK GRAIN IN TANKERS

A tanker is defined as a vessel specially designed and constructed for the carriage of liquid cargoes in bulk, and in which the cargo spaces are subdivided into smaller compartments by longitudinal and transverse bulkheads.

There are certain requirements related to safety and good cargo outturn which must be met before a tanker can be considered ready to load bulk grain. These requirements include, but are not limited to, the following:

CLEANLINESS. Compartments are to be completely clean, dry, odor-free, and gas-free. All loose scale is to be removed. In case of doubt concerning odor, the compartment should be closed and reinspected 24 hours later.

PIPELINES. All pipelines to cargo compartments must be thoroughly cleaned, drained, and blown dry. Heating coil lines and deck manifolds must be blanked. In tankers which have an independent stripping system, all pipelines, except the stripping lines, are to be blanked off in the pump room. In tankers which have the stripping lines attached to the main suction lines, all pipelines, except those forming the stripping arrangement, are to be blanked off in the pump room or other locations as necessary. In tankers where blanking is impossible due to the construction of the piping system, applicable valves must be secured by means of chains, padlocks, and seals. The time and date of this securing operation, together with the seal numbers, should be entered in the ship's Log Book.

BOXING OF SUCTIONS. Tankers that do not have bilge suction wells must be provided with an alternative arrangement to enable water to be removed. They must be fitted with boxes of 3" thick lumber or suitable perforated metal (minimum 16 gauge) constructed around the stripping line suction. Such boxes must be grain-tight, but not watertight, and have a capacity of not less than 22 cubic feet. Limbers, or openings, properly covered with burlap or mesh must be provided to permit the entry of water. Where the inside diameter of the stripping line is six inches or less, the total area of such openings should be determined by multiplying the inside cross-sectional area of the stripping line pipe by six. Where the inside diameter of the stripping line exceeds six inches, the minimum total area of the openings must be 180 square inches.

SOUNDING PIPES. Every compartment in which grain is carried must be equipped with a sounding pipe having an inside diameter of not less than 1 1/2", the lower end of which is to be made grain-tight but not watertight. Plastic pipes should have a wall thickness of not less than 0.145" (schedule 40 gauge). Such pipes are to be secured at sufficient intervals along their length to prevent bending and should be fitted with caps at the upper ends and "T" fittings at the lower ends.

STABILITY TERMS AND SYMBOLS

B	-	CENTER OF BOUYANCY (a single point within the portion of the ship's hull which is below the waterline and through which the force of buoyancy appears to operate when the ship is upright).
KB	-	Height above the keel of the Center of Buoyancy.
G	-	CENTER OF GRAVITY (a single point within the entire structure of the ship at which the total weight of the ship, and all that is in her, appears to be concentrated).
VCG (or Kg)	-	VERTICAL CENTER OF GRAVITY (height above the keel of the Center of Gravity of a cargo compartment or tank).
KG	-	Height above the keel of the Center of Gravity.
KG$_v$	-	Virtual height above the keel of a ship's Center of Gravity, obtained by adding the corrections for liquid free surfaces and vertical grain shifting moments (if applicable) to KG.
M	-	METACENTER or TRANSVERSE METACENTER (the point of intersection of vertical lines projected upwards through the Center of Buoyancy at consecutive small angles of heel).
KM	-	Height above the keel of the Transverse Metacenter.
GM	-	METACENTRIC HEIGHT (usually refers to GM corrected for free surface effect; the vertical distance between the Metacenter and the Virtual Center of Gravity, i.e. KM − KG$_v$).
MOMENT	-	The product of a weight multiplied by a distance.
HEEL	-	The transverse angle of inclination of a vessel.
HEELING MOMENT	-	The moment resulting from a transverse shift of weight through a given distance which tends to heel a vessel. Expressed as tonne-meters or foot-tons. (Also known as UPSETTING MOMENT).
VOLUMETRIC HEELING MOMENT	-	The product of a shifted volume multiplied by a transverse distance. Expressed as m^4 (m^3 x m) or ft^4 (ft^3 x ft). Converted to Heeling Moment by dividing by the Stowage Factor (or multiplying by the density) of a cargo.
GZ	-	RIGHTING ARM or RIGHTING LEVER (the horizontal distance between the force of buoyancy acting upwards through B and the force of gravity acting downwards through G).
RIGHTING MOMENT	-	The product of the Righting Arm (GZ) multiplied by the displacement (weight) of the ship.

TRIM TERMS AND SYMBOLS

TRIM	-	The longitudinal inclination of the ship. It is measured as the difference between the forward and after drafts.
LCB	-	LONGITUDINAL CENTER OF BUOYANCY (longitudinal position of Center of Buoyancy, generally expressed + or - as a distance from midships, but may be measured from the After Perpendicular).
LCG	-	LONGITUDINAL CENTER OF GRAVITY (longitudinal position of Center of Gravity, generally expressed + or - as a distance from midships, but may be measured from the After Perpendicular).
MTC (or MCTC)	-	MOMENT TO TRIM ONE CENTIMETER or Moment to Change the Trim by 1 cm.
MTI	-	MOMENT TO TRIM ONE INCH (moment to change the trim by 1").
TPC	-	TONNES PER CENTIMETER IMMERSION.
TPI	-	TONS PER INCH IMMERSION.

FORMS FOR STABILITY CALCULATIONS

Every vessel for which stability calculations are required by the Code must submit two copies of such calculations for the intended voyage to the attending National Cargo Bureau Surveyor before a Certificate of Readiness can be issued. With the exception of ships which load under A 9 of the Code, the calculations shall be drafted on the National Cargo Bureau Grain Stability Calculation Forms. The calculations must be legible, but electronic/mechanical completion is not required. The Forms, with any necessary insert sheets, will be furnished upon request by all local offices of National Cargo Bureau. They can also be downloaded in Adobe format from the National Cargo Bureau website (www.natcargo.org).

In the case of the required GM calculation for a ship loading under A 9 of the Code, the calculation shall be fully documented, although the format is not prescribed.

In each case, the calculation(s) shall be signed by the Master and by the Surveyor. One copy shall be retained on board the ship; the other copy shall be retained by the Surveyor.

The information and examples shown on the following pages are intended to assist ship Masters and Officers with proper preparation of the stability calculation.

PREPARATION OF GRAIN STABILITY CALCULATIONS

REQUISITE INFORMATION. The following information should be ascertained in order to prepare an accurate stability calculation:

1. The type and quantity of grain to be loaded.

2. An accurate estimate of the Stowage Factor.

3. The quantities of fuel and water on hand at departure, daily consumption, and amounts to be taken at bunkering ports during the voyage.

4. The Load Line Zones to be traversed during the voyage.

5. The quantities and stowage of other cargo to be carried at the same time as the grain cargo.

6. The distance and steaming time required to the port(s) of discharge.

7. Draft restrictions which may be encountered during the voyage.

With the above information on hand, the Grain Stability Calculation should be prepared, using the typical conditions shown in the Grain Loading Booklet as a guide.

UNITS. All figures used in the calculation should be shown in the same units as are used in the approved Grain Loading Booklet. (A Stowage Factor conversion table is furnished on page 100 of this booklet to assist with conversion from English to Metric units – an abbreviated conversion table appears on the Grain Stability Calculation Form itself). Tonnages and moments may be rounded off to the nearest unit.

CONDITIONS DURING THE VOYAGE. The Stability Calculation shall show:

1. The departure and arrival conditions.

2. The conditions on arrival and departure from bunkering ports. Additional insert

sheets for Part II of the National Cargo Bureau Grain Stability Calculation Form should be used as necessary for this purpose.

3.   If an arrival condition indicates ballast on board which was not shown in the departure condition, then an intermediate condition shall be included which will demonstrate compliance with the "worst" permissible stability requirement just prior to ballasting. Bunkering after departure is documented in the same way as ballasting.

FREE SURFACE OF LIQUIDS. Part II of the Grain Stability Calculation Form shall include a provision for the detrimental effect of the free surface of liquids on board. Although this may be based upon the actual condition of the tanks while the ship is at sea, it shall not be a lesser effect than is applied in the example conditions in the approved Grain Loading Booklet. In the case of U.S. flag vessels, the calculation with respect to liquid free surface shall comply with U.S. Coast Guard regulations as set forth in 46 CFR §170.285. For all vessels while at sea, the free surface of liquids should be kept to a minimum by maintaining all tanks either full or empty with the exception of those in actual use.

PARTLY FILLED COMPARTMENTS. A slack hold/compartment heeling moment value, used in the Calculations, must be at least as large as the Grain Loading Booklet value corresponding to the actual level of grain in the slack hold/compartment. To verify this requirement, ullages in slack holds/compartments will be checked by the attending NCB Surveyor upon completion of loading. Obviously, if the vessel meets the stability requirements, even when using maximum heeling moments for any slack hold/compartment, the grain can be loaded to any level within such hold/compartment without jeopardizing compliance with the Code. Checking this, while preparing the Grain Stability Calculation Form, adds an extra level of security in that, even if there are unexpected variations in the Stowage Factor or the exact amount of available cargo, the final loading condition will still comply with the Code. It should, however, be noted that use of maximum heeling moment values in the Calculations does not eliminate or reduce in any way the necessity for the grain surface in a slack hold/compartment to be leveled.

WING TANKS. When wing tanks are loaded, the maximum heeling moments for these compartments should be used in the Stability Calculation, since it is impracticable, if not impossible, to trim the tanks full. When converting Volumetric Heeling Moments to Grain Heeling Moments, the same Stowage Factor as that used in the cargo holds must be used for the wing tanks.

MAXIMUM ALLOWABLE HEELING MOMENT TABLE. This table should be used, provided it is included as part of the Grain Loading Booklet or an addendum thereto. The entering arguments are usually KG_V and Displacement. KG_V is the height of the center of gravity of the loaded ship (KG) increased by the correction for liquid free surface and the correction for vertical grain shifting moment (if applicable).

STATICAL STABILITY DIAGRAMS. In instances where the approved Grain Loading Booklet does not contain a table of Maximum Allowable Heeling Moments, Cross Curves of Stability must be utilized to prepare stability diagrams for each loading condition shown in the Stability Calculation. From these, the numerical values to be applied in the calculations, in order to demonstrate compliance with the requirements of A 7.1 of the Code, can be derived (see pages 55 and 56 of this booklet).

BALLASTING. Where, in order to meet stability requirements, ballast is required at time of departure and ballasting can not be accomplished at the loading berth due to draft restrictions or dirty harbor water, such ballasting must be completed while the vessel is in protected waters. The same condition would apply to deballasting at the port of destination.

SHIFTING BETWEEN PORTS. Vessels loading grain at two or more ports in the continental United States may, in some circumstances, be exempt from full compliance with the Code until the loading is completed at the last port before commencing the international voyage. The rules pertaining to this situation are given in Enclosure 2 to Navigation & Vessel Inspection Circular No. 5-95 (see page 10 of this booklet).

PART GRAIN CARGOES. Vessels which load part grain cargoes and subsequently load other cargo should indicate the proposed stowage location of the other cargo on the initial Grain Stability Calculation Form. If the final stowage arrangement differs from that shown in the original Calculation, a revised Stability Calculation shall be prepared.

DISCHARGE AT MORE THAN ONE PORT. When the grain cargo is discharged at more than one port (or when other cargo used to secure the grain cargo is discharged prior to the grain cargo), it shall be the responsibility of the Master to fully comply with the requirements of the vessel's Grain Loading Document and/or the requirements of local governing authorities at every stage of the voyage.

CONSTRUCTING AND MEASURING
A STATICAL STABILITY DIAGRAM

In the event that a ship's approved Grain Loading Booklet does not include a table (or curves) of Maximum Allowable Heeling Moments, it will be necessary to manually calculate the residual area and the angle of heel due to a grain shift in order to demonstrate compliance with the stability requirements of A 7 of the Code (see page 24 of this booklet).

To do this, you must first complete the calculations in Parts I, II and the first half of Part III of the National Cargo Bureau Grain Stability Calculation Form (hereinafter identified as the Form). These are the same calculations that must be performed for any grain loading and furnish the following information for each stage of the voyage, i.e. departure, arrival and, if necessary, intermediate conditions:

Displacement	*NOTE:*
KG_V	*As GM referred to is obtained*
GM	*from KG_V, it will already be*
Grain Heeling Moment	*corrected for free surface*

Next, you must draw the stability diagram for the specific displacement and KG_V. This requires use of the ship's approved Cross Curves of Stability. An example of a ship's Cross Curves of Stability is shown on page 57 of this booklet.

To facilitate the process of drawing the stability diagram and to complete the remainder of the required calculation, you should use Addendum # 1 to the Form. An example of a completed Addendum is shown on pages 55 and 56 of this booklet. The data used is taken from the example Cross Curves of Stability. Although the Addendum is intended to be self-explanatory, additional explanation is furnished in the paragraphs below, keyed to the encircled numbers on the illustration.

①   Normally the Cross Curves of Stability will be included in the approved Grain Loading Booklet. If not, they may be referenced and identified in the Booklet and furnished separately.

②   The angle of flooding is discussed on pages 25 - 26 of this booklet. For a ship which does not have a table of Maximum Allowable Heeling Moments, the angle of flooding should be included in the information furnished in the approved Grain Loading Booklet.

③   The assumed KG of the Cross Curves of Stability will be stated on the Curves. In some cases it will be identified as "pole height". It is now more common for the curves to be labeled as "KN Curves", in which case the assumed KG (pole height) is zero.

④   Since the assumed KG of the Cross Curves will probably not be identical to the actual KG_V of the ship, the correction factor determined here will need to be applied in order to adjust the Righting Arms for the difference between the two. As noted on Addendum # 1, it is important to retain the sign (+ or −).

⑤   The Angles of Inclination to be entered in the Table of Righting Arms will depend upon which angles are represented on the Curves. The angles selected should cover the range from 5° to at least 45°, preferably to 60°, in order to facilitate drawing of a smooth curve when the points are plotted. If a curve for 12° is not represented, then use the closest one to it, usually either 10° or 15°. Frequently, there is no curve for 5°. This is, however, an important angle that should not be disregarded in the plot, so enter 5° as the first angle of inclination in the Table of Righting Arms. How the value for this will be obtained is discussed in a subsequent paragraph in this section, dealing with the Plot of Stability Curve.

(6)   Using the example Cross Curves on page 57, for each angle of inclination find the point at which a vertical line projected from the appropriate position on the DISPLACEMENT scale, at the bottom, intersects the curve labeled for that angle. Project a horizontal line from that point of intersection (or set a pair of dividers) and read off the value of the GZ on the RIGHTING ARMS scale at the left.

(7)   The KG correction factor (previously determined) multiplied by the sine of the angle of inclination produces the figure that must be added or subtracted from the GZ, on the line above, in order to obtain the corrected GZ.

(8)   The corrected GZs are the righting arms at each angle of inclination for the displacement and KG_V calculated on Part II of the Form.

(9) These points, righting arms versus angle of inclination, must be plotted on the graph on page 2 of the Addendum. Note that the left side of the graph does not have a calibrated scale. The user must, therefore, calibrate the scale to accommodate the range of righting arms he is working with. In the example, the largest righting arm is 3.44 feet. Since there are four major scale divisions, mark the scale for a range from 0 to 4 feet. (If you were working in meters, the equivalent maximum righting arm would be 1.05 meters, so it may be appropriate to mark the major divisions as 0, 0.30, 0.60, 0.90 and 1.20 meters).

The corrected GZ at the 5° angle of inclination has not been defined. If a curve for 5° was included on the Cross Curves, then the procedure is the same as for the other angles. If not, and the calibrations on the left scale are of sufficient range, mark off the length of the GM on a vertical line at angle 57.3°. Mark a straight line from 0 to this point, then project a vertical line at angle 5°. Where these lines intersect establishes the 5° GZ point.

Often, to provide a reasonable scale for the righting arm values, the range of calibration entered on the graph does not permit a plot of the GM at 57.3°. In that event, the corrected GZ at 5° can be taken as GM multiplied by sine 5°. It should be noted that values obtained from both the straight line plot and use of the formula are identical.

Draw a smooth curve through the plotted points. This is the righting arm curve which describes the inherent stability characteristics of the ship at the given displacement and KG_V. Plot the grain heeling arms at angles 0° and 40°. These are the values identified as (A) and (B) on the first page of the Addendum. Draw a straight line through these two points. This line is a very close approximation of the curve of heeling moment arms generated by the assumed grain shift.

(10)   Inspection of the completed plot will reveal a point at which the heeling moment curve intersects the righting arm curve. Project a vertical line down from this point. The angle of heel can then be read off on the scale at the bottom. If an assumed grain shift should occur, with the ship loaded as described in Parts I and II of the Form, the

ship would lay over and come to rest at this angle of inclination. To satisfy A 7.1.1 of the Code, this angle must not be greater than 12°.

(11) When the ship is heeled to the angle determined above, there must still be a reserve of stability to sustain it against possible weather and/or sea conditions. The amount of this reserve is indicated on the plot by the area between the righting arm curve and the heeling arm curve within the boundaries of the angle of heel and a limiting angle, which is specified in the Code. The various conditions used to determine the limiting angle are shown on page 2 of the Addendum. Note that the limiting angle can never be greater than 40°. Also, as mentioned previously, when selecting the angles of inclination to be investigated and plotted on the curve, the last angle should always be 45° or greater. This will ensure that a smooth curve drawn through the plotted points will detect a maximum righting arm if it should occur at an angle less than 40°.

(12) The remainder of the calculation utilizes the data obtained from the graph to calculate, by Simpson's Rule, the residual area. This area provides an indication of the amount of reserve stability available and, to satisfy the requirements of A 7.1.2, it must be not less than 0.075 meter radians.

NATIONAL CARGO BUREAU, INC.

ADDENDUM # 1 TO THE GRAIN STABILITY CALCULATION FORM

TO BE COMPLETED WHEN A TABLE OF MAXIMUM ALLOWABLE HEELING MOMENTS IS NOT PROVIDED IN THE VESSEL'S APPROVED GRAIN LOADING BOOKLET. IN SUCH A CASE, COMPLIANCE WITH PERTINENT GRAIN REGULATIONS MUST BE DETERMINED FROM A PLOT OF THE STABILITY CURVE. PREPARE ONE ADDENDUM FOR EACH STAGE OF THE VOYAGE AND USE THE RESULTS TO COMPLETE THE **SUMMARY PART** OF THE GRAIN STABILITY CALCULATION FORM.

CHECK ONE:

VESSEL: **M. V. ATLANTIC**   [X] DEPARTURE FROM: **NEW ORLEANS**

PORT: **NEW ORLEANS**   DATE: **16 JULY '06**   [ ] INTERMEDIATE

                                             [ ] ARRIVAL AT: _____

① INDENTIFICATION OF CROSS CURVES OF STABILITY: **IN GRAIN LOADING BOOKLET** (SEE NOTE 1)

BASIC DATA:

DISPLACEMENT (FROM PART II) .... **14903 LT**

KG_V (FROM PART II) .... **21.70 Ft**

GM   (FROM PART II) .... **3.91 Ft**

GRAIN HEELING MOMENT (FROM PART III)............................ **11975 Ft-Tons**

② ANGLE OF FLOODING (SEE NOTE 2) .... **42°**

(A) λ_0 HEELING ARM AT ANGLE 0° (GRAIN HEELING MOMENT ÷ DISPLACEMENT). **0.804**

(B) λ_{40} HEELING ARM AT ANGLE 40° (0.8 x HEELING ARM AT 0°)..................... **0.643**

③ ASSUMED KG OF THE CROSS CURVES .... **20 Ft**

④ GZ CORRECTION FACTOR (ASSUMED KG – KG_V)........................... **- 1.70**
(MAY BE "+" OR "-", RETAIN SIGN)

TABLE OF RIGHTING ARMS (GZ): INCLUDE DATA FROM 0° TO 60° (MINIMUM)

	ANGLE OF INCLINATION θ	5°	15°	30°	45°	60°	
⑤	SINE θ	0.087	0.259	0.500	0.707	0.866	
⑥	GZ (FROM CROSS CURVES)	(GM USED)	1.52	3.30	4.16	4.15	
⑦	SINE θ x CORRECTION FACTOR (OBSERVE SIGN)	(GM) 3.91	- 0.440	- 0.850	- 1.202	- 1.472	
⑧	**CORRECTED GZ**	0.340	1.080	2.450	2.958	2.678	

NOTES:

1. THIS INFORMATION IS REQUIRED ONLY IF CROSS CURVES OF STABILITY (OR TABULAR DATA) ARE **NOT** FURNISHED IN THE VESSEL'S APPROVED GRAIN LOADING BOOKLET.

2. THE ANGLE OF FLOODING MEANS AN ANGLE OF HEEL AT WHICH OPENINGS IN THE HULL, SUPERSTRUCTURES OR DECK HOUSES, THAT CANNOT BE CLOSED WEATHER-TIGHT, IMMERSE. SMALL OPENINGS THROUGH WHICH PROGRESSIVE FLOODING CANNOT TAKE PLACE NEED NOT BE CONSIDERED.

3. THIS METHOD APPLIES IN THE USUAL CASE WHERE THREE POINTS DESCRIBE THE RIGHTING ARM CURVE BETWEEN THE ANGLE OF HEEL AND THE LIMITING ANGLE; IF NOT, APPLY SIMPSON'S RULE USING FIVE STATIONS INSTEAD OF THREE AS SHOWN.

4. METER DEGREES DIVIDED BY 57.3 = METER RADIANS; FOOT DEGREES DIVIDED BY 188 = METER RADIANS.

PLOT OF STABILITY CURVE:

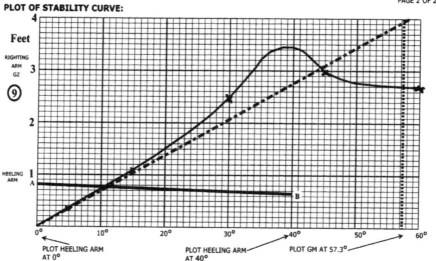

Feet

RIGHTING
ARM
GZ

⑨

HEELING
ARM

A

B

PLOT HEELING ARM
AT 0°

PLOT HEELING ARM
AT 40°

PLOT GM AT 57.3°

DETERMINE FROM THE ABOVE PLOT: **ANGLE OF HEEL** (THE FIRST INTERSECTION OF THE RIGHTING ARM CURVE WITH THE HEELING ARM CURVE)

⑩
= ___11___ **DEGREES**

⑪ **LIMITING ANGLE**   (40 DEGREES, OR
                        THE ANGLE OF FLOODING, OR   WHICHEVER IS
                        THE ANGLE AT WHICH THERE IS MAXIMUM DIFFERENCE   **LEAST**
                        BETWEEN THE RIGHTING ARM CURVE AND THE HEELING ARM CURVE)

= ___39___ **DEGREES**

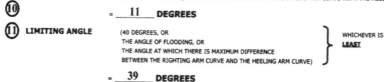

RESIDUAL AREA CALCULATION: STATION SPACING (**S**) = $\frac{\text{(LIMITING ANGLE – ANGLE OF HEEL)}}{2}$ = $\frac{39° - 11°}{2}$ = $14°$ (SEE NOTE 3)

⑫

ANGLE OF INCLINATION		RIGHTING ARM	HEELING ARM	DIFFERENCE		PRODUCT
ANGLE OF HEEL	11	–	–	0	1	0
ANGLE OF HEEL + S°	25	1.98	0.70	1.28	4	5.12
ANGLE OF HEEL + 2S° (LIMITING ANGLE)	39	3.44	0.65	2.79	1	2.79
					SUM	7.91

$\frac{\text{SUM} \times \text{S}}{3}$ = **RESIDUAL AREA** = $\frac{7.91 \times 14}{3}$ = 36.913 $\frac{ft°}{Ft°}$ = 0.196 mr (SEE NOTE 4)

*(Must comply with A 7.1.2 -
see page 24 of this booklet)*

_____   EXAMINED: _____
          MASTER   N.C.B. SURVEYOR

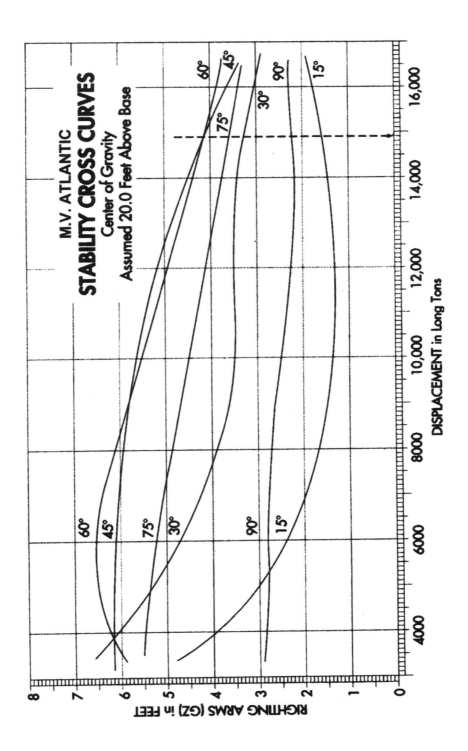

ILLUSTRATION OF
A SAUCER UTILIZING BUNDLING OF BULK GRAIN
(IN LIEU OF BAGGED)
(Specific requirements are detailed in A 15 of the Code)

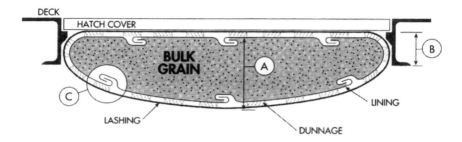

A	MOULDED BREADTH OF SHIP	DEPTH OF SAUCER
	Less than 9.1 m	1.2 m minimum
	Between 9.1 m and 18.3 m	Interpolate
	18.3 m and over	1.8 m minimum

B   Bearing contact of saucer against ship's structure:

At least one half of dimension (A)

-OR-

secured in place by transverse lashings spaced not more than 2.4 m apart.

C   To retain bulk grain within the saucer:

Lining material (strength 2687 N per 5 cm strip, i.e. 306.8 pounds per 1 inch strip) joined by sewing or double lap

-OR-

lining material (strength 1344 N per 5 cm strip, i.e. 153.5 pounds per 1 inch strip) joined by sewing or double lap, restrained by transverse lashings spaced not more than 2.4 m apart and protected from chaffing by dunnage, 25 mm minimum thickness and between 150 and 300 mm in width, placed longitudinally between the lashings and the lining material.

ILLUSTRATION OF
SECURING OF PARTLY FILLED COMPARTMENT BY STRAPPING OR LASHING

(Specific requirements are detailed in A 17 of the Code)

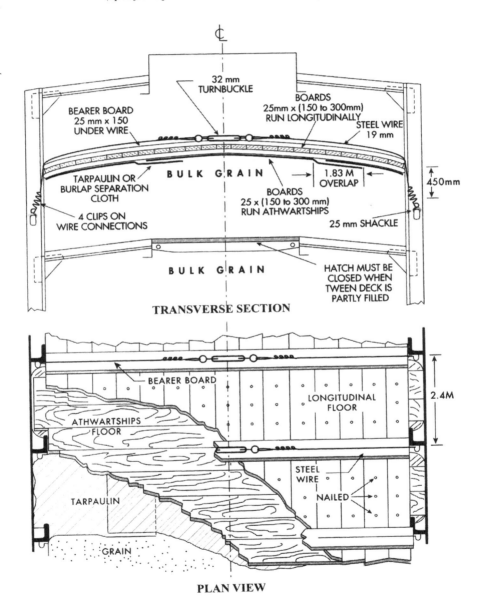

TRANSVERSE SECTION

PLAN VIEW

ILLUSTRATION OF
SECURING OF PARTLY FILLED COMPARTMENT WITH WIRE MESH
(Specific requirements are detailed in A 18 of the Code)

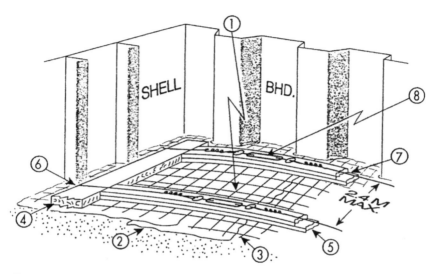

① Grain slightly crowned along fore and aft centerline of cargo hold.

② One layer of burlap, canvas or tarpaulin (sections lapped 1.8 m minimum).

③ Two layers of wire reinforcement mesh (3 mm wire welded in 150 x 150 mm squares). Bottom layer laid athwartships; top layer laid longitudinally.

④ 150 mm x 50 mm lumber bearers against frames or shell to distribute the downward thrust of wire rope lashings at the sides.

⑤ Two layers of 150 mm x 25 mm lumber bearers directly beneath the wire rope lashings.

⑥ Steel wire rope lashings, 19 mm diameter, spaced 2.4 m maximum and attached to the framing about 450 mm below grain surface.

⑦ The first and last transverse lashings to be close to forward and after bulkheads.

⑧ 32 mm turnbuckles to tension lashings.

CALCULATION OF AVERAGE VOID DEPTH (Vd)

When bulk grain is stowed so as to satisfy the requirement of A 2.2 of the Code, i.e. "filled compartment, trimmed", it must be loaded and trimmed so that the grain is at its highest possible level. Thus, the regulations recognize that, due to the settling of the grain and restricted working space, it is not feasible to fill a compartment one hundred percent. There will always be small void spaces between the trimmed surface of the grain and the overhead structure in the compartment. The regulations do not specify the depth of this void but, instead, "assume" a depth which varies, depending upon the geometry of the overhead structure.

The numerical value assigned to the average void depth (Vd) is essential to the naval architect for calculating the Grain Loading Booklet data. Details of how that value is determined are provided in B 1 of the Code. Void depth (Vd) is not, however, used by ship's personnel in any of the calculations required if the ship has a Document of Authorization and an approved Grain Loading Booklet.

In the case of a ship without a Document of Authorization which is permitted, by its Administration, to load a partial cargo of bulk grain in accordance with the provisions of A 9 (see page 28 of this booklet), the void depth, in the compartment(s) in which the grain is to be stowed, must be known as it is one of the factors to be applied in the formula for required GM.

In lieu of reference to B 1, the following tables, in Metric and English units, furnish the average void depth (Vd):

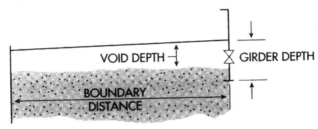

(disregard bleeder holes)

Transverse Section Through One Side of Ship

$$Vd = F_G + F_{BD}$$

Where: Vd = Average void depth
(meters for Metric, feet for English)

F_G
F_{BD} = factors from Tables I and II

AVERAGE VOID DEPTH TABLE - METRIC

Table I

Girder Depth (m)	F_G (m)
0.1	-0.375
0.2	-0.300
0.3	-0.225
0.4	-0.150
0.5	-0.075
0.6	0.000
0.7	+0.075
0.8	+0.150
0.9	+0.225
1.0	+0.300
1.1	+0.375
1.2	+0.450
1.3	+0.525
1.4	+0.600
1.5	+0.675

Table II

Boundary Distance (m)	F_{BD} (m)	Boundary Distance (m)	F_{BD} (m)
0.5	0.570	5.0	0.430
0.6	0.562	5.1	0.434
0.7	0.554	5.2	0.438
0.8	0.546	5.3	0.442
0.9	0.538	5.4	0.446
1.0	0.530	5.5	0.450
1.1	0.524	5.6	0.454
1.2	0.518	5.7	0.458
1.3	0.512	5.8	0.462
1.4	0.506	5.9	0.466
1.5	0.500	6.0	0.470
1.6	0.496	6.1	0.474
1.7	0.492	6.2	0.478
1.8	0.488	6.3	0.482
1.9	0.484	6.4	0.486
2.0	0.480	6.5	0.490
2.1	0.474	6.6	0.496
2.2	0.468	6.7	0.502
2.3	0.462	6.8	0.508
2.4	0.456	6.9	0.514
2.5	0.450	7.0	0.520
2.6	0.448	7.1	0.526
2.7	0.446	7.2	0.532
2.8	0.444	7.3	0.538
2.9	0.442	7.4	0.544
3.0	0.440	7.5	0.550
3.1	0.438	7.6	0.558
3.2	0.436	7.7	0.566
3.3	0.434	7.8	0.574
3.4	0.432	7.9	0.582
3.5 to 5.0	0.430	8.0	0.590

Example:

Girder Depth = 0.5 m
Boundary Distance = 4.2 m

$$Vd = F_G + F_{BD}$$
$$= -0.075 + 0.430$$
$$= 0.355 \text{ m}$$

IMPORTANT:

If Vd calculates as less than 0.1 m .... THEN

$$Vd = 0.1 \text{ m}$$

AVERAGE VOID DEPTH TABLE - ENGLISH

Table I

Girder Depth (inches)	F_G (feet)
6	-1.1014
9	-0.9139
12	-0.7264
15	-0.5389
18	-0.3514
21	-0.1639
24	+0.0236
27	+0.2111
30	+0.3986
33	+0.5861
36	+0.7736
39	+0.9611
42	+1.1486
45	+1.3361
48	+1.5236
51	+1.17111
54	+1.8986
57	+2.0861
60	+2.2736

Example:

Girder Depth = 36 inches
Boundary Distance
      = 19 feet 8 inches
         (19.67 feet)

$Vd = F_G + F_{BD}$
    = +0.7736 + 1.5414
    = 2.315 feet

IMPORTANT:

If Vd calculates as less
than 0.328 feet .... THEN

     Vd = 0.328 feet

Table II

Boundary Distance (feet)	F_{BD} (feet)	Boundary Distance (feet)	F_{BD} (feet)
2.00	1.8413	16.50	1.4145
2.25	1.8213	16.75	1.4246
2.50	1.8013	17.00	1.4346
2.75	1.7813	17.25	1.4446
3.00	1.7613	17.50	1.4546
3.25	1.7413	17.75	1.4646
3.50	1.7257	18.00	1.4746
3.75	1.7107	18.25	1.4846
4.00	1.6957	18.50	1.4946
4.25	1.6807	18.75	1.5046
4.50	1.6657	19.00	1.5146
4.75	1.6507	19.25	1.5246
5.00	1.6372	19.50	1.5346
5.25	1.6273	19.75	1.5446
5.50	1.6173	20.00	1.5546
5.75	1.6073	20.25	1.5646
6.00	1.5973	20.50	1.5746
6.25	1.5873	20.75	1.5846
6.50	1.5773	21.00	1.5946
6.75	1.5635	21.25	1.6046
7.00	1.5485	21.50	1.6181
7.25	1.5335	21.75	1.6331
7.50	1.5185	22.00	1.6481
7.75	1.5035	22.25	1.6631
8.00	1.4885	22.50	1.6781
8.25	1.4754	22.75	1.6931
8.50	1.4704	23.00	1.7080
8.75	1.4654	23.25	1.7225
9.00	1.4604	23.50	1.7370
9.25	1.4554	23.75	1.7516
9.50	1.4504	24.00	1.7661
9.75	1.4454	24.25	1.7806
10.00	1.4404	24.50	1.7951
10.25	1.4354	24.75	1.8159
10.50	1.4304	25.00	1.8359
10.75	1.4254	25.25	1.8559
11.00	1.4204	25.50	1.8760
11.25	1.4514	25.75	1.8960
11.50 to 16.40	1.4107	26.00	1.9160

CALCULATION IN ACCORDANCE WITH A 9

The formula for calculating the required GM in accordance with A 9 of the Code (see pages 28 - 29 of this booklet) can be simplified for solution on an electronic calculator as follows:

Let:

$$Q = \sqrt{(Vd \times B)}$$

Then:

$$GM_R = \frac{L \times Q^2 \times ((0.388 \times B) - Q)}{0.136 \times SF \times \Delta}$$

Where symbols and units are as shown in the following table:

Symbol	Meaning	Dimensions	
		Metric	English
GM_R	Required Metacentric Height	meters	feet
L	Length of Compartment	meters	feet
B	Beam of Ship	meters	feet
Vd	Average Void Depth	meters	feet
SF	Stowage Factor	m³/mt	ft³/LT
Δ	Displacement	mt	LT

Example:

Bulk grain, stowing at 1.254 m³/mt, is stowed in Nos. 2 and 4 Lower Holds. No. 2 Lower Hold is 22 meters long; No. 4 Lower Hold is 18.5 meters long. In both holds, the Girder Depth is 0.5 meters and the Boundary Distance is 4.2 meters. The Beam of the ship is 34 meters and the anticipated sailing Displacement is 23,807 metric tons.

From Tables I and II: Vd = 0.355m

Length of compartments = 22.0 + 18.5 = 40.5 m

$$Q = \sqrt{(Vd \times B)} = \sqrt{(0.355 \times 34)} \qquad Q = 3.47\ m$$

$$GM_R = \frac{L \times Q^2 \times ((0.388 \times B) - Q)}{0.136 \times SF \times \Delta}$$

$$= \frac{40.5 \times 3.47^2 \times ((0.388 \times 34) - 3.47)}{0.136 \times 1.254 \times 23807}$$

$$= \frac{40.5 \times 12.04 \times 9.72}{4060.14} \qquad GM_R = 1.17\ m$$

Required Metacentric Height (GM_R) = 1.17 meters

EXAMPLES OF LOADING CONDITIONS

Some examples of typical loading conditions, together with completed calculations on the National Cargo Bureau Stability Calculation Form, are shown on the following pages.

1. **BULK CARRIER:**

   A four hold bulk carrier, which has cargo holds that are not deemed specially suitable, is loading a part cargo of grain at a Great Lakes port (Duluth) and then completing loading (topping off) at Montreal before proceeding to sea. The loading at Duluth will be done to meet the requirements of the U.S. regulations for an exempted voyage (see page 10 of this booklet). The final loading will be done to meet the requirements of A 7 of the International Grain Code. All holds must be trimmed. (Vessel's documents in English units).

2. **BULK CARRIER:**

   A seven hold bulk carrier, which has cargo holds that are deemed specially suitable, will be loaded to meet the requirements of A 7 of the International Grain Code. The Grain Loading Booklet has been approved under the International Grain Code. The full cargo of wheat has a Stowage Factor of 1.199 m³/mt. No. 4 Hold will be slack and must be leveled. The other holds will be completely filled with the ends of the holds untrimmed. (Vessel's documents in metric units).

3. **GENERAL CARGO SHIP:**

   A two-deck general cargo ship will be loaded to meet the requirements of A 7 of the International Grain Code. Its Grain Loading Booklet was previously approved under IMO Resolution A.264(VIII). The ship is designed with permanent centerline bulkheads, forward and aft of the hatch openings, in all cargo compartments. The Grain Loading Booklet provides Volumetric Heeling Moments for all compartments, shown both without centerline divisions fitted and with centerline divisions fitted. The instructions in the Grain Loading Booklet state that the latter values may be used only when bundles, saucers, or temporary bulkheads are installed in way of the hatch openings. In this example, these arrangements are not used. The ship is loading a full cargo of wheat with a Stowage Factor of 45 ft³/LT. Loading in combination (see page 21 of this booklet), is used in No. 4 Tween Deck/Lower Hold. (Vessel's documents in English units).

4. **GENERAL CARGO SHIP:**

   A general cargo ship, similar to that in the previous example, will be loaded with a full cargo of barley with a Stowage Factor of 1.533 m³/mt, to meet the requirements of A 7 of the International Grain Code. In this case, however, bundles (see page 33 of this booklet) are fitted in the hatchways so that the tabulated Volumetric Heeling Moments with centerline divisions fitted may be utilized. Preliminary calculations of the departure and arrival conditions revealed that, on arrival, the vessel would not meet the stability requirements of the Code without taking ballast. Since the ballast was not on board at departure, an intermediate condition showing the stability available at the time of ballasting must be calculated. As the stability requirements must be complied with at every stage of the voyage, it should be apparent that the ballasting must be done while the vessel's stability is still compliant. (Vessel's documents in metric units).

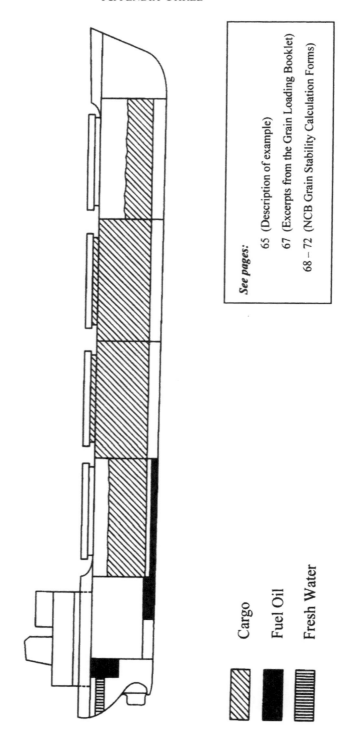

EXAMPLE 1: BULK CARRIER

See pages:

65 (Description of example)

67 (Excerpts from the Grain Loading Booklet)

68 – 72 (NCB Grain Stability Calculation Forms)

Cargo

Fuel Oil

Fresh Water

CARGO HOLDS GRAIN DATA

HOLD No.	CAPACITY (ft³)	VCG (ft)	VOLUMETRIC HEELING MOMENT Full Compartment (ft⁴)
1	138,741	24.9	38,500
2	200,875	21.7	52,300
3	201,878	21.4	52,300
4	193,873	22.1	55,700

MAXIMUM ALLOWABLE HEELING MOMENTS (FT-LT)

(Excerpt)

DISPLACEMENT (Long Tons)	VIRTUAL CENTER OF GRAVITY (KG_v) (Feet)			
	22.5	23.0	23.5	24.0
19,000	10,047	7,663	5,279	2,895
19,500	10,676	8,303	5,930	3,557
20,000	11,346	8,984	6,622	4,260
20,500	11,931	9,608	7,285	4,962

NATIONAL CARGO BUREAU, INC.
GRAIN STABILITY CALCULATION FORM
* (Required for vessels loading bulk grain in the United States of America)

M.V. SENECA	YEAR BUILT 1984
	AT CITY PASCAGOULA

COUNTRY OF REGISTRY U.S.A.	NET TONNAGE 6385	IMO NO. 1014706	IN COUNTRY U.S.A.

AGENT **MINNESOTA SHIPPING CO.**

GRAIN LOADING BOOKLET APPROVED BY **NATIONAL CARGO BUREAU**

ON BEHALF OF (FLAG STATE) **U.S.A.**

DRAWING NO. **SRN-105799** DATE OF APPROVAL **29 MAY 1984**

APPLICABLE REGULATIONS **CHAPTER VI, SOLAS 1974**

ADDENDUM FOR UNTRIMMED ENDS APPROVED BY **NATIONAL CARGO BUREAU**

DRAWING NO. **NONE** DATE OF APPROVAL **15 OCTOBER 1986**

LOADING PORT(S) **DULUTH, MN AND MONTREAL, QC**

BUNKERING PORT(S) **MONTREAL**

DISCHARGE PORT(S) **ROTTERDAM, NETHERLANDS**

STEAMING DISTANCE **3500** MILES   MILES PER DAY **350**   TIME **10.0 DAYS** (Montreal to Rotterdam)

DAILY CONSUMPTION: FUEL **25 LT**   DIESEL **3 LT**   WATER **10 LT**

	DISPLACEMENT	DEADWEIGHT	DRAFT	FREEBOARD
**WINTER				
SUMMER	20102 LT	15891 LT	29' 10"	11' 08"
**TROPICAL				

FRESH WATER ALLOWANCE **7.63"**   TPC/TPI (AT SUMMER DRAFT) **64.2 LT**

* EXCEPT FOR EXEMPTED VOYAGES
** IF APPLICABLE

THIS IS TO CERTIFY THAT:

1. THIS CALCULATION IS PREPARED IN ACCORDANCE WITH THE REQUIREMENTS OF THE VESSEL'S GRAIN LOADING BOOKLET AND THE APPLICABLE GRAIN REGULATIONS.

2. THE STABILITY OF THE VESSEL WILL BE MAINTAINED THROUGHOUT THE VOYAGE IN ACCORDANCE WITH THIS CALCULATION.

MASTER'S SIGNATURE

C. THOMPSON
MASTER'S NAME (PRINTED)

CALCULATION PREPARED BY:
(TO BE COMPLETED IF THE FORM IS PREPARED BY OTHER THAN SHIP'S PERSONNEL)

NAME (PRINT) _____
COMPANY _____
SIGNATURE _____
DATE _____

EXAMINED BY:
N.C.B. SURVEYOR'S SIGNATURE

M. BURNS
N.C.B. SURVEYOR'S NAME (PRINTED)

DATE: **1 OCTOBER 2006**

NOTE: ORIGINAL STABILITY CALCULATION AND GRAIN ARRANGEMENT PLAN TO BE SUBMITTED TO THE N.C.B. SURVEYOR. ALL TONNAGES USED IN THIS CALCULATION SHALL BE SHOWN IN THE SAME UNITS AS USED IN THE GRAIN LOADING BOOKLET.

SHIP AND CARGO CALCULATION

PART I

TYPE OF GRAIN ___**CORN**___ STOWAGE FACTOR ___ M³/MT ___**50**___ FT³/LT

COMPT. NO.	CARGO (1)	S.F. (1)	GRAIN CUBICS (2) TOTAL	USED	WEIGHT (3)	V.C.G.	MOMENT (3)
DEP. DULUTH							
1		50	138741	80000	1600	17.6	28160
2			200875	200875	4018	21.7	87191
3			201878	201878	4038	21.4	86413
4			193873	126100	2522	18.0	45396
SHIP					4211	27.3	114960
CONSTANT					129	38.3	4941
TOTALS					16518		367061
DEP. MONTREAL							
1		50	138741	138741	2775	24.9	69098
2			200875	200875	4018	21.7	87191
3			201878	201878	4038	21.4	86413
4			193873	193873	3877	22.1	85682

S.F. M³/MT	S.F. FT³/LT	DEN MT/M³
1.171	42	0.854
1.184	42.5	0.844
1.198	43	0.834
1.212	43.5	0.825
1.226	44	0.816
1.240	44.5	0.806
1.254	45	0.797
1.268	45.5	0.789
1.282	46	0.780
1.296	46.5	0.772
1.310	47	0.763
1.324	47.5	0.756
1.338	48	0.747
1.352	48.5	0.740
1.366	49	0.732
1.380	49.5	0.725
1.393	50	0.718
1.407	50.5	0.711
1.421	51	0.704
1.435	51.5	0.697
1.449	52	0.690
1.477	53	0.677
1.505	54	0.664
1.533	55	0.652
1.561	56	0.641
1.589	57	0.629
1.616	58	0.619
1.644	59	0.608
1.672	60	0.598
1.700	61	0.588
1.728	62	0.579

THIS CALCULATION IS PREPARED IN:

☐ METRIC UNITS
☒ ENGLISH UNITS

		V.C.G.	MOMENT
CARGO TOTALS	14708		328384
LIGHT SHIP	4211	27.3	114960
CONSTANT	129	38.3	4941
SHIP AND CARGO TOTALS	19048		448285

(1) COMPLETE THESE COLUMNS IF MORE THAN ONE TYPE OF CARGO IS LOADED.

(2) FOR PARTLY FILLED COMPARTMENTS, SHOW THE CUBICS USED IN ADDITION TO THE TOTAL CUBICS.

(3) WEIGHTS AND MOMENTS SHOULD BE SHOWN TO THE NEAREST WHOLE UNIT.

CARGO PLAN: INDICATE HOLDS, TWEEN DECKS, ENGINE SPACES, FITTINGS, STOWAGE, TONNAGES, ETC.

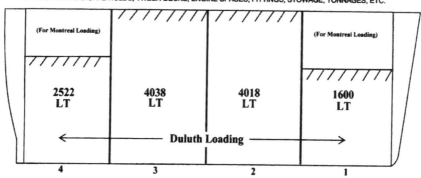

(For Montreal Loading)   (For Montreal Loading)

2522 LT	4038 LT	4018 LT	1600 LT

← Duluth Loading →

| 4 | 3 | 2 | 1 |

FUEL AND WATER CALCULATION

PART II
THE **INTERMEDIATE** SECTION MUST BE COMPLETED IF THE **ARRIVAL** SECTION SHOWS BALLAST THAT IS NOT LISTED IN THE **DEPARTURE** SECTION. THE **INTERMEDIATE** CONDITION IS IMMEDIATELY BEFORE BALLASTING AND MUST INCLUDE THE EFFECT OF FREE SURFACE, BUT NOT THE EFFECT OF ADDED WEIGHT. ADDITIONAL FUEL TAKEN AFTER DEPARTURE MUST BE SHOWN IN THE **INTERMEDIATE** SECTION IN THE SAME MANNER AS BALLAST.

TANK	TYPE LIQUID	DEPARTURE: DULUTH				INTERMEDIATE: DEP. MONTREAL				ARRIVAL: ROTTERDAM			
		WEIGHT	V.C.G.	MOMENT	F.S. MOM.	WEIGHT	V.C.G.	MOMENT	F.S. MOM.	WEIGHT	V.C.G.	MOMENT	F.S. MOM.
4DB P/S	FO	100	2.0	200	4350	300	3.5	1050	4350	100	2.0	200	4350
5DB P/S	FO	70	1.5	105	460	278	3.2	890	390	228	2.8	638	720
SETT	FO	20	31.6	632	54	20	31.6	632	54	20	31.6	632	54
SERV	FO	10	30.1	301	34	10	30.1	301	34	10	30.1	301	34
DO	DO	36	28.0	1008	176	116	30.0	3480	176	86	29.4	2528	176
FWT	FW	-				200	35.8	7160	1918	100	33.8	3380	1918
AP	FW	64	24.0	1536	1780	130	28.0	3640	-	130	28.0	3640	-

TOTALS

LIQUIDS	300	3782	6854	1054	17153	6922	674	11319	7252
SHIP AND CARGO	16518	367061		19048	448285		19048	448285	
DISPLACEMENT	16818	370843		20102	465438		19722	459604	

SAILING DRAFT 25' 06" AT DENSITY 1.000

DEPARTURE KG	22.05	INTERMEDIATE KG	23.15	ARRIVAL KG	23.30
(1) FREE SURFACE CORR. (+)	0.41	(1) FREE SURFACE CORR. (+)	0.34	(1) FREE SURFACE CORR. (+)	0.37
(2) VERT. S.M. CORR. (+)	-	(2) VERT. S.M. CORR. (+)	-	(2) VERT. S.M. CORR. (+)	-
DEPARTURE KGᵥ	22.46	INTERMEDIATE KGᵥ	23.49	ARRIVAL KGᵥ	23.67

DEPARTURE KM	28.84	INTERMEDIATE KM	29.15	ARRIVAL KM	29.06
DEPARTURE KGᵥ	22.46	INTERMEDIATE KGᵥ	23.49	ARRIVAL KGᵥ	23.67
DEPARTURE GM	6.38	INTERMEDIATE GM	5.66	ARRIVAL GM	5.39
REQUIRED MINIMUM GM	4.73	REQUIRED MINIMUM GM	1.00	REQUIRED MINIMUM GM	1.00

(See Addendum #2 - attached)

(1) FREE SURFACE CORR. = $\dfrac{\text{SUM OF FREE SURFACE MOMENTS}}{\text{DISPLACEMENT}}$

(THIS CORRECTION MUST BE APPLIED TO ALL SHIPS.)

(2) VERT. S.M. CORR. = $\dfrac{\text{SUM OF VERTICAL SHIFTING MOMENTS}}{\text{DISPLACEMENT}}$

(THIS CORRECTION APPLIES WHEN THE VOLUMETRIC HEELING MOMENT CURVES OR TABLES DO NOT SPECIFICALLY STATE THAT THE CORRECTION FOR THE RISE IN VERTICAL CENTER OF GRAVITY HAS BEEN INCLUDED, AND THE MANUAL PROVIDES VERTICAL SHIFTING MOMENTS.)

HEELING MOMENT CALCULATION

PART III

COMPT. NO	STOWAGE (1)	GRAIN ULLAGE ~~OR DEPTH~~ M/FT	VOLUMETRIC HEELING MOMENT M⁴/FT⁴	S.F. ~~OR DENSITY~~ (2)	GRAIN HEELING MOMENT ~~MT~~ M/FT–LT	VERTICAL SHIFTING MOMENT (IF PROVIDED) SEE NOTE 2 IN PART II	
						M⁴/FT⁴	MT–M/FT–LT
DEP. MONTREAL							
1	F-T	0	38500	50			
2	F-T	0	52300				
3	F-T	0	52300				
4	F-T	0	55700				
		TOTALS	198800	50	3976		

(1) UNDER STOWAGE INDICATE "F-T" FOR FILLED COMPARTMENTS TRIMMED, "F-UT" FOR FILLED COMPARTMENTS UNTRIMMED, "PF" FOR PARTLY FILLED COMPARTMENTS, AND "SEC" FOR SECURED OR OVER-STOWED COMPARTMENTS.

(2) THE STOWAGE FACTOR USED IN PART III SHALL NOT EXCEED THE ONE BASED ON THE WEIGHT PER UNIT OF VOLUME (TEST WEIGHT) OF THE GRAIN. IF THE STOWAGE FACTOR IS THE SAME IN ALL COMPARTMENTS, DIVIDE THE TOTAL VOLUMETRIC HEELING MOMENT BY THE STOWAGE FACTOR OR MULTIPLY BY THE DENSITY TO OBTAIN THE GRAIN HEELING MOMENT. IF THE STOWAGE FACTOR VARIES, OBTAIN THE GRAIN HEELING MOMENT FOR EACH COMPARTMENT.

A . FOR VESSELS APPROVED UNDER

INTERNATIONAL GRAIN CODE, Part A, 7.1
REGULATION 4, CHAPTER VI, SOLAS 1974 or
REGULATION 4, IMCO RESOLUTION A.264(VIII), NEW CHAPTER VI, SOLAS 1960
REGULATION 4, IMCO RESOLUTION A.184 AN EQUIVALENT TO CHAPTER VI, SOLAS 1960

STABILITY SUMMARY

	DEPARTURE	INTERMEDIATE	ARRIVAL
DISPLACEMENT	16818	20102	19722
KGv ~~or GM~~	22.46	23.49	23.67
TOTAL GRAIN HEELING MOMENT	SEE ADDENDUM #2 (ATTACHED)	3976	3976
MAXIMUM ALLOWABLE HEELING MOMENT		6804	5432
* ANGLE OF HEEL (12° MAX.)			
* RESIDUAL AREA 0.075 METER-RADIANS (14.1 FT° OR 4.3 M°) MINIMUM			
* GM (0.3M OR 1 FT MINIMUM)	6.38		

* TO BE COMPLETED IF VESSEL'S GRAIN LOADING BOOKLET DOES NOT INCLUDE A TABLE OF ALLOWABLE HEELING MOMENTS. IN SUCH CASE, STATICAL STABILITY DIAGRAMS DEMONSTRATING THIS INFORMATION SHALL BE ATTACHED HERETO.

B. FOR SPECIALLY SUITABLE SHIPS APPROVED UNDER

INTERNATIONAL GRAIN CODE, PART A, 8. 2
SECTION V (B) , PART B, CHAPTER VI, SOLAS 1974
SECTION V (B) , PART B, IMCO RESOLUTION A.264 (VIII), NEW CHAPTER VI, SOLAS 1960
REGULATION 12, CHAPTER VI, SOLAS 1960

$$\text{ANGLE OF HEEL} = \frac{\text{GRAIN HEELING MOMENT} \times 57.3}{\text{DISPLACEMENT} \times \text{GM}}$$

	DEPARTURE	INTERMEDIATE	ARRIVAL
TOTAL GRAIN HEELING MOMENT			
DISPLACEMENT			
GM			
ANGLE OF HEEL (5° MAX.)			

NATIONAL CARGO BUREAU, INC.
ADDENDUM #2 TO GRAIN STABILITY CALCULATION FORM
TO BE COMPLETED WHEN A VESSEL, CARRYING GRAIN IN BULK AND ENGAGED ON A VOYAGE ON THE INLAND OR COASTAL WATERS OF THE UNITED STATES, ELECTS AND IS ENTITLED TO UTILIZE THE PROVISIONS OF 46 CFR 172.030.

M.V./S.S. **SENECA**   PORT **DULUTH**

COLUMN #	1	2	3	4	5	6	7	8	9
SLACK HOLD #	L (WITHOUT C.L.)	L (WITH C.L.)	COLUMN # 2 DIVIDED BY 4	COLUMN # 1 PLUS COLUMN # 3	B	B³	COLUMN # 4 x COLUMN # 6 x 0.0661	S.F.	COLUMN # 7 DIVIDED BY COLUMN # 8
1	75	0	0	75	66	287496	1425261	50	28505
4	87	0	0	87	70	343000	1972490	50	39450
								SUM OF COLUMN 9	67955

KEY

L	=	LENGTH OF HOLD
B	=	BREADTH OF GRAIN SURFACE
C.L.	=	CENTERLINE DIVISION
S.F.	=	STOWAGE FACTOR

NOTES

1. ALL DIMENSIONS MUST BE IN METERS (M), METRIC TONS (MT), AND M³/MT OR, ALTERNATIVELY, IN FEET(FT), LONG TONS(LT), AND FT³/LT.

2. WHERE A C.L. DIVISION HALVES THE BREADTH, COLUMNS # 2 AND # 3 ADJUST THE CALCULATION FOR THIS REDUCTION.

DEPARTURE FROM: DULUTH

DISPLACEMENT = 16818

GM = 6.38

MEAN DRAFT = 25.50

FREEBOARD = 16.00

BEAM = 70.00

$r = \dfrac{\text{FREEBOARD}}{\text{BEAM}}$

$r = \dfrac{16.00}{70.00} = 0.229$

IF r < 0.268 THEN
F = 0.268 DIVIDED BY r
OTHERWISE F = 1

F = 0.268/0.229 = 1.170

REQUIRED GM = $\dfrac{\text{SUM x F}}{\text{DISPLACEMENT}}$

= $\dfrac{67955 \times 1.17}{16818}$

REQUIRED GM = 4.73

AVAILABLE GM = 6.38

ARRIVAL AT: MONTREAL

DISPLACEMENT = 16694

GM = 6.37

MEAN DRAFT = 25.33

FREEBOARD = 16.17

BEAM = 70.00

$r = \dfrac{\text{FREEBOARD}}{\text{BEAM}}$

$r = \dfrac{16.17}{70.00} = 0.231$

IF r < 0.268 THEN
F = 0.268 DIVIDED BY r
OTHERWISE F = 1

F = 0.268/0.231 = 1.160

REQUIRED GM = $\dfrac{\text{SUM x F}}{\text{DISPLACEMENT}}$

= $\dfrac{67955 \times 1.16}{16694}$

REQUIRED GM = 4.72

AVAILABLE GM = 6.37

MASTER   EXAMINED: N.C.B. SURVEYOR

EXAMPLE 2: BULK CARRIER

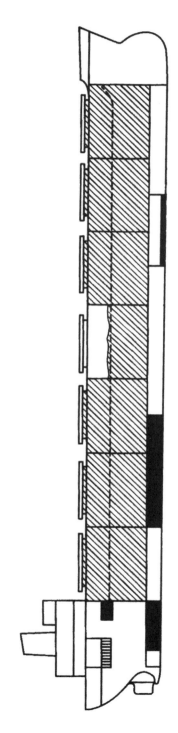

See pages:

65 (Description of example)

74 – 76 (Excerpts from the Grain Loading Booklet)

77 – 80 (NCB Grain Stability Calculation Form)

81 (Certificate of Readiness)

Cargo

Fuel Oil

Fresh Water

CARGO HOLDS GRAIN DATA

HOLD No.	FILLED ENDS TRIMMED			FILLED ENDS UNTRIMMED		
	VOLUME (m³)	VCG (m)	VOLUMETRIC HEELING MOM. (m⁴)	VOLUME (m³)	VCG (m)	VOLUMETRIC HEELING MOM. (m⁴)
1	8,343	10.20	1,143	8,129	10.20	2,085
2	10,994	9.93	1,496	10,869	9.93	2,785
3	10,993	9.89	1,496	10,868	9.89	2,785
4	10,926	9.89	1,496	10,802	9.89	2,785
5	10,999	9.90	1,496	10,874	9.90	2,785
6	10,980	9.90	1,496	10,855	9.90	2,785
7	10,383	10.19	1,229	10,223	10.19	2,576

MAXIMUM ALLOWABLE HEELING MOMENTS (MT-M)

(Excerpt)

DISPLACEMENT (mt)	VIRTUAL CENTER OF GRAVITY (KG$_v$) (m)				
	8.5	9.0	9.5	10.0	10.5
69,500	47,535	39,715	31,895	24,075	16,255
71,000	48,041	40,260	32,479	24,698	16,917
71,500	48,570	40,829	33,088	25,347	17,606
72,000	49,120	41,419	33,718	26,017	18,316
72,500	49,688	42,027	34,366	26,705	19,044
73,000	50,267	42,647	35,027	27,407	19,787

SUMMARY OF TANKS

TANK	CAPACITY (m³)	VCG (m)	FREE SURFACE MOMENT (mt-m)	
			Slack	98% Full
FUEL OIL				
2 DB P&S	1,384	0.88	11,020	144
4 DB P&S	1071	0.89	9,420	134
SETTLING	85	14.22	25	
SERVICE	80	14.39	24	
DIESEL OIL				
6 DB P&S	220	1.18	430	43
SETTLING	40	14.21	17	
SERVICE	20	14.04	11	
FRESH WATER				
DISTILLED	94	16.39	140	
F.W.T	262	16.36	520	
D.W.T.	168	16.34	330	
S.W. BALLAST				
FOREPEAK	2,756	7.52	7,704	
1 DB P&S	2,812	0.97	24,624	
3 DB P&S	3,265	0.88	24,192	
5 DB P&S	1,327	0.89	6,048	
1 TS P&S	753	16.48	1,296	
2 TS P&S	2,648	16.11	5,328	
3 TS P&S	2,652	16.11	5,328	
4 TS P&S	2,624	16.14	5,328	
AFTERPEAK	519	12.39	4,320	

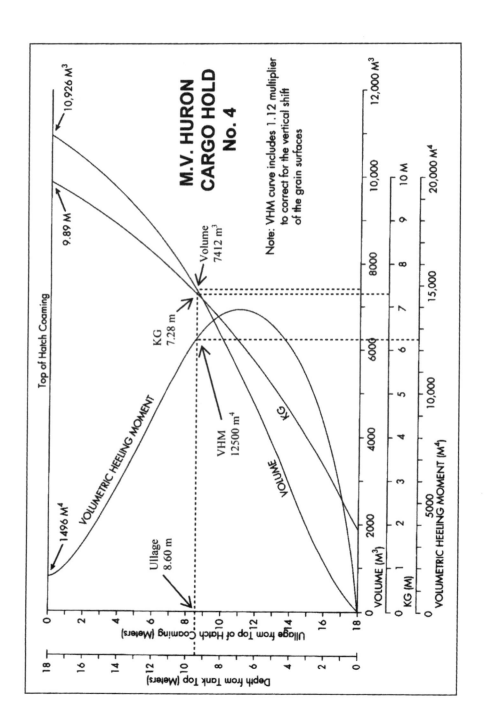

NATIONAL CARGO BUREAU, INC.
GRAIN STABILITY CALCULATION FORM
* (Required for vessels loading bulk grain in the United States of America)

M.V./S.S. **HURON**			YEAR BUILT **1995**
			AT CITY **OSHIMA**
COUNTRY OF REGISTRY **PANAMA**	NET TONNAGE **21685**	IMO NO. **1014707**	IN COUNTRY **JAPAN**

AGENT **PACIFIC STEAMSHIP AGENCIES**

GRAIN LOADING BOOKLET APPROVED BY **LLOYD'S REGISTER OF SHIPPING**

ON BEHALF OF (FLAG STATE) **PANAMA**

DRAWING NO. **1035 Rev. 1**   DATE OF APPROVAL **1 JULY 1995**

APPLICABLE REGULATIONS **INTERNATIONAL GRAIN CODE**

ADDENDUM FOR UNTRIMMED ENDS APPROVED BY **DATA IN GRAIN BOOKLET**

DRAWING NO. _____ DATE OF APPROVAL _____

LOADING PORT(S) **SEATTLE**

BUNKERING PORT(S) **-**

DISCHARGE PORT(S) **CHITTAGONG**

STEAMING DISTANCE **8750** MILES   MILES PER DAY **324**   TIME **27.0 DAYS**

DAILY CONSUMPTION: FUEL **30 MT**   DIESEL **NIL**   WATER **- 3 MT** (Evaporator)

	DISPLACEMENT	DEADWEIGHT	DRAFT	FREEBOARD
**WINTER				
SUMMER	72410 MT	60265 MT	12.44 M	2.27 M
**TROPICAL				

FRESH WATER ALLOWANCE **0.290 M**   TPC/TPI (AT SUMMER DRAFT) **62.4 MT**

• EXCEPT FOR EXEMPTED VOYAGES
** IF APPLICABLE

THIS IS TO CERTIFY THAT:

1. THIS CALCULATION IS PREPARED IN ACCORDANCE WITH THE REQUIREMENTS OF THE VESSEL'S GRAIN LOADING BOOKLET AND THE APPLICABLE GRAIN REGULATIONS.

2. THE STABILITY OF THE VESSEL WILL BE MAINTAINED THROUGHOUT THE VOYAGE IN ACCORDANCE WITH THIS CALCULATION.

MASTER'S SIGNATURE

R. LANE
MASTER'S NAME (PRINTED)

CALCULATION PREPARED BY:	
(TO BE COMPLETED IF THE FORM IS PREPARED BY OTHER THAN SHIP'S PERSONNEL)	EXAMINED BY:

N.C.B. SURVEYOR'S SIGNATURE

NAME (PRINT) _____

COMPANY _____

SIGNATURE _____

DATE _____

T. MOORE
N.C.B. SURVEYOR'S NAME (PRINTED)

DATE: **10 SEPTEMBER 2006**

NOTE: ORIGINAL STABILITY CALCULATION AND GRAIN ARRANGEMENT PLAN TO BE SUBMITTED TO THE N.C.B. SURVEYOR. ALL TONNAGES USED IN THIS CALCULATION SHALL BE SHOWN IN THE SAME UNITS AS USED IN THE GRAIN LOADING BOOKLET.

SHIP AND CARGO CALCULATION

PART I

TYPE OF GRAIN __**WHEAT**__ STOWAGE FACTOR __**1.199**__ M³/MT __**43.04**__ FT³/LT

COMPT. NO.	CARGO (1)	S.F. (1)	GRAIN CUBICS (2)		WEIGHT (3)	V.C.G.	MOMENT (3)
			TOTAL	USED			
1		1.199	8343	8343	6958	10.20	70972
2			10994	10994	9169	9.93	91048
3			10993	10993	9168	9.89	90672
4			10926	7412	6182	7.28	45005
5			10999	10999	9173	9.90	90813
6			10980	10980	9158	9.90	90664
7			10383	10383	8660	10.19	88245

S.F. $\frac{M^3}{MT}$	S.F. $\frac{FT^3}{LT}$	DEN $\frac{MT}{M^3}$
1.171	42	0.854
1.184	42.5	0.844
1.198	43	0.834
1.212	43.5	0.825
1.226	44	0.816
1.240	44.5	0.806
1.254	45	0.797
1.268	45.5	0.789
1.282	46	0.780
1.296	46.5	0.772
1.310	47	0.763
1.324	47.5	0.755
1.338	48	0.747
1.352	48.5	0.740
1.366	49	0.732
1.380	49.5	0.725
1.393	50	0.718
1.407	50.5	0.711
1.421	51	0.704
1.435	51.5	0.697
1.449	52	0.690
1.477	53	0.677
1.505	54	0.664
1.533	55	0.652
1.561	56	0.641
1.589	57	0.629
1.616	58	0.619
1.644	59	0.608
1.672	60	0.598
1.700	61	0.588
1.728	62	0.579

THIS CALCULATION IS PREPARED IN:

[X] METRIC UNITS

[ ] ENGLISH UNITS

	WEIGHT	V.C.G.	MOMENT
CARGO TOTALS	58468		567419
LIGHT SHIP	12095	10.52	127239
CONSTANT	233	11.58	2698
SHIP AND CARGO TOTALS	70796		697356

(1) COMPLETE THESE COLUMNS IF MORE THAN ONE TYPE OF CARGO IS LOADED.

(2) FOR PARTLY FILLED COMPARTMENTS, SHOW THE CUBICS USED IN ADDITION TO THE TOTAL CUBICS.

(3) WEIGHTS AND MOMENTS SHOULD BE SHOWN TO THE NEAREST WHOLE UNIT.

CARGO PLAN: INDICATE HOLDS, TWEEN DECKS, ENGINE SPACES, FITTINGS, STOWAGE, TONNAGES, ETC.

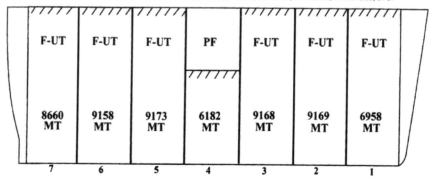

FUEL AND WATER CALCULATION

PART II

THE INTERMEDIATE SECTION MUST BE COMPLETED IF THE ARRIVAL SECTION SHOWS BALLAST THAT IS NOT LISTED IN THE DEPARTURE SECTION. THE INTERMEDIATE CONDITION IS IMMEDIATELY BEFORE BALLASTING AND MUST INCLUDE THE EFFECT OF FREE SURFACE, BUT NOT THE EFFECT OF ADDED WEIGHT. ADDITIONAL FUEL TAKEN AFTER DEPARTURE MUST BE SHOWN IN THE INTERMEDIATE SECTION IN THE SAME MANNER AS BALLAST.

TANK	TYPE LIQUID	DEPARTURE: SEATTLE				INTERMEDIATE:				ARRIVAL: CHITTAGONG			
		WEIGHT	V.C.G.	MOMENT	F.S. MOM.	WEIGHT	V.C.G.	MOMENT	F.S. MOM.	WEIGHT	V.C.G.	MOMENT	F.S. MOM.
2DB P/S	FO	103	0.88	91	11020					-			-
4DB P/S	FO	997	0.89	887	134					290	0.89	258	9420
SETT	FO	60	14.22	853	25					60	14.22	853	25
SERV	FO	40	14.39	576	24					40	14.39	576	24
6DB P/S	DO	170	1.18	201	430					170	1.18	201	430
SETT	DO	25	14.21	355	17					25	14.21	355	17
SERV	DO	12	14.04	168	11					12	14.04	168	11
DIST	FW	17	16.39	279	140					17	16.39	279	140
FWT	FW	140	16.36	2290	520					221	16.36	3616	520
DWT	FW	50	16.34	817	330					50	16.34	409	330

TOTALS

LIQUIDS	1614	6517	12651		885	6715	10917
SHIP AND CARGO	70796	697356			70796	697356	
DISPLACEMENT	72410	703873			71681	704071	

SAILING DRAFT 12.44 M AT DENSITY 1.025

DEPARTURE KG	9.72	INTERMEDIATE KG		ARRIVAL KG	9.82
(1) FREE SURFACE CORR. (+)	0.17	(1) FREE SURFACE CORR. (+)		(1) FREE SURFACE CORR. (+)	0.15
(2) VERT. S.M. CORR. (+)	-	(2) VERT. S.M. CORR. (+)		(2) VERT. S.M. CORR. (+)	-
DEPARTURE KGv	9.89	INTERMEDIATE KGv		ARRIVAL KGv	9.97
DEPARTURE KM	13.09	INTERMEDIATE KM		ARRIVAL KM	13.08
DEPARTURE KGv	9.89	INTERMEDIATE KGv		ARRIVAL KGv	9.97
DEPARTURE GM	3.20	INTERMEDIATE GM		ARRIVAL GM	3.11
REQUIRED MINIMUM GM	0.30	REQUIRED MINIMUM GM		REQUIRED MINIMUM GM	0.30

(1) FREE SURFACE CORR. = $\dfrac{\text{SUM OF FREE SURFACE MOMENTS}}{\text{DISPLACEMENT}}$

(2) VERT. S.M. CORR. = $\dfrac{\text{SUM OF VERTICAL SHIFTING MOMENTS}}{\text{DISPLACEMENT}}$

(THIS CORRECTION MUST BE APPLIED TO ALL SHIPS.)

(THIS CORRECTION APPLIES WHEN THE VOLUMETRIC HEELING MOMENT CURVES OR TABLES DO NOT SPECIFICALLY STATE THAT THE CORRECTION FOR THE RISE IN VERTICAL CENTER OF GRAVITY HAS BEEN INCLUDED, AND THE MANUAL PROVIDES VERTICAL SHIFTING MOMENTS.)

HEELING MOMENT CALCULATION

PART III

COMPT. NO	STOWAGE (1)	GRAIN ULLAGE OR DEPTH M/FT	VOLUMETRIC HEELING MOMENT M⁴/FT⁴	S.F. OR DENSITY (2)	GRAIN HEELING MOMENT MT–M/FT–LT	VERTICAL SHIFTING MOMENT (IF PROVIDED) SEE NOTE 2 IN PART II M⁴/FT⁴	MT–M/FT–LT
1	F-UT	0	2085	1.199			
2	F-UT	0	2785				
3	F-UT	0	2785				
4	PF	8.60	12500				
5	F-UT	0	2785				
6	F-UT	0	2785				
7	F-UT	0	2576				
	TOTALS	28301		1.199	23604		

(1) UNDER STOWAGE INDICATE "F-T" FOR FILLED COMPARTMENTS TRIMMED, "F-UT" FOR FILLED COMPARTMENTS UNTRIMMED, "PF" FOR PARTLY FILLED COMPARTMENTS, AND "SEC" FOR SECURED OR OVER-STOWED COMPARTMENTS.

(2) THE STOWAGE FACTOR USED IN PART III SHALL NOT EXCEED THE ONE BASED ON THE WEIGHT PER UNIT OF VOLUME (TEST WEIGHT) OF THE GRAIN. IF THE STOWAGE FACTOR IS THE SAME IN ALL COMPARTMENTS, DIVIDE THE TOTAL VOLUMETRIC HEELING MOMENT BY THE STOWAGE FACTOR OR MULTIPLY BY THE DENSITY TO OBTAIN THE GRAIN HEELING MOMENT. IF THE STOWAGE FACTOR VARIES, OBTAIN THE GRAIN HEELING MOMENT FOR EACH COMPARTMENT.

A . FOR VESSELS APPROVED UNDER
INTERNATIONAL GRAIN CODE, Part A, 7.1
REGULATION 4, CHAPTER VI, SOLAS 1974 or
REGULATION 4, IMCO RESOLUTION A.264(VIII), NEW CHAPTER VI, SOLAS 1960
REGULATION 4, IMCO RESOLUTION A.184 AN EQUIVALENT TO CHAPTER VI, SOLAS 1960

STABILITY SUMMARY

	DEPARTURE	INTERMEDIATE	ARRIVAL
DISPLACEMENT	72410		71681
KGv or GM	9.89		9.97
TOTAL GRAIN HEELING MOMENT	23604		23604
MAXIMUM ALLOWABLE HEELING MOMENT	28268		26053
* ANGLE OF HEEL (12° MAX.)			
* RESIDUAL AREA 0.075 METER-RADIANS (14.1 FT° OR 4.3 M²) MINIMUM			
* GM (0.3M OR 1 FT MINIMUM)			

* TO BE COMPLETED IF VESSEL'S GRAIN LOADING BOOKLET DOES NOT INCLUDE A TABLE OF ALLOWABLE HEELING MOMENTS. IN SUCH CASE, STATICAL STABILITY DIAGRAMS DEMONSTRATING THIS INFORMATION SHALL BE ATTACHED HERETO.

B. FOR SPECIALLY SUITABLE SHIPS APPROVED UNDER
INTERNATIONAL GRAIN CODE, PART A, 8. 2
SECTION V (B) , PART B, CHAPTER VI, SOLAS 1974
SECTION V (B) , PART B, IMCO RESOLUTION A.264 (VIII), NEW CHAPTER VI, SOLAS 1960
REGULATION 12, CHAPTER VI, SOLAS 1960

$$\text{ANGLE OF HEEL} = \frac{\text{GRAIN HEELING MOMENT} \times 57.3}{\text{DISPLACEMENT} \times \text{GM}}$$

	DEPARTURE	INTERMEDIATE	ARRIVAL
TOTAL GRAIN HEELING MOMENT			
DISPLACEMENT			
GM			
ANGLE OF HEEL (5° MAX.)			

CERTIFICATE OF READINESS
- OF -
NATIONAL CARGO BUREAU, INC.

No. _____ Port _____ **SEATTLE, WA** _____

This is to Certify, that the _____ **PANAMA** _____ **M.V. HURON** _____
                                   (flag)   (Name of Vessel)

of _____ **21685** _____ net tons, built at _____ **JAPAN** _____ in _____ **1995** _____

whereof _____ **CAPT. R. LANE** _____ is Master

and now lying at _____ **ANCHORAGE NO. 6** _____

is passed to load as follows:

GENERAL CARGO - Holds Nos. _____ **N/A** _____

BULK GRAIN - (Full Holds) Nos._____ **1, 2, 3, 5, 6 AND 7** _____

(Part Holds) Nos. _____ **4** _____

Other BULK CARGOES (Identify Cargo) _____ **NONE** _____

HOLDS Nos. _____ **N/A** _____
said holds having been prepared in accordance with the Regulations of the United States Coast Guard and the Code of Federal Regulations so far as applicable, and in accordance with the recommendations of National Cargo Bureau, Inc.

THIS CERTIFICATE VALID AT PORT OF ISSUANCE ONLY

THIS CERTIFICATE IS NOT A FORM OF INSURANCE, OR GUARANTEE, AND IS ISSUED ON THE FOLLOWING TERMS AND CONDITIONS: This Certificate and performance of services by National Cargo Bureau ("NCB") shall in no way be deemed to be a representation, statement, or warranty of seaworthiness, quality or fitness for a particular use or service, of any vessel, container, cargo, structure, item of material, or equipment. NCB shall not be liable for, and the party to whom this Certificate is issued agrees to indemnify and hold NCB harmless from and against any and all claims, demands, actions for damages, including legal fees, to persons and/or property which may be brought against NCB incidental to, arising out of, or in connection with the services to be performed hereunder, except for those claims caused solely by the negligence of NCB. NCB shall be discharged from all liability for negligent performance or non-performance of any services in connection with issuance of this Certificate, unless the same is discovered prior to and is claimed in writing made to NCB within 180 days and litigation is commenced within one year after performance of survey services. THE COMBINED LIABILITY OF NCB, ITS OFFICERS, EMPLOYEES, AGENTS OR SUBCONTRACTORS FOR ANY LOSS, CLAIM, OR DAMAGE ARISING FROM NEGLIGENT PERFORMANCE OR NON-PERFORMANCE OF ANY SERVICES IN CONNECTION WITH THE ISSUANCE OF THIS CERTIFICATE, OR FROM BREACH OF ANY IMPLIED OR EXPRESS WARRANTY OF WORKMANLIKE PERFORMANCE, OR ANY OTHER REASON, SHALL NOT EXCEED IN THE AGGREGATE $10,000. IN NO EVENT SHALL NCB BE LIABLE FOR ANY CONSEQUENTIAL DAMAGES, INCLUDING, BUT WITHOUT LIMITATION, DELAY, DETENTION, LOSS OF USE, OR CUSTOMARY PORT CHARGES TO THE PARTY TO WHOM THIS CERTIFICATE IS ISSUED OR TO ANY OTHER PERSON, CORPORATION OR BUSINESS ENTITY FOR WHOSE BENEFIT THIS CERTIFICATE MAY BE ISSUED.

AGENT _____

OPERATOR _____

DATE ____ **10 SEPTEMBER 2006** ____

Time passed ____ **15:30 HOURS** ____

____ *T. Moore* ____ Surveyor
              T. MOORE

Rev. 9/94

EXAMPLE 3: GENERAL CARGO SHIP

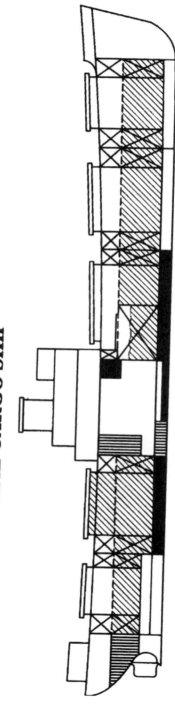

See pages:

65 (Description of example)

83 – 84 (Excerpts from the Grain Loading Booklet)

85 – 88 (NCB Grain Stability Calculation Form)

89 (Certificate of Loading)

Cargo

Fuel Oil

Fresh Water

VOLUMETRIC HEELING MOMENTS (FT⁴)

HOLD	CAPACITY (ft³)	VCG (ft)	LOADED SEPARATELY			LOADED IN COMBINATION	
			WITHOUT C.L. DIVISION	WITH C.L. DIVISION	MAXIMUM SLACK	WITHOUT C.L. DIVISION	WITH C.L. DIVISION
1 LH	60,780	20.2	25,000	18,800	174,500	49,100	47,000
1 TD	35,900	39.4	26,500	20,600	178,100		
2 LH	112,610	17.5	75,400	51,700	576,300	129,200	112,000
2 TD	47,400	36.5	52,200	40,300	299,900		
3 LH	51,020	16.8	30,636	17,900	292,300	70,813	58,900
3 TD	35,010	35.0	47,400	36,900	271,300		
3 DT	50,600	16.8		23,500	75,300		
4 LH	96,540	18.5	58,900	41,600	434,000	100,800	91,000
4 TD	36,380	36.1	43,000	33,400	254,200		
5 LH	42,160	24.3	30,500	21,800	151,900	54,400	50,800
5 TD	24,460	37.6	25,700	19,400	168,300		

NOTE: This vessel has permanently installed underdeck centerline divisions. The above table shows heeling moments with and without temporary centerline divisions installed in hatchways.

MAXIMUM ALLOWABLE HEELING MOMENTS (FT-LT)

DISPLACEMENT (LT)	VIRTUAL CENTER OF GRAVITY (KG_v) (ft)						KM (ft)
	21.50	22.00	22.50	23.00	23.50	24.00	
14,400	12,764	11,172	9,580	7,988	6,398	4,804	25.38
14,600	13,138	11,525	9,910	8,296	6,682	5,068	25.45
14,800	13,613	11,976	10,339	8,702	7,065	5,428	25.51
15,000	13,905	12,245	10,585	8,925	7,265	5,605	25.57
15,130	14,107	12,433	10,759	9,085	7,411	5,737	25.61

SUMMARY OF TANKS

TANK	CAPACITY (ft³)	VCG (ft)	FREE SURFACE MOMENT (ft-LT)	
			Slack	98% Full
FUEL OIL				
3 DB P&S	12,464	2.0	5,690	1,897
6 DB P&S	8,170	2.0	2,208	736
SETTLING	1,586	34.0	44	
SERVICE	1,586	34.0	44	
DIESEL OIL				
4DB P&S	6,796	2.1	1,550	529
SERVICE	464	34.0	8	
FRESH WATER				
5 DB P&S	1,220	2.1	182	
FWT	5,382	17.1	326	
AFTERPEAK	7,176	27.8	817	
S.W. BALLAST				
1 DB	8,156	3.5	3,348	
2 DB P&S	10,852	2.0	3,883	
7 DB	1,855	2.2	489	
5 DT P&S	8,366	9.5	504	
FOREPEAK	10,782	24.0	296	

NATIONAL CARGO BUREAU, INC.
GRAIN STABILITY CALCULATION FORM

* (Required for vessels loading bulk grain in the United States of America)

M.V. / S.S. ATLANTIC			YEAR BUILT 1977 AT CITY BATH
COUNTRY OF REGISTRY U.S.A.	NET TONNAGE 4572	IMO NO. 1014708	IN COUNTRY U.S.A.

AGENT **NORTHWEST AGENCIES, INC.**

GRAIN LOADING BOOKLET APPROVED BY __NATIONAL CARGO BUREAU__

ON BEHALF OF (FLAG STATE) __U.S.A.__

DRAWING NO. __GW-348__ DATE OF APPROVAL __10 NOVEMBER 1977__

APPLICABLE REGULATIONS __RESOLUTION A.264(VIII)__

ADDENDUM FOR UNTRIMMED ENDS APPROVED BY __NONE__

DRAWING NO. __—__ DATE OF APPROVAL __—__

LOADING PORT(S) __PORTLAND, OR__

BUNKERING PORT(S) __—__

DISCHARGE PORT(S) __VALPARAISO, CHILE__

STEAMING DISTANCE __5300__ MILES   MILES PER DAY __350__   TIME __15.14 DAYS__

DAILY CONSUMPTION: FUEL __30 LT__   DIESEL __3 LT__   WATER __12 LT__

	DISPLACEMENT	DEADWEIGHT	DRAFT	FREEBOARD
**WINTER				
SUMMER	15130 LT	11014 LT	28' 00"	10' 08"
**TROPICAL				

FRESH WATER ALLOWANCE __7"__   TPC/TPI (AT SUMMER DRAFT) __52.5 LT__

• EXCEPT FOR EXEMPTED VOYAGES
** IF APPLICABLE

THIS IS TO CERTIFY THAT:

1. THIS CALCULATION IS PREPARED IN ACCORDANCE WITH THE REQUIREMENTS OF THE VESSEL'S GRAIN LOADING BOOKLET AND THE APPLICABLE GRAIN REGULATIONS.

2. THE STABILITY OF THE VESSEL WILL BE MAINTAINED THROUGHOUT THE VOYAGE IN ACCORDANCE WITH THIS CALCULATION.

J. Z___
MASTER'S SIGNATURE

CALCULATION PREPARED BY: (TO BE COMPLETED IF THE FORM IS PREPARED BY OTHER THAN SHIP'S PERSONNEL)	**J. JONES** MASTER'S NAME (PRINTED)
	EXAMINED BY: *R L Smith* N.C.B. SURVEYOR'S SIGNATURE
NAME (PRINT) _____	
COMPANY _____	**R. L. SMITH** N.C.B. SURVEYOR'S NAME (PRINTED)
SIGNATURE _____	
DATE _____	DATE: **10 OCTOBER 2006**

NOTE: ORIGINAL STABILITY CALCULATION AND GRAIN ARRANGEMENT PLAN TO BE SUBMITTED TO THE N.C.B. SURVEYOR. ALL TONNAGES USED IN THIS CALCULATION SHALL BE SHOWN IN THE SAME UNITS AS USED IN THE GRAIN LOADING BOOKLET.

SHIP AND CARGO CALCULATION

PART I

TYPE OF GRAIN _____**WHEAT**_____ STOWAGE FACTOR _____ MT 〜 **45** _____ FT³/LT

COMPT. NO.	CARGO (1)	S.F. (1)	GRAIN CUBICS (2) TOTAL	GRAIN CUBICS (2) USED	WEIGHT (3)	V.C.G.	MOMENT (3)
1 LH		45	60780	60780	1351	20.2	27290
2 LH			112610	112610	2502	17.5	43785
3 LH			51020	51020	1134	16.8	19051
3 DT P&S			50600	46035	1023	16.8	17186
4 LH			96540	96540	2145	18.5	39683
4 TD			36380	36380	808	36.1	29169
5 LH			42160	42160	937	24.3	22769

S.F. $\frac{M^3}{MT}$	S.F. $\frac{FT^3}{LT}$	DEN $\frac{MT}{M^3}$
1.171	42	0.854
1.184	42.5	0.844
1.198	43	0.834
1.212	43.5	0.825
1.226	44	0.816
1.240	44.5	0.806
1.254	45	0.797
1.268	45.5	0.789
1.282	46	0.780
1.296	46.5	0.772
1.310	47	0.763
1.324	47.5	0.755
1.338	48	0.747
1.352	48.5	0.740
1.366	49	0.732
1.380	49.5	0.725
1.393	50	0.718
1.407	50.5	0.711
1.421	51	0.704
1.435	51.5	0.697
1.449	52	0.690
1.477	53	0.677
1.505	54	0.664
1.533	55	0.652
1.561	56	0.641
1.589	57	0.629
1.616	58	0.619
1.644	59	0.608
1.672	60	0.598
1.700	61	0.588
1.728	62	0.579

THIS CALCULATION IS PREPARED IN:

☐ METRIC UNITS

☒ ENGLISH UNITS

CARGO TOTALS	9900		198933
LIGHT SHIP	4116	26.1	107428
CONSTANT	150	35.0	5250
SHIP AND CARGO TOTALS	14166		311611

(1) COMPLETE THESE COLUMNS IF MORE THAN ONE TYPE OF CARGO IS LOADED.

(2) FOR PARTLY FILLED COMPARTMENTS, SHOW THE CUBICS USED IN ADDITION TO THE TOTAL CUBICS.

(3) WEIGHTS AND MOMENTS SHOULD BE SHOWN TO THE NEAREST WHOLE UNIT.

CARGO PLAN: INDICATE HOLDS, TWEEN DECKS, ENGINE SPACES, FITTINGS, STOWAGE, TONNAGES, ETC.

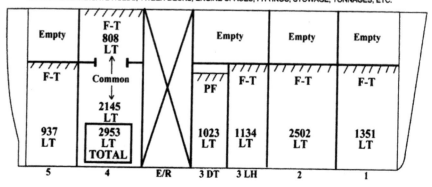

FUEL AND WATER CALCULATION

PART II
THE **INTERMEDIATE** SECTION MUST BE COMPLETED IF THE **ARRIVAL** SECTION SHOWS BALLAST THAT IS NOT LISTED IN THE **DEPARTURE** SECTION. THE **INTERMEDIATE** CONDITION IS IMMEDIATELY BEFORE BALLASTING AND MUST INCLUDE THE EFFECT OF FREE SURFACE, BUT **NOT** THE EFFECT OF ADDED WEIGHT. ADDITIONAL FUEL TAKEN AFTER DEPARTURE MUST BE SHOWN IN THE **INTERMEDIATE** SECTION IN THE SAME MANNER AS BALLAST.

TANK	TYPE LIQUID	DEPARTURE: PORTLAND				INTERMEDIATE:				ARRIVAL: VALPARAISO			
		WEIGHT	V.C.G.	MOMENT	F.S. MOM.	WEIGHT	V.C.G.	MOMENT	F.S. MOM.	WEIGHT	V.C.G.	MOMENT	F.S. MOM.
3DB P/S	FO	302	2.0	604	5690					60	2.0	120	5690
6DB P/S	FO	212	2.0	414	736					-		-	-
SETT	FO	40	34.0	1360	44					40	34.0	1360	44
SERV	FO	30	34.0	1020	44					30	34.0	1020	44
4DB P/S	DO	98	2.1	206	1550					53	2.1	111	1550
SERV	DO	10	34.0	340	8					10	34.0	340	8
5DB P/S	FW	34	2.1	71	-					34	2.1	71	-
FWT	FW	138	17.1	2360	326					-		-	-
AP	FW	100	27.8	2780	817					56	27.8	1557	817

TOTALS

LIQUIDS	964	9155	9215			283	4579	8153
SHIP AND CARGO	14166	311611				14166	311611	
DISPLACEMENT	15130	320766				14449	316190	

SAILING DRAFT   28' 07"   AT DENSITY   1.000

DEPARTURE KG	21.20	INTERMEDIATE KG		ARRIVAL KG	21.88
(1) FREE SURFACE CORR. (+)	0.61	(1) FREE SURFACE CORR. (+)		(1) FREE SURFACE CORR. (+)	0.56
(2) VERT. S.M. CORR. (+)	-	(2) VERT. S.M. CORR. (+)		(2) VERT. S.M. CORR. (+)	-
DEPARTURE KGv	21.81	INTERMEDIATE KGv		ARRIVAL KGv	22.44
DEPARTURE KM	25.61	INTERMEDIATE KM		ARRIVAL KM	25.40
DEPARTURE KGv	21.81	INTERMEDIATE KGv		ARRIVAL KGv	22.44
DEPARTURE GM	3.80	INTERMEDIATE GM		ARRIVAL GM	2.96
REQUIRED MINIMUM GM	1.00	REQUIRED MINIMUM GM		REQUIRED MINIMUM GM	1.00

(1) FREE SURFACE CORR. = $\dfrac{\text{SUM OF FREE SURFACE MOMENTS}}{\text{DISPLACEMENT}}$

(THIS CORRECTION MUST BE APPLIED TO ALL SHIPS.)

(2) VERT. S.M. CORR. = $\dfrac{\text{SUM OF VERTICAL SHIFTING MOMENTS}}{\text{DISPLACEMENT}}$

(THIS CORRECTION APPLIES WHEN THE VOLUMETRIC HEELING MOMENT CURVES OR TABLES DO NOT SPECIFICALLY STATE THAT THE CORRECTION FOR THE RISE IN VERTICAL CENTER OF GRAVITY HAS BEEN INCLUDED, AND THE MANUAL PROVIDES VERTICAL SHIFTING MOMENTS.)

HEELING MOMENT CALCULATION

PART III

COMPT. NO	STOWAGE (1)	GRAIN ULLAGE OR DEPTH M/FT	VOLUMETRIC HEELING MOMENT M⁴/FT⁴	S.F. OR DENSITY (2)	GRAIN HEELING MOMENT MT-M/FT-LT	VERTICAL SHIFTING MOMENT (IF PROVIDED) SEE NOTE 2 IN PART II M⁴/FT⁴	MT-M/FT-LT
1 LH	F-T	0	25000	45			
2 LH	F-T	0	75400				
3 LH	F-T	0	30636				
3 DT	PF	2.4	75300 (Max)				
4 TD/LH	F-T	0	100800				
5 LH	F-T	0	30500				
TOTALS			**337636**	**45**	**7503**		

(1) UNDER STOWAGE INDICATE "F-T" FOR FILLED COMPARTMENTS TRIMMED, "F-UT" FOR FILLED COMPARTMENTS UNTRIMMED,
"PF" FOR PARTLY FILLED COMPARTMENTS, AND "SEC" FOR SECURED OR OVER-STOWED COMPARTMENTS.

(2) THE STOWAGE FACTOR USED IN PART III SHALL NOT EXCEED THE ONE BASED ON THE WEIGHT PER UNIT OF VOLUME (TEST WEIGHT) OF
THE GRAIN. IF THE STOWAGE FACTOR IS THE SAME IN ALL COMPARTMENTS, DIVIDE THE TOTAL VOLUMETRIC HEELING MOMENT BY THE STOWAGE
FACTOR OR MULTIPLY BY THE DENSITY TO OBTAIN THE GRAIN HEELING MOMENT. IF THE STOWAGE FACTOR VARIES, OBTAIN THE GRAIN HEELING
MOMENT FOR EACH COMPARTMENT.

A . FOR VESSELS APPROVED UNDER

INTERNATIONAL GRAIN CODE, Part A, 7.1
REGULATION 4, CHAPTER VI, SOLAS 1974 or
REGULATION 4, IMCO RESOLUTION A.264(VIII), NEW CHAPTER VI, SOLAS 1960
REGULATION 4, IMCO RESOLUTION A.184 AN EQUIVALENT TO CHAPTER VI, SOLAS 1960

STABILITY SUMMARY

	DEPARTURE	INTERMEDIATE	ARRIVAL
DISPLACEMENT	15130		14449
KGᵥ or GM	21.81		22.44
TOTAL GRAIN HEELING MOMENT	7503		7503
MAXIMUM ALLOWABLE HEELING MOMENT	13069		9853
* ANGLE OF HEEL (12° MAX.)			
* RESIDUAL AREA 0.075 METER-RADIANS (14.1 FT° OR 4.3 M°) MINIMUM			
* GM (0.3M OR 1 FT MINIMUM)			

* TO BE COMPLETED IF VESSEL'S GRAIN LOADING BOOKLET DOES NOT INCLUDE A TABLE OF ALLOWABLE HEELING MOMENTS. IN SUCH
CASE, STATICAL STABILITY DIAGRAMS DEMONSTRATING THIS INFORMATION SHALL BE ATTACHED HERETO.

B. FOR SPECIALLY SUITABLE SHIPS APPROVED UNDER

INTERNATIONAL GRAIN CODE, PART A, 8. 2
SECTION V (B) , PART B, CHAPTER VI, SOLAS 1974
SECTION V (B) , PART B, IMCO RESOLUTION A.264 (VIII), NEW CHAPTER VI, SOLAS 1960
REGULATION 12, CHAPTER VI, SOLAS 1960

$$\text{ANGLE OF HEEL} = \frac{\text{GRAIN HEELING MOMENT} \times 57.3}{\text{DISPLACEMENT} \times GM}$$

	DEPARTURE	INTERMEDIATE	ARRIVAL
TOTAL GRAIN HEELING MOMENT			
DISPLACEMENT			
GM			
ANGLE OF HEEL (5° MAX.)			

CERTIFICATE OF LOADING
(Bulk Grain Only)
- OF -
NATIONAL CARGO BUREAU, INC.

This is to Certify, that the _____ U.S.A. _____ S.S. ATLANTIC ___
(flag) (Name of Vessel)

whereof _____ CAPT. J. JONES _____ is Master, of _____ 4572 _____ Net Tons,

built at _____ U.S.A. _____ in _____ 1977 _____, said to be bound for _____ CHILE _____

via _____ DIRECT _____

has been under the inspection of a surveyor or surveyors of NATIONAL CARGO BUREAU, INC. at this port from time to time during the course and in respect of the loading of grain in bulk; that so far as said cargo came under the observation of such surveyor or surveyors, the stowage was in accordance with the regulations of the United States Coast Guard.

**THIS CERTIFICATE IS NOT A CERTIFICATE OF SEAWORTHINESS
AND RELATES ONLY TO THE ABOVE CARGO**

THIS CERTIFICATE IS NOT A FORM OF INSURANCE, OR GUARANTEE, AND IS ISSUED ON THE FOLLOWING TERMS AND CONDITIONS: This Certificate and performance of services by National Cargo Bureau ("NCB") shall in no way be deemed to be a representation, statement, or warranty of seaworthiness, quality or fitness for a particular use or service, of any vessel, container, cargo, structure, item of material, or equipment. NCB shall not be liable for, and the party to whom this Certificate is issued agrees to indemnify and hold NCB harmless from and against any and all claims, demands, actions for damages, including legal fees, to persons and/or property which may be brought against NCB incidental to, arising out of, or in connection with the services to be performed hereunder, except for those claims caused solely by the negligence of NCB. NCB shall be discharged from all liability for negligent performance or non-performance of any services in connection with issuance of this Certificate, unless the same is discovered prior to and is claimed in writing made to NCB within 180 days and litigation is commenced within one year after performance of survey services. THE COMBINED LIABILITY OF NCB, ITS OFFICERS, EMPLOYEES, AGENTS OR SUBCONTRACTORS FOR ANY LOSS, CLAIM, OR DAMAGE ARISING FROM NEGLIGENT PERFORMANCE OR NON-PERFORMANCE OF ANY SERVICES IN CONNECTION WITH THE ISSUANCE OF THIS CERTIFICATE, OR FROM BREACH OF ANY IMPLIED OR EXPRESS WARRANTY OF WORKMANLIKE PERFORMANCE, OR ANY OTHER REASON, SHALL NOT EXCEED IN THE AGGREGATE $10,000. IN NO EVENT SHALL NCB BE LIABLE FOR ANY CONSEQUENTIAL DAMAGES, INCLUDING, BUT WITHOUT LIMITATION, DELAY, DETENTION, LOSS OF USE, OR CUSTOMARY PORT CHARGES TO THE PARTY TO WHOM THIS CERTIFICATE IS ISSUED OR TO ANY OTHER PERSON, CORPORATION OR BUSINESS ENTITY FOR WHOSE BENEFIT THIS CERTIFICATE MAY BE ISSUED.

Issued at _____ PORTLAND, OR _____
Port

14:45 HOURS _____ 15 OCTOBER 2006
Time Date

_____ J. JONES _____ Master _____ R. L. SMITH _____ Surveyor

Rev. 6/94 A final Certificate of Loading will be issued in due course.

EXAMPLE 4: GENERAL CARGO SHIP

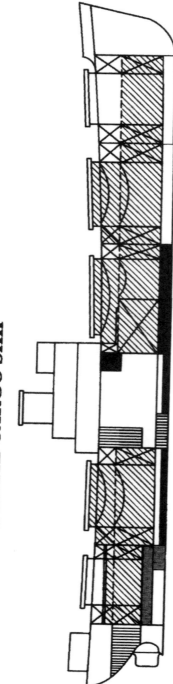

See pages:

65 (Description of example)

91 – 92 (Excerpts from the Grain Loading Booklet)

93 – 96 (NCB Grain Stability Calculation Form)

Cargo

Fuel Oil

Fresh Water

Ballast (to be taken at sea)

VOLUMETRIC HEELING MOMENTS (M⁴)

HOLD	CAPACITY (m³)	VCG (m)	LOADED SEPARATELY			LOADED IN COMBINATION	
			WITHOUT C.L. DIVISION	WITH C.L. DIVISION	MAX. SLACK	WITHOUT C.L. DIVISION	WITH C.L. DIVISION
1 LH	1,721	6.16	216	162	1,506	424	406
1 TD	1,017	12.01	229	178	1,537		
2 LH	3,189	5.33	651	446	4,974	1,115	967
2 TD	1,342	11.13	451	348	2,588		
3 LH	1,445	5.12	264	154	2,523	611	508
3 TD	991	10.67	409	318	2,342		
3 DT	1,433	5.12		203	650		
4 LH	2,734	5.64	508	359	3,746	870	785
4 TD	1,030	11.00	371	288	2,194		
5 LH	1,194	7.41	263	188	1,311	470	438
5 TD	693	11.46	222	167	1,453		

NOTE: This vessel has permanently installed underdeck centerline divisions. The above table shows heeling moments with and without temporary centerline divisions installed in hatchways.

MAXIMUM ALLOWABLE HEELING MOMENTS (MT-M)

DISPLACEMENT (mt)	VIRTUAL CENTER OF GRAVITY (KG_v) (m)					KM (m)
	6.50	6.75	7.00	7.25	7.50	
14,600	3,934	4,049	2,343	1,536	728	7.73
14,800	4,198	3,255	2,437	1,619	801	7.75
15,000	4,368	3,386	2,556	1,701	898	7.77
15,200	4,471	3,476	2,635	1,788	953	7.79
15,373	4,556	3,549	2,699	1,848	998	7.81

SUMMARY OF TANKS

TANK	CAPACITY (m³)	VCG (m)	FREE SURFACE MOMENT (mt-m)	
			Slack	98% Full
FUEL OIL				
3 DB P&S	360	0.61	1,762	587
6 DB P&S	215	0.61	684	228
SETTLING	43	10.36	14	
SERVICE	43	10.36	14	
DIESEL OIL				
4DB P&S	164	0.64	480	164
SERVICE	13	10.36	2	
FRESH WATER				
5 DB P&S	35	0.64	56	
FWT	152	5.21	101	
AFTERPEAK	203	8.47	253	
S.W. BALLAST				
1 DB	237	1.07	1,037	
2 DB P&S	315	0.61	1,203	
7 DB	53	0.67	151	
5 DT P&S	237	2.90	156	
FOREPEAK	313	7.32	92	

NATIONAL CARGO BUREAU, INC.
GRAIN STABILITY CALCULATION FORM
* (Required for vessels loading bulk grain in the United States of America)

M.V.	PACIFIC		YEAR BUILT 1976
COUNTRY OF REGISTRY	NET TONNAGE	IMO NO.	AT CITY GREENOCK
MALTA	4572	1014710	IN COUNTRY U.K.

AGENT **ORLEANS SHIPPING CO.**

GRAIN LOADING BOOKLET APPROVED BY __BUREAU VERITAS__

ON BEHALF OF (FLAG STATE) __MALTA__

DRAWING NO. __GW-348A__   DATE OF APPROVAL __19 MARCH 1997__

APPLICABLE REGULATIONS __RESOLUTION A.264(VIII)__

ADDENDUM FOR UNTRIMMED ENDS APPROVED BY __NONE__

DRAWING NO. __—__   DATE OF APPROVAL __—__

LOADING PORT(S) __NEW ORLEANS, LA__

BUNKERING PORT(S) __—__

DISCHARGE PORT(S) __BIZERTE, TUNISIA__

STEAMING DISTANCE __5300__ MILES   MILES PER DAY __350__   TIME __15.14 DAYS__

DAILY CONSUMPTION: FUEL __25 MT__   DIESEL __3 MT__   WATER __12 MT__

	DISPLACEMENT	DEADWEIGHT	DRAFT	FREEBOARD
**WINTER				
SUMMER	15373 MT	11191 MT	8.53 M	3.25 M
**TROPICAL				

FRESH WATER ALLOWANCE __0.191 M__   TPC/TPI (AT SUMMER DRAFT) __53.3 MT__

* EXCEPT FOR EXEMPTED VOYAGES
** IF APPLICABLE

THIS IS TO CERTIFY THAT:

1. THIS CALCULATION IS PREPARED IN ACCORDANCE WITH THE REQUIREMENTS OF THE VESSEL'S GRAIN LOADING BOOKLET AND THE APPLICABLE GRAIN REGULATIONS.

2. THE STABILITY OF THE VESSEL WILL BE MAINTAINED THROUGHOUT THE VOYAGE IN ACCORDANCE WITH THIS CALCULATION.

MASTER'S SIGNATURE

B. KARLOV
MASTER'S NAME (PRINTED)

CALCULATION PREPARED BY:	
(TO BE COMPLETED IF THE FORM IS PREPARED BY OTHER THAN SHIP'S PERSONNEL)	EXAMINED BY:

N.C.B. SURVEYOR'S SIGNATURE

D. DAVIDSON
N.C.B. SURVEYOR'S NAME (PRINTED)

NAME (PRINT) _____

COMPANY _____

SIGNATURE _____

DATE _____

DATE: __14 JULY 2006__

NOTE: ORIGINAL STABILITY CALCULATION AND GRAIN ARRANGEMENT PLAN TO BE SUBMITTED TO THE N.C.B. SURVEYOR. ALL TONNAGES USED IN THIS CALCULATION SHALL BE SHOWN IN THE SAME UNITS AS USED IN THE GRAIN LOADING BOOKLET.

REV 07/06   HTTP://WWW.NATCARGO.ORG (212) 785-8300

SHIP AND CARGO CALCULATION

PART I

TYPE OF GRAIN **BARLEY**   STOWAGE FACTOR   **1.533** M³/MT   **55** FT³/LT

COMPT. NO.	CARGO (1)	S.F. (1)	GRAIN CUBICS (2) TOTAL	USED	WEIGHT (3)	V.C.G.	MOMENT (3)
1 LH		1.533	1721	1721	1123	6.16	6918
2 LH			3189	3189	2080	5.33	11086
2 TD			1342	1342	875	11.13	9739
3 LH			1445	1445	943	5.12	4828
3 TD			991	991	646	10.67	6893
3 DT P&S			1433	1433	935	5.12	4787
4 LH			2734	2734	1783	5.64	10056
4 TD			1030	1030	672	11.00	7392
5 LH			1194	1194	779	7.41	5772
5 TD			693	340	222	11.46	2544

Density conversion table:

S.F. M³/MT	S.F. FT³/LT	DEN MT/M³
1.171	42	0.854
1.184	42.5	0.844
1.198	43	0.834
1.212	43.5	0.825
1.226	44	0.816
1.240	44.5	0.806
1.254	45	0.797
1.268	45.5	0.789
1.282	46	0.780
1.296	46.5	0.772
1.310	47	0.763
1.324	47.5	0.755
1.338	48	0.747
1.352	48.5	0.740
1.366	49	0.732
1.380	49.5	0.725
1.393	50	0.718
1.407	50.5	0.711
1.421	51	0.704
1.435	51.5	0.697
1.449	52	0.690
1.477	53	0.677
1.505	54	0.664
1.533	55	0.652
1.561	56	0.641
1.589	57	0.629
1.616	58	0.619
1.644	59	0.608
1.672	60	0.598
1.700	61	0.588
1.728	62	0.579

THIS CALCULATION IS PREPARED IN:

[X] METRIC UNITS

[ ] ENGLISH UNITS

	WEIGHT	V.C.G.	MOMENT
CARGO TOTALS	10058		70015
LIGHT SHIP	4182	7.96	33289
CONSTANT	152	10.67	1622
SHIP AND CARGO TOTALS	14392		104926

(1) COMPLETE THESE COLUMNS IF MORE THAN ONE TYPE OF CARGO IS LOADED.

(2) FOR PARTLY FILLED COMPARTMENTS, SHOW THE CUBICS USED IN ADDITION TO THE TOTAL CUBICS.

(3) WEIGHTS AND MOMENTS SHOULD BE SHOWN TO THE NEAREST WHOLE UNIT.

CARGO PLAN: INDICATE HOLDS, TWEEN DECKS, ENGINE SPACES, FITTINGS, STOWAGE, TONNAGES, ETC.

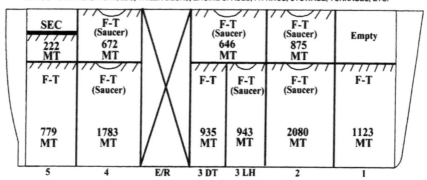

FUEL AND WATER CALCULATION

PART II
THE INTERMEDIATE SECTION MUST BE COMPLETED IF THE ARRIVAL SECTION SHOWS BALLAST THAT IS NOT LISTED IN THE DEPARTURE SECTION. THE INTERMEDIATE CONDITION IS IMMEDIATELY BEFORE BALLASTING AND MUST INCLUDE THE EFFECT OF FREE SURFACE, BUT NOT THE EFFECT OF ADDED WEIGHT. ADDITIONAL FUEL TAKEN AFTER DEPARTURE MUST BE SHOWN IN THE INTERMEDIATE SECTION IN THE SAME MANNER AS BALLAST.

TANK	TYPE LIQUID	DEPARTURE: NEW ORLEANS				INTERMEDIATE: AT BALLAST POINT (After 297 MT consumption)				ARRIVAL: BIZERTE			
		WEIGHT	V.C.G.	MOMENT	F.S. MOM.	WEIGHT	V.C.G.	MOMENT	F.S. MOM.	WEIGHT	V.C.G.	MOMENT	F.S. MOM.
3DB P/S	FO	335	0.61	204	587	335	0.61	204	587	146	0.61	89	1762
6DB P/S	FO	190	0.61	116	684	4	0.61	2	684	-			-
SETT	FO	41	10.36	425	14	41	10.36	425	14	41	10.36	425	14
SERV	FO	30	10.36	311	14	30	10.36	311	14	30	10.36	311	14
4DB P/S	DO	100	0.64	64	480	78	0.64	50	480	55	0.64	35	480
SERV	DO	10	10.36	104	2	10	10.36	104	2	10	10.36	104	2
5DB P/S	FW	35	0.64	22	-	35	0.64	22	-	35	0.64	22	-
FWT	FW	140	5.21	729	101	140	5.21	729	101	58	5.21	302	101
AP	FW	100	8.47	847	253	11	8.47	93	253	-			-
5DT P/S	SWB	-			-	-				156	243	2.90	705	-
7DB	SWB	-			-	-				151	54	0.67	36	-

TOTALS

LIQUIDS		981		2822	2135	684		1940	2442	672		2029	2373
SHIP AND CARGO		14392		104926		14392		104926		14392		104926	
DISPLACEMENT		15373		107748		15076		106866		15064		106955	

SAILING DRAFT **8.721 M** AT DENSITY **1.000**

DEPARTURE KG	7.01	INTERMEDIATE KG	7.09	ARRIVAL KG	7.10
(1) FREE SURFACE CORR. (+)	0.14	(1) FREE SURFACE CORR. (+)	0.16	(1) FREE SURFACE CORR. (+)	0.16
(2) VERT. S.M. CORR. (+)	-	(2) VERT. S.M. CORR. (+)	-	(2) VERT. S.M. CORR. (+)	-
DEPARTURE KGv	7.15	INTERMEDIATE KGv	7.25	ARRIVAL KGv	7.26

DEPARTURE KM	7.81	INTERMEDIATE KM	7.78	ARRIVAL KM	7.77
DEPARTURE KGv	7.15	INTERMEDIATE KGv	7.25	ARRIVAL KGv	7.26
DEPARTURE GM	0.66	INTERMEDIATE GM	0.53	ARRIVAL GM	0.51
REQUIRED MINIMUM GM	0.30	REQUIRED MINIMUM GM	0.30	REQUIRED MINIMUM GM	0.30

(1) FREE SURFACE CORR. = SUM OF FREE SURFACE MOMENTS / DISPLACEMENT

(2) VERT. S.M. CORR. = SUM OF VERTICAL SHIFTING MOMENTS / DISPLACEMENT

(THIS CORRECTION MUST BE APPLIED TO ALL SHIPS.)

(THIS CORRECTION APPLIES WHEN THE VOLUMETRIC HEELING MOMENT CURVES OR TABLES DO NOT SPECIFICALLY STATE THAT THE CORRECTION FOR THE RISE IN VERTICAL CENTER OF GRAVITY HAS BEEN INCLUDED, AND THE MANUAL PROVIDES VERTICAL SHIFTING MOMENTS.)

HEELING MOMENT CALCULATION

PART III

COMPT. NO	STOWAGE (1)	GRAIN ULLAGE OR DEPTH M/FT	VOLUMETRIC HEELING MOMENT M³/FT⁴	S.F. OR DENSITY (2)	GRAIN HEELING MOMENT MT- M / FT- LT	VERTICAL SHIFTING MOMENT (IF PROVIDED) SEE NOTE 2 IN PART II M³/FT⁴	MT- M / FT- LT
1 LH	F-T	0	216	1.533			
* 2 LH	F-T	-	446				
* 2 TD	F-T	-	348				
* 3 LH	F-T	-	154				
* 3 TD	F-T	-	318				
3 DT	F-T	0	203				
* 4 LH	F-T	-	359				
* 4 TD	F-T	-	288				
5 LH	F-T	0	263				
5 TD	SEC	-	0				
* SAUCER USED	TOTALS		2595	1.533	1693		

(1) UNDER STOWAGE INDICATE "F-T" FOR FILLED COMPARTMENTS TRIMMED, "F-UT" FOR FILLED COMPARTMENTS UNTRIMMED, "PF" FOR PARTLY FILLED COMPARTMENTS, AND "SEC" FOR SECURED OR OVER-STOWED COMPARTMENTS.

(2) THE STOWAGE FACTOR USED IN PART III SHALL NOT EXCEED THE ONE BASED ON THE WEIGHT PER UNIT OF VOLUME (TEST WEIGHT) OF THE GRAIN. IF THE STOWAGE FACTOR IS THE SAME IN ALL COMPARTMENTS, DIVIDE THE TOTAL VOLUMETRIC HEELING MOMENT BY THE STOWAGE FACTOR OR MULTIPLY BY THE DENSITY TO OBTAIN THE GRAIN HEELING MOMENT. IF THE STOWAGE FACTOR VARIES, OBTAIN THE GRAIN HEELING MOMENT FOR EACH COMPARTMENT.

A . FOR VESSELS APPROVED UNDER

INTERNATIONAL GRAIN CODE, Part A, 7.1
REGULATION 4, CHAPTER VI, SOLAS 1974 or
REGULATION 4, IMCO RESOLUTION A.264(VIII), NEW CHAPTER VI, SOLAS 1960
REGULATION 4, IMCO RESOLUTION A.184 AN EQUIVALENT TO CHAPTER VI, SOLAS 1960

STABILITY SUMMARY

	DEPARTURE	INTERMEDIATE	ARRIVAL
DISPLACEMENT	15373	15076	15064
KGv or GM	7.15	7.25	7.26
TOTAL GRAIN HEELING MOMENT	1693	1693	1693
MAXIMUM ALLOWABLE HEELING MOMENT	2188	1734	1696
* ANGLE OF HEEL (12° MAX.)			
* RESIDUAL AREA 0.075 METER-RADIANS (14.1 FT° OR 4.3 M°) MINIMUM			
* GM (0.3M OR 1 FT MINIMUM)			

* TO BE COMPLETED IF VESSEL'S GRAIN LOADING BOOKLET DOES NOT INCLUDE A TABLE OF ALLOWABLE HEELING MOMENTS. IN SUCH CASE, STATICAL STABILITY DIAGRAMS DEMONSTRATING THIS INFORMATION SHALL BE ATTACHED HERETO.

B . FOR SPECIALLY SUITABLE SHIPS APPROVED UNDER

INTERNATIONAL GRAIN CODE, PART A, 8. 2
SECTION V (B) , PART B, CHAPTER VI, SOLAS 1974
SECTION V (B) , PART B, IMCO RESOLUTION A.264 (VIII), NEW CHAPTER VI, SOLAS 1960
REGULATION 12, CHAPTER VI, SOLAS 1960

$$\text{ANGLE OF HEEL} = \frac{\text{GRAIN HEELING MOMENT} \times 57.3}{\text{DISPLACEMENT} \times \text{GM}}$$

	DEPARTURE	INTERMEDIATE	ARRIVAL
TOTAL GRAIN HEELING MOMENT			
DISPLACEMENT			
GM			
ANGLE OF HEEL (5° MAX.)			

STANDARD BUSHEL WEIGHTS

WHEAT, SOYBEANS, RICE
      60 lbs. per Bushel
      37.33 Bushels per Long Ton
      1,000 Bushels = 26.7857 LT

$$LT = Bushels \times \frac{3}{112}$$

$$Bushels = LT \times \frac{112}{3}$$

CORN, RYE, SORGHUM, FLAX
      56 lbs. per Bushel
      40 Bushels per Long Ton
      1,000 Bushels = 25 LT

$$LT = Bushels \times \frac{3}{120}$$

$$Bushels = LT \times \frac{120}{3}$$

BARLEY
      48 lbs. per Bushel
      46.67 Bushels per Long Ton
      1,000 Bushels = 21.4286 LT

$$LT = Bushels \times \frac{3}{140}$$

$$Bushels = LT \times \frac{140}{3}$$

NOTE: The above are standard Bushel Weight Units used in the Grain Trade and should not be confused with Bushel Volume Units used to determine Test Weights.

APPROXIMATE TEST WEIGHTS OF THE PRINCIPAL GRAINS LOADED AT UNITED STATES PORTS

The Test Weight of a particular grain is the actual weight in pounds of a U.S. (Winchester) Bushel which is a unit of volume (dry measure) equaling 2,150.42 cubic inches or 1.2445 cubic feet.

Pounds per bushel		Pounds per bushel	
BARLEY	49	SORGHUM (MILO)	58
CORN	56	SOYBEANS	55
LINSEED	50	SUNFLOWER SEED	28
MILLET	57	WHEAT, AMBER DURUM	61
OATS	35	WHEAT, HARD WINTER	62
PEANUTS	51	WHEAT, NORTHERN SPRING	60
RICE	60	WHEAT, SOFT RED	59
RYE	58	WHEAT, WHITE	61
SAFFLOWER SEED	41	CANOLA/RAPE SEED	51

NOTE: The above Test Weights are approximate figures based on information obtained from grain loading ports. The specific Test Weights of particular grain cargoes may vary from the figures shown. Data on Test Weights is usually available from grain inspection offices at shipping elevators.

The above Test Weights when used in conjunction with the Stowage Factor table on the following page will give the approximate Stowage Factor for a conventional general cargo vessel with one tween deck.

The Stowage Factor for a specially suitable bulk carrier will generally be from one to two cubic feet per long ton less due to compaction and the configuration of the holds.

PRODUCTS REGULATED AS GRAIN

Products considered to be 'Grain', and regulated as such, include the following:

Barley	Oats (including Oat Groats)
Barley Malt	Pulses (includes edible seeds such
Canola	as peas, beans or lentils)
Canola Pellets	Rapeseed
Cocoa Beans	Rapeseed Pellets
Coffee Beans	Rice
Corn (Maize)	Rye
Cottonseed, de-linted	Safflower Seed
(linted Cottonseed is not included)	Screenings and Hulls
Flaxseed *or* Solin *or* Linola	Sorghum (Milo)
Linseed	Soybeans
Maize (Corn)	Sunflower Seed
Millet	Wheat
Milo (Sorghum)	
Mustard Seed	
Nuts (including peanuts)	
with shells removed (decorticated)	

GRAIN STOWAGE FACTORS (SF)

1 U.S. Bushel = 1.2445 ft³

$$\frac{2240 \text{ lbs}}{\text{Test Weight / Bushel (lbs)}} \times 1.2445 \text{ ft}^3 = \text{ft}^3 / \text{Long Ton}$$

Test Weight (lbs/Bushel)	SF (m³/mt)	SF (ft³/LT)	Test Weight (lbs/Bushel)	SF (m³/mt)	SF (ft³/LT)
32	2.428	87.11	50	1.554	55.75
33	2.354	84.47	51	1.523	54.66
34	2.285	81.99	52	1.494	53.61
35	2.220	79.65	53	1.466	52.60
36	2.158	77.43	54	1.439	51.62
37	2.100	75.34	55	1.413	50.68
38	2.045	73.36	56	1.387	49.78
39	1.992	71.48	57	1.363	48.91
40	1.942	w69.69	58	1.340	48.06
41	1.895	67.99	59	1.317	47.25
42	1.850	66.37	60	1.295	46.46
43	1.807	64.83	61	1.274	45.70
44	1.766	63.36	62	1.253	44.96
45	1.726	61.95	63	1.233	44.25
46	1.689	60.60	64	1.214	43.56
47	1.653	59.31	65	1.195	42.89
48	1.619	58.08	66	1.177	42.24
49	1.586	56.89	67	1.160	41.61

When Test Weights are for Canadian Imperial Bushels, multiply the above Stowage Factors by 1.0315 (1 Canadian Imperial Bushel = 1.2837 ft³).

CONVERSION TABLE FOR GRAIN STOWAGE FACTORS

Stowage Factors		Equivalent Densities	
ft³/LT (2240 lbs)	m³/mt (1000 kg)	LT/ft³	mt/m³
40	1.115	0.02500	0.897
41	1.143	0.02439	0.875
42	1.171	0.02381	0.854
43	1.198	0.02326	0.834
44	1.226	0.02273	0.816
45	1.254	0.02222	0.797
46	1.282	0.02174	0.780
47	1.310	0.02128	0.763
48	1.338	0.02083	0.747
49	1.366	0.02041	0.732
50	1.393	0.02000	0.718
52	1.449	0.01923	0.690
54	1.505	0.01852	0.664
56	1.561	0.01786	0.641
58	1.616	0.01724	0.619
60	1.672	0.01667	0.598
62	1.728	0.01613	0.579
64	1.784	0.01563	0.560
66	1.839	0.01515	0.544
68	1.895	0.01471	0.528
70	1.951	0.01429	0.513
72	2.007	0.01389	0.498
74	2.062	0.01351	0.485
76	2.118	0.01316	0.472
78	2.174	0.01282	0.460
80	2.230	0.01250	0.448
82	2.285	0.01220	0.438
84	2.341	0.01190	0.427
86	2.397	0.01163	0.417
88	2.453	0.01136	0.408
90	2.508	0.01111	0.399

Note: Stowage Factor as applied in grain stability calculations is defined in A 2.6 of the International Grain Code.

METRIC CONVERSIONS

Use of Conversion Factors: $C = A \times B$

$$or \quad A = \frac{C}{B}$$

	A	B	C
Length	Centimeters (1/100 meter)	0.03281 0.3937	Feet Inches
	Meters	3.28084 0.001	Feet Kilometers
	Kilometers (1000 meters)	3280.839 0.62137 0.53997	Feet Statute Miles Nautical Miles
Area	Square Centimeters	0.155	Square Inches
	Square Meters	10.7639	Square Feet
Volume	Cubic Centimeters	0.061024 0.001 0.033814	Cubic Inches Liters Fluid Ounces
	Cubic Meters	35.31467 264.17205 28.3776	Cubic Feet Gallons (U.S.) Bushels (U.S.)
	Liters	33.81 0.26417 0.03531 61.02553	Fluid Ounces Gallons (U.S.) Cubic Feet Cubic Inches
Mass (Weight)	Kilograms	2.20462 0.001 0.000984 0.0011	Pounds Metric Tons Long Tons Short Tons
	Tonnes (metric tons)	2204.623 1000.0 0.98421 1.10231	Pounds Kilograms Long Tons Short Tons
Force	Kilonewton (1000 Newtons)	101.94 224.739 0.10033 0.11237	Kilograms Pounds Long Tons Short Tons
Pressure	Kilogram per Square Centimeter	14.22333	Pounds Per Square Inch
	Kilograms per Square Meter	0.204816	Pounds Per Square Foot
Moment	Meters^4 Meter – Tonnes	115.8618 3.22904	Feet^4 Foot – Long Tons

USEFUL CONVERSIONS

WATER:
  1 U.S. gallon = 231 cubic inches
  1 U.S. gallon = 0.13368 cubic foot
  1 U.S. gallon = 8.3456 pounds
  1 cubic foot of salt water = 64 pounds
  1 cubic foot of fresh water = 62.43 pounds
  1 cubic foot of water = 28.375 liters
  1 cubic meter of water = 1 metric ton
  1 cubic foot of ice = 57 pounds
  Specific gravity of salt water = 1.025 (approx.)
  Specific gravity of fresh water = 1.000 (at 4° Celsius)

HYDROSTATICS:
  Displacement: Long tons (SW) x 35 = cubic feet
                  Long tons (FW) x 35.88 = cubic feet
  Tons Per Inch (TPI) x 0.40 = Tonnes Per Centimeter (TPC)
  Moment to Trim 1 Inch (MTI) x 0.12192 = Moment to Trim 1 Cm
                                       (MTC *or* MCTC)

NAUTICAL MEASURE:
  1 nautical mile = 6,076 feet = 1,852 meters
  1 knot = 1 nautical mile per hour
  1 fathom = 6 feet = 1.83 meters
  1 shot (chain) = 15 fathoms = 90 feet

MISCELLANEOUS:
  1 long ton = 2240 pounds
  1 short ton = 2000 pounds
  1 metric ton (tonne) = 1000 kilograms
  Long tons x 1.016 = metric tons (tonnes)
  Metric tons (tonnes) x 0.9842 = long tons
  Long tons x 1.12 = short tons
  Short tons x 0.893 = long tons
  1 Measurement Ton = 40 cubic feet
  1 barrel = 42 gallons
  1 barrel = 5.61 cubic feet
  1 cubic foot = 7.48 gallons
  Barrels x Specific Gravity x 0.15648 = long tons
  Pounds per square inch x 0.070307 = kilograms per square centimeter
  Kilograms per square centimeter x 14.22333 = pounds per square inch

INDEX

ABOUT THE AUTHOR

ROBERT J. MEURN, MASTER MARINER and captain, U.S. Naval Reserve (Ret.), received his bachelor of science in nautical science from the U.S. Merchant Marine Academy (USMMA) Kings Point, New York, and his master of arts in higher education from the George Washington University, Washington, DC. He taught at Texas Maritime Academy, was commandant of cadets and executive officer of the TS *Texas Clipper*, and was selected as teacher of the year in 1978. In 1983 and 2003 he was honored as teacher of the year at the USMMA. He is also the author of the second edition of *Watchstanding Guide for the Merchant Officer* and *Survival Guide for the Mariner*, Second Edition.

Meurn has sailed with the U.S. Lines, Farrell Lines, American Export Lines, Moore McCormick Lines, Grace Lines, and Military Sealift Command. In the U.S. Navy he had active duty as a gunnery officer aboard a destroyer and executive officer aboard a LST.

A relief chief mate and a master with the Military Sealift Command, Atlantic, he was an active member of the U.S. naval reserve, where he was commanding officer of Convoy Commodore and Naval Control of Shipping Units in addition to two other commands. His last active duty was as vice commodore during a convoy exercise in December 1989 in Diego Garcia.

Meurn is a member of, and has presented papers to, the International Marine Simulation Forum and the International Navigation Simulator Lecturers Conference. He was also chairman of the Maritime Academy Simulator Committee (MASC) and a member of the International Maritime Lecturers Association and the Marine Board, National Research Council's committee on ship/bridge simulation training. Currently, he is professor emeritus in the department of marine transportation at USMMA and recipient of the U.S. Merchant Marine Distinguished Service Medal.

ABOUT THE BOOK

MARINE CARGO OPERATIONS CLEARLY INSTRUCTS merchant officers with the techniques of cargo operations and the principles of stowage and their application. Based on the author's half century of experience, the book singles out the most practical methods, procedures, and philosophies and presents them in thorough detail. Over 160 photographs and drawings enhance these discussions. The book provides a complete understanding of the shipping cycle so all associated personnel can work as a team in observing the "three Cs" of shipping: communication, cooperation and coordination.

The fourth edition emphasizes innovations in cargo operations over the last five decades, particularly containerization and the responsibilities of the ship's officers for the proper and safe carriage of their cargo. Chapters include discussions on innovations to carriage of goods at sea, cargo responsibility, materials handling and stowage principles, planning the stowage and preparing cargo spaces, stowage of general and hazardous cargo, proper cargo care and hold ventilation, and marine materials handling equipment. This edition provides vital information for candidates taking a U.S. Merchant Marine license examination, and is an important refresher for those who have already received their licenses.

US $50.00

9 780870 336232   5 5 0 0 0

ISBN: 978-0-87033-623-2